ROUTLEDGE HANDBOOK OF SUSTAINABILITY AND FASHION

The clothing industry employs 25 million people globally, contributing to many livelihoods and the prosperity of communities, women's independence and the establishment of significant infrastructures in poorer countries. Yet the fashion industry is also a significant contributor to the degradation of natural systems, with the associated environmental footprint of clothing high in comparison with other products.

Routledge Handbook of Sustainability and Fashion recognizes the complexity of aligning fashion with sustainability. It explores fashion and sustainability at the levels of products, processes and paradigms and takes a truly multidisciplinary approach to critically question and suggest creative responses to issues of:

- fashion in a post-growth society;
- fashion, diversity and equity;
- fashion, fluidity and balance across natural, social and economic systems.

This handbook is a unique resource for a wide range of scholars and students, in the social sciences, arts and humanities, interested in sustainability and fashion.

Kate Fletcher is Professor of Sustainability, Design, Fashion at the Centre for Sustainable Fashion, University of the Arts London, UK.

Mathilda Tham is Professor of Design at Linnaeus University, Sweden, and metadesign researcher at Goldsmiths, University of London, UK.

ROUTLEDGE HANDBOOK OF SUSTAINABILITY AND FASHION

Edited by Kate Fletcher and Mathilda Tham

LONDON AND NEW YORK

from Routledge

First published 2015
by Routledge
2 Park Square, Milton Park, Abingdon, Oxfordshire OX14 4RN

and by Routledge
711 Third Avenue, New York, NY 10017

First issued in paperback 2016

Routledge is an imprint of the Taylor & Francis Group, an informa business

British Library Cataloguing-in-Publication Data
A catalogue record for this book is available from the British Library

Library of Congress Cataloging-in-Publication Data
Routledge handbook of sustainability and fashion/edited by
Kate Fletcher and Mathilda Tham.
pages cm. – (Routledge international handbooks)
Includes bibliographical references and index.
1. Fashion – Environmental aspects. 2. Clothing trade – Environmental
aspects. 3. Sustainability. I. Fletcher, Kate, 1971- editor of compilation.
II. Tham, Mathilda., editor of compilation. III. Title: Handbook of
sustainability and fashion.
TT515.R8317 2015
338.4'7687 – dc23
2014007889

ISBN 13: 978-1-138-23226-6 (pbk)
ISBN 13: 978-0-415-82859-8 (hbk)

Typeset in Bembo and Minion Pro
by Florence Production Ltd, Stoodleigh, Devon, UK

To our kids (J, C, P, RL) and all others

CONTENTS

Contents

FIGURES

TABLES

CONTRIBUTORS

Kate Fletcher has been a researcher, writer and design activist working in sustainability and fashion for two decades. She is Professor of Sustainability, Design, Fashion at the Centre for Sustainable Fashion, University of Arts, London.

Joanne Entwistle has published extensively on the sociology of fashion and dress, the sociology of body, aesthetic markets and aesthetic economy. Her current research is examining the configuring of light in everyday life.

Louise St. Pierre is an Associate Professor of Design at Emily Carr University in Vancouver, Canada. She is the recipient of numerous grants and awards for her work on sustainable design and is the co-author of the internationally recognized texts, *Okala Ecological Design* and *Okala Practitioner: integrating ecological design*.

John Thackara, the director of Doors of Perception, is a writer, philosopher and event producer.

John R. Ehrenfeld is an MIT retired faculty member and is the author of the recently published, *Flourish: a frank conversation about sustainability* (with Andrew Hoffman).

Ann Thorpe is a design strategist and author based in London.

Jonathan Chapman is Professor of Sustainable Design at the University of Brighton. He is Course Director of the MA Sustainable Design, and author of *Emotionally Durable Design: objects, experiences and empathy* (Earthscan, 2005).

Carolyn Strauss is a design researcher and curator with a focus on Slow (design) knowledge. She is the founder and director of slowLab (US/NL), a nonprofit organization that explores and catalyses Slow design thinking, learning and activism through research, public dialogues, creative initiatives and academic programmes.

Amanda Ericsson is a PhD student in Up-cycling Textile Management at The Swedish School of Textiles, exploring capacity building and second-hand clothing business development through the action-based project The Life of a Dress and dreamandawake brand.

Andrew Brooks is a Lecturer in Development Geography at King's College London. His research maps connections between places of production and spaces of consumption in Africa.

Dr Mirjam Southwell is a designer and researcher with a background working in international development and education. She provides expertise to third sector organizations advising on project development, monitoring and evaluation and, when she's not doing that, she knits.

Dr Sue Thomas is Course Leader of the Bachelor in Fashion (Apparel Engineering and Design) course at Holmesglen Institute, Melbourne, having taught in the UK and Aotearoa New Zealand. A public speaker, writer and broadcaster, her interests are ethics and sustainability in the fashion industry. She is writing a book: *Fashion Ethics*, for Routledge.

Ingun Grimstad Klepp is a Research Professor and works at the National Institute for Consumer Research (SIFO) in Oslo, with research on sustainable textile, clothing, laundry and leisure consumption. She currently works with wool, both with consumption and questions regarding the value chain. The relationship between textiles' social and physical characteristics is at the core of her interest.

Kirsi Laitala has an MSc in Textile, fiber and clothing engineering, and is a PhD candidate at the National Institute for Consumer Research (SIFO). She has researched and published on areas related to clothing quality, maintenance, safety, as well as fit and size issues. Currently, she is working on sustainability of clothing consumption.

Sophie Woodward is a Lecturer in Sociology at the University of Manchester. She carries out research into material culture and everyday clothing practices and has a particular interest in developing novel methodological approaches. She is the author of several books, including *Why Women Wear What They Wear* (Berg, 2007) and *Blue Jeans: the art of the ordinary* (University of California Press, 2012).

Joe Smith is Senior Lecturer in Geography at the Open University and writes about the history, policy and politics of environmental change. He is a specialist in environmental communications and has advised on over 30 hours of BBC TV and radio broadcasts, as well as playing more strategic roles in the field.

Sasha Rabin Wallinger is an entrepreneur, artist and catalyst for social change who works to create future-facing programmes that connect the people and processes behind sustainable design and innovation through her (US-based) consulting firm, Haute Verte Couture. Sasha completed her Masters at Reed College, where she traced the environmental and social history of the business of fashion.

Simonetta Carbonaro is a consumer psychologist, expert in strategic marketing and design management, and a partner at the business consulting firm REALISE. She is a Professor of Design Management and Humanistic Marketing at The Swedish School of Textiles at the University of Borås, and a Visiting Professor at the London College of Fashion.

David Goldsmith is a PhD candidate at The Swedish School of Textiles, in Borås, and Adjunct Professor at Parsons The New School for Design, New York. His research focus is design management toward sustainability.

Else Skjold is currently a PhD candidate at Kolding School of Design/Copenhagen Business School. Her thesis, *The Daily Selection*, evolves around the relationship between people and their wardrobes.

Greg Peters is a chemical engineer and Associate Professor at Chalmers University of Technology. He brings a perspective built on the application of sustainability assessment tools in the water, chemicals and agricultural industries.

Hjalmar Granberg has a PhD in physics and works as a senior research associate at Innventia AB. His research focuses on designing new materials based on wood, including cellulose electronics and mechano-active materials that respond to the environment.

Susanne Sweet is Associate Professor of Business Administration at Stockholm School of Economics. Her research explores the interconnections in a global world that provide inspiration but also unsustainable economical, technological and behavioural lock-ins.

Carole Collet is a Reader and Deputy Director of the Textile Futures Research Centre at the University of the Arts London. She has also recently set up the Design With Living Systems Research Lab at Central Saint Martins, which aims at exploring emerging and disruptive technologies through design to create a more sustainable future.

Timo Rissanen is an Australian-trained Finnish fashion designer. He is currently the Assistant Professor of Fashion Design and Sustainability at Parsons The New School for Design.

Liz Parker is an Associate Lecturer in sustainable fashion at London College of Fashion and a freelance activist and project manager in workers' rights in garment supply chains. Previously, she has held positions with the Clean Clothes Campaign, including project manager of Fashioning an Ethical Industry.

Lynda Grose, designer, consultant and educator, has engaged cross-sector to further sustainability in fashion for over two decades. She co-founded ESPRIT's ecollection, launched in 1992, has worked with such clients as Sustainable Cotton Project, Gap Inc, Patagonia and Aid to Artisans and is currently Assistant Professor at California College of the Arts, San Francisco.

Dilys Williams is a fashion designer, collaborator and creator of the Centre for Sustainable Fashion. She engages translational leadership to devise and align emergent ideas towards sustainability through fashion's artistic and business practices. Through high-profile design positions and academic leadership roles, she explores empathy and interconnectivity to find means to support human fulfilment and nature's resilience. Manifestations of her work are applied to academic research, education, government and industry interactions.

Lizzie Harrison is a designer and researcher who uses an entrepreneurial approach to explore fashion, community and sustainability through her label Antiform and social enterprise ReMade in Leeds. Lizzie also teaches and researches at SustainRCA at the Royal College of Art.

Amy Twigger Holroyd is a designer, maker and researcher who has explored fashion and sustainability through her knitwear label, Keep & Share, since 2004. Amy completed her PhD at Birmingham City University in 2013 and is now Research Fellow at the University of Leeds.

Jonnet Middleton is a UK artist and mending activist currently writing a PhD on mending at Lancaster University. She turned down a career as a fashion designer and, in 2008, took a pledge to wear only the clothes she already owned for the rest of her life.

Otto von Busch is Professor of Design at Konstfack University College of Arts, Crafts and Design (Stockholm) and Assistant Professor in Integrated Design at Parsons the New School for Design (New York).

Mathilda Tham's work sits in a positive, creative and activist space at a convergence between fashion, futures studies and sustainability. She is Professor of Design at Linnaeus University, Sweden, and metadesign researcher at Goldsmiths, University of London.

INTRODUCTION

Dear reader and collaborator of fashion, it is an honour to share with you a body of work that celebrates fashion futures for sustainability.

This edited volume of contributions from over thirty scholars from around the world explores interconnections between sustainability and fashion, a web of relationships that are, at one and the same time, global and also domestic, personal and also industrial, a basic need and also a luxury, essential to the fashion sector and also challenging to its very nature. It does so by bringing together different experiences and perspectives of fashion: some emerging from within fashion itself, and others from the sustainability community. The chapters reflect a wide range of influences as varied as everyday actions, scholarly practice, technological innovation, direct experience, industrial knowledge and creative activity, many of which are different to what has gone before, and some of which are *radical* in the original sense of the word, that is *forming the roots*, back to the bare and essential aspects of ideas and practice of fashion found within a thriving – a sustainability – future.

We believe the contribution of this volume to be new, vibrant and unique in a number of ways, including that:

- it opens up the fashion and sustainability discourse, and hopefully practice, by inviting a range of perspectives from scholars and disciplines hitherto outside this remit;
- it integrates theoretical fashion perspectives, pushing the engagement in understandings of sustainability towards relating with, embracing and even celebrating the complex symbolic rationales that underpin the fashion experience;
- it asks scholars and practitioners to step beyond what they *know* and, from their advanced vantage point, speculate and offer visions for fashion and sustainability, as well as sketching out further territories of research and practice;
- it integrates insights from research and practice, dissolving some boundaries between, and also honours insights coming from the personal realm of the contributors;
- it focuses on solutions and possibilities, seeking to offer agency and a range of ideas;
- it draws on collaborative processes, where each contributor has been invited to shape the ethos and direction of the book.

The contributions to fashion and sustainability offered by this volume are of different types. They range from fresh findings from empirical research, which should prompt new emphases going forward; to reconceptualizations of fashion and sustainability, which invite novel understanding of the alignment of fashion and sustainability stakeholders, identify new actors to involve, or redistribute power and open up new territories for research and practice. The wide range of academic and professional disciplines meeting (and hopefully attracting a similarly wide readership) is also reflected in the diversity in terms of conventions of voice and research.

Context and rationale

The urgent need to engage systemically with environmental, social and economic considerations is formally and globally recognized (see e.g. Stern, 2006; IPCC, 2013). In 2009, a comprehensive piece of research was published identifying nine planetary boundaries that, if transgressed, would lead to unpredictable instability in Earth systems (Rockström *et al.*, 2009). Alarmingly, at least three planetary boundaries have already been crossed, specifically climate change, the rate of biodiversity loss and the rate of human interference in the nitrogen cycles, with others being approached at a rapid pace. Each transgression is serious in its own right; however, because changes in Earth systems are non-linear, their potential effects include the dramatic and asymmetrical impact upon other boundaries, threatening the collapse of the larger systems. The research, however, reflects hope and agency in how it describes the presence, within the planetary boundaries, of 'a safe operating space for humanity' (ibid.). While adhering to the boundaries, within this space a diversity of initiatives and approaches to sustainability are not only possible, but needed.

The role played by the fashion sector in contributing to degradation of natural systems is increasingly acknowledged. To further contextualize fashion in the larger picture, the associated environmental footprint of clothing is high in comparison with other products (Chapman, 2010) and should be framed within projections that, by 2050, as a global society, we will be facing a tripling of annual resource extraction and consumption (UNEP, 2011: xv), and, in order to maintain relative climate stability, 'substantial reductions in the resource requirements of economic activities are necessary if the growing world population can expect to live under conditions of sustainable resource management' (ibid.).

Environmental effects of each individual garment are attributed to the resource drawdown, pollution effects and waste generated within a total industrial and sociocultural system that is large and growing larger. The picture achieves even further complexity with the implications of the fashion industry's major relocation of production from the global North to the South and East in search of low labour costs over the last 50 years, and the effects of a 'fast' fashion business model, where economies of scale deliver standardized fashion at high volume and low price. The economic imperative behind these shifts creates downward pressure on standards – a 'race to the bottom' – where workers, production facilities, their environments and communities are impacted hard, as mills and factories compete on price for contracts. Greenpeace's recent campaign to highlight the use of toxic chemicals in fibre and fabric processing (Greenpeace, 2011, 2012) has revealed, in some parts of the industry, ill-informed tolerance of the use of damaging process chemicals, because production decisions are made on the basis of low unit price and exclude broader conceptions of costs. The collapse of the Rana Plaza factory in Bangladesh in 2013, with the appalling toll of death and injury, and repercussions across families and communities, is but one example of the wide-ranging social toll of the fashion sector.

Yet the industry also contributes to livelihoods and communities. The sector's size and the manual dexterity of the work of fashioning garments mean that the clothing industry employs over 25 million workers worldwide, especially women, and adds to their independence and the establishment of infrastructure in poorer countries. Thus, fashion can also be seen to constitute a vibrant and innovative economic and sociocultural field, offering values at individual, community, corporate and national levels. The omnipresence of fashion, its alluring emotional language and its pivotal role in the experimentation with identity formation and communication position it, as well as a driver of consumption, as a potentially auspicious agent of change.

In the last decade, the realm of fashion and sustainability has grown in scale, tone, approach and acceptability, from a place often at the margins to one of cohesive strategies to manage resource flows in industry and co-ordinate action with competitors (for example, the Sustainable Apparel Coalition; www.apparelcoalition.org), and it has become an emerging academic field in its own right – confirmed by the existence of this reference work in your hands. Yet, although the field has matured, corporate strategies towards sustainability have become increasingly standardized often lacking nuance, and the literature reflects a response largely of accommodation of ideas of sustainability, where efforts are directed to maintaining the status quo with key adaptations, at the level of lessening the resource profile of existing products and processes. Although constituting important improvements and worthy of attention and effort, this approach fails to engage with fundamental underlying structures contributing to the unsustainability of fashion, such as the economic imperative of continuous growth and the increasing marketization of all aspects of society. It further fails to engage with emerging bodies of knowledge and practice that can offer insights and creative opportunities beyond a current paradigm.

Aims of the book

The ambition of this book is to offer a range of perspectives that both recognize the complexity of aligning fashion with sustainability values, action and futures and offer strong visions. It is concerned with long-term futures, not just transitional strategies, with the effect that, although the book often engages with fashion and sustainability at the level of products, processes and services, it is predominantly occupied with the deeper levels of systems and paradigms. This volume also has a pragmatic goal: to infuse and apprise the world of fashion with insights from multiple, plural, complex points of view. While revealing fundamental underlying structures and conflicts, say between economies of scale and the fragility of natural systems, it also seeks to promote agency by offering inspiring examples, tangible strategies and strategic platforms for new enquiry. The book's bold ambition is to set out a research agenda for the next 10 years. Another aim of the book is to shift the perception of fashion as problem to fashion as a resource for sustainability futures.

Cumulatively, the book is a broad, oftentimes deep and singularly distinctive, sounding of the field. It is also one that is aware of its own limitations: we openly acknowledge that this sounding reflects but a moment of time and the voices of a particular range of perspectives in the territory. Just as there are trends in fashion clothes, there are trends in discourses also, with a marked shift in recent years away from framing 'fashion and sustainability' as a material phenomenon to one instead influenced by human actions, relationships and their material effects. We also firmly believe that a fuller mapping of the field is necessarily an ongoing activity, more emergent, more multidimensional, more fervent. Yet this book offers clues as to how this process of charting might unfold over time, how it may look and feel, and what it might reveal about what we value and how we extend an ethic of care to others and the natural world, through and within fashion.

The book's ethos and the working process behind it

Early in the planning of the book, many of the contributors met in an exploratory workshop, sharing ideas on the shape and requirements of a new reference book in the field of 'fashion and sustainability', including its ambition and ethos. It was especially clear from this session that the book, both as product and process, should, in so far as was possible, embody some core understandings of a paradigm of sustainability. An example of this is the continuous collaborative approach used in writing the book, reflecting the essential participatory nature of the sustainability imperative, the complexity of which is such that no individual or organization can alone hold problems or their solutions. Accordingly, authors have been part of writing groups and worked to shape the book's total ethos and direction, as well as their own distinctive contributions. As editors, we felt this was an important way to seed and cultivate an edited work about a field that is shared, relational, and where knowledge is not fixed, nor beyond contest. Another example is how value explicitness and self-reflexivity have been encouraged. Each contributor was asked to introduce her/himself and her/his perspective in the chapter, as well as to present a research agenda reflecting personal and/or professional viewpoints. In the same vein, we have encouraged authors to use a voice and language they feel comfortable with and that embody the points of view and visions they bring to the book. Contributors were also urged to draw on a wide epistemology – theory, personal and professional experience, practice – and, from this robust basis, generously experiment and speculate towards suggestions for the future.

We feel convinced that the shared process of creating this book has produced neither a consensual volume nor one that is populist; but rather a title that is a dynamic compendium of perspectives, ideas and practices of fashion and sustainability, including a lived sense or understanding of what it is to know about this field of study. The reader will find chapters offering contrasting or complementary understandings of approaches to change, ranging from the pragmatic to the radical, technological to behavioural, and we invite you, as you read, to hold the tension between perspectives, explore amid the emerging relationships and not necessarily seek to resolve the differences between them.

The book celebrates a wide epistemology, or knowing about fashion and sustainability, in the many themes and disciplines it brings together, and includes perspectives of both scholars and practitioners, established and distinguished, as well as new voices. We must share the reflection that the format of a handbook such as this is not always optimal for practitioners, who perhaps are short on experience of scholarly writing, to share their expertise. Significantly, the sustainability imperative prompts us to question the hierarchies in knowledge creation and sharing and ask how the scholarly format constitutes a barrier, to both the distribution and accessing of vital information. We are especially proud of the strong voices and important perspectives offered by practitioners of fashion in this volume.

Important to our collaborators and to us was to make this book accessible to a wide readership. Therefore, we have sought to create a volume with language that is inclusive and that does not shy away from complex ideas and terms, but also explains them. This is especially important, as the book bridges many fields, each with its own particular terminology and jargon. The reader will also find new language emerging in this volume that both expresses and shapes ideas in fashion and sustainability. We see this developing lexicon as asking different questions and opening up new understandings and ways of thinking about the field. For example, beyond its tangible application to the fixing of broken cloth, 'mending' (see Chapter 26) as metaphor encourages us to explore what capabilities are needed to make a fashion system whole. A list of emerging language is included at the end of this introduction, and we invite you to notice the use of these words and others as you read the contributions, and to build them into your own language, ideas and approach as appropriate. That a new language of fashion and sustainability might develop through the creation of this book is, for us, an important possibility, for words influence how we perceive and imagine the world. They convey material, individual, social and political creativity and action. Much of the lexicon of opportunity around fashion and sustainability captured in this book is emerging in places other than industry boardrooms and corporate social responsibility conferences. Some of this language is rising up from the streets, from ordinary people and everyday fashion practices. Some of these terms are technical and numeric language, but mostly they are not the nomenclature of problem minimization. Rather, they are the words of creation. They speak of the qualities that foster what Aristotle called *eudaimonia*, the language and ideas of well-being, capabilities and flourishing.

Essential also is a note on the use of the terms 'sustainability' and 'sustainable'; often employed as synonyms (including by many contributors here). We distinguish between the terms thus: *sustainability* names an idea, a system property that is dependent on the relationships between things that evolve through time and towards an aspirational goal of thriving; *sustainable*, by contrast, describes the process of attempting to achieve this goal, often in instrumental, bounded, static ways. That the two are sometimes used interchangeably betrays, perhaps, the relative youth and linguistic awkwardness of the field, yet often, in these pages, the experiences to which these terms point are moments of shared values and common sites of departure, underscoring the need to read both words and underlying praxis.

Fashion and sustainability: definitions respectively and together

The book employs a generous definition of fashion, celebrating its co-creative and fluid nature and acknowledging its wide range of stakeholders. The definition encompasses fashion's formalized and institution-based activities and 'hard' production, and the subtler and more elusive domains of emotion, symbols and identity, and practices springing from individual or vernacular creativity and resourcefulness.

Similarly, for us, the editors, and for many of the contributors to this volume, the working experience of sustainability in these pages is very broad. We frame it as a magical territory of possibilities and aspiration, where words such as love, empathy, care, hope, creativity, imagination and play have an important place.

The territory of this book, fashion and sustainability, often elicits strong responses and, most notably, an often-repeated view about the apparent paradoxical nature of the field. That fashion contributes to unsustainability is incontestable: it is readily characterized by the superfluity of mass production and unlimited consumption and often targeted, rightly, as in need of a greater moral conscience. Moreover, it is seen as a cipher: frivolous, evanescent and a sector that delivers change without development. Thus, fashion and sustainability are framed, as is typical in Western thought, as a pair of contrasting ideas, as two separate and antagonistic concepts and experiences. Seen as opposite ends of a linear continuum, sustainability and fashion are fixed in a relationship of enmity: more fashion equates to less sustainability (and vice versa). This book attempts to diversify the understandings of both sustainability and fashion, thereby reaching beyond such dichotomies and polarizations to explore synergistic vantage points across a range of themes and concerns. That the field of fashion and sustainability is mired in the language and thinking of the oxymoron reflects, not the field's potential, but the hold and influence of one particular experience of fashion on our collective imagination – of fashion as commerce, novelty, premature product obsolescence – and the narrow spectrum of fashion this values and promotes. Indeed, this restricted view has also tempered the sustainability response in the sector and still trains a lens on a production agenda where interventions are understood in units and judged in numbers, and actions are framed as mitigation. Alert or not to this febrile backdrop, first views of fashion and sustainability are often formed quickly from preconceived ideas and tinged with bemusement, hectoring and, occasionally, conceit. Yet it quickly becomes clear that the field is a space of complex, additive independencies, a place at a nexus of contemporary culture, economic ideology, creative expression, social processes, fundamental human needs and personal pleasure, which places many of us outside our intellectual comfort zones. The broadly held ethic of care evoked within these pages circles around and uncovers views of fashion as varied as: collective and normatively regulated practices in everyday life; clothes that endure (not just new items); industrial activity; a process of identity formation; the 'craft of use'; agent of change; creative practice; function and driver of consumerist society; physical garment; and form of political democracy, among others.

Our previous experiences have confronted us with a series of powerful stereotypes of fashion and its practitioners, which can be summarized in the terms flippant, superficial and insubstantial – an experience reflected in some of the chapters of this volume, including that of Joanne Entwistle (Chapter 2). We believe this to be a contributing factor to the slow mobilization of expertise to fashion futures for sustainability, and feel confident that this volume is a positive force in dissolving some of the lingering suspicions of the credibility, rigour and responsibility of the field of fashion. At the same time, it is remarkable how pockets of fashion have remained non-analytical havens, with fashion professionals hiding from deep analysis and action. Again, we hope that this volume contributes to a far wider dissemination of the urgency of the sustainability imperative and the participation of many perspectives and capabilities, as well as the many rewards of engaging with it.

Scope and limitations

This book draws together a wide range of themes crucial to a deeper discourse of fashion and sustainability; it also blends micro and macro perspectives, levels of products, systems and paradigms, and short- and long-term futures. Its explicit starting point is that, in order to work towards an experience of sustainability, for humans and nonhuman systems, change in the fashion sector needs to be comprehensive – at least systemic, and maybe even paradigmatic. Some of the discrete themes that this book explores and unpacks include:

- Fashion and systems thinking – how can we use knowledge of synthesis and holism to build theory and practice in fashion that reflect how systems and their stakeholders work together?
- Fashion and relationships – how can we both acknowledge and empower understanding of fashion and sustainability as relational and evolving?
- Fashion in a post-growth society – how can we mobilize creativity and foresight to achieve thriving fashion systems that develop qualitatively, decoupled from accelerating material throughput?
- Fashion, diversity and equity – how can we draw from extended epistemologies, celebrate the wisdom of a plurality of voices and transcend the limitations of Western biases and world-views, to achieve futures of sustainability in the context of fashion?
- Fashion, fluidity and balance – how can we achieve a sophisticated, integrated understanding and a more transparent narrative of highly complex resource and information flows, across natural, social and economic systems?
- Fashion and ecological literacy – how can experiences of nature, language, garments and the way fashion systems are felt reflect interdependency, complexity, balance and change?

We are conscious also of the book's quirks, of what is not included, and the biases in its contributions. That the book has partialities is inevitable and also revealing, because, for the editors and authors collaborating on this project, they underscore our finitude, the limitations of our network of contacts, the haphazard, imperfect and often chance nature of knowledge building, and the realization that sustainability ideas are not fixed, nor is knowledge permanent. The biases in this *Handbook* reflect a Western perspective, the ideas and work of privileged academics and practitioners, and a gender imbalance – more than two-thirds of our authors are women, a fact that should be considered alongside the stereotyped views of what work in this area entails and who does it. Also revealed in these pages is an emphasis on the softer aspects of the fashion sustainability challenge, perhaps reflecting a recent trend in discourse that empha-sizes social processes over material flows in the fashion and sustainability field. This slant is obvious in the relative lack of chapters here exploring technical aspects of fashion's materials and production and the technology and science that facilitate this, though other edited works explore this approach almost exclusively (see, for example, Blackburn, 2009; Gardetti and Torres, 2013). That science and technology are not the focus in this book is not because we see them as unimportant, but is rather reflective of our ecocentric philosophical approach to sustain-ability, which invests in a holistic world-view integrating spiritual, social and environmental dimensions and frames questions as nature- and people-centred. Also, perhaps, it reveals that the fashion and sustainability community is not as integrated as we would like, and that work in science and technology on the one hand, and design and social practice on the other, continues to be undertaken independently.

Here, we wish also to evoke the insightful words of a woman who was both an environmental pioneer and a champion of systems thinking, Donella Meadows. In her text *Places to Intervene in a System* (1997), she eloquently described how change directed at the paradigm of a system is more effective than any other change and can happen in a very instant. But, of course, such change is also scary! It is appropriate to mention Meadows here, as many of the contributors explicitly or implicitly draw on her work and that of other systems thinkers. Systems thinking, since it was first introduced to the realm of fashion (Fletcher, 2008), has provided a helpful perspective on an area characterized by complexity, intricate interdependencies and flux, and a wide span, geographically, epistemologically and in terms of the many types of disciplines and discourses it draws together. Systems thinking continues to yield insights and vibrant ideas, as evidenced in the chapters.

The book's structure

As we have lived with this book, and tried to organize its many perspectives, we realized that a metaphor of the perspective itself, the vision or the point of view, was a helpful organizing principle for the contributions (although, just like any linear format, a little clunky at times). Accordingly, the book's parts represent different ways of looking at fashion and sustainability, providing different sorts of sight and insight (see Figure I.1). Not unlike the different types of photoreceptive cell in the human eye that are responsible for vision of different qualities in different conditions, the book builds towards a total vision by drawing on complementary parts: see Figure I.1.

The first part, 'Framing and expanding fashion and sustainability', represents the broad and keen eagle-eye view, scanning a field from above, revealing larger patterns and flows, complex systems of which 'fashion and sustainability' form an interconnected whole. This part reveals some of the foundations of what it means to know about and work in this area.

The second part, 'Sustainability and fashion as seen from other places and disciplines', comprises a series of outlooks on fashion and sustainability from thinkers and researchers from disciplines outside fashion. This is important, as these chapters both contribute significant insights from

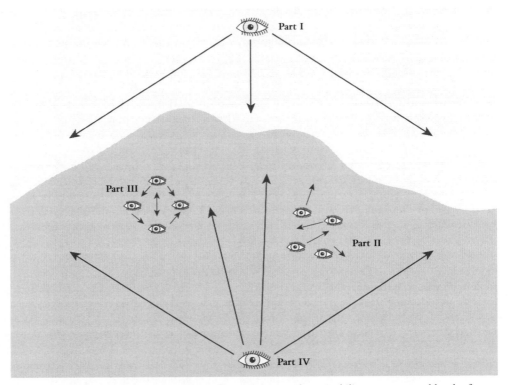

Figure I.1 Different perspectives and approaches to fashion and sustainability as represented by the four parts of this book

fields, such as ethnography, that can enrich the 'fashion and sustainability' discourse and practice, and also lay bare some residual perceptions and assumptions of fashion and 'fashion and sustainability'.

The third part, 'Perspectives on refining fashion from within', comprises scholars and practitioners working inside the fashion systems, using their rich experience and knowledge and a magnifying glass to illuminate and suggest alternatives to practices in the field.

Finally, the fourth part, 'Visions of sustainability from within the fashion space', opens up the field of 'fashion and sustainability' through a series of chapters with far-reaching suggestions for fashion–sustainability futures.

From a collection of a sometimes unruly series of perspectives, we have sought to create a curated whole. Each part is briefly introduced, key themes and terminology are highlighted, and discourses are contextualized. The book ends with a conclusion that summarizes the research agendas and discusses some of their implications for futures of 'fashion and sustainability'.

There are, of course, other reading paths that can be charted through this volume. One reader may, for example, wish to navigate the volume's contributions with a political eye and mind; others may choose to read chapters written by young researchers; others still may seek out those pieces that dig deeply into material flows, innovations and natural systems, or wish to follow papers that reflect on gender, or those that draw heavily on theory. We have highlighted some of the possible reading paths in Figure I.2; there are, of course, many others, as varied as the minds and hands that pick up this book.

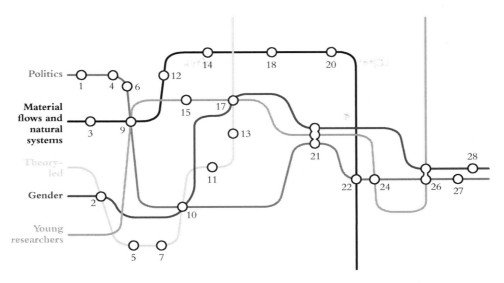

Figure I.2 Possible reading paths through the book (numbers correspond to chapter numbers)

We would like to thank the contributors to the book for their generosity with insight, time and commitment, in a process that has asked more (and perhaps also returned more) than is usual in the creation of a book of this type. We also would like to thank a large community of peers and colleagues, friends and families, who have in various ways supported its coming into being. Huge gratitude to Julia Crew for her sensitive and careful organization of both us and the book. We are also grateful to the excellent team at Routledge, including Khanam Virjee and Helen Bell.

It is wonderful to hand over to you, the reader and collaborator of fashion. This book is now yours. We hope that you take it forward with you.

Emerging lexicon

Here, we present emerging language from the chapters. Some of the terms are new, and others are old but with an invigorated understanding. The lexicon spans language that evokes glimpses of new possibilities for fashion and sustainability, but also such terms that may help us express and understand the extreme seriousness of unsustainability. The lexicon is, of course, not exhaustive, and we encourage the reader to enjoy a continuous search for words that can help us create futures of fashion and sustainability.

Accidental sustainability
Adaptive resilience
Anthropocene
Assemblage, fashion as
Awareness
Balance
Care
Change as usual

Cognitive dissonance
Commodity activism
Commons, commoning, conceptual commons, open fashion commons
Community
Confidence
Consideration
Correspondences
Craft of use
Cultures of repair
Democratization
Democratized fashion supremacy
Desire
Dissenting imagination
Eco-stress
Ecological literacy
Emotional durability
Empowerment
Enclosure
Endurance
Ethics, ethic of care
Eudaimonia
Fashion-ability
Fashion supremacy
Fast fashion
Fear
Fearlessness
Feminization of responsibility
Flows
Flourishing
Gender
Generosity
Gestation
'Good value'
Joint liability
Joy
Leadership
Love
Luck
Mending, mend follows matter
Micro-aggressions
Micro-kindnesses
Micro-practices
Openness
Paradigm change
Patience
Peace
Politics, political power

Post-growth
Prosumers, prosumption
Psychic rewards
Quiet sustainability
Re-knitting
Receptivity
Relational
Relationships
Resourcefulness
Resilience
Response-ability
Self-respect
Sorrow
Speciesism
Spirit
Stable fashion
Style
Superabundance
Thriving
Value, good value
Violence
Wardrobe studies

References

Blackburn, R. S. (2009), *Sustainable Textiles: Lifecycle and Environmental Impact*, Oxford, UK: Woodhead Publishing.

Chapman, A. (2010), *Mistra Future Fashion – Review of Life Cycle Assessments of Clothing*, Stockholm: Oakdene Hollins for Mistra. [Online] Available at: www.oakdenehollins.co.uk/media/232/2010_mistra_review_of_life_cycle_assessments_of_clothing.pdf (accessed 31 January 2014).

Fletcher, K. (2008), *Sustainable Fashion and Textiles: Design Journeys*, London: Earthscan.

Gardetti, M. A. and Torres, A. L. (2013), *Sustainability in Fashion and Textiles*, Sheffield, UK: Greenleaf.

Greenpeace (2011), *Dirty Laundry, Unravelling the Corporate Connections to Toxic Water Pollution in China*, Amsterdam: Greenpeace International. [Online] Available at: www.greenpeace.org/international/Global/international/publications/toxics/Water%202011/dirty-laundry-report.pdf (accessed 31 January 2014).

Greenpeace (2012), *Toxic Threads: The Big Fashion Stitch-Up*, Amsterdam: Greenpeace. [Online] Available at: http://issuu.com/greenpeaceinternational/docs/toxic-threads-1/1?e=2537715/1440427 (accessed 31 January 2014).

IPCC (2013), *Climate Change 2013*, New York: Cambridge University Press. [Online] Available at: www.climatechange2013.org/images/report/WG1AR5_ALL_FINAL.pdf (accessed 31 January 2014).

Meadows, D. H. (1997), 'Places to Intervene in a System.' *Whole Earth*, Winter. [Online] Available at: www.wholeearthmag.com/ArticleBin/109.html (accessed 12 December 2012).

Rockström, J., Steffen, W., Noone, K., Persson, Å., Chapin III, F. S., Lambin, E., Lenton, T. M., Scheffer, M., Folke, C., Schellnhuber, H., Nykvist, B., De Wit, C. A., Hughes, T., van der Leeuw, S. Rodhe, H., Sörlin, S., Snyder, P. K., Costanza, R., Svedin, U., Falkenmark, M., Karlberg, L., Corell, R. W., Fabry, V. J., Hansen, J., Walker, B., Liverman, D., Richardson, K., Crutzen, P. and Foley, J. (2009), 'Planetary boundaries: exploring the safe operating space for humanity.' *Ecology and Society*, 14, 2. [Online] Available at: www. ecologyandsociety.org/vol14/iss2/art32/ (accessed 31 January 2014).

Stern, N. (2006), *The Stern Review: Economics of Climate Change*. [Online] Available at: http://webarchive.nationalarchives.gov.uk/+/www.hm-treasury.gov.uk/media/3/6/Chapter_1_The_Science_of_Climate_Change.pdf (accessed 31 January 2014).

UNEP (2011), *Decoupling Natural Resource Use and Environmental Impacts from Economic Growth*. [Online] Available at: www.unep.org/resourcepanel/decoupling/files/pdf/decoupling_report_english.pdf (accessed 25 January 2014), p30.

PART I

Framing and expanding sustainability and fashion

We open this book with a view of fashion and sustainability that is both targeted and also telescopic. An alert but encompassing bird's eye view of a field that is alive to the dynamic whole: attentive to the lie of the land, the area's broad, underlying shaping forces, but also the small disturbances, flashes of movement, new growth. From such a vantage point above our emerging field we can discern patterns and flows of the fashion space and the intricate interplay of complex systems. We see synergies developing, both at the centre and on the periphery of the territory, stretching the field in new directions and depths and yielding new insights that shape our understanding and practice of fashion and sustainability. Here, the depth, breadth, complexity and interconnected nature of ecological, social and cultural understandings within the field are visible.

For us, such vision is vital, for, in a sector such as fashion that is powerfully shaped by commercial imperatives, this view acts as a countervailing voice and perspective. In fashion, action around ecological, social and cultural issues has predominantly operationalized sustainability from a perspective of commerce – where growth becomes the chief criterion for all programmes of improvement. The authors in this part see things differently, unfolding alternative narratives and possibilities, offering synergistic and continuous instead of divisive understandings of economic, ecological and sociocultural remits.

By looking to the fashion–sustainability 'offing', enabling a comprehensive view of the big perspectives, underlying patterns and, most urgently, relationships, **Kate Fletcher** (Chapter 1) reveals to what extent our fashion (and sustainability) awareness is shaped in a commercial guise. This repeated and common experience of fashion and sustainability as commerce can readily emerge as the defining narrative of the territory, suggesting, in subtle (or not so subtle) reinforcement of particular actions and approaches, their importance in focus and actions, and thereby shaping future action and imagination in its likeness. Yet, the status quo is not the only possible state of affairs. As revealed by her experimental exploration of the 'craft of use', it is but one, limited and limiting, story of fashion (and sustainability). Other parallel and powerful narratives, insights and practices exist that, if we invite and accept them, can show us ways for fashion and sustainability guided by dependencies on people and time and a deep sense of care, instead of commerce; and for these to liberate fashion into 'reality', that is, into a world of ecological limits, capabilities and deeper understanding of the human condition.

It was important for us that this volume should include a strong theoretical perspective on fashion, as the deeper understanding of the field and its complex motivations has – at a cost – often been lacking from the fashion and sustainability discourse. **Joanne Entwistle** (Chapter 2), therefore, concisely situates the sustainability imperative within an expanding fashion theory, remarking on the failure to effectively integrate perspectives from sociology with, for example, material flows. Fashion theory's association with gender has a long lineage, and Entwistle explores gender through two branches of literature focused variously on production and consumption. She then moves beyond this 'simplistic' analysis for a fuller account of fashion and sustainability and, drawing on the work of Bruno Latour, and actor network theory, she proposes an exploration of fashion as nature–culture hybrid to allow us 'the opportunity to see the continuities between our dress practices and their wider environmental impact'.

Louise St. Pierre (Chapter 3) complementarily illuminates fashion within the context of ecology. She powerfully and expressively reminds us that natural systems cannot be controlled by humans; instead, we must learn to manage ourselves within their boundaries. She outlines changes to natural systems, reflecting specifically on climate change. As a fundamental part of fostering a different relationship with the Earth, she calls for the development of an ecological literacy, the understanding of principles of ecology and natural systems in the fashion and sustainability community. For St. Pierre, these 'visceral, tangible and unshakeable relationships with the Earth' influence the current social imaginary of the modern West and include the ecological imagination, a precursor to deep and significant change, and only with this renewed sensibility can we make fashion futures of sustainability.

This section concludes with **John Thackara** (Chapter 4) treating us to a contextualization of fashion and sustainability in global political systems. He ignites our understandings of unsustainability by citing the detrimental effect of converting sustainability value into monetary values and then marketizing it, and the pervasive dualism of Western thought, which separates humankind from her surroundings. Foremost, he offers alternative ways to conceptualize and organize the world, building rich and diverse accounts of democracy in the context of sustainability, and drawing on commons as a way for 'constellations' of people and interested parties to cohabit successfully in 'social–ecological systems'. He points to the Latin American notion of *buen vivir* to argue for a politics that lets modern humans thrive *with* indigenous people, society *with* nature, and that favours stewardship instead of extraction: '*Buen Vivir* is not just about the individual, but the individual in the context of their unique environmental situation'.

1

OTHER FASHION SYSTEMS

Kate Fletcher

Introduction

In the summer of 2013, I was lucky enough to be part of a research trip that involved sailing around the Western Isles of Scotland. It was a transformatory experience in many ways, not least because, a few days into the voyage, I developed extreme longsightedness and could no longer see to read or sew. So many were the seascapes, wildlife sightings, changing colours of a waxing and waning moon, glimpses of magical light creeping around the edges of the sky, that my optical lenses fixed in long-view mode. Close work in books, with needle and thread, on a computer – the things that dominate so many hours of so many of my days – were shuffled unceremoniously by my body's optics into a back room. And the door closed firmly behind them. With it, my life was shown up for its relentless myopic bias, for the dominance within it of things close to eye – things I could now no longer see to do. Life then became different for me. I took the eyes' cue (what else could I do?) and started to look long and look far, to look to the 'offing' – the physical place that is the distant part of the sea.

Back on dry land and in the vicinity of an optician, I now have glasses. But the sea's legacy is, for me, a permanent physical reminder of the need to move my metaphorical field of vision beyond that which is close at hand; to shift gauge of focus, scale, rhythm, place and timeframe. To look to distant, broad perspectives, to underlying patterns, to gathering relationships and to subtle changes in 'weather' – that is, to look to the fashion–sustainability offing – in order to better understand the tides, channels of navigation and conditions nearby. In this chapter, I try to do just this. I should say that I have been attempting this big view for most of the two decades of my work exploring design for sustainability in fashion and textiles as a design researcher and consultant; that is, to understand things holistically, to work from the whole down to the level of the parts and detail; but longsightedness has leant this task an uncommon edge, for it is now the clearest vision I have. Hence, like many of my fellow authors in this book, I seek to explore the interplay of fashion and sustainability in the context of the dominant societal organizing forces affecting fashion, economic growth and consumerism. I investigate how these structures and behaviours and the complex or aggregate relationships of people in society reveal some – and obscure other – sustainability routes ahead for fashion, for such structures and behavioural patterns are like a partial nautical chart, mapping some features and currents, but failing to note others. Attempting to sketch in some of the other fashion geographies and practices that draw on a broader spectrum of activity than the buying and selling of new garments, I try to show that other systems of fashion provision and expression are both real and possible. This chapter seeks to tell stories of fashion with different emphases, allegiances, beliefs and visions from those most often experienced today, and, in so doing, to chart a course for other ways of doing things. I start with two tales of garment use from the general public, drawn from the *Local Wisdom* project.

Multiple functions take time

This top is made out of two shirts, two men's shirts . . . half of it is silk and half of it is polyester. You can totally unbutton the two halves from each other. So it means that you can wash [the two halves] separately, but it actually means that one side crinkles much more than the other, so I only have to iron half of that [laughs].

And I guess because it had a life as something else, it has this kind of memory that comes with it and whether that's the feeling that I get from always knowing that the pockets are in this slightly awkward position and also other people's recognition of that when they see me in it.

Figure 1.1 Multiple functions take time
Source: *Local Wisdom* project; photography by Paul Allister

I've also found that when I've had pieces like this which have multiple functions I don't really find the second function until I've owned it for a number of years. It is not something that I necessarily interchange, weekly. It might be I wear it one way for a year or two and then I discover how the other way now works. That sort of helps the longevity of a piece that might not be immediately apparent.

Size doesn't matter

This shirt belonged to my friend and flatmate who moved to Sydney about three years ago and he's about 5'5" or 5'6" maybe but we shared clothes even though he'd be small and skinny. I'm about 6'3" . . . the sleeves [of the shirt] are a bit short but I wear them rolled up so you wouldn't notice, but the rest of it fits fine. And then the jacket is my Dad's . . . part of a suit that he wore. He'd be a bit smaller than me as well. I think he was around 5'11" or that.

Figure 1.2 Size doesn't matter
Source: *Local Wisdom* project; photography by Des Moriaty

Fashion is consumption

In contrast to the view and practices of fashion evinced by these two stories, in neo-liberal market economies such as the UK (my home), the language and expression of the consumer society are so overriding in fashion that we hardly notice them. In the collective cultural consciousness, fashion *is* consumption, materialism, commercialization and marketing. It is buying high street and high end. It is watching, browsing, purchasing. Fashion comes to be anything that emerges from a certain consumerist machine. This is, somewhat predictably, also the view of fashion from many within the sustainability lobby, where there persists a reluctance to imagine fashion outside a commercial context that trades on novelty and status anxiety for economic return. In fact, it seems almost impossible to take this psychic leap, for the prevailing consumerist fashion style and story appear 'natural' to our way of thinking and behaviour: it is normal to access and engage with fashion primarily by exchanging money for product; it is expected that these same products will look dated and stylistically incongruous in six months; it is usual to discard, rather than repair.

Dig a little deeper, and we see other forces at play. It soon becomes apparent that consumerist fashion is locked into a cycle of self-justification, creating the very conditions by which it becomes both dominant and credible. Consumers see an ever more rapid cycle of new products introduced in stores (up to twelve seasons per year and moving towards a strategy of continuous replenishment; Anson, 2010: 4), because retailers compete on novelty. They buy items increasingly often, because the garments' inferior materials and construction means they fall apart quickly and need to be replaced (see also Chapter 12). They grow their reliance on fashion that can be made into and traded as a commodity, because the consumer society fails to value activities that cannot be marketed. In the consumer society, ideas about fashion are organized around commerce and consumerism, and most of those involved – that is, those of us who are creating fashion or wearing it – end up becoming dependent on them. In the consumer culture in which we live, we communicate through the social language of position and status determined by what we buy, and we capitulate to and reinforce the commercial and ideological pressure of the market as *the* route through which to organize our lives (Thorpe, 2012). In the creed of market economics, growth is essential in order to maintain stability of the economy, and, as such, ideas of 'progress' have become tied to a societal narrative of growth through buying more material goods, many of them shaped in garment form.

The fashion industry itself has evolved under this narrative. The dynamics of the sector, its business models and manufacturing approaches have been reshaped by tenets of growth, globalization and 'more and cheaper'. In the first decade of the twenty-first century, clothing prices in Europe fell by 26.2 per cent and in the US by 17.1 per cent (Anson, 2010: 5), and cheap garments have changed patterns of consumption: during that same decade, the number of pieces bought in the UK has increased by one-third (Allwood *et al.*, 2006: 11), that is, to a volume of 2 million tonnes per annum (*Textile Outlook International*, 2009: 99). In a merging of free-market ideology, changing business practices and technological development – which has seen the relaxing of global tariffs on trade of textiles and clothing; the relocation of the majority of production to low-labour-cost nations; the return of manufacturing of some trend-sensitive pieces to regions of high consumption to quicken their time to market; just-in-time manufacturing co-ordinated with electronic sales receipts to trigger replenishment production and more frequent stock drops in store – the sector has generated more opportunities to consume. For fashion brands, success is measured in retail sales figures reported as a percentage growth year on year, a success that is evidenced by data that suggest that nearly 70 per cent of garments in a wardrobe are inactive (Pure Profile, 2013), a surfeit that proves no barrier to producers manufacturing more clothes and to consumers buying additional new pieces.

Within this distinctive hierarchy of fashion provision based almost exclusively on an ideology of more consumption of new clothes, independent and shared expectations of creating fashion have been increasingly forgotten. Home sewing and mending habits that used to be relatively common across social classes, ages and genders have become less practiced, as the economic incentive to transform cloth into clothing and keep it clean and serviceable has been undercut by the cheap price of, and ready access to, new garments. Where they are still practised, home sewing and knitting, which have enjoyed a revival in recent years of recession, are often either the preserve of the ProAm (the Professional Amateur, that is highly skilled) maker (Leadbeater and Miller, 2004), or a badge of youthful experimentation, rather than a widespread and accepted fashion practice on a par with shopping for clothes. Further, sewing-machine-repair services, drapers and haberdashers are marginalized in town centres, away from the stores selling new garments, thereby isolating the business of maintaining and caring for garments from their purchase and thus making it difficult to experience fashion as autonomous from consumerist values. Elsewhere in this volume, Amy Twigger Holroyd (Chapter 25) discusses the ambiguous relationship many people have with garments they have made themselves, but it seems that market expectations reinforce the marginal aspect and individual idiosyncrasy of such engagements with fashion, framing them as temporary involvements, practised for a few short years before progression to new, shop-bought clothes.

Consumerist fashion: fashion's governing story

In a piece about the marginalization of cycling within societies designed for car transportation, environmental politics scholar Justin Williams (2010: 251) calls upon Herbert Marcuse's insights into the key factors that influence the governing story, technology or 'project of realization' in society. It is, Marcuse via Williams argues, related to dominant interests. The interests of the dominant parties favour one particular story and way of experiencing (in our case) fashion, and, in the process of favouring one story, these parties deny and reject others. The almost total influence of consumerist fashion within the fashion mindset means that alternatives are squeezed out (see also Chapter 28). Other options seem unworkable. In such a context, alternatives become seen as little valued, because cultural conditions and economic inducements create desire for the current set-up. Alternatives from outside the status quo appear inferior, impractical, expensive and unattractive. Yet the key point here is that the status quo is not the only possible state of affairs. The prevailing system is the result of intentional, political choice, and, as such, consumerist fashion is revealed as a power structure, rather than an expression of our desire for dressing ourselves in multiples of cheap garments. It is unveiled as a way to maintain and even expand the position of those with influence, not a reflection of fashion's wider potential and practice. To return again to the arguments made by Justin Williams (and reinterpreting them from his context of cycling to ours): consumerist fashion is not freely chosen by shoppers (it is the only option), nor are the fashion alternatives freely ignored (consumers do not know about them) (2010: 256); instead, it is dominant economic logic, business models, organizational structures and culture that dictate the prevailing view of fashion provision and expression – and repress other perspectives. There is, of course, nothing inevitable about this view. It is a result of the decisions we do or do not make.

These models and structures have also shaped expectations about the sorts of action that can be taken around sustainability. Industry, for its part, has concentrated on fine-tuning, making market adjustments to and engineering its growth model. Adjustments can be identified across the piece: reductions in the resource intensity of fibre production; developments that minimize use of energy and water in production; some improvements in conditions for workers; support for consumers to reduce the impact of the laundering process; reclamation and reuse of waste materials (see, for example, Fletcher and Grose, 2012). The logic that dominates fashion – growth economics and supporting business practices – has shaped the supply-side view of action on sustainability as a task of delivering efficiency improvements within the bounds of current practices. And yet a different vantage point offers the view that, improved as it is, the sector's relationship with growth will act to limit the success of efforts to improve its individual products and activities, setting up a self-defeating circle (see Ehrenfeld, Chapter 5). Although improvements have likely led to a decline in impact per garment – in Chapter 22, Lynda Grose cites a figure of 30 per cent for material efficiency improvement over the last 30 years – higher levels of consumption have overshadowed this reduction. Attempts to lessen the net impact of the fashion sector have been eroded by an increase in the number of garments in circulation. Consumers, even those buying 'eco' alternatives, are still locked into a relationship with fashion based on buying new clothes. In such a relationship, not only is consumption increased, but also dependency on capital exchange and commodity products as the representative fashion experience.

Relational fashion systems

Thus, it seems that we have allowed our fashion ideas, expectations and actions to be shaped by consumerism's view of a world that is individualistic, autonomous and drawn into the market. And this has meant that both fashion and fashion and sustainability have been understood *in separation* from the big picture view; at a distance from a clear view about what it is in the fashion sector we actually want to sustain into the future; apart from real understanding of individual and collective behaviour; afar from the social contexts of people's lives; unconnected to natural systems and planetary boundaries; and, I am certain, worse for it. By contrast, when we broaden the agenda for fashion beyond production and consumption of new clothes, goals for fashion and sustainability cease to be described merely in functional terms and, I suggest, emerge instead as a set of practices animated by concern for others. A key term here is practice, which, in the words of American poet Gary Snyder (1990: viii) is, 'a deliberate sustained and conscious effort to be more finely tuned to ourselves and to the way the actual existing world is'. In contrast to consumerist fashion, other fashion systems are rooted in experience and reality of the world and its contexts; *they are relational*.

Arguments, rehearsed in this volume and elsewhere, set out the need to base our underlying political economy on ideas other than growth and efficiency (Jackson, 2009), and to reimagine our relationship with materialistic consumption, particularly given the understanding that, beyond sufficient levels of accumulation, materialistic values undermine our well-being (Kasser, 2002; Offer, 2006). Here it seems vital to do two things. First, to develop knowledge that grounds and places us in our actual condition; that acknowledges the deep-rooted political and structural influence of the market and individualistic consumption on our ideas about fashion, in order to better understand its influence on us. And second, to stray outside this understanding: to re-appreciate the potential of fashion to nourish and foster other actions – to remake these charged political choices through our design and production decisions, through our wardrobes and as we dress. There is jeopardy at this contingent, complex interplay, for it involves a radical re-engagement with fashion on terms different from those that dominate it today, and these changed terms are widely distributed. Many of these different terms are explored in this book and range from a fashion commons, to a politics of mending, to new forms of togetherness in fashion. The riskiness of such a course of action, both for those who provide fashion and those who experience it, is perhaps essential preparation for life in a world whose climate is changing unpredictably and that is deciding new behaviours across the globe (McKibben, 2010). To deal with uncertainty of both natural and human systems is to cleave directly to the heart of the work of fashion and sustainability. That is to breed responses that move ideas and practices of fashion out of a space of fixed and narrow expectations, isolated individuals and organizations; out of rigid, 'permanent' fashion knowledge that prioritizes industrial information, fashion ideals, the primacy of the visual, the object and the sovereignty of consumers; but, rather, to steer expectations and provision of fashion to a place where fashion systems are relationally bound to others in ways that absorb disturbance and adapt with integrity in response to changing circumstances – to 'adaptive resilience' (Robinson, 2010).

As I have come to understand it, the relational process of fashion in sustainability is fundamentally based on a broadly held morality linked to caring for others and 'especially a kind of care that entails limiting oneself so that others can have the ecological space to live out their lives' (Wapner, 2010: 35). A mandate of care and its associated politics of thriving and fulfilment, which finds expression in terms of our own sense of what it is to be human, of relationships to others and the natural world (Ehrenfeld, 2008), provides direction to the fashion and sustainability discourse by broadening the spectrum of fashion activity that is seen as valuable. Here, alternatives are seeded, nourished and reared in open acknowledgement of – not subjugation to – conventional expectations of fashion. By highlighting other fashion systems, we see ourselves in a relational web that weakens an autonomous, socially indifferent view of fashion and explores a new set of social relationships based on responsibility to others. The sum of these alternatives' forces is what we can loosely call the spirit of fashion and sustainability, and they find form in both the individual and the system.

The 'craft of use'

For my own part, I have sought to explore these relational expressions of fashion and the behaviours and ideas of care most recently in a project called *Local Wisdom*.[1] The project explores the tending, fixing and satisfying use of clothing – described as the 'craft of use'[2] – attempting to direct attention to these practices at a time and in a sector that privileges creation of new items over maintenance and use of what we already have. The project draws on ethnographic methods, alongside design processes, to open up the 'deep inner space of the wardrobe' and amplify its insights, so as to drive change towards practices of sustainability in fashion in ways that see an increase in the qualitative experiences of fashion without quantitative growth. The study of the craft of use attempts to connect the world of material relationships, so often the preserve of industrial activity, with that of social relationships, the majority of which, 'belong to the consumer's life world' (Skov, 2011: n.p.). It then seeks to frame design and use as a single whole and infuse the practices of use into design thinking; that is, to investigate the honed skills of use and the informal pathways of influence in fashion that spring from wardrobes, in order to start the process of recognizing where widespread action can take place.

Many examples of resourceful, creative and connected fashion activity already exist and emerge out of domestic provisioning, thrift, care for others and a sense of community, reflecting what has been called a 'quiet sustainability' (Smith and Jehlička, 2013) (also see Chapter 15). Typically, they require some practical skill to enact, occasionally they are politically motivated, mostly they are personal, slow to develop and charged with social significance, and rarely do they require much in the way of materials or finance to carry them through. Yet their value is little regarded; to the extent that the main arena for formulating the self through fashion is the marketplace, such practices are driven underground. Moreover, actors from across the fashion system are unaware that such behaviours are missing from the fashion landscape and why. Recognizing such practices as valuable to fashion builds an awareness of fashion as a shared enterprise, as something that cannot be understood solely by its suitability for commoditization and trade, but rather as something that unfolds across time, space, between people and in the midst of real lives, a site of material and social exchange. Perhaps this is evidence that garments are not stationary objects, but rather are *matter in motion* (Simms and Potts, 2012: 11, from Lucretius), in an action of continual adaption of fashion provision and expression in and through our lives.

In his superlative book about peregrine falcons (part of my eclectic reading about the natural world since my trip to Scotland), J. A. Baker describes this shift from static to dynamic as the difference between a picture of the falcon and experience of the living bird:

> Books about birds show pictures of the peregrine. . . . Large and isolated in the gleaming whiteness of the page, the hawk stares back at you, bold, statuesque, brightly coloured. But when you have shut the book, you will never see that bird again. . . . The living bird will never be so large, so shiny-bright. It will be deep in landscape, and always sinking further back. . . . Pictures are waxworks beside the passionate mobility of the living bird.
>
> *(1967: 19)*

The same observation can be made of fashion. Fashion on a catwalk, in a magazine, on a mannequin, is an isolated waxwork, a still life beside the varied, unpredictable, fervent, 'deep landscape' of use practices of clothes experienced in the course of life. Fashion is created and presented in ways that do not refer to, or imagine, use over time, and it is different for it. Drawing on the work of Jeremy Till (2009: 77), who has explored similar ideas in architecture, we can see that fashion is constructed and promoted for the idealized moment *before* a person slips on a piece, before time and life enter the sleeves, mark the collar and crease the fabric at the front hip of the trouser leg. Severed from its context of use, fashion is reduced to an object, to a vehicle for trade, reinforcing the expression of fashion as a fleeting and never complete construction of self. Yet a more relational understanding of fashion converts the garment from waxwork to a frame within which a 'passionate mobile' life can unfold, through building an understanding of fashion based on people and time. This is a profoundly difficult challenge for a sector that has been – and continues to be – realized in separation from everyday use through time and around the models and rules of modern society. Stewart Brand (1994: 71), also writing about the built environment, describes this transition as: 'a leap from the certainties of controllable things in space to the self-organising complexities of an endlessly ravelling and unravelling skein of relationships over time'. In the hands of users, garments have a life of their own. Here, fashion has a new opportunity, to, as perfectly phrased by Evans, 'improve the human condition', compared with the opportunity of consumerist fashion to display and 'express the human condition' (in Till, 2009: 88). That is to perhaps recognize and facilitate practices such as those that express the craft of use:

Button vertebrae (from the Local Wisdom project)

This is a very old cashmere cardigan which has quite a strong connection with my Mum. She's quite a hoarder and I've inherited that off her . . . I've customised it by sewing on these buttons. I found that when I wore it, I actually liked to wear it back to front with the buttons done up the back. But to make it look more purposeful I decided to sew on all these little shell buttons here which are from a sort of collection of buttons that again my mum had that I think as she's worn through cardigans she tends to snip the buttons off. And I quite like the

Figure 1.3 Button vertebrae
Source: *Local Wisdom* project; photography by Tim Mitchell

way that if you wear it the right way round you end up with buttons sort of running down your spine like vertebrae. But then if you wear it that wrong way round its sort of in the place of where the buttons would go. And on the front, I've sewn some additional buttons onto the button stand which sort of makes up for the fact that some buttons are missing from where they should be and other ones are sort of extra so that it's all done up so that it's a little kooky here.

Conclusions

Ideas and expectations of fashion are 'locked in' to conventions, habits, social norms and industry structures that reflect a vision of our fashionable selves as individuals consuming new clothes, but, as the tales and images of garment use from *Local Wisdom* reveal, other forms of fashion expression and provision exist and reflect resourceful, fulfilling and empowering engagement with garments. Tentatively, this points to a situation where ideas of progress are no longer only tied to a societal narrative of economic growth through market transactions. For a sector such as fashion, which sees the purchasing and possessing of garments as a key way to construct freedom and individuality, this loosening of the fashion narrative's ties to growth is a radical move of hitherto unknown scope, and one that will necessarily form a central part of a research agenda for fashion and sustainability over the next decade. Yet this agenda is not for the academy alone. It is only when it is applied and actioned in the fashion sector, and the products generated are in active use, that the sustainability potential of a more broadly defined fashion economy will be released. Work of a foundational order is also the process of mapping, storytelling and developing of skills and capabilities that build a relational fashion economy of community shaped by an understanding about how our world is and the interdependencies that we face. We have always used (fashion) clothes to insulate, protect and shield us from the world; to thrive, we also need to use them to embrace and further that world.

Notes

1   www.localwisdom.info
2   www.craftofuse.org

References

Allwood, J. M., Laursen, S. E., Malvido de Rodriguez, C. and Bocken, N. M. P. (2006), *Well Dressed?* Cambridge: University of Cambridge Institute of Manufacturing.

Anson, R. (2010), 'End of the line for cheap clothing?' *Textile Outlook International*, 147: 4–10.

Baker, J. A. (1967), *The Peregrine*, New York: New York Review of Books.

Brand, S. (1994), *How Buildings Learn*, London: Penguin.

Ehrenfeld, J. (2008), *Sustainability by Design*, New Haven, CT: Yale.

Fletcher, K. and Grose, L. (2012), *Fashion and Sustainability: Design for Change*, London: Laurence King.

Jackson, T. (2009), *Prosperity without Growth*, London: Sustainable Development Commission.

Kasser, T. (2002), *The High Price of Materialism*, Cambridge, MA: MIT Press.

Leadbeater, C. and Miller, P. (2004), *The Pro-Am Revolution*, London: Demos.

McKibben, B. (2010), *Eaarth: Making a Life on a Tough New Planet*, New York: St Martin's Griffin.

Offer, A. (2006), *The Challenge of Affluence*, Oxford, UK: Oxford University Press.

Pure Profile (2013), *ahm Fashion Exchange* (research conducted in September 2013 on a sample of over 1,250 Australians across the country), Sydney: ahm.

Simms, A. and Potts, R. (2012), *The New Materialism*, London: Bread Print Roses.

Smith, J. and Jehlička, P. (2013), 'Quiet sustainability: fertile lessons from Europe's productive gardeners.' *Journal of Rural Studies*, 32: 148–57.

Robinson, M. (2010), *Making Adaptive Resilience Real*, London: Arts Council England. [Online] Available at: www.artscouncil.org.uk/media/uploads/making_adaptive_resilience_real.pdf (accessed 3 June 2013).

Skov, L. (2011), *Entering the Space of the Wardrobe*, Creative Encounters Working Paper 58, Copenhagen: Copenhagen Business School.

Snyder, G. (1990), *The Practice of the Wild*, Berkeley, CA: Counterpoint Press.

Textile Outlook International, (2009), 'Textiles and clothing: opportunities for recycling', 139: 94–113.

Thorpe, A. (2012), *Architecture versus Consumerism*, London: Earthscan.

Till, J. (2009), *Architecture Depends*, Cambridge, MA: MIT Press.

Wapner, P. (2010), Sacrifice in an age of comfort, in Maniates, M. and Meyer, J. M. (eds), *The Environmental Politics of Sacrifice*, Cambridge, MA: MIT Press: 33–59.

Williams, J. (2010), Bikes, sticks, carrots, in Maniates, M. and Meyer, J. M. (eds), *The Environmental Politics of Sacrifice*, Cambridge, MA: MIT Press: 247–69.

2

SUSTAINABILITY AND FASHION

Joanne Entwistle

Introduction

In this chapter, I want to examine some of the ways in which fashion has been analysed and criticised within the social sciences, particularly from my own discipline, sociology, and explore what connections we might make between fashion and sustainability that have not been fully addressed within this literature. What I suggest is that much critical analysis of fashion from social science scholars, from the late nineteenth century onwards, chimes with contemporary sustainability debates and criticisms, even though the term sustainability isn't used in this early literature. Broadly speaking, the association with femininity has done much to diminish and discredit fashion, with early tendencies to see fashion as immoral and not worthy of intellectual analysis. This classic literature has been challenged more recently with the growth of fashion studies in Europe and North America. This literature is summarised in the first part of the chapter. In the second part of the chapter, I want to consider how we might bring fashion and sustainability together for a more comprehensive analysis. I argue that we need to find new and innovative ways to examine these in a more integrated way and argue for an actor–network-theory (ANT) approach.

Part I: fashion research within the social sciences

Although it has often been marginalised and considered 'trivial' or irrelevant, fashion has a long history within the social sciences, drawing the attention of sociologists, psychologists and cultural studies theorists in particular (see, for example, Flugel, 1930; Veblen 1953 [1899]; Simmel, 1950, 1971; Wilson and Taylor, 1989; Entwistle, 2000; Entwistle and Wilson, 2001; Wilson, 2003). The low status of fashion, vis-à-vis other more supposedly 'serious' topics, has, to some extent, changed more recently with a growing recognition of fashion's multi-million-pound significance as a major cultural industry and employer (Pratt, 2004, 2008). Sustainability, on the other hand, has received relatively little attention by social scientists, and the connections between fashion and sustainability have not been fully explored, despite the fact that fashion's sustainability (or not) is now a hot topic within mainstream media and a major issue more broadly, as I argue below.

When reviewing the now vast and constantly expanding literature on fashion, it is apparent that the social meanings and practices around modern fashionable dress are key concerns. Much of this literature is concerned with questions of identity, examined from the point of view of gender (Veblen, 1953 [1899]), 'race' and ethnicity (Kondo, 1997; Kawamura, 2004), class identity (Veblen, 1953 [1899]; Simmel, 1971; Cohen, 1972; Hall and Jefferson, 1976), sexuality (Lewis and Rolley, 1997; Geczy and Karaminas, 2013) and religion (Lewis, 2013). The association with gender has perhaps the longest pedigree within the literature, with fashion associated more closely with women. This is historically inaccurate, as aristocratic men and women were both engaged in fashion in the early years of its development. That said, by the nineteenth century, a close association of femininity with fashion was firmly established, along with the idea of 'separate spheres' – men in the world of production and work, and women in the world of consumption and the home. In addition, the idea of a 'great masculine renunciation' of finery in dress was widely accepted among scholars (Flugel, 1930; Kutcha, 2002), although it has since been challenged as too simplistic (Wilson, 2003; Shannon, 2006).

What does this concern with gender have to do with issues of sustainability? We can begin to answer this question by dividing it into two branches of literature, one that is focused on production and the other concerned with consumption, and examine the ways in which femininity has been closely associated with fashion on both sides of this equation.

Taking production first, it is a simple fact that fashionable dress has, historically, been produced by female seamstresses, sitting at an individual sewing machine. This work has, notoriously, been conducted under harsh 'sweated' conditions: long hours in hot, dangerous, poorly regulated factories for low pay (see also Chapter 21). Even when not produced in factories, home-working seamstresses are also poorly paid and have to work long hours (Phizacklea, 1990). These production characteristics have long been a source of concern and condemnation and closely associated questions of sustainability today. Thus, Karl Marx's critique of capitalism (1976) attended to the problems of both the textile industry and the sweated labour conditions in factories producing garments (see Harris, 2005, for a fuller discussion of nineteenth-century needlewomen).

As production of garments, alongside many other products, now happens across vast global distance, in search of the cheapest labour, more recent, Marxist-inspired literature has focused attention on global commodity chains, or GCCs, which emphasise the connections within any commodity system, linking up all parts of production across the chain – what is referred to as a 'vertical' chain. Commodity chain analysis traces the entire trajectory of the product within a political economy of development perspective (Hughes and Reimer, 2004; Raghuram, 2004), and there are broadly two approaches – world systems theory and systems of provision.

Taking the former first, 'world systems theory' (Wallerstein, 1974; Hopkins and Wallerstein 1986; Gereffi and Korzeniewicz, 1994; Gereffi 1994, 1999) has its roots in Marxist theory and aims to trace the connections between production in 'peripheral' regions (where there is cheap labour) to 'core' or Western retail and consumption areas. Here we have arrived at one of the heartland issues of sustainability: working pay and conditions and the human toll that Western appetites for shiny new consumer goods, such as cheap fashions, takes on the workers who toil to produce. Much as fashion was a driver of industrialisation in the nineteenth century in countries such as Britain, it is now a driver of development in the countries located in the global South and East. And, just as with nineteenth-century industrialisation, it is women, predominantly, who bear the brunt of the harsh industrial systems of production. Thus, whereas, in the nineteenth century when Marx was writing, the workforce being exploited for its labour in the cramped and unhealthy environment of the sweatshop was formed of home-grown women and children, today's sweated labour is much further away. Indeed, this has been part of the problem. The rise of 'fast fashion' – cheap fashion garments in large retail chains – has brought with it a need to find ever cheaper labour, as the workforce at home became too expensive. This sourcing of labour abroad, in factories of India and Bangladesh and in newly capitalist countries such as Poland, not only makes for a longer supply chain, often with subcontractors pushing the responsibility and duty of care for workers' health and well-being further away, it has also meant a greater distance between Western consumers and the Eastern and Southern producers, putting it 'out of sight, out of mind'. What academic writing and global activism since the 1990s have done (Ross, 1997; Klein, 2000) is bring this murky production out into the light, forcing many of the bigger brands such as Nike and Gap to alter their relationships to subcontractors. However, wave after wave of scandal continues to put labour practices in the spotlight, as when a fire in a Bangladeshi factory hit the headlines in 2013. These awful stories provide moments in which to reflect on the harsh working environment that feeds the Western fashion system, although fashion is by no means the only problematic industry.

Although commodity chain approaches examine vertical relationships between production and consumption and are sensitive to the power dynamics between 'core' and 'peripheral' nations, it is not exclusively linear relations we need to consider when trying to understand the relationships within any system of production. Some of the literature within sociology and geography has argued that we should also consider the 'horizontal' features, which might relate different commodity chains (Leslie and Reimer, 1999; Hughes and Reimer, 2004). Indeed, Leslie and Reimer (1999: 407) ask, 'Is there a vertical uniqueness to individual commodity chains? Does a vertical approach neglect the interconnections between different systems of provision?' Some workers in fashion might have more in common with workers in other design/aesthetic production – say in furniture design – than they do with other workers in the same industry, further along the chain. For example, a fashion buyer in London probably has more in common with an urban-based architect or interior designer than they do with workers in India who make the clothes they buy. This point about horizontal connections may also caution us from seeing fashion as the only industry with labour practice problems: in the IT industry, workers in India producing iPads and smartphones have been shown to endure similarly bad working conditions and poor labour practices as workers in the fashion industry. We might ask why it is that fashion is often singled out for more condemnation, as against other manufactured goods: could it be something to do with the lingering suspicion that fashion is more 'trivial', that some-how consumption of fashionable dress is more problematic and immoral than consumption of the obligatory smartphone or tablet? Is there a lingering gendered prejudice at work here? (See also Chapter 28.)

Another form of commodity chain analysis is the systems of provision (SOPS) approach, which traces the 'vertical' connections between production and consumption, but, whereas GCC tends to move linearly from production to consumption, SOPS tends to see a more dialectical relationship between production and consumption that recognises the cultural significance of commodities and acknowledges the important dynamics between production and consumption (Hughes and Reimer, 2004). A SOPS approach to fashion has been most fully examined by Fine and Leopold (Leopold, 1992; Fine and Leopold, 1993; Fine, 1995). Their 'systems' approach takes into account the importance of consumers in determining some of what appear as com-modities within any system and also recognises the critical importance of distribution systems and 'middlemen' (*sic*) as 'linchpins' within systems of provision.

What does all this focus on 'systems' and 'commodity chains' tell us about the ways in which fashion has been thought about and how we might connect it up to concerns about sustainability? For one thing, this way of approaching fashion focuses attention on the importance of thinking about the entire fashion cycle, from production through to distribution, retail and consumption. Production is only one side of the story: a second body of literature has dealt with the relationships between gender and consumption.

Indeed, the literature on gender and consumption is extensive. From cultural histories (Vickery, 1993; de Grazia and Furlough, 1996; Jones, 1996, 2014) to contemporary accounts of women's relationship with dress (Entwistle, 1997, 2001; Woodward, 2007), we find there is a concern with the gendered identity of fashion consumers. Fashion has long been criticised as a cruel, exploitative industry, one that is oppressive to women in particular, as it is women who, in the eyes of some social and cultural theorists, are 'victims' of the (supposedly) 'frivolous' and 'ridiculous' pendulum swings of fashion. This line of criticism dates far back through the centuries, but, by the nineteenth century, it sparked a number of dress reform movements that attempted to eradicate fashion and introduce a new, more 'rational' and 'healthy' system of dress (see Newton, 1974, for a fuller discussion).

One academic associated with this critical stance towards fashion is Thorstein Veblen (1953 [1899]). For Veblen, writing at the end of the nineteenth century in the United States, it was the fashions of the nouveau riche that were a problem and that he criticised for their 'irrational' fashionable dress. In his view, fashion is about class competition, worn by women in the newly emerging urban petite bourgeoisie for the vicarious display of the wealth of their husbands. As he sees it, to be 'in fashion', one has to be wealthy enough to follow the incessant pendulum swings of style, which involves discarding garments before they are worn out, something he argued is inherently irrational and wasteful. Further, the fashions themselves display this wealth by being demonstratively constraining – corsets, heavy skirts and so on – suggesting the woman is not able to work and, therefore, further demonstrating the pecuniary strength of the husband.

Although Veblen's analysis was directed at a small social milieu at the turn of the nineteenth century, some of the central tenets of his analysis have had wider application. His view of the fashionable bourgeoisie women as the 'chattels' of men seems outdated now, although feminists from the first wave in the early part of the twentieth century through to second-wave feminism in the late twentieth century have also had cause to criticise the seemingly oppressive strictures of the Western fashion system, and there has been a tendency to see women as unwitting 'victims' of fashion, whereas men, on the other hand, are somehow placed above or beyond it. This is, indeed, a simplification of fashion; plenty of scholars (Breward, 1995; Edwards, 1997; Shannon, 2006) have demonstrated male engagement with fashion throughout history, and a whole host of dandies have graced the last few centuries (see, for example, Baudelaire, 1986 [1863]). Further, women are not necessarily unwitting and passive recipients of fashion messages and styles, but active and engaged in their choices and practices of dress, as much contemporary fashion scholarship has demonstrated (Woodward 2007). That said, suspicion permanently hovers over fashion, and there remains a lingering idea that women are 'passive' and easily swayed by fashion: one only has to think about concerns about 'size zero' fashion models and eating disorders to see a similar construction of young women as vulnerable followers of fashion.

Perhaps of continued relevance today is Veblen's basic premise – that fashion is about social competition and emulation – which has retained analytical power, albeit with some degree of scepticism from some theorists (Campbell, 1997). Indeed, Veblen's critique, although challenged by fashion scholars as both historically inaccurate and too simplistic (Wilson, 2003), chimes with some contemporary unease with fashion and the lingering feeling that it is an inherently irrational and wasteful system.

More recently, however, a new 'fashion studies' challenges this simplistic analysis, as well as shifting academic attention to new concerns. One significant area focuses on fashion as a 'creative' industry, examining the nature of production and labour in this sector (McRobbie, 2000; Pratt and Jeffcutt, 2002). Here, there is a concern with the sustainability of careers in the so-called 'creative industries/sector', which depend upon a willingness to identify with 'creative' work and put up with poor conditions – freelance and contract-based work, low pay, long and irregular working hours (McRobbie, 2002; Mears and Finlay, 2005; Entwistle and Wissinger, 2006). However, we have yet to see a fuller account of fashion and sustainability from within a social science perspective.

Part II: fashion and sustainability – where to now?

Indeed, in contrast to a growing literature on fashion in general, there has been much less written on the issue of sustainability and fashion from a sociological perspective. What literature there is tends to be within business and management studies and is concerned with corporate social responsibility, or CSR (Dickson *et al.*, 2009). Although sociological attention has yet to catch up with these issues, there is, at least, growing recognition of the need to examine fashion and sustainability: for example, the Nordic Fashion Association now brings together designers and academics across the Nordic countries and beyond (with collaborations in the UK as well). In the remaining part of this chapter I focus on how we might develop a more integrated account of fashion and sustainability, deriving from recent work within actor–network theory and practice theory. Both offer ways of connecting up different actors and practices to provide a more integrated approach to the analysis of fashion and sustainability.

Of all the pressing issues with sustainability, the one that perhaps dominates discussion is the environment and the cost of our production and consumption practices on natural resources such as air and water. Indeed, from high water usage in such things as cotton production, to the cost of transporting clothes across vast territories in search of the cheapest labour to stitch knickers (or whatever!), to the problems of our over-consumption of fast fashion and the amount of landfill we create, fashion has been under the spotlight in the popular press in recent years on account of its high environmental costs. This issue is definitely something that warrants attention from social scientists.

One explanation as to why sustainability has only recently come to the attention of traditional social science might be down to the sharp division traditionally drawn between the natural and the social world. Environmental costs have, therefore, been placed on the 'nature' side of the division and, as a result, tend to be under-analysed, as sociologists focus on 'social' concerns. There are exceptions to this, of course – the work of sociologist Ted Benton (1993) stands out in particular, both for his critiquing this nature/culture division within sociological thought and for putting the environment and ecology on the academic agenda. That said, we have still very few studies that examine sustainability issues alongside fashion.

What perhaps is needed is to think more radically about how we connect up nature and culture, if we are to try to fully map the relationships between our clothing and the surrounding environment. ANT provides some fruitful avenues of enquiry. To understand the radical intervention this approach has made in social science, we need to acknowledge the work of French theorist, Bruno Latour. Latour (1993) challenges our preconceptions about what it is to be 'modern', which, he argues, depends upon an artificial distinction between 'nature' and 'culture' that sustains the view of 'culture' as superior and active and 'nature' as inferior and passive. As he powerfully points out, the objects we label as 'natural' are actually products of our particular historical/social ways of seeing and are, therefore, not simple, natural objects, but nature–culture artefacts, or *hybrids*. For example, modern science depends upon various instruments and devices that enable us to 'see' things: microscopes that allow us to see bacteria or cells invisible to the naked eye, for example. This has led biology into areas of human 'culture' – examining the human genome for example. In this sense, then, nature is no longer seen as merely 'out there', separate and different to us, but we are continuous with nature, a part of it, and our apparently 'social' world is in fact a hybrid of nature–culture (see Entwistle and Slater, 2013; Entwistle, forthcoming 2015, for fuller discussion). Latour's approach has helped to open up this dialogue between science and culture, referred to as Science and Technology Studies or STS.

If we follow this logic, something seemingly 'cultural' such as fashion is shown to be a hybrid creation, in part 'natural', made up of natural materials – such as cotton and water, for example – which are 'assembled' (an ANT word) into our 'social/cultural' world in complex ways. Thus, we need not see a sharp distinction between the 'natural' and 'cultural' dimensions of fashion at all, but simply examine the continuous flow of materials, objects and actors that make up fashionable dress. Indeed, if we are trying to think more ecologically – that is, see ourselves as part of the Earth's ecology, not somehow separate or 'above' it – then to think about fashion as a nature–culture hybrid is highly beneficial. This way of thinking depends upon a different understanding of the meaning of 'actor'. For ANT, an 'actor' is anything with an ability to act in some capacity; hence, water is an actor, as it is an active component of the materials that make up fashion (and, indeed, just about everything else as well).

ANT provides us with a methodology for 'tracing' these connections, by instructing us to closely observe and 'follow the actors', in order to see where they go, what they do. If we do this for fashion garments, we might start with fields of cotton in India, or production factories somewhere in Asia, and follow the actors – from the production of textiles to their construction into garments, their distribution to shops and on to consumers, and beyond consumption to disposal and waste. As we follow them, 'natural' actors come into contact with 'cultural' actors, in complex 'assemblages' or hybrids.

This careful attention to materiality and practice evident in STS/ANT has been extended in the work of Shove and others (Shove *et al.*, 2007) to focus attention on design and consumption practices. Shove (2003) examines how everyday objects are utilised in everyday practice, often creatively, and she argues that this feeds into the design of objects. 'Practice theory' has tended to examine such things as domestic appliances and everyday technologies – for example, 'Nordic walking' (Shove, 2005; see also Pantzar and Shove, 2005) – but there is plenty of scope for extending this way of thinking to fashion consumption, to examine the life cycle of clothes as part of our everyday material culture and look into ways of making our fashion production and consumption more sustainable.

Conclusion

As I have argued in this chapter, there is a long tradition of social science writing on fashion, and we can find within it some themes that touch on issues we now call sustainability. However, we urgently need to think through fashion and sustainability in more sustained and integrated ways if we are to fully understand our relationship to fashionable clothing. I have suggested that ANT and practice theory offer innovative ways of thinking through fashion and sustainability, although the potential of these approaches has yet to be fully applied. They both attend to the importance of materiality and our relationships to objects that enable us to think through fashion as a material practice. Thinking of fashion as a nature–culture hybrid affords us the opportunity to see the continuities between our dress practices and their wider environmental impact. Practice theory attends to the many different ways in which our use of objects feeds back into their design. Brought together, we can use these two approaches to develop a more comprehensive and global account of fashion as not simply about 'identity' or 'meaning' or 'consumption' – those buzz words in many sociological texts on fashion – but as stretched across the entire range of practices, from production to distribution and consumption, and find more productive ways of tying these together.

References

Baudelaire, C. (1986 [1863]), *My Heart Laid Bare and Other Prose Writings*, London: Soho Book Company.

Benton, T. (1993), *Natural Relations?: Animal Rights, Human Rights and the Environment*, London: Verso Books.

Breward, C. (1995), *The Culture of Fashion*, Manchester, UK: Manchester University Press.

Campbell, C. (1997), When the meaning is not a message: a critique of the consumption as communication thesis, in Nava, M., Blake, A., MacRury, I. and Richards, B. (eds), *Buy this Book: Studies in Advertising and Consumption*, London: Routledge: 239–54.

Cohen, S. (1972), *Folk Devils and Moral Panics: The Creation of the Mods and Rockers*, London: Paladin.

de Grazia, V. and Furlough, E. (eds) (1996), *The Sex of Things: Gender and Consumption in Historical Perspective*, London: University of California Press.

Dickson, M. A., Locker, S. and Eckman, M. (eds.) (2009), *Social Responsibility in the Global Apparel Industry*, New York: Fairchild Books.

Edwards, T. (1997), *Men in the Mirror: Men's Fashions and Consumer Society*, London: Cassell.

Entwistle, J. (1997), Power dressing and the fashioning of the career woman, in Nava, M., MacRury, I., Blake, A. and Richards, B. (eds), *Buy this Book: Studies in Advertising and Consumption*, London: Routledge.

Entwistle, J. (2000), Fashioning the career woman: power dressing as a strategy of consumption, in Andrews, M. and Talbot. M. (eds), *All the World and Her Husband: Women, Consumption and Power*, London: Continuum International Publishing Group: 224–38.

Entwistle, J. (2001), Fashioning of the career woman: power dressing as a strategy of consumption, in Talbot, M. and Andrews, M. (eds), *All the World and Her Husband: Women and Consumption in the Twentieth Century*, London: Cassell: 224–38.

Entwistle, J. (forthcoming 2015), Latour, actor–network–theory and fashion, in Rocamora, A. (ed.), *Thinking Through Fashion*, London: I. B. Tauris.

Entwistle, J. and Slater, D. (2013), 'Reassembling the cultural: fashion models, brands and the meaning of "culture" after ANT.' *Journal of Cultural Economy*, 7 (2): 161–77.

Entwistle, J. and Wilson, E. (eds) (2001), *Body Dressing*, Oxford, UK: Berg.

Entwistle, J. and Wissinger, E. (2006), 'Keeping up appearances: aesthetic labour in the fashion modelling industries of London and New York.' *Sociological Review*, 54 (4): 774–94.

Fine, B. (1995), From political economy to consumption, in Miller, D. (ed.), *Acknowledging Consumption: A Review of New Studies*, London: Routledge: 127–63.

Fine, B. and Leopold, E. (1993), *The World of Consumption*, London: Routledge.

Flugel, J. C. (1930), *The Psychology of Clothes*, London: The Hogarth Press.

Geczy, A. and Karaminis, V. (eds) (2013), *Queer Style*, London: Bloomsbury Academic.

Gereffi, G. (1994), The organization of buyer-driven global commodity chains: how US retailers shape overseas production networks, in Gereffi, G. and Korzeniewicz, M. (eds), *Commodity Chains and Global Capitalism*, Westport, CT: Greenwood Press: 95–122.

Gereffi, G. (1999), 'International trade and industrial upgrading in the apparel commodity chain.' *Journal of International Economics*, 48: 37–70.

Gereffi, G. and Korzeniewicz, M. (eds) (1994), *Commodity Chains and Global Capitalism*, Westport, CT: Greenwood Press.

Hall, S. and Jefferson, T. (eds) (1976), *Resistance Through Rituals: Youth Subcultures in Post-war Britain*, London: Hutchinson.

Harris, B. (ed.) (2005), *Famine and Fashion: Needlewomen in the Nineteenth Century*, Aldershot, UK: Ashgate.

Hopkins, T. K. and Wallerstein, I. (1986), 'Commodity chains in the world economy.' *Review*, 10: 157–70.

Hughes, A. and Reimer, S. (eds) (2004), *Geographies of Commodity Chains*, London: Routledge.

Jones, J. (1996), Coquettes and grisettes: women buying and selling in *ancien régime* Paris, in de Grazia, V. and Furlough, E. (eds), *The Sex of Things: Gender and Consumption in Historical Perspective*, London: University of California Press: 25–53.

Jones, J. (2014), Gender and eighteenth-century fashion, in Black, S., de la Haye, A., Entwistle, J. et al. *The Handbook of Fashion Studies*, London: Bloomsbury Academic: 121–36.

Kawamura, Y. (2004), *The Japanese Revolution in Paris Fashion*, Oxford, UK: Berg.

Kutcha, D. (2002), *The Three-Piece Suit and Modern Masculinity*, Berkeley, CA: University of California Press.

Klein, N. (2000), *No Logo*, London: HarperCollins.

Kondo, D. (1997), *About Face: Performing Race in Fashion and Theatre*, London: Routledge.

Latour, B. (1993), *We Have Never Been Modern*, London: Harvester/Wheatsheaf.

Leopold, E. (1992), The manufacture of the fashion system, in Ash, J. and Wilson, E. (eds) *Chic Thrills*, London: Pandora: 101–17.

Leslie, D. and Reimer, S. (1999), 'Spatializing commodity chains.' *Progress in Human Geography*, 23 (3): 401–20.

Lewis, R. (2013), *Modest Fashion: Styling Bodies, Mediating Faith*, London: I. B. Tauris.

Lewis, R. and Rolley, K. (1997), (Ad)dressing the dyke: lesbian looks and lesbian looking, in Nava, M., Blake, A., MacRury, I. and Richards (eds), *Buy this Book: Studies in Advertising and Consumption*, London: Routledge: 259–309.

McRobbie, A. (2000), Fashion as a culture industry, in Bruzzi, S. and Church Gibson, P. (eds), *Fashion Cultures: Theories, Explanations and Analysis*, London: Routledge.

McRobbie, A. (2002), 'Clubs to companies: notes on the decline of political culture in speeded up creative worlds.' *Journal of Cultural Studies*, 16 (4): 516–31.

Marx, K. (1976), *Capital*, Vol. I, London: Penguin/New Left Review.

Mears, A. and Finlay, W. (2005), 'Not just a paper doll: how models manage bodily capital and why they perform emotional labor.' *Journal of Contemporary Ethnography*, 34: 317.

Newton, S. M. (1974), *Health, Art and Reason: Dress Reformers of the 19th Century*, London: John Murray.

Pantzar, M. and Shove, E. (2005), 'Understanding innovation in practice: a discussion of the production and reproduction of Nordic walking.' *Technology Analysis and Strategic Management*, 22 (4): 447–62.

Phizacklea, A. (1990), *Unpacking the Fashion Industry: Gender, Racism and Class in Production*, London: Routledge.

Pratt, A. (2004), Mapping the cultural industries: regionalisation; the example of South East England, in Scott, A. J. and Power, D. (eds), *The Cultural Industries and the Production of Culture*, London: Routledge: 19–36.

Pratt, A. (2008), Locating the cultural economy, in Anheier, H. and Isar, Y. R. (eds), *The Cultural Economy*, London: Sage: 42–51.

Pratt, A. and Jeffcutt, P. (2002), 'Managing creativity in the cultural industries.' *Creativity and Innovation Management*, 11 (4): 225–33.

Raghuram, P. (2004), Initiating the commodity chain: South Asian women and fashion in the diaspora, in Hughes, A. and Reimer, S. (eds), *Geographies of Commodity Chains*, London: Routledge: 120–36.

Ross, A. (ed.) (1997), *No Sweat: Fashion, Free Trade and the Rights of Garment Workers*, London: Verso.

Shannon, B. (2006), *The Cut of his Coat: Men, Dress and Consumer Culture in Britain, 1860–1914*, Athens, OH: University of Ohio Press.

Shove, E. (2003), *Comfort, Cleanliness and Convenience: The Social Organization of Normality*, Oxford, UK: Berg.

Shove, E. (2005), 'Consumers, producers and practices: understanding the invention and reinvention of Nordic walking.' *Journal of Consumer Culture*, 5 (1): 43–64.

Shove, E., Watson, M., Hand, M. and Ingram, J. (2007), *The Design of Everyday Life*, Oxford, UK: Berg.

Simmel, G. (1950), *The Sociology of Georg Simmel*, London: Collier-MacMillan.

Simmel, G. (1971), *Fashion. On Individuality and Social Forms*. Levine, D. (ed.), London: University of Chicago Press.

Veblen, T. (1953 [1899]) *The Theory of the Leisure Class: An Economic Study of Institutions*, New York: Macmillan.

Vickery, A. (1993), Women and the world of goods: a Lancashire consumer and her possessions, 1751–81, in Brewer, J. and Porter, R. (eds), *Consumption and the World of Goods*, London: Routledge: 274–301.

Wallerstein, I. (1974), *The Modern World System*, London: London Academic Press.

Wilson, E. (2003), *Adorned in Dreams: Fashion and Modernity*, London: I. B. Tauris.

Wilson, E. and Taylor, L. (1989), *Through the Looking Glass: A History of Dress from 1860 to the Present Day*, London: BBC Books.

Woodward, S. (2007), *Why Women Wear What They Wear*, Oxford, UK: Berg.

3

NATURE'S SYSTEMS

Louise St. Pierre

Introduction

I write here as both an industrial designer and a farmer's daughter. My connection to the land means that I see nature's systems as inviolable, a view that has resulted in great internal conflict throughout my 30-year industrial design career. I have seen creative energy poured into projects that prioritized industry over the environment and noted time and again how chains of seemingly small decisions created momentum to carry us further and further from sustaining our natural world. From this perspective, I wonder: can we appreciate how urgent it is that we become more ecologically knowledgeable? Could greater ecological literacy then help us to distinguish industry rhetoric from ideas that genuinely steward the Earth? Ultimately, can we, as designers, producers and shapers of culture, shift the momentum of the fashion industry to support natural systems?

Countless texts throughout history offer insight into the beauty and power of natural systems, and yet their wisdom eludes contemporary understanding. Most of us in Western society continue to work through the day unaware of natural processes that nourish life and natural processes that transmit our industrial-age mistakes around the planet. With this limited knowledge, we are participating in industrial systems that have tremendous impact on the natural world that we rely on for survival. Our lack of ecological understanding has contributed to the compromise or demise of many natural systems.

In this chapter, I briefly outline core ecological principles and call for research that actively probes for methods to viscerally engage all levels of society with the Earth. I believe this is how to engender the commitment needed to reorganize the way that we design, produce, sell, distribute and consume artefacts in alignment with the requirements of the ecosphere.

Ecological literacy

Ecological literacy, or ecoliteracy, begins with understanding the principles of ecology and natural systems. In my experience, this involves more than academic understanding. Ecoliteracy is most functional when it emerges from a tangible engagement with nature's processes. 'We can be ethical only in relation to something we can see, feel, understand, love, or otherwise have faith in' (Leopold, 1949: 214). Educational initiatives offer ecoliteracy opportunities for children that are based in tactile and experiential learning (Stone and Barlow, 2005; Goleman *et al.*, 2012; Center for Ecoliteracy, 2013). There are, however, few of these initiatives directed at adults, which unfortunately implies that engaged ecoliteracy is either childish or unimportant. Further, existing initiatives do not reach many of today's decision-makers. According to Bill McKibben, the widespread notion that global warming was going to be an issue 'for our grandchildren' was deceptively lulling: the crisis is well ahead of schedule (McKibben, 2011: 51), and it is adults who have the most immediate need of ecological literacy.

Ecoliteracy theory highlights gaps in our knowledge:

> There are laws of sustainability which are natural laws, just as the law of gravity is a natural law. In our science in past centuries, we have learned a lot about the law of gravity and similar laws of physics, but we have not learned very much about the laws of sustainability.
>
> *(Capra, 2013)*

This knowledge gap is highly problematic. Michael Decleris, writing about the laws of sustainable development for the European Commission, articulates the principle that all citizens should act as stewards of the Earth, and that, in order to do so, they have a basic right to information about the environment (Decleris, 2000: 123). However, biologist Søren Nielsen claims that most ecology textbooks fail to include accurate information on the behaviour of ecosystems (2007). To compound this, the media are often manipulated to offer misleading environmental information (Oreskes and Conway, 2011). Many citizens may have a superficial ecological understanding at best, and others are labouring under misinformation.

Although the general population may have grown cynical about advertising's overuse of the terms 'green' and 'eco', industry's solutions to environmental problems are often still welcomed uncritically. For example, consider so-called compostable plastics. Most 'compostable' plastics decompose in industrially manufactured, fossil-fuel-powered equipment under strict temperature and humidity conditions and can't be composted at home (Royte, 2006). Chemical additives find their way into food chains as toxins, a complex issue that is avoided by regulatory agencies (Sullivan, 2011). Industrial compost processing consumes energy and generates contaminated refuse. Garden composting methods do the reverse: they generate thermal energy and nutrients. The acceptance of 'compostable' plastics in place of an ecological system illustrates how gaps in critical understanding permit misuse of resources and ongoing degradation of ecological systems: from producer to designer to consumer.

Changes to natural systems

The degree to which the Earth has changed is an indication of how important it is to understand the way natural systems work. Environmentalist and scholar Bill McKibben has been observing and documenting climate change since he wrote *The End of Nature* in 1989. He reflects in his recent book *Eaarth* (not Earth – the name was modified to convey how different things are now): 'The planet on which our civilization evolved no longer exists. The [climatic] stability that produced that civilization has vanished; epic changes have begun' (McKibben, 2011: 27). McKibben's despair about society's collective inability to redirect our efforts comes through as he lists example after example of the consequences: the spread of Lyme disease, increasing numbers of parasites, stronger storms, high death tolls from heat waves, reduced crop yields, crops unable to germinate in the heat, intensified and more frequent floods, and more (2011). A more conservative view from the Intergovernmental Panel on Climate Change (IPCC) was once available for those who wished to catch their breath and take in information more slowly (2007). However, the IPCC's 2007 predictions have already been proven optimistic. As an example, the Arctic ice melt began in 2007, instead of the predicted 2050 (Lovelock, 2010: 42), 43 years ahead of schedule. The early release of the IPCC's next assessment report asserts that planetary warming is certain, noting attendant problems that confirm McKibben's view (Intergovernmental Panel on Climate Change, 2013). All of this adds up: Earth is altering rapidly.

Scientist James Lovelock recently asserted that, as humans are the only species with the capacity to be self-reflective and redirect our own futures, we have the unique potential to carry our species forward into a different kind of relationship with the Earth (2010). This insight links to what systems theorist Donella Meadows described as high meta-meta resilience: 'feedback loops that can *learn, create, design, and evolve* ever more complex restorative structures' (2005: 76). In other words, ecoliteracy, informed by feedback loops that effectively convey information about the state of ecosystems, would engender our ability to steward and restore the biosphere.

Principles of natural systems

Darwin embodied engaged ecoliteracy in his decades-long study of worms. He brought them into his home in pots of earth and documented diverse experiments to understand if they smell (not much), hear (they don't) and learn (they do) (1976 [1881]). Through this study, he approached what today is called 'earth systems science – the holistic study of how our planet works' (Flannery, 2011: 8). All of the key characteristics of ecosystems (flows, transformations, and storage of energy and matter) can be observed in the 5–10-cm-deep network of humus, nutrients and micro-organisms that is home for those worms that Darwin tracked. Worms emerge 'in the darkest hours with their tail securely hooked into their burrow entrance and drag detritus into their burrows' (Flannery, 2011: 9) for disassembly, assisted by microorganisms, fungi and decomposers, into elements that we know as nutrients. Natural systems cycle and transform matter at both small and large scales. Darwin also observed worms building soil mass; a natural system cycle transforming at the microscopic and macro level.

Flannery calls captured sunlight 'the Earth's energy budget' (2011: 42). This energy powers photosynthesis and enables plants to extract nutrients (nutrient cycle) carbon (carbon cycle) and water (hydrologic cycle) from their surroundings. Elements and nutrients are available to other organisms up the food chain, including humans, until they finally cycle back to the decomposers and then begin these cycles again. The term 'waste' does not apply at any point in nature's systems. Waste has been introduced by human activities and constitutes shifting elements at large scales to the wrong place in the system: excess carbon is accumulating in the atmosphere, nutrients are flowing into lakes instead of our foods, industrially produced chemicals are entering the nutrient cycle and minerals are becoming concentrated at toxic levels in the biosphere (McNeill, 2000).

The interrelationship between plants, animals and microorganisms (biotic) and the non-living (abiotic) environment comprises an ecosystem. Usually, the term refers to a geographically recognizable unit, but a drop of water that contains microorganisms may meet the conditions to be described as an ecosystem. The smallest ecosystem is nested within progressively larger ecosystems, i.e. nested systems. Cycles are also nested. For example, at the small scale, plants capture and sequester carbon, and, on a larger scale, carbon cycles throughout the atmosphere. Interactions, cycles and flows take place internally within ecosystems, vertically, from the small to the largest nested system, and horizontally between them. The resulting complexity of relationships is described by Fritjof Capra as, 'a pattern that is common to all life. Wherever we see life, we see networks' (2002: 9). The largest living system that we know is the Earth system, which James Lovelock calls Gaia, to connote that it is a living entity (2010).

Lovelock (among others) holds that Earth evolved over time, in reciprocal dialogue with the smallest biota; microorganisms in the soil and plankton in the oceans were evolving in tandem (2010). Roughly 10,000 years ago, the amount of mineral material below the Earth's crust and the composition of the thin layer of air at the surface reached the conditions uniquely suited to support life (Suzuki, 1997). These qualities define the epoch known as the Holocene. The Earth was able to self-regulate to maintain the stable climate that has allowed the flourishing of human civilizations throughout the Holocene, until recently, when we began to shift high volumes of carbon dioxide from below the Earth's crust into the atmosphere (Rockström *et al.*, 2009). In the ultimate demonstration of interdependence, Gaia is responding with changes to temperature, biosphere and cycles.

To signify that humans are now the dominant driver of change to the Earth's system, the current era is referred to as the Anthropocene (Rockström *et al.*, 2009). 'Humanity has co-opted, or taken over, more than 40% of the photosynthetic activity on the planet' (Suzuki, 2010: 27). Much of our impact is due to numbers alone. According to Lovelock, 'the exhalations of breath and other gaseous emissions by the nearly 7 billion people on earth, their pets and their livestock are responsible for 23% of all greenhouse gas emissions' (2010: 47). Our growing population exceeds the Earth's carrying capacity (Lovelock, 2010), and our accelerated methods of production and consumption have huge impacts on the Earth system.

In 2009, Johan Rockström and his colleagues at the Stockholm Resilience Centre identified nine systems that are essential to the functioning of the Earth, in the Planetary Boundaries Report (see Figure 3.1). This makes it apparent that, despite our understandable focus on climate

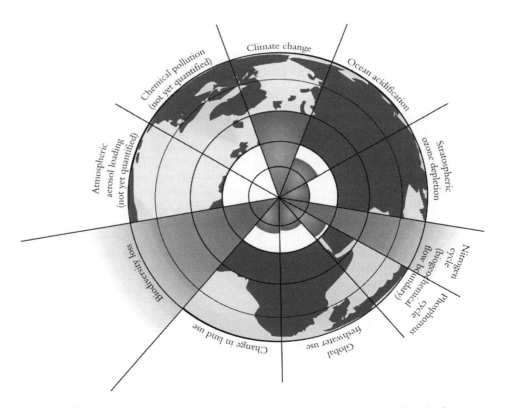

Figure 3.1 The Planetary Boundaries Report identifies nine systems that are essential to the functioning of the Earth. Green denotes the boundary of safety that each system should not exceed

Source: Azote Images/Stockholm Reslience Centre

change, there are multiple challenges to the health of the Earth system. The authors estimate a threshold for each system that we should not transgress, in order to keep the Earth as close as possible to the stable conditions of the Holocene. However, they are clear that each of these boundaries overlaps the others, and that changes in one might have unexpected impacts on another. Interacting processes can take place at more than one scale and can trigger a domino effect of changes across the globe. This is sometimes known as the 'butterfly effect'. The authors note that interactions can trigger non-linear changes: changes that are abrupt, large, complex and irreversible (Rockström *et al.*, 2009).

We see that interdependence defines natural systems: from the microscopic, earthbound cycles of decomposers to large-scale system processes. In healthy, natural systems, interdependence is highly functional. Where there is adequate biodiversity, an abundance of ever-changing, interdependent relationships maintains ecosystem resilience.

Ecosystem resilience

Ecosystem resilience involves creative flexibility. Resilience has been defined as stasis, or 'rebounding to a prior state'. However, resilience is *actually* the capacity of a system to evolve productively in response to crisis or stimuli. 'Living networks continually create, or re-create, themselves by transforming or replacing their components' (Capra, 2002: 10). Characteristics that support resilient systems include networks, feedback loops, and biodiversity and redundancy. Within this network of flows and feedback loops, biodiversity and redundancy are essential. Biodiversity supports resilience by providing what Nielsen calls a 'library' of life forms that can step in and provide alternative functions necessary for an ecosystem to evolve (Nielsen, 2007). Redundancy is slightly different. Here, species may fulfil the same functions and have other, minor, differences. For example, two species of bee may fulfil the identical function of pollinating a specific group of plants, but have different nesting habits. Destruction of the habitat of one might cause that species to crash, but leave the other relatively untouched. The surviving bees can continue to perform the pollination function, enabling the whole system to continue. A healthy complement of diverse and redundant species supports the productive evolution and ongoing functioning of an ecosystem.

Western industrial culture is challenged by the idea of biodiversity. We don't know how to value life forms that provide no known direct benefit to humanity, or have no known value to ecosystems. However, we need to find a way: biodiversity and redundancy serve resilience at the large, planetary scale, as well as at the smaller, ecosystem scale. According to Flannery, 'It's clear from major extinction events in the fossil record that if Earth's energy budget and ecosystem resilience fall below certain thresholds, a fully functioning Earth system cannot be maintained' (Flannery, 2011: 43). The authors of the Planetary Boundaries Report concur that the biodiversity threshold has been transgressed to a greater degree than the other thresholds, including climate change. According to Carl Folke, the planetary boundary of biodiversity loss is 'currently exceeded by two orders of magnitude or more' (Folke, 2013: 34). Biodiversity and redundancy are seriously threatened, with grave implications for ecosystem resilience and the future of the Earth.

Fashion and biodiversity

The relationship between fashion and biodiversity is most easily apparent in the search for 'natural' fibres as lower-impact alternatives to petroleum-based fibres. This focus supports a system that threatens biodiversity: most natural fibres are sourced from industrial agriculture, which reduces biodiversity by planting large swathes of monocultures, eroding habitat and impacting ecosystems with pesticides, herbicides and artificial fertilizers. Soil is compacted, eroded and depleted by these methods, even though it hosts one of nature's most valuable processes: the cycle that provides nutrients to feed all species (Pollan, 2006). Studies show that nutritional values in human foods have declined steadily since we began tracking them in the 1950s (Marler and Wallin, 2006; Pollan, 2006). By extension, the nutrient value for the ecosystem is also compromised.

Textile fibres such as flax, hemp, jute, ramie and wool that grow rapidly usually rely on industrial agricultural production methods. Biofibres (such as PLA or Triexta) are plant-based plastics synthesized from corn or other carbohydrate sources that are grown industrially. Their production reduces biodiversity, and they bring additional problems. Processing biofibres requires inputs of chemicals and energy (Fletcher and Grose, 2012) and generates toxins (Madival *et al.*, 2009). However, owing to general confusion and media promotion, biofibres masquerade as 'natural' solutions. The resulting support from misled purchasers has contributed to the growth of an industry that now has momentum. Ronald Wright calls this a 'progress trap': a purported solution that creates new problems and also sets conditions from which it becomes difficult to extricate ourselves (Roy and Crooks, 2011). This returns us again to the deficit that allows progress traps to unfold: the deficit of ecological literacy.

Building adult ecoliteracy

When Michael Pollan visited a prairie farmer to learn about organic food production, he found himself on his hands and knees with his cheek to the ground, naming the diverse species that comprise a grassland (2006). Like Pollan and Darwin, my preferred route to ecoliteracy is nose to the ground. There are other ways. Adults who work with the land, are professionally engaged with the environment and are of land-based faith can be expected to have higher ecoliteracy levels. Other professions also incline naturally to ecoliterate thinking.

The creative sector has unique capacities to assist the perceptual shifts that are central to ecological literacy: from linear to non-linear thinking, and from a focus on objects to a focus on patterns, systems and context. Azby Brown contends that artists and designers who are trained to see 'negative space', the shapes between things, are able to imagine the invisible interactions between biological elements (Brown, 2009). They can also help others decode intangibles. The team of Grose, Cara and Imhoff of the Sustainable Cotton Project developed visual tools that translated the language of local farmers into the patterns and systems that the fashion sector could implement (Fletcher and Grose, 2012). Trend and colour forecasting in the fashion industry is a long-standing example of pattern-analysis expertise in the creative sector. These talents and disciplines could be further empowered to help others make the conceptual shifts towards ecological literacy.

Many adults are 'primed' for ecoliteracy through outdoor recreation or hobbies. The sportswear manufacturer Patagonia attracts employees who share an outdoor lifestyle that places high value on the natural world. This sector is easily inspired by founder Yvon Chouinard's passion for ethical work (Chouinard, 2006). Patagonia has pioneered recycled fabrics for sporting goods and promoted the purchase of durable goods for longevity rather than quick turn-around. Interface Carpets, an industry leader in researching non-toxic carpet products, is also recognized for high levels of ecological commitment, from the shop floor to executive leadership. According to Interface designer David Oakey, this began with exposure to the Biomimicry Institute in the 1990s. Initiated by visionary founder Ray Anderson, Interface Carpets instituted a learning process that spread ecological understanding throughout the workforce. Commitment to natural systems has become an unquestioned part of the culture at Interface and extends outside the company via volunteer work in neighbouring parks (Oakey, 2013).

The core values of companies such as Patagonia and Interface transmit to their community of customers, employees and suppliers and set the conditions for ongoing shared learning.

Goleman, Bennett and Barlow suggest that this is an important route to ecoliteracy: 'ecological intelligence is inherently *collective*. Socially and emotionally engaged ecoliteracy, therefore, encourages us to gather and share information collectively, and to collectively take action to foster sustainable living' (Goleman *et al.*, 2012: 7). The Fibershed movement offers a strong example of collective knowledge building. A Fibershed is a network that manufactures textile products from resources and labour sourced from a geographic region no larger than a 300-mile footprint. These networks model the interdependence, diversity and resilience of natural systems.

Fibersheds envision 'regional textile supply chains that enliven individual community connection and ownership of "Soil-to-Skin" processes' (Fibershed, n.d.). Originating in California, Fibersheds have spread throughout the Western world. They emulate natural systems to produce textile products and, in doing so, embrace interdependence with local microclimates, cycles and nested systems (Swenson Dunlap, 2013). Many principles of natural systems are adhered to in the use of natural dyes and the safe composting of organically grown materials. Further, a strong community building programme establishes a feedback loop for the ongoing learning and adaptation that are key to a resilient system (Fibershed, n.d.). The flagship Fibershed fosters ecoliteracy by inviting tours that connect the general public and consumers with all who are engaged with the growing, harvesting, dyeing, composting and crafting of fibre goods. Significantly, the community has developed the collective wisdom and strength to oppose false solutions, as evidenced by the Fibershed's stand against biofibres (Kahn, 2013).

Janine Benyus, founder of biomimicry (1997), and Fritjof Capra, co-founder of the Center for Ecological Literacy (2002, 2005), offer lists that encapsulate principles of natural systems. Taken as a whole, this set of criteria can propel interdependent systems (see Table 3.1). Comprehensive engagement with this set of criteria would lead to the increasingly radical and systemic change that is needed to tend the ecosphere. For example, a 'meta-fibershed' guided

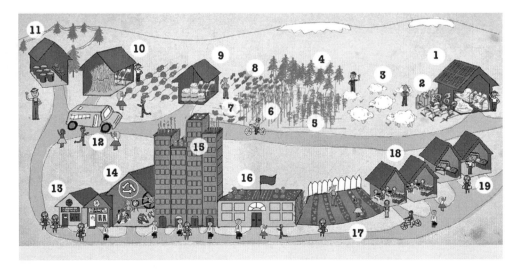

Figure 3.2 A flourishing Fibershed might include solar-powered mills, sheep, farmlands, gardens for food, fibre and dyes, small-scale equipment, tours, retail, recycling and artisanal workshops

Source: Donna Roggi

Table 3.1 Nature's criteria: insights from Benyus and Capra about the functioning of nature's systems can radically transform the fashion industry

Benyus: design checklist (adapted from Benyus, 1997: 291–2)	Capra: principles (adapted from Capra: 2002: 231, 2005: 23–9)	Ecoliterate design approach
Will it fit in?	Interdependence: the sustainability of individual populations and the sustainability of the entire ecosystem are interdependent. No organism can exist in isolation	Knowing that interdependence means a complexity of impacts, design to meet real needs. Consider ecosystem needs on par or prioritized more highly than other stakeholders
Will it last?	Dynamic balance: ecosystems exist in dynamic balance, a relatively steady state that also has continual fluctuations	Lasting is one good solution, transforming appropriately is another. The design can be modifiable and adaptable, or should biodegrade safely, without the addition of energy and technology
Does it run on sunlight?	Flows: solar energy, transformed into chemical energy by the photosynthesis of green plants, drives the ecological cycles, and sustains life	Alternatives to fossil fuels include wind, solar, biomass, hydropower, geothermal, human power and animal power
Does it use only the energy it needs?	Flows: a sustainable society would only use as much energy as it could capture from the sun	Avoid approaches that consume fossil-fuel energy either directly or hidden via the embodied energy in artefacts or tools
Does it recycle everything?	Cycles: all living organisms must feed on continual flows of matter and energy. One species' waste is another species' food. Thus, matter cycles continuously	Design artefacts to cycle. Nutrients should return to a location where they can be used, and/or artefacts can evolve to become something new and relevant
Does it reward cooperation?	Networks: the exchange of energy and resources in an ecosystem is sustained by pervasive cooperation and enabled by partnering and open networks. All living systems share resources across their boundaries	Create reciprocal flows of goods and information through open networks, with low barriers to entry (i.e. no new skills required, not dependent on new software)
Does it support biodiversity?	Diversity: the greater the diversity, richness and complexity, the more stability and resilience there are in an ecosystem	Develop diverse designs rather than focusing efforts on single perceived 'best' solutions. Ensure that the design supports existing ecosystems and habitat
Does it utilize local supply and expertise?	Nested systems: systems and cycles are nested within systems, from the small and local, to increasingly larger and more complex regional and global cycles. Each system is an integrated whole and at the same time part of the others	Local systems often minimize energy consumption and tailor solutions to contextual needs. Learn more about local supply and expertise, in order to work with it effectively
Does it curb excess from within?	Dynamic balance: dynamic balance is enabled by multiple feedback loops that regulate the ecological community. No single variable is maximized; all variables fluctuate around their optimal values	Foster exchange of information by setting up effective local feedback loops. Ensure that information is open and accessible
Does it tap the power of limits?		Limits inspire innovation and drive risk-taking.
	Development: all life evolves over time; species adapt and evolve, and organisms co-evolve. Ecosystems pass through successive stages, and each stage represents a distinctive community in its own right. Development is non-linear	Re-examine ideas about ecoliterate design regularly, and learn from each other to evolve better approaches, through a meta-feedback loop

by these criteria would eliminate reliance on fossil fuels. They would also gather, reprocess or remanufacture discarded fibre products that accumulate in the region from other sources. These substantial challenges can only be met through commitment to ongoing experimentation and exploration, supported by individuals and communities who have the critical capacity to determine when a solution genuinely supports ecological systems.

Concluding thoughts

I approach the topic of nature's systems with humility, inspired by the awe of spending long days and nights on the expanse of the Canadian prairie. Despite the lists proffered by experts and the insight of scientists, I believe that we do not know enough. If the fundamentals of ecoliterate thinking include the ability to connect the dots in our interconnected system, perhaps it also includes appreciating that natural systems have a larger power. They are not subject to society's economic and technological constructs or limitations. The human capacity to invent and our current dominance of global ecological systems do not confer the ability to manage or control nature. That will always be out of our reach. We can, however, learn to manage *ourselves*, so that natural systems can recover and thrive. We can change our relationship with the Earth, and this includes changing our relationship with fashion.

Adult ecoliteracy is central to this change. Individuals can choose to become students of the natural world, and collectives can deepen our learning. Ecoliterate communities such as Patagonia, Interface and Fibershed are only beginning to explore ways to align different parts of the fashion and fibre industry with nature's systems. These communities, and others like them, can support the considered decision-making that increases the probability of genuine solutions. They can help us learn to prioritize the environment over industry, and to strengthen our resolve to make the greater changes needed to heal the ecosphere.

I grew up in a family attuned to the cycles of nature. This left me with an implicit understanding of the primacy of natural systems. How can others acquire a similar certainty? Research should focus on developing ways to help all of us build visceral, tangible and unshakeable relationships with the Earth: an embodied ecological literacy, where fashion is part of a vital relationship with nature.

References

Benyus, J. (1997), *Biomimicry: Innovation Inspired by Nature*, 1st edn, New York: William Morrow.

Brown, A. (2009), *Just Enough: Lessons in Living Green From Traditional Japan*, Tokyo and New York: Kodansha International.

Capra, F. (2002), *The Hidden Connections: Integrating the Biological, Cognitive, and Social Dimensions of Life Into a Science of Sustainability*, 1st edn, New York: Doubleday.

Capra, F. (2005), Speaking nature's language, in Stone, M.K. and Barlow, Z. (eds), *Ecological Literacy*, San Francisco, CA: Sierra Club Books: 18–29.

Capra, F. (2013), *Ecology and Community*. [Online] Available at: www.ecoliteracy.org/essays/ecology-and-community (accessed 9 July 2013).

Center for Ecoliteracy (2013), *What We Do*. [Online] Available at: www.ecoliteracy.org/about-us/what-we-do (accessed 9 July 2013).

Chouinard, Y. (2006), *Let My People Go Surfing: The Education of a Reluctant Businessman*, New York: Penguin Group.

Darwin, C. (1976 [1881]), *The Formation of Vegetable Mould Through the Action of Worms, with Observations on their Habits* [reprint]. Ontario, CA: Bookworm Publishing Company. First published 1881, London: Faber and Faber.

Decleris, M. (2000), *The Law of Sustainable Development: General Principles*, European Commission. [Online] Available at: www.woodlandleague.org/documents/sustainability/sustlaw.pdf (accessed 7 July 2013).

Fibershed (n.d.), *About Fibershed*. [Online] Available at: www.fibershed.com/about (accessed 16 October 2013).

Flannery, T. (2011), *Here on Earth: A Natural History of the Planet*, New York: Atlantic Monthly Press.

Fletcher, K. and Grose, L. (2012), *Fashion and Sustainability: Design for Change*, London: Laurence King.

Folke, C. (2013), Respecting planetary boundaries and reconnecting to the biosphere, in Starke, L., Assadourian, E. and Prugh, T. (eds), *State of the World 2013: Is Sustainability Still Possible?* Washington DC: Island Press: 19–27.

Goleman, D., Bennett, L. and Barlow, Z. (2012), *Ecoliterate: How Educators Are Cultivating Emotional, Social, and Ecological Intelligence*, 1st edn, San Francisco, CA: Jossey-Bass.

Intergovernmental Panel on Climate Change (2007), *Final Report*. [Online] Available at: www.ipcc.ch/pdf/assessment-report/ar4/syr/ar4_syr_spm.pdf (accessed 4 May 2013).

Intergovernmental Panel on Climate Change (2013), *Summary for Policymakers*. [Online] Available at: www.ipcc.ch (accessed 4 October 2013).

Kahn, D. (2013), *Fibershed Questions* [Email] St. Pierre, L., 1 October.

Leopold, A. (1949), *A Sand County Almanac: And Sketches Here and There*, 2nd edn, Oxford, UK: Oxford University Press.

Lovelock, J. (2010), *The Vanishing Face of Gaia: A Final Warning*, 1st trade paper edn, New York: Basic Books.

McKibben, B. (2003 [1989]), *The End of Nature*, 2nd edn, London: Bloomsbury.

McKibben, B. (2011), *Eaarth: Making a Life on a Tough New Planet*, 1st edn, New York: St. Martin's Griffin.

McNeill, J. R. (2000), *Something New Under the Sun: An Environmental History of the Twentieth-Century World*. New York: W.W. Norton.

Madival, S., Rafael, A., Sher, P. and Ramani, N. (2009), 'Assessment of the environmental profile of PLA, PET and PS clamshell containers using LCA methodology.' *Journal of Cleaner Production*, 17: 1183–94.

Marler, J. B. and Wallin, J. R. (2006), *Human Health, the Nutritional Quality of Harvested Food and Sustainable Farming Systems*. [Online] Available at: www.nutritionsecurity.org/PDF/NSI_White%20Paper_Web.pdf (accessed 5 July 2013).

Meadows, D. H. (2005), Dancing with systems, in Stone, M. K. and Barlow, Z. (eds), *Ecological Literacy*, San Francisco, CA: Sierra Club Books: 193–205.

Nielsen, S. N. (2007), 'What has modern ecosystem theory to offer to cleaner production, industrial ecology and society? The views of an ecologist.' *Journal of Cleaner Production*, 15: 1639–53.

Oakey, D. (2013), Importance of nature at interface [interview by telephone]. 4 October.

Oreskes, N. and Conway, E. M. M. (2011), *Merchants of Doubt: How a Handful of Scientists Obscured the Truth on Issues From Tobacco Smoke to Global Warming*, reprint edn, New York: Bloomsbury Press.

Pollan, M. (2006), *The Omnivore's Dilemma: A Natural History of Four Meals*, New York: Penguin Group.

Rockström, J., Steffen W., Noone, K., Persson, Å., Chapin III, F. S., Lambin, E., Lenton, T. M., Scheffer, M., Folke, C., Schellnhuber, H., Nykvist, B., De Wit, C. A., Hughes, T., van der Leeuw, S. Rodhe, H., Sörlin, S., Snyder, P. K., Costanza, R., Svedin, U. Falkenmark, M., Karlberg, L., Corell, R. W., Fabry, V. J., Hansen, J., Walker, B., Liverman, D., Richardson, K., Crutzen, P. and Foley, J. (2009), 'Planetary boundaries: exploring the safe operating space for humanity.' *Ecology and Society*, 14 (2): 32. [Online] Available at: www.ecologyandsociety.org/vol14/iss2/art32/ (accessed 27 April 2013).

Roy, M. and Crooks, H. (2011), *Surviving Progress* [film], Canada: National Film Board of Canada.

Royte, E. (2006), 'Corn plastic to the rescue.' *Smithsonian*, August. [Online] Available at: www.smithsonianmag.com/science-nature/plastic.html (accessed 4 October 2013).

Stone, M. K. and Barlow, Z. (2005), *Ecological Literacy: Educating Our Children for a Sustainable World*, San Francisco, CA: Sierra Club Books.

Sullivan, D. (2011), 'Compostable plastics and organic farming.' *BioCycle*, 52 (3): 36. [Online] Available at: www.biocycle.net/2011/03/23/compostable-plastics-and-organic-farming (accessed 30 September 2013).

Suzuki, D. (1997), *The Sacred Balance: Rediscovering Our Place in Nature*, 3rd edn, Vancouver: Greystone Books.

Suzuki, D. (2010), *The Legacy: An Elder's Vision for Our Sustainable Future*, Vancouver: Greystone Books.

Swenson Dunlap, A. (2013), 'Fibershed; creating an interdependent community of farmers, makers and wearers.' *Wild Fibers Magazine*. [Online] Available at: www.fibershed.com/WildFibersMag2013.pdf (accessed 30 September 2013).

4

A WHOLE NEW CLOTH

Politics and the fashion system

John Thackara

You probably need to be naked to read this paragraph with a clear conscience. Its author, for one, felt like stripping off as his exploration of the fashion system progressed. It took 700 gallons of fresh water to make my cotton T-shirt, I learned. It's partly down to me that 85 per cent of the Aral Sea in Uzbekistan has disappeared (because its water is used to grow cotton in the desert). A quarter of all the insecticides in the world are used on cotton crops. Nearly all the textiles in my life will end up in landfill – clothes, household textiles, carpets, the lot (Fletcher and Grose, 2012).

Thanks to the tireless work of activists and advocates, millions of people like me are learning about the social and environmental harm wrought by industrial systems – including the textile and fashion ones. As our awareness and concern has grown, many fashion brands have committed to do less harm – and a few have even committed themselves to a 'leave things better' course. But, despite decades of campaigning and advocacy, the overall condition of the biosphere continues to worsen. The reason for this is simple: we've been addressing symptoms, but not their principal cause – an economic system whose core logic is perpetual growth in a finite world.

I experienced the grim consequence of this underlying reality at a meeting of 200 sustainability managers at a famous home-furnishing giant in Sweden (Thackara, 2012). During 20 years of uninterrupted work on sustainability, this famous company has made thousands of rigorously tested improvements that are recorded on a 'list without end'. The range of improvements is startling – even admirable – except for one fact: this huge company has never thought even to question whether it should grow. On the contrary: it is committed to double in size by 2020. By this date, the number of customers visiting their giant blue sheds will increase from from 650 million a year to *1.5 billion* a year. And why? The senior manager who briefed our meeting on this plan (in 2012) put this growth into context: 'Growth is needed', she explained, 'to finance the sustainability improvements we all want to make'.

The problem with this narrative is best explained if I talk about wood. The company, as the third largest user of wood in the world, has promised that, by 2017, half of all the the wood it uses – up from 17 per cent now – will either be recycled, or come from forests that are responsibly managed. Now 50 per cent is a vast improvement, but it also begs the question: What about the *second* half of all that wood? As the company doubles in size, that second pile of wood – the *un*-certified half, the unreliably-sourced-at-best half – will soon be twice as big as all the wood it uses today. The impact on the world's forests, of one company's ravenous hunger for resources, will be catastrophic.

The committed and gifted people I met in Sweden – along with sustainability teams in hundreds of the world's major companies, including fashion and textile ones – are trapped on a similar deadly path: their incremental sustainability improvements consistently take second place to the prime directive of perpetual growth. However hard they work, however many innovations they come up with, the net negative impact of these firms' activities, on the world's living systems, will be *greater* in the years ahead than it is today.

Many fashion brands proclaim that their products are verified, accredited or certified as being sustainable. But, with no shared definition of what 'sustainable' actually means, the barrier to adherence is low. More than a hundred different textile and clothing industry sustainability labels and standards commit merely to 'minimize' negative economic, environmental and social impacts (Ethical Fashion Forum, n.d.). There are no binding targets, no collective governance of this vast and fragmented industry. The result is an empty promise to leave the world 'as unspoilt as possible' (Kleinod, 2011).

If a lack of transparency were the problem, help would be at hand: a system to measure the impacts of business on biodiversity and ecosystems is now emerging. The Economics of Ecosystems and Biodiversity – TEEB – is a set of accounting tools that puts a price on the ecosystem services provided by nature and used by industry (www.teebweb.org). The thinking behind TEEB is that knowing the price of ecosystems will cause companies to look after them, and many governments and companies are signing up to this thinking and the TEEB framework. There is troubling evidence, however, that this well-intentioned project will backfire. TEEB's numbers, acting like blood in the water, have attracted the attention of predatory investors bent on 'financializing' environmental assets; these investors are now busily describing natural resources such as land, ecosystems and riversheds in the abstract language of commodities. Natural assets, once converted into this abstract new language, can be 'securitized' and then traded. An especially deadly feature of this financialization of nature is that powerful incentives are designed into these financial products in such a way that they *accelerate* the rate of exploitation of the world's soils, water and biodiversity. For EKO Asset Management, an early mover in this nature grab, 'sustainability means running the global environment like a corporation'.

A new story

All is not bleak. Across the world, a multitude of social movements and grass-roots projects are animated by a growing recognition that our lives are codependent with the plants, animals, air, water and soils. These are the green shoots of a leave-things-better economy. The eco-philosopher Joanna Macy describes the appearance of this new story as 'The Great Turning' – a profound shift in our perception of who we are, and a reawakening to the fact that we are not separate from the Earth as a living system (Macy, n.d.). From sub-microscopic viruses, to the vast subsoil networks that support trees, awareness is spreading that the entire Earth is animated by complex interactions between its life forms, rocks, atmosphere and water (Merryweather, 2006). Understood in this way – by science, as much as by philosophy – the Earth no longer presents itself as a repository of resources. On the contrary: this new story about the interdependence of healthy soils and living systems – and the ways we can help them regenerate – finally addresses the 'why' of economic activity we've been lacking (Collis, 2012). This narrative also points to the one kind of growth that makes sense, and that we can afford: the regeneration of life on Earth.

How systems change

At first, the language used by Joanna Macy and others to describe a politics of regeneration and reconnection strikes some people as being naive. But Macy's approach turns out, on reflection, to be consistent with the ways complex systems – including belief systems – change. 'All the great transformations or creations have been unthinkable until they actually came to pass', confirms the French philosopher Edgar Morin (Morin, in Bauwens, 2013); 'the fact that a belief system is deeply rooted does not mean it cannot change' (ibid.). Transformation can unfold quietly as a variety of changes, interventions and disruptions accumulate across time. At a certain moment – a moment that is impossible to predict – a tipping point, or phase shift, is reached, and the system as a whole changes. Sustainability, in other words, is not something best campaigned for as a political demand. Rather, it's a condition that emerges as the effects of incremental change, at many different scales, accumulate.

There's mounting evidence that a new narrative is ready to emerge on a mass scale. According to the German Advisory Council on Climate Change (WBGU), the heavyweight scientific body that advises the German federal government on 'Earth system megatrends', a 'global transformation of values' has already begun (WBGU, 2011). In the North as in the South, a significant majority would 'welcome a new economic system' that supports ambitious climate protection measures. What the WGBU terms 'post-materialist thinking' is not limited to the well-off and educated: its studies also found a 'latent willingness to act' among the citizens of South Korea, Mexico, Brazil, India and China.

There's a cheering consequence of this account: our passionate but puny efforts in support of sustainability so far may not have been in vain: in an age of networks, even the smallest actions can contribute to transformation of the system as a whole – even if none of us had that outcome explicitly in mind (Nesta, 2013).

From dirt to shirt, from soil to skin

Practical consequences are following from this bottom–up change in consciousness. Food and fibre systems, for example, which were once thought to be too big and too hard to change, are being discovered as design projects with the potential to drive ecological regeneration when reconfigured at a bioregional scale. In food, advanced prototypes are already being tested. The Food Commons, for example, launched in the US in 2009, is the world's first prototype for a designed regional food system. The Food Commons platform (www.thefoodcommons.org) is a physical, financial and organizational infrastructure designed to connect myriad small-to-mid-sized enterprises: farms, food processors, distributors, retailers. The platform helps these foodshed actors to collaborate by providing advanced communications platforms, community-based economic models, and scientific knowledge about sustainable agriculture. For Professor Larry Lee, founder of the Food Commons, 'the Food Commons represents a whole new cloth; it's woven from threads of several successful organizations, business enterprises, and disciplines.'

Rebecca Burgess, founder of Fibershed (www.fibershed.com) in California, is confident that 'fiber will follow food' in public awareness. She began Fibershed with a challenge, to herself, to wear clothes, sourced and dyed within a 150-mile radius from her front door, for a year. The essential elements for a bioregional fibershed were in place, Burgess discovered: animals, plants and people, skills, spinning wheels, knitting needles, floor looms. But there was a lack of connectivity between the many different actors. The many small farmers and producers within her region were doing great work – but on a small scale and, for the most part, below the radar. 'Our priority is to integrate vertically', explains Burgess, 'from soil to skin'. As a first step in connecting the Fibershed's actors, an inaugural Wool and Fine Fiber Symposium in 2012 brought together the region's producers, shearers, artisans, designers, knitters, fibre entrepreneurs and clothes-wearing citizens to discuss what it would it take to bring 'farm-fresh clothing' to the region (Braslow, 2012). All manner of fine-grain issues emerged: flock health, rotational grazing, weed management, predator issues, breeding for fibre, colour attributes, and milling and fibre processing capacity. A Wool Inventory Mapping Project was then launched to collect data on everyone operating a dairy, ranch, farm or homestead with one or more fibre-producing animals. Data from the Wool Inventory Map will be used to assess the scale, scope and location of future fibre-processing facilities. Also in development is a prototyping and education facility, called FiberLab (ibid.).

Can Fibershed-scale production feasibly clothe today's large human populations, and affordably? It depends on how you define and measure human 'needs'. Rebecca Burgess concedes that Fibershed systems are small scale right now, and that locally grown, dyed and made garments can therefore be expensive and scarce. But these are early days: as shared production facilities and network coordination improve, she says, small Fibersheds will link together in pan-regional networks to share knowledge and facilities in ways that improve supply. The growth of food and Fibershed mosaics will not be fast: these are democratic and community-driven projects whose vitality depends on the steady growth of trust – in a place, and through time. But momentum is growing.

Call of the commons

The framing idea that connects and gives shared meaning to projects such as Fibersheds is the commons (Bollier and Helfrich, 2012) – the natural, genetic, material, physical, social, cultural, intellectual and creative resources, all the things that we inherited from past generations, which enable our livelihood. The maintenance, health and sustainability of these resources are in our shared interest, as they have always been (Finidori, 2012) (see also Chapter 25). No individual, company or government created these common goods; therefore, none has a right to claim them as private property. On the contrary: we inherited them from previous generations and have a moral obligation to look after them for future generations.

The commons are not just an ideological proposition. Numerous scientific studies confirm that sharing is in our genes. Psychologists at Harvard, for example, have confirmed that humans seem to possess 'a strong propensity to cooperate rather than compete over limited resources, trusting that they'll benefit in the end'. Swiss scientists, too, discovered that children above a certain age are driven by both genes and social factors to share with others – even if they don't have to (Marsh, 2011). The commons as an idea crops up throughout history: The shared management of water, for example – a hugely stressful issue for textile production today – dates back 8,000 years; the earliest records of collectively managed irrigation have been found in the regions of the Middle East that we now know as Iraq and Iran. In Bali, too, a complex 'irrigation society' that dates back 1,000 years still thrives as what the ecological anthropologist Stephen Lansing (2012) calls a 'coupled social–ecological system'.

The spirit and practice of commoning is reviving once again – and on a global scale. It has new names – such as the sharing economy, transition towns, or the peer-to-peer (P2P) economy – but the principle is unchanged: citizens are organizing to take charge of their lives and resources. For Rob Hopkins, founder of the Transition movement, 'once you put the glasses of the commons on, you see it all over'.

That said, commons do not run themselves (Burke, 2012) and no universal rulebook exists for commons governance. But in her 1990 book *Governing the Commons* Nobel laureate Elinor

Ostrom identified a number of principles that she had discovered were common in successful examples of self-governance. Based on a systematic study of fisheries, irrigation, groundwater and forestry systems, she found a number of shared values: commons are not commodities to be sold for money; anyone who takes from the commons has to contribute to the commons; knowledge, skills and tools should be free, open and shared; and they should be organized by the people who benefit from them (Ostrom, 1990).

In the years since Ostrom's pioneering work, scholars in real-world contexts have deepened our understanding of what it takes for people and living systems to co-exist sustainably (Andries and Janssen, 2013). Whether the context be coral reefs in Australia, arid lands in Brazil, or farmers markets in Europe, the pattern of governance to emerge is described as *adaptive co-management* – an approach found when 'constellations' of people and interested parties cohabit successfully in 'social–ecological systems'.

Dealing with difference

An important lesson has emerged from study of these diverse experiments: paying attention to the *process by which groups work together* is just as important as deciding what needs to be done – perhaps more. It's not enough simply to proclaim the moral superiority of sharing, for example, and expect everyone to fall in line. Tough questions must be confronted, and not brushed under the carpet. Among these are: how to define, map and name the resources to be shared; determining who is entitled to what; designing rules and sanctions; designing how to make the rules. For Massimo De Angelis (2010), how to deal with difference is the most important by far:

> We have to go beyond the idea that democracy means: 'here is my view, there is yours, let's see who wins'. We need to acknowledge differences, allow those who don't want to share with us, or with whom we do not want to share, to be heard.

Dealing with difference involves a lot of consensus building, collective participation and transparent decision-making. All this takes time, and a politics that involves endless meetings is neither attractive nor practicable for most people. New ways of doing politics are needed that are shaped by the ways people live now – not the other way round.

Our inner states are just as important to a healthy political movement as are its external activities. For Sophie Banks, who leads a programme on 'inner transition' for the Transition movement, 'we have a global system that's depleting the planet, and we're burning out ourselves; it's no coincidence. We have to change the culture of how we do things' (Banks, in Hopkins, 2013). For Banks, one indicator of healthy politics is the quality of meetings. In healthy meetings, she observes, people feel relaxed and connected to each other. Even when there's a lot to discuss, time is found to discuss how the group is working, how people are dealing with differences. These events are celebratory and not just about building and doing things.

A common thread in this new approach to politics is the need for some kind of caretaker, or steward. The steward's job is to nurture communication between members of the community, make sure that everyone understands and abides by the rules, and generally foster a shared spirit of reciprocity and cooperation. None of these skills is taught in mainstream education, but, around the world, individuals with these special qualities have started to emerge. Cheryl Dahle, founder of the Future of Fish, is one such steward. 'When I began my journey to understand global overfishing, I knew that it was a sprawling and complex tangle of intertwining problems touching the spheres of policy, commerce, environment and livelihood', she recalls.

Now, almost five years in, I see its complexity through the stories of people I've met who live in that tangle: Each of the players in this system has an incredibly personal stake in how we humans choose to rethink the way we hunt, eat and protect fish.

(Dahle, 2013)

For Dahle, what she names the 'people platform' question became the core design challenge: How do you design interactions between competitors – folk who've been enemies on opposite sides of policy debate, scientists and business people who don't speak the same language – to enlist their help and collaboration? For insight, Dahle turned to the work of Adam Kahane, one of the pioneers of collaboration design. 'What might seem at first glance to be abstract theory has proved incredibly instructive', says Dahle (ibid.).

When we convene any group – fishers, processors or financiers – we set up the conversation so there's something in it for them. We acknowledge the interests of everyone in the room, and we never ask anyone to sacrifice their self-interest. We work to show – to *prove* – that there is a reason for them to shift their thinking and behavior.

(ibid.)

As for fish, so, too, for fibre. Another technique with potential for fashion systems is Appreciative Inquiry (AI). In AI, rather than compile lists of all the problems that need to be fixed, the group focuses first on what is working; it then explores which successful ingredients might be used elsewhere, and how. A variety of next-generation institutes, now emerging, will teach you these kinds of skill. At the Presencing Institute (www.presencing.com), for example, founder Otto Scharmer runs Theory U workshops that teach people how to 'co-sense and co-create positive change'. The Alia Institute (www.aliainstitute.org), based in Halifax, Nova Scotia, offers skill-building courses with names such as Change Lab and Human Systems Dynamics. Another network, Art of Hosting (www.artofhosting.org) teaches people 'how be successful in complex circumstances when we can't predict what ten, five or even two years down the road will look like'. Likewise in Brazil: the Elos Institute, founded in 2000 by young architects (www.walkoutwalkon.net/brazil/), runs a collaborative game called Oasis that's designed 'to awake and give impulse to communities through fast actions with high impact'. A cross between an architectural charrette and an Amish-style barn-raising, Oasis games typically end with a square, a park, a day-care centre or a cultural centre being built – there and then.

Wild law

Although grass-roots projects are driving transformational change and action, their capacity to thrive is still influenced by institutional frameworks – especially legal ones. Right now, in most of the world's legal systems today, only humans have rights. Our laws are based on the Enlightenment notion that the universe is a repository of dead resources that we can exploit, as and when we like, for the exclusive benefit of our own species (Animate Earth, 2011). In contradiction to ecological principles of wholeness and interconnection (see also Chapter 3), legal notions of property perpetuate the division of land into discrete parcels. Nature's inherent diversity is at odds, too, with free-trade treaties that support large-scale monoculture projects; these, as we know, destroy biodiversity. Laws – and the institutions that impose them – are what people mean by the 'hard-wiring' that locks us into damaging relationships with living systems.

In *The Great Work*, Thomas Berry calls for a new jurisprudence to redefine the relationship between the human community and the Earth community in which it lives (Berry, 1999). We need a legal system that governs the relationship between humans and the natural world as a totality, not as a collection of parts, he argues, and that respects equally the rights of the natural world to exist and thrive.

Is a transformation of our legal systems along these lines feasible? The South African lawyer Cormac Cullinan (2011), a pioneer in Earth jurisprudence, compares our situation now with the abolition of slavery. Even when American public opinion came to regard slavery as morally abhorrent, the concept of slaves as property remained hard-wired into the legal system. It took a tremendous political effort – not to mention a civil war – before laws were changed, and slavery was finally abolished.

Changes to the legal status of living systems and property rights are emerging in a wide variety of legal systems around the world – including unexpected ones. In 1996, for example, a celebrated legal text in the United States, called *Should Trees have Standing?*, gave serious consideration to the proposition that trees might be given legal rights, in the same way that minors or corporations are given artificial legal personalities. To most people's surprise, the Supreme Court, although it voted against the proposal, also found that there was some merit to these arguments (Stone, 1996). More recently, a dozen US municipalities have introduced ordinances that grant equal rights to human and natural communities. In 2009, the city of Spokane became one of the first cities in the world to legislate for the rights of nature (envisionspokane.org). The measures declared:

> Ecosystems, including but not limited to, all groundwater systems, surface water systems, and aquifers, have the right to exist and flourish. River systems have the right to flow, and to contain water of a quality necessary to provide habitat for native plants and animals, and to provide clean drinking water. Aquifers have the right to sustainable recharge, flow, and water quality.

Then, in 2013, Santa Monica passed a Sustainability Rights Ordinance which recognizes that, 'natural communities and ecosystems possess fundamental and inalienable rights to exist and flourish in the City' (Biggs, 2013). The Ordinance includes protections for this right from acts by 'corporate entities' that, it states, 'do not enjoy special privileges or powers under the law that subordinate the community's rights to their private interests'. The Ordinance also articulates the rights of people to self-governance, a healthy environment and sustainable living. It is, of course, true that state and federal authorities often veto such measures – but the political lesson is that such measures are being passed at an increasing rate.

At the scale of the nation-state, radical legal expressions of a new world-view are emerging in Latin America. Ecuador's national constitution was revised in 2008 to recognize and protect rights of nature. Indigenous elders played a critical part in the revision of the new constitution, which grants to Mother Earth 'the right to exist, persist, maintain and regenerate its vital cycles, structure, functions and restoration'. A key concept in the new thinking is *buen vivir*, a term that translates loosely into English as 'good living' or 'well living'. The Uruguayan ecologist Eduardo Gudynas (2011), a leading scholar on the subject, emphasizes that *buen vivir* is less human-centric than Western notions of well-being, or welfare: 'Buen Vivir is not just about the individual, but the individual in the context of their unique environmental situation. The dualism in Western knowledge that separates society from nature vanishes under this perspective.' With *buen vivir*, the *polis* is expanded, and the concept of citizenship is widened to include these other actors within environmental settings.

Ecuador's new constitution is not a one-off. In 2010, when Bolivia hosted a World People's Conference on Climate Change and Rights of Mother Earth, it was attended by 30,000 people, from 100 countries. One outcome, a 'Universal Declaration on Rights of Mother Earth', was presented to the UN. Furthermore, a Global Alliance for the Rights of Nature has been created, with an initial sixty member organizations from around the world. Bolivia itself went on to introduce its own new legislation, an 'Act of the Rights of Mother Earth', and created a new ministry to oversee the Act.

Buen vivir has been welcomed by many as an alternative project for civilization,[1] but its critics portray the concept as a mystical return to an indigenous past and charge that it lacks any practical strategy. They also point out that it has been accompanied by new plans, enthusiastically promoted by the same government, for energy, road-building and extractive-industry mega projects. Official rhetoric even talks about 'Oil exploration to live well' or 'hydroelectric plants in the Amazon to live well'. Gudynas counters by citing examples of legal and tax reform and the introduction of environmental accounting, right across South America. 'The Buen Vivir perspective is not only post-capitalist, but also post-socialist', he argues; 'It departs from the uncritical faith in progress of the modernist world view. It reconnects nature and society, modern and indigenous peoples.'

A shift away from seeing Earth solely in terms of 'resources' to be exploited for our own use is beginning to appear in international law and governance at a global level, too. An Earth Charter along these lines has been formally recognized by many transnational organizations, and a large number of universities are involved in the Earth System Governance Project (www.earthsystem governance.org), which was launched in 2009. This multidisciplinary network of scholars and practitioners, working across the global North and South, is forging new connections between the social and natural sciences in exploring new models of environmental governance.

A new concept of the world

In this between-two-worlds period of history, myriad details of a new economy are emerging whose core value is stewardship, rather than extraction. A new kind of political participation means appreciating the potential of the places where we live now, adapting what we can of the apparatus of modern life – but with a different mental model of what can, and should, be done. Some of our assets are technological solutions. Some are to be found in the natural world, thanks to millions of years of natural evolution. Many more assets are social practices – some of them very old ones – learned by other societies and in other times. The more pieces we fit in – each piece a new way to feed, shelter and heal ourselves, in partnership with living processes – the easier it becomes. In the words of Arundhati Roy (2003): 'Another world is not only possible, she is on her way. On a quiet day, I can hear her breathing.'

Note

1   www.shareable.net/blog/el-buen-vivir-and-the-commons

References

Andries, J. M. and Janssen, M. A. (2013), *Sustaining the Commons* [online]. Available at: http://sustaining thecommons.asu.edu/wp-content/uploads/2013/07/Sustaining-the-Commons-v101.pdf (accessed 29 November 2013).
Animate Earth (2011), *Animate Earth: Science, Intuition & Gaia* [online]. Available at: www.animateearth. com/Animate_Earth/the_film.html (accessed 29 November 2013).

Bauwens, M. (2013), *The Manifesto for Homeland Earth, by Edgar Morin* [online]. Available at: http://blog.p2pfoundation.net/the-manifesto-for-homeland-earth-by-edgar-morin/2013/07/27 (accessed 29 November 2013).

Berry, T. (1999), *The Great Work: Our Way into the Future*. New York: Bell Tower.

Biggs, S. (2013), *Legalizing Sustainability? Santa Monica Recognizes Rights of Nature* [online]. Available at: www.globalexchange.org/blogs/peopletopeople/2013/04/11/legalizing-sustainability-santa-monica-recognizes-rights-of-nature (accessed 29 November 2013).

Bollier, D. and Helfrich, S. (eds) (2012), *The Wealth of the Commons: A World Beyond Market and State*. Amherst, MA: Levellers Press.

Braslow, J. (2012), *Fibershed Bringing 'Farm Fresh' Clothing to the Region* [online]. Available at: http://ucanr.edu/sites/Grown_in_Marin/Grown_In_Marin_News/Grown_in_Marin_News_Winter_2012/Fibershed_bringing_farm-fresh_clothing_to_the_region (accessed 29 November 2013).

Burke, L. (2012), *Book Review: The Wealth of the Commons: A World Beyond Market and State* [online]. Available at: www.kosmosjournal.org/articles/book-review-the-wealth-of-the-commons-a-world-beyond-market-state#sthash.qF06Fdpy.dpuf (accessed 29 November 2013).

Collis, S. (2012), *The Metabolic Commons or, From Occupying to Commoning Through Decolonization* [online]. Previously available at: http://thefutureofoccupy.org/2012/04/the-metabolic-commons-or-from-occupying-to-commoning-through-decolonization/ (accessed 29 November 2013).

Cullinan, C. (2011), *Wild Law: A Manifesto for Earth Justice*. White River Junction, VT: Chelsea Green Publishing.

Dahle, C. (2013), *What the Future of Fish Can Teach Us About Designing Systems* [online]. Available at: www.core77.com/blog/sustainable_design/what_the_future_of_fish_can_teach_us_about_designing_systems_by_cheryl_dahle_24407.asp (accessed 29 November 2013).

De Angelis, M. (2010), *On the Commons: A Public Interview with Massimo De Angelis and Stavros Stavrides*, interviewed by Architektur, A. [online]. Available at: www.e-flux.com/journal/on-the-commons-a-public-interview-with-massimo-de-angelis-and-stavros-stavrides/ (accessed 29 November 2013).

Ethical Fashion Forum (n.d.), *Standards & Labelling* [online]. Available at: www.ethicalfashionforum.com/the-issues/standards-labelling (accessed 29 November 2013).

Finidori, H. (2012), *The Commons at the Core of our Next Economic Models?* [online]. Available at: http://menemania.typepad.com/helene_finidori/2012/04/the-commons-at-the-core-of-our-next-economic-models.html (accessed 29 November 2013).

Fletcher, K. and Grose, L. (2012), *Fashion and Sustainability: Design for Change*. London: Laurence King.

Gudynas, E. (2011), Buen vivir: today's tomorrow, *Development*, 54 (4): 441–7.

Hopkins, R. (2013), *Sophy Banks on the Power of Not Doing Stuff*, Transition Network [online]. Available at: http://transitionnetwork.org/blogs/rob-hopkins/2013–07/sophy-banks-power-not-doing-stuff (accessed 29 November 2013).

Kleinod, M. (2011), As unspoilt as possible – a framework for the critical analysis of ecotourism, *Transcience*, 2 (2) [online]. Available at: www2.hu-berlin.de/transcience/Vol2_Issue2_2011_44_58.pdf (accessed 29 November 2013).

Lansing, S. (2012), *Bali's Water Temples*. Presentation at Toward Resilience, Poptech 2012, June 27–29. Reykjavik, Iceland. Available at: http://poptech.org/iceland_videos (accessed 29 November 2013).

Macy, J. (n.d.), *The Great Turning* [online]. Available at: www.ecoliteracy.org/essays/great-turning (accessed 29 November 2013).

Marsh, J. (2011), *Does Sharing Come Naturally to Kids?* [online]. Available at: http://greatergood.berkeley.edu/article/item/does_sharing_come_naturally_to_kids (accessed 29 November 2013).

Merryweather, J. (2006), Secrets of the Soil, *Resurgence*, 235: 26–8.

Nesta (2013), *Systems Innovation Discussion Paper* [online]. Available at: www.nesta.org.uk/publications/systems-innovation-discussion-paper (accessed 29 November 2013).

Ostrom, E. (1990) *Governing the Commons – The Evolution of Institutions for Collective Action*. Cambridge, UK: Cambridge University Press.

Roy, A. (2003), *Confronting Empire* [online]. Available at: http://ratical.org/ratville/CAH/AR012703.html (accessed 29 November 2013).

Stone, C. D. (1996), *Should Trees Have Standing? And Other Essays on Law, Morals and the Environment*. New York: Oceana Publications.

Thackara, J. (2012), *Old Growth* [online]. Available at: www.doorsofperception.com/sustainability-design/old-growth/ (accessed 29 November 2013).

WBGU (2011), *World in Transition: A Social Contract for Sustainability* [online]. Available at: www.wbgu.de/fileadmin/templates/dateien/veroeffentlichungen/hauptgutachten/jg2011/wbgu_jg2011_en.pdf (accessed 29 November 2013).

PART II

Sustainability and fashion as seen from other places and disciplines

Whereas the previous part of this book offered a bird's-eye view on fashion and sustainability, discerning larger patterns and flows that are residual, dominant and emerging, this part looks at the field from the 'side'. It draws upon perspectives from scholars and practitioners predominately from outside the remit of fashion, and also those who are using approaches or views cultivated elsewhere, and invites this external gaze to provide a variety of discernment, penetration and exposure often difficult to achieve from within. As mentioned in the introduction to this volume, we have found it important to include these 'outsiders' in a handbook of fashion and sustainability, first because of the valuable insights their experiences from other specialisms and perspectives can offer. Also, interdisciplinarity (or working across silos of knowledge) is often hailed as the holy grail of sustainability work, although, in practice, it can turn out to be impractical, messy and slow to enact. It is our conviction that interdisciplinarity is essential to meeting the sustainability challenge. We believe this section highlights both the many benefits of 'unleashing' new perspectives on fashion and sustainability, but also some of the hurdles, such as a stereotypical understanding of 'fashion' and of 'fashion and sustainability', that such work has to cross in order to be truly successful.

Thus, this part comprises an eclectic range of voices and themes. The first four authors can be termed 'design thinkers' – using an approach that is strategic, experimental, collaborative and geared towards evolving systems. Their chapters highlight both similarities between fashion and other forms of design, and motivations and conditions unique to fashion.

John R. Ehrenfeld (Chapter 5) argues the futility of such work, in fashion and beyond, that, in the manner of 'sustaino-efficiency', only reduces unsustainability. For Ehrenfeld, only a new set of beliefs, leading to a new set of cultural habits, can create what he calls sustainability-as-flourishing. Here, Ehrenfeld explores the language and associated ideas and action around sustainability, usefully posing and then problematizing the question about what it is we are proposing to sustain. He critiques technological and technocratic 'fixes' and favours epistemological and cultural shifts based on connectedness with the natural world, relationships between people and also a change in the beliefs held about what it is to be human. He articulates a role for designers in this new realm, where they regard themselves as in service of 'cares' instead of wants, and supports Erich Fromm's notion of *being* instead of *having*.

Ann Thorpe (Chapter 6) explores the role of economic systems and frameworks for fashion and sustainability, by contextualizing fashion sustainability in terms of consumer-led economic growth. Central tenets of her piece constitute the failure of a marketplace to acknowledge social and environmental values, and the dominant growth agenda's intrinsic incompatibility with long-term sustainability. This is a theme evoked, in different ways, by many of this volume's contributors. She cites Avner Offer's notion of a vicious cycle of 'diminishing returns of novelty and psychic rewards' that fuels over-consumption and alienates consumers from deeper needs, and from natural and social health. Importantly, drawing on emerging theory and tentative practices, Thorpe sketches pathways towards slower consumption cycles, alternative indexes of success, social metrics, as well as models for making clothes available to an end user that decouple use and enjoyment from ownership and high material throughput.

Citing Bateson, **Jonathan Chapman** (Chapter 7) refers to the dire social and environmental predicament – in fashion and beyond – as the result of an *epistemological error* – in essence, an error in the deep, motivational origins of the experience of being human, and our search for meaning in sociocultural contexts. Chapman proposes a recalibration of the parameters of good design, to foster different epistemological underpinnings, which should result in a stronger commitment to the objects of design, and thus reverse their associated detrimental effect on Earth systems. By drawing on resilience theory, we can understand the objects of design as being in constant flux, and the designer can nurture their enfolding over time, as well as the perceived value of them to a user.

A recurrent theme in the fashion and sustainability discourse is the attribution of blame to the advent of fast fashion. For **Carolyn Strauss** (Chapter 8), founder of slowLab, the best response is not a total paradigm of slowness. Instead, in her thought-provoking and rich chapter, she encourages engagement with a number of registers of pace. She proposes that designers – and others – work towards a more even distribution of products, services and systems across this spectrum: 'Thinking–learning–sensing–designing–relating at a range of speeds equips us with far greater breadth of knowledge from which to draw inspiration, make connections and propose new directions for our lives and for our world.' In a series of cases, she situates notions of patience, gestation and receptivity as key facets in shaping fashion and societies of diversities of speed. Like several other contributors in this volume, Strauss denotes the education system's importance for fashion and sustainability. She powerfully exemplifies how introducing new contexts for fashion design to students, such as the effects of an environmental calamity on a particular community, can enable shifts and reattunements in fashion awarenesses, sensibilities and skill sets, from personal curiosity or career towards self-preservation and community well-being.

The next two chapters in this part illuminate two specific remits of diversity often lacking from, or superficially treated in, a fashion and sustainability discourse.

Informed by political economy and the field of textile up-cycling, **Amanda Ericsson** and **Andrew Brooks** (Chapter 9) describe how the imbalance of affluence in the North and poverty in Africa is manifested in, and aggravated by, the flow of second-hand clothing from the former to the latter. Whether organized by charities or commercial outfits, this cements economic dependency, as well as undermining an African clothing industry. Yet, as exemplified in the case of *Mima-te* in Mozambique, there are possibilities for value creation, for both the individual and communities, and to challenge socio-economic relationships, when passive reception turns to creative initiatives for up-cycling. The authors make a strong argument for augmented research efforts dedicated to understanding complex global commodity chains and the export of Western second-hand clothing, a phenomenon that, despite its distinct place in the economy of many poorer regions, has remained invisible in the dominant fashion and sustainability discourse.

This volume features a bias towards female authors, and it is well known that the fashion industry is similarly gender skewed, with, as has been argued, a reverse distribution of power.

Gender features as a recurrent theme in the dominant construction of fashion itself, fashion as consumption and body ideals (see Joanne Entwistle, Chapter 2). However, as **Mirjam Southwell** shows, in Chapter 10, the role of gender in fashion and sustainability has been hitherto underexplored. She offers a feminist perspective on the integration of sustainability into fashion, by drawing on literature and examining fashion and sustainability blogs, twitter feeds and their commentaries. This reveals a series of conflicts. Responsibility for the environment has become feminized, with women more likely to steer domestic consumption towards ethical and environmental options. This is also reflected in the corporate realm, which shows a correlation between female leaders and sustainability endeavours. Yet, women are dominantly constructed as instigators of consumption in general and of fashion in particular. This causes both individual cognitive dissonance and, alongside other pressures, women to experience 'eco-stress'. Southwell calls for an understanding that there is no gender-neutral consumer (nor fashion agent) and for an advancement in knowledge about a generation now stepping into adulthood – both here and in emerging economies – that, from a young age, has learned (or been taught) identity through consumption, at the same time as the environmental predicament reaches a peak of urgency.

If gender has been underexplored in the quest for futures of fashion and sustainability, **Sue Thomas** (Chapter 11) terms spirituality as the last taboo in the fashion industry supply chain, particularly in the hard-fought rationalism of corporate social responsibility. In a thought-provoking chapter, she argues that engagement with spirituality is essential for theoretical and practical sustainability work in fashion. She evokes the experience of cognitive dissonance from the previous chapter, here the result of conflicting personal and professional beliefs, as fashion designers and their colleagues must make choices with social and environmental impacts – choices explained as ultimately ethical. She persuasively explains the lack of engagement with spirituality-based ethics as a fear of loss of rationality, which, in juxtaposition with prevailing understandings of fashion as already irrational, opens up a rich space of enquiry. Drawing on existing businesses that are explicitly guided by spirituality, and the success of interfaith initiatives in peace work, Thomas sees the potential for pluralistic ethics in spirituality to, at the minimum, provoke important reflections within the remit of fashion business and, more ambitiously, drive fashion business towards sustainability.

The three last chapters in this part bring us closer to the object of fashion, clothing, and its most mundane – and perhaps potent – setting, the home, and the unfolding, complex behaviour of users of clothing.

From the realm of consumption studies, **Ingun Grimstad Klepp** and **Kirsi Laitala** (Chapter 12) argue the value of research into everyday clothes consumption, to counteract perspectives from marketing, elicit a range of real narratives and, of course, inform strategy and policy. After Alan Warde, they understand 'consumption mainly as collective and normatively regulated practices in everyday life'. Klepp and Laitala describe a repertoire of tools and methods they use that draw on touch, smell and linguistic descriptions, alongside fieldwork and user diaries, to arrive at a very nuanced understanding of clothing usage, care and disposal and the parameters for placing value on clothing employed by users. This can inform design strategies, textile waste management, business models, as well as, significantly, timely and palatable information given to consumers. The research has yielded powerful insights, oftentimes in conflict with persistent assumptions or myths about clothes use. One such refuted myth (also evoked in this volume) is that of fashion being an important reason why clothes are discarded – it isn't(!).

In a manner complementary to the preceding chapter, **Sophie Woodward** (Chapter 13) homes in on ethnographic approaches where clothing is contextualized within people's lives and relationships more broadly. Not originally 'in service' of sustainability, Woodward saw the potential of her work and field to contribute towards an understanding of 'the potentials in people's already existing practices to be sustainable rather than inherently problematic, and . . . to enhance these possibilities' (see also Fletcher, Chapter 1). Woodward shares important insights into how, contrary to a frequent construction of fashion consumers as passive victims, clothing practice entails a careful and nuanced creation of fashions or styles using both old and new – and often in conflict with social categories or fashion rules. These practices also evoke the diversity of paces called for by Carolyn Strauss (Chapter 8).

Like the previous two contributors, **Joe Smith**, in this part's concluding chapter, Chapter 14, takes us to the personal remit of clothing usage, drawing on the example of the century-long lifetime use and care of garments of one woman – his grandmother – to shed light on a history, politics and geography of consumption. Exploring garments in this way demonstrates the deep interdependence of choice, use and care of clothes with external events, such as war, technological advances and changes in social structures. This is, in many ways, a story of liberation (from corsets, social conventions, dependence on a service economy), but also, of course, of decreased care and resourcefulness, as celebration of progress turns to financial and ecological debt and social cost. Through masterful storytelling, Smith encourages us to see this history as a resource to draw on for fashion and sustainability, and proof 'that system changes are possible, and can be determined by positive goals'.

5

THE REAL CHALLENGE OF SUSTAINABILITY

John R. Ehrenfeld

Sustainability does not refer only to the state of the environment. It has come to refer to the state of human life on the planet as well. The health of the global society can be assessed in systemic terms such as poverty or inequality, or individual measures such as mental health or obesity. On these and other measures, Earth is not doing well. Over 80 percent of the global population lives in poverty, on less than US$10 per day. In practical terms, sustainability refers to some condition that is to be maintained over a prolonged period. Surely, we do not mean to maintain the present levels of human suffering and environmental breakdown.

Sustainability, unlike greening, is a commonly used word with a clear and specific meaning. Sustainability is defined as the capacity of a system or object to produce something desired over an extended period. Without naming the something, sustainability belongs to the class of so-called empty words—words that lack specificity until some contextual reference is added. One such, common, word is the preposition "to." Without naming a "what" or "where," the word has no practical significance—practical in the sense of coordinating action. Similarly, sustainability must have a reference to what is to be maintained to have any practical significance. Otherwise, as has been noted by many in business and elsewhere, the word has no commonly understood meaning. Many business leaders and others have complained that, because it means whatever suits the speaker, it means nothing at all.

Given its history, sustainability, with no further elaboration, generally relates to mitigating the deterioration of the Earth in its role as a life-support system for humans and non-humans. Of course, this is a very good and important idea, but still begs the question of what we want from the Earth. Is it only to provide a materialistic, hedonistically comfortable life for human beings—the primary goal of Western societies since John Locke, Adam Smith, and other modernist political philosophers proposed their new theories? This goal has been a primary driver in the fashion industry. These ideas of the Enlightenment thinkers led to an affluent, dynamic culture for a handful of Western-thinking developed nations.

At the time these thinkers proposed the new ideas for designing society, the world was much less populated, and the technological forces of modernity were just beginning to uncover and exploit the vast natural resources that have powered our modern societies. Science and its handmaiden, technology, were seen as providing freedom from the chains of dogma that had enslaved human settlements for centuries and from the rigors of a harsh world that, in his classic book, *Leviathan*, Thomas Hobbes described as making "the life of man, solitary, poore, nasty, brutish, and short."

Now, some three and one-half centuries later, the world has become densely populated, and the plentiful natural resources are now being stressed and depleted. Earth scientists claim we are now moving from the Holocene era, in which the evolutionary forces of nature created unheard-of new life forms, including our own species, to what is being called the *Anthropocene*, in which human activities have begun to exert significant destructive impacts on the Earth (Rockström *et al.*, 2009). Climate change is perhaps the most significant of these impacts, but not the only one. Habitat destruction, accelerated species extinction, and failures of potable water systems are among others.

Sustainability might be understood only by reference to the maintenance of the planetary life-support system, but it has also become associated with the social conditions of human societies, particularly the poverty levels of at least one-third of the world's population. Even in affluent countries, poverty affects large numbers of people. Other social pathologies, such as crime, obesity, or mental illness, have been rising, even as affluence has grown. Inequality is on the rise and has been invoked as a strong factor underlying these pathologies (Wilkinson and Pickett, 2009).

Given this current context for life on Planet Earth, it is critical to ask, what should we be striving to sustain? If living conditions were believed to be wonderful everywhere, we would have an implicit, normative sense of where we want the future to take us. But it isn't, and so it is meaningless to talk about sustainability without an explicit vision of the future for all life on Earth. All life needs to be included, as the human species is but a single part of the complex, highly interconnected global system. We cannot deal with sustainability in terms of isolated species or polities. The conventional technological tools mustered to stem the tide of unsustainability have proven inadequate to offset the unintended consequences of economic growth, the framework presumed by policymakers to solve all of our social problems. (Eco-efficient) growth, fueled by technological innovation, is implicit in the well-known Brundtland definition of sustainable development (World Commission on Environment and Development, 1987). As I have written elsewhere, expecting technology to overcome unsustainability is one of the primary causes of the problems we now face (Ehrenfeld, 2008; Ehrenfeld and Hoffman, 2013).

Pinning hopes on technological (eco-efficiency) or technocratic (rules and regulations) fixes is a losing approach. Unsustainability is a set of unintended consequences of modern cultures. We have had policies and institutions in place, many going back to the Enlightenment thinkers, to perfect the state of humankind. Our political economies have been designed and evolved according to materialistic measures of human well-being. For a few centuries, the cultural structure built on the beliefs rising from those great thinkers and on the power of the new sciences was able to continuously improve the lot of humans in the West, where such beliefs and knowledge were to be found. No longer was life restricted to a Hobbesian existence; new measures of well-being kept increasing.

Our political institutions followed the successes and now are deeply engrained in the culture. No one paid much attention to the negative outcomes that accompanied all the progress, especially for the natural world. Unalleviated or increased human suffering was noticed—for example, in the works of Dickens and others who portrayed the underside of life—and attempts to mitigate it were introduced into the societal institutions. In recent years, stemming from demographic and economic growth and from new technologies that consume vast amounts of energy and material resources, unintended consequences (always there) have grown to a point where they cannot be and have not been ignored. But action beyond attempts to relieve the symptoms has not followed and will not, until a meaningful definition of sustainability is used to guide such action.

Finding a meaningful quality to sustain is no easy task. The usual economic measure of well-being, Gross Domestic Product (GDP) or something equivalent, is inadequate. Economists and others have demonstrated that subjective measures of well-being tail off once some level of affluence has been reached (Easterlin, 1974, 2003). Maslow's famous hierarchy of needs transitioned from materialistically based categories to existential measures, once the basic subsistence and safety needs were met (Maslow, 1954). His highest level is self-actualization, which has unfortunately become equated to material wealth as a cultural norm. Erich Fromm noted that affluent societies, especially the United States, have elevated *having* far above *being*, with disastrous consequences to themselves and the world (Fromm, 1976). The implications for, and challenges to, the fashion industry should be obvious.

As a start along the right path, I offer this definition: Sustainability is the possibility that humans and other life will flourish on the planet forever (Ehrenfeld, 2008). Flourishing is the normative goal or vision to attain and sustain. Flourishing has been considered an ideal goal of human life over history. This word is found in some form in virtually all cultures. To emphasize the importance of naming something to sustain, I use the compound form, sustainability-as-flourishing. Once the reference to flourishing is understood by all as an essential part of the definition, the word, sustainability, can be used without the hyphenated parts. Others may choose to use a different normative outcome than flourishing, but some property must always be designated. Sustainability-as-GDP, the implicit, conventional meaning, doesn't make sense. What level of GDP is to be normatively appropriate? Can the quality of human well-being really be measured by a number? GDP is a poor proxy for human well-being.

So, the key question for those who will be reading and applying the ideas in this *Handbook* is what, if any, is the role, or roles, for designers and producers of fashion in any program aimed at creating sustainability-as-flourishing? It is not the present program to reduce unsustainability. Only a very minor role can be assigned to this objective, because, simply on a relative basis, the volume of fashion objects is but a very small percentage of all the commodity goods that are made and sold. There is, however, little to be lost, and something to be gained, if only for its symbolic value, in reducing unsustainability through application of conventional design for sustainability or design for environment, that is, by enabling reuse or recycling or toxics elimination, and so forth (Braungart and McDonough, 2002; Bhamra and Lofthouse, 2007; Shedroff, 2009).

Having said this, however, there is an important error often made in acting toward sustainability in this way, and that is believing that you are really "saving" the Earth. At best, reducing the impact through conventional "technical" design features will only slow down the inevitable march toward the abyss. At its worst, such measures will fool the designers, manufacturers, and consumers into believing that they are doing all it takes to create sustainability-as-flourishing. This latter outcome is exacerbated by misleading advertising promoting sustainable fashion or sustainable anything. Phrases such as "environmentally friendly" are misleading. Nothing we make is friendly, so to speak, to the environment. Mother Nature would not be pleased.

There is much the fashion industry can do, however, but only after the players, such as those in all other institutions, learn what sustainability is really all about. Let's go back to the generic definition of sustaining something. The choice should not be, as I noted above, about the present state of the world. There is too much out of kilter and out of sorts to seek to preserve the status quo. And, as the next part will assert, the roots of unsustainability remain untouched by the current approach. The fashion industry and all of its leaders need to know and acknowledge two important aspects of sustainability: first, a meaningful definition and goal, and, second, an understanding of the roots of unsustainability and a commitment to replace them with cultural drivers that both eliminate or greatly reduce the impacts of everyday life and begin to bring flourishing forth.

If the fashion industry, like any other institutional sector, wants to make a commitment to sustainability as I have defined it, it must focus its "sustainability" efforts on the roots of unsustainability beyond those intended to mitigate or remedy the damage already done and continuing to be produced. This means it must develop strategies to change the basic beliefs that keep unsustainability in place and inhibit the creation of flourishing. If, as I argue, that unsustainability is an unintended consequence of our current cultural beliefs and practices, only a new set beliefs, leading to a new set of cultural habits, can eliminate the negative consequences. Without such a change, we are limited to playing catch-up and clean-up.

Such practices—termed eco-efficiency—have been the so-called sustainability strategy of industry (and other sectors) ever since sustainable development introduced the term into everyday practice. Eco-efficiency means simply providing more or equal value in the offering, but at less environmental impact. This metric is almost always used in reference to environmental factors, but, in theory, it could be expanded to include measures of social damages and become a "sustaino-efficiency" measure. Social impacts are conventionally managed under the rubric of corporate social responsibility (CSR) and are not, like eco-efficiency, measured in terms of specific products. Practices such as fair-traded goods are among the most common of such CSR practices. In the wake of the tragedies in Bangladesh, in the apparel industry, calls for a more aggressive form of CSR have come forth.

As important as all of the eco-efficiency and CSR activities are, they will not produce sustainability-as-flourishing. The fundamental coupling between efficiency and growth will not allow significant reductions in environmental harms. Known as the Jevons paradox, economists have known for more than a century that efficiency gains in production are overwhelmed by overall economic growth, putting the lie to the possibility of continuing growth in a finite world of material resources (Jackson, 2009). I will not comment further on this, except to say that the fashion industry, like all other sectors, should not label any of its sustaino-efficient actions as producing sustainability, saying instead only that they are reducing unsustainability. And to the extent the fashion industry is truly committed to create flourishing, it must not let these mitigating fixes blind it to the need for change at the roots. The defocusing that comes by continuing to treat only the symptoms and not the roots is endemic. Systems dynamicists have named it an archetype of everyday activities and given it a name—shifting-the-burden (Kim, 1994).

So, let me leave eco-efficiency and CSR behind and get to the heart of the challenge facing the fashion (and every) industry. What are the root causes of unsustainability, and what can you do about eliminating them? Root causes are those that, if properly addressed, make the problematic situation disappear. Solutions aimed at the symptoms, eco-efficiency in this case, are no longer necessary. Of course, new kinds of problem are likely to show up, simply because the world keeps changing, or what we thought were the root causes were, in fact, not the whole story.

I have already covered the first challenge facing the fashion industry—the failure to understand what sustainability means—and so fashion has followed the industry crowd from every sector. The second failing—the absence of practices to change the underlying causes of unsustainability—I will discuss below.

Suppose a fashion product produced two categories of effects, instead of the usual single set of user satisfactions. Appropriate sustaino-efficient designs, as I have called the combination of addressing both social and environment problems, can do the latter, reaching even beyond the ultimate user to other stakeholders as well. What if, however, design produced a change in the belief system of the ultimate user and others observing how the user behaved? In particular, what if the design raised consciousness of the user's multiple connections to the world, and further guided subsequent behaviour toward a caring, responsible stance toward that world.

A shift toward sustainability-as-flourishing requires that the underlying modernist beliefs about the nature of our species become transformed to a new set, based on care as the fundamental way of being human. A conscious sense of responsibility to act in a caring way has the power to embed whatever practices arise as new cultural norms, which, combining with reflection, can also embed this new belief. This process of transformative change is not new; it is found in education, therapy, organization learning, and so on. In recent years, it has been applied to the design of artifacts and the design process itself.

The concept of transformative design, such practices being applied by designers, is now becoming recognized as a necessary adjunct to conventional practices in dealing with the complex problems we face today (Burns *et al.*, 2006). H. Rittel and M. Webber coined the term "wicked problem" in a classic paper directed at the planning profession (Rittel and Webber, 1973). Among the ten defining features in their paper, several points are highly relevant to this discussion:

- Solutions to wicked problems are not true-or-false but good-or-bad.
- Every implemented solution to a wicked problem has consequences.
- Wicked problems do not have a well-described set of potential solutions.
- Every wicked problem can be considered a symptom of another problem.

Sustainability-as-flourishing is the epitome of a wicked problem. Planning can be considered to be simply a form of design, if one uses the definition of design as a process that arises in a breakdown, cessation, or any equivalent word denoting a failure to produce satisfaction. Anyone can be and is a designer when he or she creates a solution to a persistent problem that has resisted normal forms of solution.

I first came across transformational practice in the work of Jaap Jelsma while I was spending a year in the Netherlands (Jelsma, 2000). Jelsma calls it "behaviour-steering design" and uses the two-button toilet as his model. People encountering a two-button toilet (now quite common in Europe, but not so elsewhere) for the first time will stop and reflectively ask themselves what is going on. Most will figure out what the small and large buttons are to be used for and, in the process, may also become conscious of the place the wastes go and the amount of water being used to transport the wastes there. Some may even develop a conscious sense of responsibility for taking care of water, both as an essential resource and also as the repository for human wastes. Speed bumps do the same thing by interrupting the unconscious act of driving momentarily and causing the driver to slow down and perhaps also look around for pedestrians. After a few encounters without slowing down, most drivers will start to take care as they see a speed bump ahead. This kind of design process, which involves changing norms and their underlying beliefs, goes by other names in addition to the two above. The design studio, IDEO, speaks of "design thinking" and has embodied that framework in a toolkit called Human Centred Design.

Patagonia took a step in the direction of sustainability, with their "Don't buy this shirt" campaign of the past two years, but stopped short. Their ads did create a reflective moment, but stopped at asking if the customer really needed the object right then. The real opportunity would have been to get even deeper and use the rather startling message to get the customer to think more fundamentally about what he or she really cares about. "Manicare Stop That" is a safe and non-toxic habit-breaking nail polish formulation, designed to help cure the habit of nail biting by incorporating a harmless but bitter taste. What if the bottle carried a message, "Think about why you bite your nails"? Now the behavioural change the bad taste produces might be accompanied by a deeper reflection that eventually eliminates the bad habit and, thus, the need for the symptomatic remedy.

Although there are certainly several beliefs that could serve as a target for transformation, the one that seems most critical to the fashion industry is the belief we hold about what it is to be human. Flourishing is not something that can or does show up in the narcissistic, selfish, insatiably needy, mechanistic persona that modern humans beings think they possess. Flourishing always carries some sense of completion—the satisfaction of one's immediate cares. Flourishing produces a sense of authenticity, knowing that one is acting from within, not responding to the pressures of society. Can fashion designers produce such a reflection and learning experience?

This is what sustainability-as-flourishing needs. It places new roles and responsibilities on the shoulders of designers. They acquire a responsibility for the outcomes of the design. They must have a stake in that outcome. I am not talking about "persuasive design" here (Fogg, 2002). Persuasive design aims at changing habits but not beliefs, and is based on a manipulative, not an interactive, reflective encounter. Persuasive design shows up in advertising and, currently, in the design of social media technology. It is designed to get people to do what the vendor wants them to. It can affect widely held beliefs, as used in Facebook, for example, with the meaning of "friend." Such persuasive design practices tend to reinforce our basic belief as insatiable consumers. More friends are better than fewer. The quality and meaningfulness of friendship get diminished.

I make no claims to being a professional designer, but do often think about what "design" is and does. Design, in my thinking, does not just solve problems; it makes them go away. New ones will eventually crop up. Design co-involves the designer and those with the problem. This mix is essential in getting the problem right. The focus of the process should be the problem out there in the world, not whatever lives in the designer's context. That is what is missing in the usual meaning of persuasive design. The designer is shaping technology to make users do what the business wants, often opposing what they might do in the absence of the technology. This is why I prefer to use the more expansive term, transformational design or technology. All design in this sense must be able to create a breakdown and induce reflection. Only when the action has gotten out of the mindless mode can the actor begin to probe what is going on. Perhaps actors can figure out what is going wrong and adopt new ideas and practices on their own, but the designer can provide positive guidance.

In the case of sustainability-as-flourishing, the force of habits is so strongly embedded in the culture that people will always need both intervention and guidance. The designer of speed bumps did that, as did the one who created the two-button toilet. If the fashion industry wants to take on the real sustainability challenge, its designers will have to learn how to embed its messages in the designs that end up in the market. Stunning garments must become more than something that fires up critics and customers. Design must stop the action, so as to raise questions about the nature of human being and offer an alternative to the present economistic belief. If flourishing is the end, the new belief must turn to caring, instead of needing. For starters, fashion designers can think about satisfying what people can use to address their cares, instead of what they think they need.

References

Bhamra, T. and Lofthouse, V. (2007), *Design for Sustainability: A Practical Approach*, Farnham, UK: Ashgate.

Braungart, M. and McDonough, W. (2002), *Cradle to Cradle: Remaking the Way We Make Things*, New York: North Point Press.

Burns, C., Cottam, H., Vanstone, C. and Winhall, J. (2006), *Transformation Design-RED Paper 2*, London: The Design Council-UK.

Easterlin, R. A. (1974), Does economic growth improve the human lot?, in W. E. Melvin (ed.), *Nations and Households in Economic Growth*, Palo Alto, CA: Stanford University Press: 98–125.

Easterlin, R. A. (2003), Explaining happiness, *Proceedings of the National Academy of Sciences*, 100 (19): 11176–83.

Ehrenfeld, J. R. (2008), *Sustainability by Design: A Subversive Strategy for Transforming Our Consumer Culture*, New Haven, CT: Yale University Press.

Ehrenfeld, J. R. and Hoffman, A. (2013), *Flourishing: A Frank Conversation about Sustainability*, Palo Alto, CA: Stanford University Press.

Fogg, B. J. (2002) *Persuasive Technology: Using Computers to Change What We Think and Do*, San Francisco, CA: Morgan Kaufmann.

Fromm, E. (1976), *To Have or To Be?*, ed. Ruth Nanda Anshen, World Perspectives; New York: Harper & Row.

Jackson, T. (2009), *Prosperity Without Growth*, London: Earthscan.

Jelsma, J. (2000), Design of behaviour steering technology, *International Summer Academy on Technology Studies*, Graz (Deutschlandsberg), Austria.

Kim, D. H. (1994), *Systems Archetypes I*, Cambridge, MA: Pegasus Communications.

Maslow, A. H. (1954), *Motivation and Personality*, New York: Longman.

Rittel, H. W. J. and Webber, M. M. (1973), Dilemmas in a general theory of planning, *Policy Sciences*, 4: 155–69.

Rockström, J., Steffen, W., Noone, K., Persson, Å., Chapin, F. S., Lambin, E. F., Lenton, T. M. *et al.* (2009), A safe operating space for humanity, *Nature*, 461 (7263): 472–75.

Shedroff, N. (2009), *Design Is the Problem: The Future of Design Must Be Sustainable*, Brooklyn, NY: Rosenfeld Media.

Wilkinson, R. and Pickett, K. (2009), *The Spirit Level: Why Greater Equality Makes Societies Stronger*, London: Bloomsbury Press.

World Commission on Environment and Development (1987), *Our Common Future*, Oxford, UK: Oxford University Press.

6

ECONOMIC GROWTH AND THE SHAPE OF SUSTAINABLE FASHION

Contextualizing fashion sustainability in terms of consumer-led economic growth

Ann Thorpe

Our ideas of progress have become tied largely to economic growth in a societal narrative where consuming more is better. In this narrative, we view more and larger market transactions as an indicator of increasing well-being. We view "consumer choice" as the most important way that people express and meet their needs.

The pressure for growth is expressed in economic practices that increase consumption. Such practices include reducing costs, increasing sales, expanding markets, and attracting investment. Every aspect of our daily lives, including fashion, is under this pressure, which shapes the fashion sector in a number of problematic ways.

This chapter stems from an examination of how growth and consumerism shape, and are shaped by, material culture and the industries that provide them (Thorpe, 2012). We begin with background on growth and then look at how consumer-driven growth is problematic for sustainability in the fashion sector. We ask where fashion products and processes can address sustainability at this intersection of fashion and the economy.

Economic growth

Since the 1950s, economic growth has been a central organizing principle in many countries (Offer, 2006: 15). In affluent countries, 60–70 percent of growth comes directly from consumer demand (Organisation for Economic Co-operation and Development, 2009). Growth is seen as the key to adequate levels of employment, among other things. In turn, consumer choice is hailed as an important freedom and consumption as the duty of good citizens. Economic growth has been taken as a proxy for overall well-being in a sort of "market triumphalism" (Sandel, 2012: 6).

In recent decades, however, research and experience have led many people to question the benefits of continuous economic growth (Victor, 2008; Jackson, 2009; Sandel, 2012). A central question is whether we can afford economic growth, which is expensive in resource and material terms, but also in social terms.

In material terms, every unit of growth uses up resources and creates waste. What if improved efficiency could outrun the harmful ecological effects of growth? This concept is known by names such as green growth, eco-efficiency, de-materialization or decoupling (the process of detaching economic growth from growth in resource consumption). Yet, even with improved material efficiency over the years, we haven't been able to "outrun" the increasing resource use required by growth (Fischer-Kowalski *et al.*, 2011).

Consider, for example, how automobile travel outpaces gains in efficiency. Between 1970 and 1990, fuel efficiency increased by 34 percent, but total fuel consumption rose by 7 percent. There was just too much growth in car ownership (cars per household), vehicle size, and miles driven per car (Manno, 2002: 68). Economist Peter Victor also notes that, "if the adverse effects on the environment [from growth] are cumulative, decoupling slows down the rate at which things get worse, but it does not turn them around" (Victor, 2008: 40).

There is also evidence that individual consumers use their efficiency gains to increase consumption, an effect known as "rebound" (Sorrell, 2007). For example, savings from a more efficient car may enable a cheap airline flight. The rebound may be calculated purely on budgetary terms, but there's some evidence that consumers trade "good" behavior off against "bad"; for example, consumers may reason that, if they recycle or buy an eco product, they're entitled to use more of other resources (Catlin and Wang, 2013).

Nevertheless, green growth is a step in the right direction. In the fashion sector we see green-growth initiatives that aim to increase profits while decreasing environmental costs. Common examples include sourcing organic and other environmentally superior materials, taking back and reusing clothing or shoes, or striving to eliminate waste from production processes.

The green-growth approach, although important as part of an overall sustainable solution, particularly in developing countries, is not enough in itself to overcome the environmental and social costs of growth. Currently, green growth, particularly eco-efficiency, can't outrun sheer growth in material use. Green growth also does little to address the problems of convenience and inertia of habit, the human weakness for temptation, and the effects of peer pressure and social networks.

Despite the troubles with economic growth, it remains central and is rarely challenged; but two recent reports suggest that there is another way. Tim Jackson's *Prosperity Without Growth* (2009) examined key issues around the idea of maintaining well-being ("prosperity") in conditions of a steady-state economy. Jackson's work was based in part on Peter Victor's *Managing Without Growth* (2008), in which Victor reports on a model for a steady-state, or low-growth, Canadian economy. These authors are both suggesting that it is possible, particularly in affluent countries, to have an economy that works on principles different than continuous economic growth based on consumerism—this is the idea of a "post-growth" era and the possibility of maintaining and improving well-being without continuous economic growth.

In this chapter, we explore some of Jackson's and Victor's central themes. For example, we look at how human nature, long ignored by the economic assumption of a "rational man," amplifies the negative effects of a society focused on private consumption. We investigate how "development"—growth and improvement in well-being—is different than "economic growth" and requires a robust public realm. We explore how real costs are left out of the prices we pay in the realm of private consumption. We address the underlying question of how we might use fashion design products and processes to relieve pressures for growth as a step toward a post-growth economy.

The following sections briefly explore some of the social and environmental problems and solutions associated with growth, focusing on the context of textiles and fashion. Our focus is on affluent countries, where, most experts agree, consumption must level off or decrease. By contrast, many poorer countries need absolute increases in consumption to reach decent standards of living.

Inaccurate prices and hidden costs

It is now broadly understood that what we think of as "the economy" and often call "the market," including its resources (money, buildings, or equipment), sits within a much wider economy made up of ecological and social resources. But, over hundreds of years, we've gradually structured a market that doesn't account for damage to ecological and social resources (Hawken *et al.*, 1999).

In many cases, there is no direct price on natural and social resources, and that hides the true cost of most garments. Environmental damages, such as heavy pesticides on cotton, and social damages, such as child labor, are simply invisible to many actors in the system, including consumers. Laws and practices to protect workers and the environment in industrial countries typically add costs to production that don't exist in developing countries, which is why much production takes place overseas. Even in industrialized countries, many types of pollution are allowed to some degree, and this level of pollution is "free." Many companies will pollute up to the allowable limit, rather than spend money to eliminate "free" pollution. Pushing costs on to distant communities or on to the environment is central to keeping garment purchase prices low, which also expands markets.

Shifting costs on to distant communities is one way to hide them, but other hidden costs are closer to home. The pressure to find new ways to profit from fashion outpaces our understanding of the health effects of new methods of growing and processing fabric fibers. Consider chemicals used in plastics and fibers to make them more versatile, which allows for more new kinds of fabric and clothing—and consequent growth.

But testing chemicals is expensive, and huge profits might be at risk if the 1,000 or so new chemicals introduced each year had to be proven safe. Ninety-two percent of chemicals in use are unregulated, and most also aren't tested. Rather, they are presumed innocent until proven guilty (Snell, 2008). One textile-relevant example comes from fire retardants such as chlorinated TRIS, assumed safe until research found them to be mutagenic and they were removed from children's sleepwear in 1977 (Blum and Ames, 1977). The European Union's REACH (Registration, Evaluation and Authorisation of Chemicals) initiative is only just beginning to require some testing. All actors in the fashion system, up against both economic pressure and this invisibility of chemicals, are susceptible to using standard materials that have hidden costs.

Making costs visible

Two common ways for fashion to "show" these hidden costs are through the creation of issue-specific labels or rating systems aimed at informing consumer purchases. Both of these approaches offer a way to indicate the social and environmental performance of products and processes. Examples of widely known labels that are sometimes used in fashion include "fair trade" and "organic." Stakeholders in the fashion industry have experimented with other labeling approaches as well: for example, the Made-By blue button label intends to show consumers that a fashion label or collection is pursuing sustainability across the supply chain (Fletcher, 2008: 67–9).

To date, consumer labels have gained the most traction in markets for appliances and green or energy-efficient buildings, arguably because the up-front cost, as well as the money-saving potential for the consumer, is relatively high. Yet the viability of fair-trade and organic labels suggests that, with the right comparative framework, which is yet to be developed for fashion, these labels can shift the market even for lower-cost goods.

It's worth mentioning that, at the level of producer and designer, there also exist a number of standards that describe how products and processes should perform, if they aim to be sustainable. Consumers won't normally "see" these standards, unless they are captured through consumer-oriented labels or ratings. Producer-level standards originate with groups such as the Fair Wear Foundation, the Global Recycle Standard, or Worldwide Responsible Apparel Production.

Pace

A prominent way to increase sales and improve growth in the fashion industry, like others, is to encourage and supply frequently updated and new styles. Otto von Busch reports that the pace of fashion design is escalating so much that major retail brands such as H&M update their collections ever more frequently, sometimes monthly (von Busch, 2009: 31–4). The need for businesses to demonstrate growth quickly is aggravated by a reporting system that expects results every 3 months in quarterly reporting. The fast pace of fashion has obvious implications for environmental sustainability in terms of resource consumption and waste, but it also has significant negative social impact.

Avner Offer argues that the fast pace of the market is problematic because, in affluent consumer culture, the easy availability of novel stimulation is overwhelming. Offer calls this stimulation "psychic reward" and notes that, just as the availability of these rewards has burgeoned, our ability to resist their temptations has waned (Offer, 2006: 37). We find it harder to keep long-term commitments—to prudently study, save or exercise (for example). Our traditional ways of committing to our own future well-being have eroded, whereas new systems (that account for overwhelming short-term stimulation) have not yet evolved. We are less able to pace ourselves; our ability to maximize our own well-being *across time* is failing.

Historically, our methods of committing to the future involved both our own internal willpower (self-control or self-discipline), as well as social and community constraints related to family structure, social traditions, religion, or other "social contracts." One of Offer's key observations is that our strategies for committing to the future, whether internal or community-based, are costly and difficult to cultivate. They take time to build up and often involve a process of social learning and education. The strategies require regular training to maintain.

Alongside that, Offer outlines the problem of the diminishing returns of novelty and psychic rewards. He suggests that there is a relationship between "reward" and "satisfaction," where more reward leads to more satisfaction, creating a "pleasure zone," but only up to a point. After that point, satisfaction is replaced by habituation—we become too used to the reward for it to yield much satisfaction, and so we move to new rewards (Offer, 2006: 56).

Slowing the pace in satisfying ways

Fashion and other designers confront the fast pace of consumerism through "slow design"—approaches that highlight the appeal and pleasure of taking our time and making our consumption more gradual.

One mode of slow design alters private consumption by attaching meaning to deeper, long-term content. An example is Flock knitwear by designer Christien Meindertsma. The knitwear

Figure 6.1 Connecting to the material source of clothing; wool for Flock knitwear by Christien Meindertsma

aims to put people back in touch with the source of their clothing: the fibers are traced back to specific animals (sheep and goats), and the clothing tag provides information about the animal, such as its name, location, and breeding (Nowacek, 2006). It is a form of "slow" clothing, connecting people to the environment to generate meaning.

Another approach is collaborative or shared consumption. In this model, the emphasis shifts from the immediate rewards based on purchase and ownership—my car, my dress, my house—to a model where reward potentially comes from what Kate Fletcher calls "the craft of use" (Fletcher, 2011). Reward and stimulation in this model are paced by new patterns of access that derive from human relationships, such as planning ahead to reserve a car or working together with sharing partners. The quality of stimulation is also different, shifting from the acquisition and care of things, to the development of relationships. Relationships involve connecting with others and giving to others, both of which have repeatedly been shown to increase well-being (Michaelson *et al.*, 2009).

Other forms of slow design, which we might think about as slow and "long" design, focus more on helping us make and keep long-term commitments by rejigging the infrastructure of daily life. For example, a bicycle lane makes it easier to commit to cycling instead of driving. Designer Kate Ludwig's expandable urban mobility jacket provides a built-in alternative to plastic carrier bags (2005). The jacket's normally hidden pocket–bag zips out as needed and includes an interior shoulder strap, making it easier to commit to re-usable shopping bags. Another example is clothing company Iva Jean's fashion clothing for cycling, such as a pencil skirt that unzips for cycling leg movement. The skirt preserves a woman's fashionable presence, without compromising her functional capability to ride a bike, which, again, makes it easier to commit to cycling.

Durable design is another way to support long-term commitment. Designers have done a reasonably good job of linking durability to the notion of heirlooms and products that tell a story. Examples include products with lifetime guarantees, alluring aging processes (patterned on the aging of leather and denim), or elements that the user can update or modify over time (van Hinte and Bonekamp, 1997).

The fast pace of novelty—frequent new styles—is a key result of pressures for economic growth. Slow and long design responds by attaching novelty to the deeper meaning of consumption, for example through connections to nature or to the wider community. This type of design also addresses infrastructure that makes it easier to shift our long-term commitments.

Status anxiety

Consumerism provides a form of social language based on private consumption. Using this language, we gain social status, avoid shame, even shape our identities. We "keep up" our social position through "positional consumption," in a race that can never be won. As Peter Victor explains, "People think that a higher income will make them happier, but overlook the rising aspirations that will accompany such an increase" (Victor, 2008: 128). As people experience rises in income, they begin to compare themselves with a new, higher-income group, which then requires a new round of positional consumption.

Positional consumption amplifies the societal narrative that well-being is expressed, even increased, through individual ownership. We sell more power tools, ball gowns, cars, and washing machines when each individual or household owns one. Research shows, however, that many material goods are used rarely, or used at a fraction of their capacity. Power tools and four- and five-seat automobiles fall in to this category, but so do many clothes (Fletcher and Tham, 2004).

Figure 6.2 Iva Jean pencil skirt designed by Ann DeOtte

Woodward's small study found that less than 40 percent of a woman's clothing is actively worn, about 50 percent has the potential to be worn (it fits and is in good repair), and the remainder is inactive (Woodward, 2007: 45). Yet the priority on increasing sales, driven by a societal narrative favoring private ownership, filters into design research and production that then concentrate on privatized approaches.

In light of the social language of goods, as standard styles become "norms," they allow us to both belong, by owning something that's the norm, but also to distinguish ourselves through different "brands" of this norm. In this sense, norms and standards in themselves serve social purposes, but become problematic when they are governed by profits in a context of affluence. Important elements of social meaning and purpose are framed through the advertising and marketing of profit-maximizing entities. Novelty (stimulation-as-reward) and social anxiety (striving for position or belonging through goods) are two key factors that drive consumerism.

Building on this point and drawing on the work of Amartya Sen, Tim Jackson points out the social trap, in which, at the individual level, it makes sense to seek social position and avoid shame through the language of goods, but, at the societal level, it leads only to "fragmentation and anomie." He continues,

> Most worrying of all is that there is no escape from this social trap within the existing paradigm. While social progress depends on the self-reinforcing cycle of novelty and anxiety, the problem can only get worse. Material throughput will inevitably grow. And the prospects for flourishing within ecological limits evaporate.
>
> *(Jackson, 2009: 88)*

Relieving anxiety through the civic realm

A key response to the social anxiety surrounding positional consumption and ownership is to re-invigorate the public or civic realm. One approach is to use skills, rather than possessions, to build social position. Examples here include both "hacking" and "open source."

Open-source approaches put blueprints and patterns into the commons for people to use and adapt. Pattern-sharing has a long history in fashion terms, but a contemporary example is the group DIY Couture, which creates and shares patterns online. MIT's fabrication laboratories, "fablabs," pioneered by Neil Gershenfeld, are another "open" example. Fablabs bring, not only tools, but also non-commercial spaces, where communities often choose to make locally relevant objects. Gershenfeld comments, "personal fabrication is a new kind of literacy that can be brought to the community," which facilitates local, grass-roots invention (Beck, 2005: 58).

Not only do these "commons" approaches address social anxiety, but they also address well-being through positive development, in ways that growth can't. Peter Victor argues that, in affluent countries, where there are no shortages of goods, and "positional consumption" is the dominant form of consumption, high-quality public goods and public spaces are a central component of "development," because they offer relief from the consumption race (Victor, 2008: 128).

So far, we've looked at a few key problems and solutions at the intersection of fashion and economic growth, including hidden costs, pace, and status anxiety. In the next sections, we examine ways of organizing our work and measuring our impact in scenarios where economic growth is not our prime metric.

Restructure design practices and organizations

As we find ourselves needing to address values that aren't captured in the marketplace, we can continue with traditional business models, but we also need new ways to structure our work. Ultimately, profit-driven businesses tied to a growth agenda may limit our scope for sustainable actions.

Social enterprise, a newly emerging form, aims to maximize social good without losing money. It turns the traditional profit-maximizing agenda on its head by framing the objective as a "non-loss" business. Some earnings might be distributed to shareholders, but earnings are also plowed into the social agenda. Slow-clothing consultancy Rewardrobe and handbag-maker Bottletop are two fashion companies working to a social enterprise model and addressing ethical production (Sloan, 2013).

Nonprofits also direct resources into social good, but they tend to rely on grants or member donations. Membership networks, certification (or rating) agencies, and independent educational institutions are springing up in the nonprofit category to promote and implement sustainable fashion. An example is advocacy group Clean Clothes Campaign, which aims to improve working conditions in the global garment industry.

By moving into nonprofit or social enterprise formats that are "excused" from growth requirements, we can often pursue an expanded sustainability agenda. However, in moving away from economic growth as a guiding measurement, how should we measure success?

Measure social impact

No matter how our work is structured, we have to find ways to measure our social and environmental impacts and check that the value we create builds toward long-term, higher-level goals.

As labels and rating systems typically signal feasible or best available techniques, such as percentage of organic cotton or ethical labor practices, they often don't represent our higher-level goals. An example of such a goal is: keep the concentration of carbon dioxide in the atmosphere below 350 parts per million. Another example is: reduce income inequality. To reach these goals, we need to measure our impacts and ensure they're adding up.

Social and environmental values are much more complex and difficult to measure than money and profits (Wood and Leighton, 2010). But, as we know financial markets don't capture important social and environmental values, we need to find social metrics that can help us decide how to invest in, compare, and evaluate social and environmental solutions (Tuan, 2008). For example, carbon-based budgets would help shift societal measurement to better reflect energy flows.

Carbon budgets may not tell as much of the social story. For example, if our goal is to strengthen social networks in a disadvantaged neighborhood through a make-and-mend project, how do we measure success or failure? In terms of friendships made? Skills gained? Here, it's useful to note the difference between what the project produced, such as mended garments or a mending handbook, and the longer-term outcomes, such as friendships or new skills. Even if friendships form during the project, what additional factors made that possible?

Although social metrics are thorny and difficult, we should keep working on how to measure them for sustainable fashion. We also need to learn how project-level metrics relate to higher-level goals. Ultimately, social metrics should provide a way to link project impacts to longer-term goals for a sustainable economy.

Along these lines, some analysts have tried to assemble alternate, high-level measures of societal well-being, measures that can replace Gross Domestic Product (a measure of a the financial transactions within a country). Examples include the Genuine Progress Indicator or the Gross National Happiness index (Michaelson *et al.*, 2009). These efforts can be useful in lending credibility to the whole idea of social metrics.

Conclusion

The examples above begin to show how fashion can shift from being a "problem" to a "resource" for transitioning away from "growth" economics. A broad-brush research agenda in the area of fashion and sustainable consumption should explore the concepts outlined above, using fashion to:

- increase the visibility of social and environmental costs of the current system;
- explore ways to slow the pace of consumerism and rekindle long-term commitment; and
- reinvigorate the civic realm as an important resource for relieving pressures from the realm of private consumption.

Green economic growth will continue to play a role in moving toward a sustainable economy, but, in affluent countries, we must move more quickly to opportunities for fashion products and processes to reduce consumption, rather than simply green it.

References

Beck, E. (2005), Customize this. *ID*, 6 (June): 56–9.

Blum, A. and Ames, B. N. (1977), Flame retardant additives as possible cancer hazards: The main flame retardant in children's pajamas is a mutagen and should not be used. *Science*, 195: 17.

von Busch, O. (2009), *Fashion-able: Hacktivism and Engaged Fashion Design*, Gothenburg, Sweden: Camino Forlag.

Catlin, J. R. and Wang, Y. (2013), Recycling gone bad: When the option to recycle increases resource consumption. *Journal of Consumer Psychology*, 23: 122–27.

Fischer-Kowalski, M., Swilling, M., von Weizsäcker, E. U., Ren, Y., Moriguchi, Y., Crane, W., Krausmann, F., Eisenmenger, N., Giljum, S., Hennicke, P., Romero Lankao, P., and Siriban Manalang, A. (2011), Decoupling Natural Resource Use and Environmental Impacts from Economic Growth, A Report of the Working Group on Decoupling to the International Resource Panel. United Nations Environment Program.

Fletcher, K. (2008), *Sustainable Fashion and Textiles: Design Journeys*, London: Earthscan.

Fletcher, K. (2011), Post Growth Fashion and the Craft of Users, in Gwilt, A. and Rissannen, T. (eds) *Shaping Sustainable Fashion*, London: Earthscan: 165–75.

Fletcher, K. and Tham, M. (2004), Clothing Rhythms, in van Hinte, E. (ed.) *Eternally Yours: Time in Design*, Rotterdam: 010 Publishers: 254–74.

Hawken, P., Lovins, A., and Lovins, L. H. (1999), *Natural Capitalism*, New York: Little, Brown.

van Hinte, E. and Bonekamp, L. (eds) (1997), *Eternally Yours*, Rotterdam, the Netherlands: 010 Publishers.

Jackson, T. (2009), *Prosperity without Growth? A Transition to a Sustainable Economy*. London: Sustainable Development Commission.

Ludwig, K. (2005) Expandable Urban Mobility Jacket/Kate Ludwig. *ID*, September/October.

Manno, J. (2002), Commoditization: Consumption Efficiency and an Economy of Care and Connection, in Princen, T., Maniates, M., and Conca, K. (eds) *Confronting Consumption*, Cambridge, MA: MIT Press: 67–100.

Michaelson, J., Abdallah, S., Steuer, M., Thompson, S., and Marks, N. (2009), National Accounts of Well-being: Bringing Real Wealth onto the Balance Sheet, New Economics Foundation, London: 48.

Nowacek, N. (2006), From farm to closet. *Metropolis*, December.

Offer, A. (2006), *The Challenge of Affluence: Self-Control and Well-Being in the United States and Britain since 1950*, Oxford, UK: Oxford University Press.

Organisation for Economic Co-operation and Development (2009), National Accounts of OECD Countries 2009, Volume I, Main Aggregates, "Household Consumption," OECD Publishing, OECD library [online]. Available at: http://dx.doi.org/10.1787/na_vol_1–2009-en-fr (accessed August 26, 2011).

Sandel, M. (2012), *What Money Can't Buy*, London: Allen Lane.

Sloan, A. (2013), How social enterprise can succeed in the world of high fashion. *The Guardian* [online]. Available at: www.theguardian.com/social-enterprise-network/2013/apr/23/social-enterprise-world-fashion (accessed April 9, 2014).

Snell, M. B. (2008), Mr. Clean: Michael Wilson wants the chemical industry to make products safe before they get to the market. *California Magazine*, Sept/Oct.

Sorrell, S. (2007), The Rebound Effect: An assessment of the evidence for economy-wide energy savings from improved energy efficiency. UK Energy Research Centre.

Tuan, M. T. (2008), *Measuring and/or Estimating Social Value Creation: Insights into Eight Integrated Cost Approaches*, Seattle, WA: Bill & Melinda Gates Foundation.

Thorpe, A. (2012), *Architecture & Design versus Consumerism: How Design Activism Confronts Growth*, London: Routledge.

Victor, P. A. (2008), *Managing without Growth: Slower by Design, not Disaster*, Cheltenham, UK: Edward Elgar.

Wood, C. and Leighton, D. (2010), *Measuring Social Value: The Gap Between Policy and Practice*, London: Demos.

Woodward, S. (2007), *Why Women Wear What They Wear*, Oxford, UK: Berg.

7

PROSPECT, SEED AND ACTIVATE

Advancing design for sustainability in fashion

Jonathan Chapman

Positioning statement

No designer ever knowingly set out to make the world a worse place. No designer ever jumped out of bed one Monday morning saying, 'Hey, I'm going to design a really unsustainable, meaningless product today!' The desire to produce lasting value and meaning in the world, through the things we create, is in the very DNA of all creative minds. It's actually very easy to design and manufacture a T-shirt that will last physically for 15 years; that can be done with relative ease. What's not so easy is to design and manufacture a T-shirt that someone will want to keep for 15 years. This is because, as consumers of material things, we haven't been trained to have that kind of long-term relationship with our stuff.

Coming from a background in product design, interaction design and human factors, I examine the psychological phenomena that shape patterns of consumption and waste. My work develops strategic counterpoints to a throwaway society by developing design tools, methods and frameworks that build resilience into the relationships between people and things. This research manipulates the meaning of objects and materials to challenge established systems of value and define and apply new forms of design for the twenty-first century, pioneering new routes to waste reduction, while enhancing the perceived value of products, materials and the brands we associate with them.

A cultural phenomenon

At its best, the fashion system is an incredibly dynamic and vibrant cultural phenomenon, yet it can also be an extremely wasteful and destructive one, as is commonly the case. This is largely owing to its ephemeral nature, fuelled by a ceaseless hunt for change, novelty and just noticeable difference. Of course, it is this constant restless shifting that makes fashion such an animated and beguiling field.

In his analysis of the fashion as a system, Barthes describes how calculating for industrial society forms consumers who don't calculate; if clothing's producers and consumers had the same consciousness, clothing would be bought (and produced) only at the very slow rate of its dilapidation (Barthes, 1992).

Indeed, beyond the largely out-of-reach world of 'high fashion', the concept of seasonality is becoming increasingly obsolete, as brands increase the number of annual collections to drive sales (Ethical Fashion Forum, 2012). Collections of ever-so-slightly different versions of hats, jackets, tops, scarves, knickers, trousers, shoes and skirts spill out of the commercial fashion system, with an increasing familiarity and pace. In this way, we can see how the everyday social practice of shopping connects us to one of the most ecologically destructive systems in the world, a system that wreaks havoc throughout the natural world (Chapman, 2013).

So how can we continue to engage with fashion, as a rich and fulfilling cultural phenomenon, while separating ourselves from the destructive systems underpinning its formation?

Human destruction of the natural world is a crisis of behaviour, and not one simply of energy and material alone, as is often assumed; the decisions we make as an industry, the values we share as a society and the dreams we pursue as individuals collectively drive all that we accomplish, while shaping the ecological impact of our development as a species.

The Earth is finite, balanced, synergistic and reactive, and yet we design the world as though it were separable, mechanical and lasting. This dualism between ecological and mechanistic world-views is born from a fundamental crisis of behaviour, which itself is shaped by the deeper motivational origins of the human condition (encompassing the experience of being human, and the ongoing search for ultimate meaning in social, cultural and personal contexts), leading to what Bateson refers to as a fundamental *epistemological error* (Bateson, 1972) that shapes practically all that we do, and one that can be found at the very root of unsustainability. Design for sustainability drills to the core of this *epistemological error*, first to understand why we are the way we are, and then to propose how we could and should move forward.

Of course, the design business is steadily shifting its perception of sustainability, moving from risk to opportunity, from mere compliance to a leadership issue (Sherwin, 2012). These *weak signals* indicate a departure from the tired 'doom and gloom' rhetoric of sustainability discourse, to reveal a more optimistic, inspirational and creative vision that places sustainability and innovation side by side. Fashion design has made the transition from a 'world-making' to a 'world-breaking' enterprise. As the complexity, pace and scale of the industry have increased, so too have its social, economic and ecological impacts. This has put it in a position of flux, in which urgent re-examination of the potential of fashion as an agent of positive change continues to gather in intensity.

Change is natural

If you take a look around you, everything (and I mean everything) that your eyes fall on will change – from material on the upper of your shoes and the glass in those windows to the concrete of the building you can see through them. All of this is changing. Of course, our experience of the everyday tends to happen through a series of fleeting glimpses, which provide a fragmented, artificial portrayal of reality. These passing snapshots capture isolated moments in a far longer and more complex timeline of an object, material or building, for example.

As if to disprove this argument, we fabricate the material world as though it can be fixed, set in place and frozen. Through this, we form expectations of permanence, of things that last for centuries, unchanged. In an attempt to transcend the inevitability of change, we fabricated an alien world of durable textiles, metals, polymers and composite materials: 'immune to the glare of biological decay, these materials grossly outlive our desire for them' (Chapman, 2005: 47), largely owing to their inability to change and evolve.

This *thinking-error* – sometimes referred to as *cognitive distortion* (Burns, 1989) – is so engrained within us that, even with thoughts and ideas, the pursuit of fixed, solidified ideologies is highly prized. The level of value assigned to theories, for example, often relates directly to their longevity, and how well they have stood the test of time. This 'resilience' is greatly valued and serves to illustrate just how afraid of change we really are. When describing the metaphysics of rigour, Professor John Wood tells us how,

> our desire to believe in 'rigour' coincides with a popular idea of rigidity as a paradigm of the so-called real world . . . we continue to speak of 'firm foundations' and use metaphors such as 'concrete', and 'material' to elevate the status of thoughts and opinions.
>
> *(Wood, 2000)*

Change, and the impermanence of all things, has forever troubled us humans – that whispered taunt, just beneath the level of awareness, that reminds us of our own mortality, and that of all things on Earth. As streams of matter and energy flow continuously in and out of each other, we realize that the one constant in all of this is change itself. The more we attempt to overcome this fact, the less in tune with natural processes our thinking becomes, and the more alien our resulting practices are. In this way, the continually adaptive and Darwinian character of fashion can be understood in terms of principles and laws, but no one really knows what is going to happen next. What we do know, though, is that change is natural – and inevitable – and so the best approach we can take is to embrace it and begin defining the social, economic, cultural and ecological parameters upon which this change should be founded.

One might instantly assume that trend is a negative thing. However, for a fashion designer to approach the creation of garments without considering trend, it would be like an architect approaching the creation of buildings without considering gravity. Trend is pervasive, it's out there, whether you like it or not. Where a cultural trend is said to last 10 years or more, fashion trends are far more fleeting, often occupying a handful of weeks in any given year. Indeed, trend is a constantly evolving reality that is both followed and defined by fashion brands. This fact alone is at the heart of fashion's obsession with pace, newness and ephemera.

Adaptive resilience

If you know how to be nimble, think in an elastic way and evolve your creative practice as a matter of course, you will be resilient to whatever comes next. In fact, you will probably look forward to it.

In evolutionary biology, it is not the strongest species that survive, nor the most intelligent, but the most responsive to change (Darwin, 1859). In resilience thinking, this innate capacity to absorb disturbance and accept change (rather than defensively resist and block it) is key to success. In the designed world, however, this idea is sorely misunderstood, and the ever-present tension that exists between states of change and stability means they are generally considered to be at odds with one another.

Adaptive resilience, says Robinson, is the capacity to remain productive and true to core purpose and identity, while absorbing disturbance and adapting with integrity in response to changing circumstances (Robinson, 2010). To engage with this concept, you must first be able to define and know your core purpose and identity, and those things that are peripheral to them. Of course, the core and the periphery are connected; they are simply different regions of the whole system. Change at the periphery is felt at the core, and yet the pace of this change differs greatly, with the majority of it happening at the periphery. The core holds fast, whereas the periphery can be understood as a flux space – a space for negotiation, adaption and innovation. In this way, innovation and novelty tend to happen at the edges, where paradigms collide and grate.

The notion of adaptive resilience is far more helpful than *sustainability*, argues Robinson, who reminds us that central to the notion of resilience is that change is normal and necessary, and that to maintain any system in a fixed – arguably efficient or optimal – state contains risks, and this can ultimately be counter-productive. We need to provide new opportunities to build resilience, without becoming defensive or static. As Thackara (2005) urges: 'we are facing an array of wicked problems that are simultaneously complex, uncertain and urgent. We have to learn how to adapt to unpredictable and possibly catastrophic disruptions to climate, financial systems, and resource flows.' A single-vision, top–down approach to design and planning simply does not work in the face of so much uncertainty (Robinson, 2010). Striving to preserve the present, keeping things just the way they are, could be the greatest risk we are taking. Change is upon us; it's time to adapt.

Wake of destruction

Sociologist Robert Bocock tells us that consumption is founded on a lack – a desire always for something not there. Consumers, therefore, will never be satisfied. The more they consume, the more they will desire to consume (Bocock, 1993). Bocock – whose work examines the contribution of leading writers in the field, including Veblen, Simmel, Marx, Gramsci, Weber, Bourdieu, Lacan and Baudrillard – claims that consumer motivation, or the awakening of human need, is catalysed by a sense of imbalance or lack that steadily cultivates a restless state of being; material consumption is, therefore, motivated when discrepancies are experienced between actual and desired conditions. The types of consumptive behaviour that these conditions provoke range in scale from major lifestyle shifts, such as buying a larger property in a more affluent part of town, or something less dramatic, such as treating yourself to a new pair of slippers. Indeed, the myriad forms of consumption that derive from this phenomenon are varied, and yet the root motivation of the consumption is surprisingly consistent.

As the design and formation of the fashion system race opportunistically forward, we as consumers eagerly await the next, next thing. Duped by the illusion of *progress* we continue to spend money we don't have on things we don't need . . . and the wheels of conventional capitalism rotate with a familiar ease. This continual making and remaking (or selling and reselling) of the world ensure that the consumer appetite for fresh material experiences is sustained; swarms of just noticeably different garments hold us in a frenzied, child-like state of suspension, reminiscent of bedtime on Christmas Eve. Anxious to keep up, consumers scramble to update their wardrobes, replace their trainers and evolve their look. However, the much-sought-after experience of being up to date is a fleeting one, and it isn't long before the dark side to this story pulls into view.

Through such continual drives towards identity formation and update, we have wreaked unprecedented levels of destruction throughout all natural systems that support life on this planet. Since the mid eighteenth century, more of nature has been destroyed than in all prior human history (Hawken *et al.*, 1999: 2). Our species reached full behavioural modernity about 50,000 years ago, and yet, during the past 60 years alone, we have stripped the world of a quarter of its topsoil and a third of its forest cover. In total, one-third of all the planet's resources have been consumed within the past four decades (Burnie, 1999: 40), all in the name of *human development* and *progress*.

Resources (as we like to call matter for which we have a commercial use) are being transformed at a speed far beyond the natural self-renewing rate of the biosphere. In the past six decades, we have consumed, poisoned, corrupted, destroyed or incinerated the vast majority of them. Despite the enormity of these problems, it is important to remember that they are symptoms of a deeper behavioural ailment, latent in us all. Furthermore, in a post-awareness-raising era, it is essential that we do not scream, shout and thump tables over this. As the Navajo proverb goes: you can't wake a person who is pretending to be asleep. Most people are already aware of this, though they might not be familiar with the fine-grain detail of the facts and figures.

Furthermore, people find it hard to relate to data and the patter fed through our TV screens by alarmist newsreaders, with their doom and gloom statistics. Somehow, this abstract language is alienating and falls short of connecting us to the crisis in question, which, for most of us, takes place on the high street (or surfing ASOS online with a mug of tea). Instead, the language and methods of communication used often serve to forge separations between consciousness and the issues in question.

Short-term relations

Of course, when new things are acquired, older things must be ejected from one's material empire, to make room, so to speak – out with the old, in with the new. This has led to the development of an increasingly 'disposable' character in fashion culture and design. Indeed, it was the fashion sector that first pushed the idea of disposability, back in the early 1900s (Slade, 2007).

Just over a century ago, disposability referred to small, low-cost products such as the Gillette disposable razor or paper napkins, whereas today – largely through the efforts of industrial strategy and advertising – it is culturally permissible to throw away anything, from TV sets and vacuum cleaners to automobiles and an entire fitted bathroom. It should come as no surprise, then, that landfill sites and waste recycling facilities are packed with stratum upon stratum of durable goods that slowly compact and surrender working order beneath a substantial volume of similar scrap. Even waste that does find its way to recycling and sorting centres frequently ends up in stockpiles, as the economic systems that support recycling and disassembly fail to support them. For example, about 250,000 tons of discarded but still usable mobile phones sit in stockpiles in America, awaiting disposal (Slade, 2007).

In 1932, Bernard London first introduced the term *planned obsolescence* (also known as 'death dating'). In London's text, *Ending the Depression Through Planned Obsolescence*, he blamed the US Great Depression (1929–33) on consumers who used their old cars, their old radios and their old clothing much longer than statisticians had expected (London, 1932). Since then, interest in the lifespan of material experiences – from pantyhose to pavilions – has steadily increased to become a crucial constituent of contemporary design discourse today (Cooper, 2002: 15–27).

In the context of fashion, different forms of obsolescence motivate replacement, including: technical obsolescence (where materials fail, stain or become damaged), style obsolescence (where shifts in trend relocate possessions outside the fashion cycle) and psychological obsolescence (where the items fail to both project and mirror an up-to-date self-image). Fletcher (2012) also describes these phenomena through her research, which examines the processes and practices of use.

The process of consumption is, and has always been, motivated by complex emotional drivers, and is about far more than just the mindless purchasing of newer and shinier things; it is a journey towards the ideal or desired self, that through cyclical loops of desire and disappointment, becomes a seemingly endless process of serial destruction (Chapman, 2005).

As Slade forcefully argues in his rousing book, *Made to Break: Technology and Obsolescence in America*, the concept of disposability was, in fact, a necessary condition for America's rejection of tradition and our acceptance of change and impermanence (Slade, 2007). By choosing to support ever-shorter product lives, he argues that we may well be shortening the future of our way of life as well, with perilous implications for the very near future.

As we shop our way giddily forth in the seemingly inexhaustible pursuit of newer, trendier material experiences, we leave behind a wake of devastation. The majority of these abandoned fashion goods are neither broken nor dysfunctional. Rather, these orphans have been cast aside before their time, to make way for newer, younger models in an adulterous swing we call consumerism. Indeed, as the emotional needs of consumers relentlessly grow and flex, the plethora of stuff deployed to satisfy those needs remains relatively frozen in time; the mountain of waste and ecological destruction this single inconsistency generates have yet to be fully understood.

Emotional durability

Emotionally durable design (Chapman, 2005) explores the idea of creating a deeper, more sustainable bond between people and their material things. The ultimate aim is to reduce the consumption and waste of resources by increasing the durability of relationships between consumers and products. This approach presents important counterpoints to our *throwaway society* by developing design tools, methods and frameworks that build resilience into subject–object relationships, presenting a call to arms for professionals, students and academic creatives to think about designing things we would cherish and keep, rather than throw away.

Take, for example, a dress that lasts about 12 months. If you can extend that use-career to 18 months through emotionally durable design, you have brought about a 50 per cent reduction in waste consumption in all the materials and energy and systems associated with the production and distribution of that product – this is a significant impact. Of course, this does not factor in the environmental cost of laundry, occurring during the use-phase. We, therefore, need to consider a no-/low-laundry solution at the design stage, so that ecological impacts can be minimized at different points along a product's timeline.

Fashion businesses are also thinking how they can get customers to shop with them more regularly. The idea is to use product and brand as talking points: the product becomes a conversation piece that creates a lasting connection between the business and its customers and, ultimately, increases loyalty to the brand and drives future sales (Webb, 2013).

Emotionally durable fashion is adaptable and capable of modification, it uses materials that age well and grow old gracefully, it is designed to be repaired with low levels of skill, and it avoids fleeting trend to occupy a slower and more enriching style space. In this way, designers can reduce the need to consume by making stuff that lasts, things that withstand the test of time, with durable meanings and values that people want to keep and look after – a more fulfilling and satisfying fashion space, founded on relationships and an abundance of meaning and value.

As a strategic approach, therefore, emotionally durable design provides a useful language to describe the contemporary relevance of designing responsible, well-made, tactile products, which the user can get to know and assign value to in the long term (Lacey, 2009: 87–92). On a corporate level, the desire is also evident, as customer satisfaction and consequent loyalty are tied in to such issues (Chapman, 2013).

Take denim jeans, for example: you have a close relationship with your jeans. Your jeans are like a second skin, worn and moulded and torn by your everyday experiences. Purchased like blank canvases, jeans are worked on, sculpted and personified over time. It is clear that the shift towards designing longer-lasting products is something that most designers are already behind.

This builds on the work of Tham and Fletcher (2004), matching fast and slow garments with fast and slow rhythms of use to save resources, while simultaneously providing for people's symbolic *and* material needs.

Prospect, seed and activate

If you want people to change behaviour, the new thing needs to be more fulfilling, meaningful, fun and rewarding than the previous thing. Expecting people to 'care' is a risky approach.

Whether you care about the environment or not, the future success of design will be increasingly dependent on how well you deal with some pretty big questions, such as: How will the industry react to shortages of raw materials, and subsequent rises in material prices? How could the workforce be affected by shifting supply chains and technological development? How might technology influence and change the way products are manufactured and sold? How will people care for their things in a future of water shortages and high energy prices? How could reuse and remanufacturing of old and unwanted products develop as a response to higher demand and prices? (Forum for the Future, 2013). Each of us needs to engage with these questions in our own way and bring our own particular skills and values to them.

As a sustainable designer, you contribute to a dynamic and emerging field that recalibrates the parameters of 'good design' in an unsustainable age. It *prospects*, *seeds* and *activates* the power of design in creating social, economic and ecological resilience, in an increasingly unstable world. To achieve this, we need to get better at working with people outside our own disciplinary silo. At its best, design has a broad epistemological base, drawing together different forms of knowledge (economic, scientific, social, medical and cultural, for example); converging around the locus of design agency, it is a means to identify ways in which we can reconsider and know the world better and contribute to its advancement. This approach reframes design as both a prospective and transformative activity, underpinned by a rich repertoire of tools, methods and approaches, which strengthen the transformative power of design to establish a clear social, economic and ecological purpose.

References

Barthes, R. (1992*)*, *The Fashion System*, Berkeley, CA: University of California Press.

Bateson, G. (1972), *Steps to an Ecology of Mind*, Chicago, IL: University of Chicago Press.

Bocock, R. (1993), *Consumption*, London: Routledge.

Burnie, D. (1999), *Get a Grip on Ecology*, Lewes, UK: The Ivy Press.

Burns, D. (1989), *The Feeling Good Handbook*, New York: William Morrow.

Chapman, J. (2005), *Emotionally Durable Design: Objects, Experiences & Empathy*, London: Earthscan: 47.

Chapman, J. (2013), *Textile Toolbox blog* [online]. Available at: www.textiletoolbox.com/posts/design-reduce-the-need-consume-2 (accessed 1 July 2013).

Cooper, T. (2002), Durable consumption: reflections on product life cycles and the throwaway society, in Hertwich, E. (ed.), *Life-cycle Approaches to Sustainable Consumption* (Workshop Proceedings), Austria, November: 15–27.

Darwin, C. (1859), *On the Origin of Species: By Means of Natural Selection*, UK: Dover Publications.

Ethical Fashion Forum (2012), *Fast Fashion, 'Value' Fashion* [online]. Available at: www.ethicalfashion forum.com/the-issues/fast-fashion-cheap-fashion (accessed 25 September 2012).

Fletcher, K. (2012), Durability, fashion, sustainability: the processes and practices of use, *Fashion Practice*, 4 (2): 221–38.

Forum for the Future (2013), *Fashion Futures* [online]. Available at: www.forumforthefuture.org/project/fashion-futures-2025/overview (accessed 21 June 2013).

Hawken, P., Lovins, A. and Hunter Lovins, L. (1999), *Natural Capitalism: Creating the Next Industrial Revolution*, Boston, MA: Little, Brown.

Lacey, E. (2009), Contemporary ceramic design for meaningful interaction and emotional durability: a case study, *International Journal of Design*, 3 (2): 87–92.

London, B. (1932), *Ending the Depression Through Planned Obsolescence* [pamphlet], US.

Robinson, M. (2010), *Making Adaptive Resilience Real*, London: Arts Council.

Sherwin, C. (2012), *Seymour Powell Blog* [online]. Available at: http://blog.seymourpowell.com/2012/01/seymourpowell-hires-chris-sherwin-as-head-of-sustainability/#.UkLPMGRNay8 (accessed 10 April 2012).

Slade, G. (2007), *Made to Break: Technology and Obsolescence in America*, Cambridge, MA: Harvard University Press.

Thackara, J. (2005), *In the Bubble: Designing in a Complex World*, Cambridge, MA: MIT Press.

Tham, M. and Fletcher, K. (2004), Clothing rhythms, in Hinte, E. (ed.) *Eternally Yours: Time in Design*, Rotterdam, the Netherlands: 010 Publishers: 254–74.

Webb, F. (2013) Time for new business models based on durable design? *Guardian Sustainable Business*, 18 January.

Wood, J. (2000), The culture of academic rigour: does design research really need it? *The Design Journal*, 3 (1): 44–57.

8

SPEED

Carolyn Strauss

Slow urgency

Look at us! We are still untired! Our hearts know no weariness because they are fed with fire, hatred, and speed! Does that amaze you? It should, because you can never remember having lived! Erect on the summit of the world, once again we hurl our defiance at the stars!

(Marinetti, 1909)

In February 1909, the French newspaper *Le Figaro* published Filippo Marinetti's "Manifesto of Futurism," a passionate proclamation of the virtues of the machine world, the glory of war and the dominance of man[1] over Nature. Marinetti and his Futurist colleagues were by no means unique in staking their quest for modernity on such ideas, but they were perhaps the first to assign them a name that we now know so well: "speed."

Just 20 years after the Futurists' raucous coming-out party, the philosopher Ivan Illich used another French daily, *Le Monde*, to deliver his contradictory (and *much* more sober) observation on the same topic. In that essay, titled "Energy and equity," Illich cautioned that the new era of ever-faster speeds was taking its toll on people's lives and on the human spirit: "We are so enamored by speed, and especially by the idea of getting somewhere quickly, that our personal agency and creativity have been stunned into submission." He saw the individual duly seduced and swept up by speed as steadily being stripped of "physical, social and psychic powers" and at risk of losing his or her very center of being (Illich, 1929).

Since then (and in spite of such warnings from Illich and countless others), the world has proceeded along the path of acceleration at a rate unimaginable perhaps even by Marinetti and his bunch. Speed has been responsible for huge swathes of progress, but it also has wreaked its fair share of destruction. Fashion sits squarely in the midst of those mixed results.

As founder and director of the design research organization slowLab,[2] I've spent the past decade exploring "Slower" forms of thinking, learning and sharing that I believe are essential to sensing and moving *toward* more sustainable forms of living. The point of this chapter is neither to celebrate nor to censure the "fast" aspects of fashion, but rather to make the case for its real and potential impacts at other registers of speed, especially the Slower ones, because, although it's true that the sheer scale and pace of change of the fashion industry make it one of the worst fast offenders, at the same time, I believe fashion is overflowing with promise and positive potential for restoring balance in a now-too-fast world.

People often believe that the goal of my work of advancing the field of Slow design is to reject or attempt to subvert the fast world. In fact, the primary objective is to see how design can help open things up along the speed spectrum: to create space for reflection, for dialogue, for new forms of engagement and relationship, because I know that the only real way to break the "tyranny" of speed (Zardini, 2009) is not to be set against it, but rather to be proactive in considering, experimenting with and striving to get a deep sense of many different tempos and rhythms of experience.

Thinking–learning–sensing–designing–relating at a range of speeds equips us with far greater breadth of knowledge from which to draw inspiration, make connections and propose new directions for our lives and for our world. And those fuller ways of knowing give us both the competence and agility—what I like to call "response-ability"—to live consciously, effectively and collectively, with grace, humanity and appropriate timing.

Deceleration

Several years ago, I came across this diagram (see Figure 8.1) by Stewart Brand of the Long Now Foundation, an organization whose mission is "to provide a counterpoint to today's accelerating culture and help make long-term thinking more common."[3] The diagram is of what Brand calls a "pace-layered cross section of civilization," illustrating a bottom-to-top progression from what he regards as the Slowest-moving, stablest force of all, Nature, to the liveliest and most erratic one, Fashion. In reference to this diagram, Brand explains that,

> The combination of fast and slow components makes the system resilient, along with the way the different paced parts affect each other. Fast learns, slow remembers. Fast proposes, slow disposes. Fast is discontinuous, slow is continuous. [. . .] The total effect of the pace layers is that they provide many-leveled corrective, stabilizing, negative feedback throughout the system. It is precisely in the apparent contradictions of pace that civilization finds its surest health.
>
> *(Brand, 1999)*

Brand's idea of those interconnected, mutually balancing elements is compelling, but I'm not sure that civilization these days can count on the stability that he describes. Today's monoculture of the fast is taking an enormous and mounting toll on the supposedly more solid areas of the diagram. And, if Brand's portrayal is any indication, it also has got disproportionate hold on how we think about fashion's role in our world. It is true that the industry of fashion operates predominantly in the upper echelons of the diagram (note that squiggly line he's drawn to represent the fickleness of consumer taste and the rapid-fire commercial forces that both encourage and indulge those fleeting wants), but I would argue that fashion has many other aspects, expressions and impacts within what Brand has identified as the Slow and sustaining territories of his map.

Yes, fashion is exciting, impulsive and unpredictable,[4] but it also can be steady, mindful and reliable (see the discussion in Chapter 12). It is able to both turn on a dime and spread deep and enduring roots. When we embrace the Slow (and "Slowing")[5] potentials of fashion, we come upon something extremely fertile and infinitely more inspiring than the bits of it that Brand says "get all the attention."

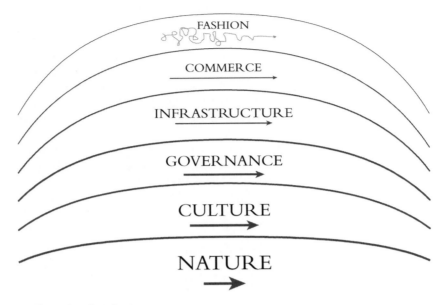

Figure 8.1 The order of civilization

Source: Stewart Brand, "The order of civilization," adapted with permission from *The Clock of the Long Now: Time and Responsibility* (Basic Books, New York, 1999)

Here are three suggestions I have for beginning to explore that field of possibility:

1. A Slower, more expansive view of fashion means moving beyond discrete focus on the material object in and of itself to include the vast territory of real and imagined experiences that it can deliver.

All of us who produce and wear fashion need to start thinking about it as something that expands awareness of both self and context, creates a space of dialogue and enables new forms of participation. That includes more fully acknowledging (and celebrating!) the intricate web of people, places, sensations, memories, emotions and aspirations that surround it, all of which influence how we view, experience and affect the world we live in.

I like pointing people to Ruby Hoette and Elisa van Joolen's research project "dress-series" that registers acts of everyday creativity expressed through dress. For Hoette and van Joolen, the mere act of paying closer attention to clothing in the everyday is the starting point for what they call pushing fashion "beyond accepted forms of production and presentation to a more inclusive reality."[6] In their project, what people wear acts as a kind of mnemonic trigger, so that even the most fleeting of fashion encounters has the power to awaken and relocate us firmly in the here and now of our lives. Who can forget a pair of flourescent pumps on a New York City subway train? (The individual who's looking out at the world and *not* down at his/her so-called "smartphone" is the clear winner here.)

Design educator and activist Jogi Panghaal calls the medium through which such subtle, new levels of consciousness and participation are born as "play."[7] He explains it as beginning with the body and extending out through relationships the body creates with the materials, contexts and other bodies it encounters in life. In his talk *Body, Movement, Joy*, delivered at the Doors of Perception conference in Amsterdam in 2005, Panghaal said, "Play makes us curious, it helps to stretch limits, exploring risks, breaking rules and conventions and founding new fields and

Figure 8.2 Fleeting encounters with dress can help locate us in the here and now of our lives

Source: Ruby Hoette and Elisa van Joolen, film still from the project "dress-series/measure" (2011), edited by Sunanda Sachatrakul

boundaries" (Panghaal, 2005). Importantly, the "fields" that he's talking about are both the inner and the outer, the personal and the shared, through which we come to know ourselves, affirm our connections with others and move more consciously in the world.

A beautiful illustration of the role that the designer can have in all this is the work of Dutch multidisciplinary artist Maria Blaisse. Blaisse describes her rigorous investigations of form and material (for clients ranging from Issey Miyake to Camper) as both sculptures and costumes, where the human body enters into play with a material object to reveal a dynamic range of new expressions.

The image shown in Figure 8.3 is from her 2008 research project "Moving meshes," where thin, pliable stalks of bamboo, intricately woven together, become flexible, responsive structures in direct resonance with their environment. On their own, these delicate constructions subtly breathe and pulse. When animated by human touch, they respond with surprising grace and fluidity. But most astonishing is how the mesh forms behave when inhabited by a human body in motion: the two move in seamless unison, the body animating the material form, the form animating the body, one seemingly becoming an extension of the other. The dance between the two is graceful, surprising and utterly beautiful. Panghaal would say that, through play, the two bodies are searching for each other's centers.

Watching one of Blaisse's mesh forms in symbiotic interplay with a human counterpart,[8] we easily begin to imagine it as an article of clothing, as a room, as a form of transport, as the shape of a city. Fashion can learn a lot from this expansive vision for how our bodies relate to the material world, with intimacy and co-dependence, creating new layers of physicality and awareness that then might extend out further in dialogue with the context around it. Here is the ingenuity (and generosity) of the designer in Slow dialogue with material, with the body, with the space around and, importantly, with the larger framework of living.

2. Embracing fashion in terms of multiple registers of speed also means drawing a more comprehensive map of its assets and stakeholders.

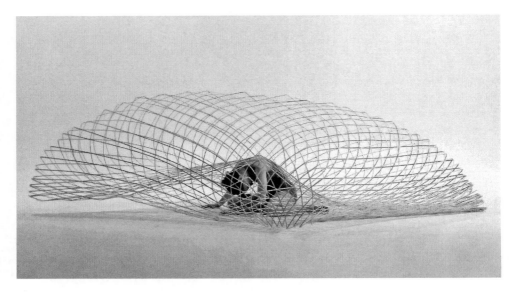

Figure 8.3 Dancer and oloid form share a moment of rest
Source: Maria Blaisse, "Moving meshes" (2008)

Such a map reaches well beyond narrowly defined interests linked to a specific product or service, such as short-term economic gain or the temporary welfare of people directly engaged along a given line of production and consumption. Instead, it considers broader markers of prosperity and well-being, including the enduring health and happiness of *all* people, communities and natural systems affected by that chain in any way across space and time. Clearly, that's a lot harder to quantify, but all of these are vital to a truly robust system, and we need to at least try to imagine them and sketch them on to our maps.

This was a central tenet of slowLab's "Slow Lloyd" research program, a multi-year collaboration with the Lloyd Hotel and Cultural Embassy in Amsterdam, the Netherlands. That program set out to investigate how Slow design ideas, tools and values might enhance the Lloyd's current enterprise and cultural offerings, while reaching out to include a broader network of resources and relationships from the local area and the city at large.

What ensued was a series of "Slowing experiments" conducted by hundreds of designers, architects, social and environmental innovators, students and members of the local community. Individually and in groups, they were challenged to conceive of "Slow Lloyd" as a multifaceted and ever-evolving ecology within which a diverse collection of stakeholders think, dream and operate. They were asked to explore the unique tempo of each idea, circumstance, person, place and thing they encountered, and to carefully consider appropriate forms and timing for engaging them. For inspiration, participants looked to the myriad of physical and social traces from the Lloyd's varied historical past, they sought out the know-how embedded in the local community of today, and they imagined the lives and livelihoods of future inhabitants. They questioned and redrew the Lloyd's physical borders and reappraised its assets to include dormant potentials of people and place. The result was a wide-ranging agenda for a Slower Lloyd, comprehensive of new functional, spatial, temporal, sensorial and social site layers. Waste from the hotel became food for more sustainable local energy flows. Hallways of the building were reimagined as spaces of communal ownership. Notions of "hospitality" reached inward to enhance the well-being of hotel staff and cast outward to fuel the desires of the surrounding neighborhood.[9]

Did all of this render the Lloyd a "Slow hotel"? Not exactly. Or, at least, not in directly quantifiable terms. But Slow Lloyd's success is that it created a context within which an enormously *creative* research process could take place, one that encouraged participants to be more reflective and reflexive as they looked Slow-ly, not only at the layers of the Lloyd, but also at the layers of their own lives: from their personal habits and beliefs to the larger stories and value systems that influence how and where they operate in the world. The impact of so many people partaking in such a process, of adding those new and imaginative methodologies to their life- and design-toolkits, is impossible to measure, but it is certainly meaningful. What this program proved is that, when we approach any circumstance of our world more fully, critically and creatively (read: Slow-ly), amazing possibilities can open up. Fashion can be a powerful device for leading such investigations, and for persuading others to join in.

3. Last, but certainly not least, if we are to fully appreciate and leverage fashion's potential at multiple registers of speed, fashion education needs to be on board.

An important way that fashion education can be Slower is by focusing less on the marketplace and more on collective well-being, cultivating approaches to thinking and making that can help people flourish together into the future. This was one of the directions slowLab tested out in 2010, when we hosted a Slow design workshop for Bachelor- and Masters-level fashion students. The workshop, called "Prikkelend Slow," was intended to confront and stimulate the students to move out of their comfort zones in taking a Slower view of their chosen field. (The Dutch word *prikkel* has to do with provoking people in a way that's both exciting and slightly agitating.)

That day, I co-facilitated a break-out session with the American artist Julia Mandle, who I had come to know and admire for her urban interventions in New York City that often included clothing as a tool for engaging the public.[10] When Mandle and I asked the students gathered at our table why they chose to attend the workshop, most of them talked about their interests in what are typically perceived as the "Slow" areas of fashion: handcraft, use of recycled and/or local materials, reworking of old garments, and so on. But the tone around the table got significantly Slower (in the more holistic terms I've been describing) when, in introducing principles from the Transition movement,[11] we issued the students the following challenge: "A calamity has struck and the gates of your city are flooded. No people or material resources can go in or out. You are a fashion designer. What is your contribution going to be?"

This was a huge turning point. Confronted by such a scenario, these students' sense of identity, and not least their work as designers, could no longer be seen merely from the perspective of their personal curiosity, isolated interests or self-serving career goals, but rather from that of self-preservation and community well-being. They were being asked to see themselves and their unique talents as part of an interconnected whole: a place they needed and a place that needed them. What was surprising (and encouraging) is how they jumped right in. One student talked about how she might apply her knowledge of weaving and manipulating textiles to the construction of shelter. Another one imagined how clothing could serve as a silent tool for communicating needs and emotions, while retaining dignity. For yet another student, this challenge triggered thoughts about the ritual uses of fashion in her home country, and she wondered what new kinds of fashion ritual might support people's adjustment to living under the conditions of this hypothetical scenario.

What this example means for fashion education is how much value can be derived from regarding the creative thinking and skills we teach, not merely as means to a fashion product or preconceived career path, but rather as essential life skills that enhance the individual learner and can make for his or her larger contributions to society. This, combined with open and horizontal models of mentorship and knowledge-building, will equip the fashion practitioners of tomorrow with both a healthy dose of personal agency and a more robust set of tools with which to navigate the complexity they will encounter in their lifetimes.

Fashion forward

> To undertake Slow learning, we need to feel comfortable being at sea for a while.
> *(Claxton, 1997)*

How to move this agenda for fashion (and for our lives) forward?

The quotation from psychologist Guy Claxton, above, provides a clue. The first step is acknowledging that, for many, this is unknown territory. That makes it feel like a risk and makes people feel vulnerable. From a Slow perspective, those feelings create an opening; they are an opportunity. Maria Blaisse calls this "the freedom of not giving a name to things, to see what emerges from one form/inciting the flow of continuous creation" (Blaisse, 2008).

People who are serious about moving fashion in more sustainable and fulfilling directions—whether as individuals, educational institutions, professional organizations or enterprises—need to be committed to the *not-knowing* that is essential to any learning and growing process. Part of that is acknowledging that every individual or group, circumstance or system has unique requirements in terms of what Ivan Illich called "space, time and personal pace" (Illich, 1929). That means creating ample room for reflection and dialogue that help people renew their understandings of self, context, relationship and responsibility, which includes allowing (indeed, encouraging) them to press against boundaries and move out of their comfort zones. This is especially true for teaching and learning environments, whether formal (schools) or informal (the rest of life).

For educators and professionals, this probably requires some recalibrating of the way they think, reconsidering how they've grown accustomed to getting things done and re-examining inherited belief systems and practices at the very heart of their chosen fields. Mutual respect, trust and listening are key to accommodating everyone involved, bringing the collective knowledge and creativity of the group to fruition. Organizations, enterprises and schools that support these Slower pedagogical models provide both a structure and a buffer zone for amazing new things to happen. And they also bolster participants' resilience, so that they stay the course when, inevitably, they encounter resistance from people comfortably situated (and earning their keep) within the fast status quo.

What's at stake here is not the success or demise of a Spring/Summer collection, but rather the very fate of humanity. Learning to embrace and operate at multiple levels of speed is, in my opinion, one of the best chances we have for surviving and thriving into the future. Fashion can play an important role in that evolution, but first it needs to Slow down.

I'm reminded of a performance I saw many years ago in New York. Mikhail Baryshnikov, with wireless electronic sensors attached to his chest, danced to a piece of music, the tempo of which was his own beating heart.[12] The heartbeat was transmitted over a loudspeaker system, for both dancer and musicians to keep time to. As the dancer moved, and his heart rate increased, the music too got faster. The amazing part was Baryshnikov's mastery of the whole thing, his deep attunement to his body making it possible for him, not only to calm his heart when he so desired, but to modulate the full complexity of the arrangement so as to enjoy an artful interplay with the musicians, the audience and the space of the stage.

It's an apt metaphor for the human condition in a world racing at perpetually higher speeds. Like inexperienced dancers, most of us today are just trying to keep up with that progressively faster tempo, spinning and whirling toward an unknown (and predictably unstable) outcome.

The fact is that either we can keep rushing along with the rest of the world—drowning in a sea of information, consuming ever greater amounts of nonrenewable resources and desperately gulping up the diminishing returns of an ever-faster existence—or we can choose to be Slower: cultivating new knowledge that allows us to perceive and leverage a much wider spectrum of individual and collective potentialities in the people, places and systems that surround us, thereby gaining both insight and impetus to propose new ways forward.

Importantly, just as Baryshnikov didn't develop his deep body knowledge overnight, neither can we expect to shift effortlessly into Slower ways of engaging the people, places and information around us. It takes time, practice and sustained involvement. It requires patience, dedication and receptivity. Accomplished dancers, athletes, yogis and anyone who has truly mastered anything all attest that hard work, determination and humility are the only way to the deep state of knowing from which true freedom of movement (and joy!) can flow.

What better field than fashion to initiate us on the path? What better stimulant to make us curious and critical, confident and playful? What better instrument to open up new dimensions of awareness, to take us from one level of (intellectual, material, relational, spiritual) consciousness to the next? What better platform to inspire us to step up as vibrant, responsible and response-able participants in the world?

And what better time than now?

Let's begin . . . Slow-ly.

Notes

1 I deliberately use the word 'man,' as Marinetti was notorious for his loathing of women. Not only did he fail to include them in his vision of Futurism (though some women did enlist on their own terms later on), his manifesto specifically cites "contempt for women" and "fighting [. . .] feminism."

2 Founded in 2003, slowLab is an interdisciplinary design laboratory that explores Slow design thinking, learning and activism. Learn more at: www.slowlab.net

3 Long Now Foundation: http://longnow.org/about/

4 Brand proposes that, "The job of fashion is to be froth: quick, irrelevant, engaging, self-preoccupied, and cruel. [. . . It is] cut free to experiment as creatively and irresponsibly as society can bear."

5 At a slowLab gathering in London in 2010, design educator, author and activist Stuart Walker proposed the terms "Slowing" and "doing Slowing" to describe processes of actively pursuing more reflective thinking, expressions and relationships by design.

6 Learn more about Hoette and van Joolen's project at: http://dress-series.com/

7 In Panghaal's native India, one of the overriding concepts for participation in the world is Lila, referring to "play," "sport," "spontaneity" or "drama."

8 Watch the incredible video of "Moving meshes" at: http://vimeo.com/7381953

9 An incomplete archive of this program's results is at: www.slowlloyd.slowlab.net

10 Mandle's work has explored issues of urban identity, civic responsibility and community renewal, posing questions such as, "How do we, through our daily activities and thoughts, affect the environment around us?". See: www.juliamandle.com

11 The Transition movement is a grassroots network that supports community-led responses to climate change and shrinking supplies of cheap energy, building resilience and happiness. Learn more at: www.transitionnetwork.org/

12 The piece, titled "heartbeat: mb," was created by interactive artist and composer Christopher Janney in collaboration with choreographer Sara Rudner. It was based on the project "Heartbeat," originally conceived by Janney in 1981, when he was a Research Fellow at MIT's Center for Advanced Visual Studies.

References

Blaisse, M. (2008), *Vouwblad 5*, from the series Vouwblad, Amstelveen: Lenoirschuring.

Brand, S. (1999), *The Clock of the Long Now: Time and Responsibility*, New York: Basic Books: 37.

Claxton, G. (1997), "The speed of thought," in *Hare Brain Tortoise Mind*, New York: HarperCollins: 9.

Illich, I. (1929), "Energy and Equity," *Le Monde*, Paris [online]. Available at: http://clevercycles.com/energy_and_equity/index.html (accessed 23 September 2013).

Marinetti, F. T. (1909), "Manifesto of Futurism," *Le Figaro*, Paris. English-language translation ©1973 London: Thames and Hudson Ltd [online]. Available at: www.italianfuturism.org/manifestos/founding manifesto/ (accessed 23 September 2013).

Panghaal, J. (2005), *Body, Movement and Joy*, Conference paper: Doors of Perception 5 [online]. Available at: http://museum.doorsofperception.com/doors5/content/panghaal.html (accessed 23 September 2013).

Zardini, M. (2009), "Speeds and their limits," *Speed Limits*, Montreal: Canadian Centre for Architecture: 23.

9

AFRICAN SECOND-HAND CLOTHES

Mima-te *and the development of sustainable fashion*

Amanda Ericsson and Andrew Brooks

Introduction

Clothing has long been reused, and garments have been retailored, to create new textures of value and give unwanted things a second life. Social and cultural research has focused on remaking in Western societies, but here we switch attention to Africa and explore how unwanted clothes are resold to some of the world's poorest countries and both how they influence economic development, and how they can be retailored to create new value. Through this chapter we explore trends in up-cycling and how second-hand clothes circulate in and beyond Europe and North America. Many second-hand clothes are exported to Africa, and we investigate the links between poverty and dependency. Later in the chapter, we show how two Mozambican designers, Nelly and Nelsa Guambe, are creating value and producing vintage fashion from low-value, used garments.

The authors are Amanda Ericsson, a PhD student in Up-cycling Textile Management at the Swedish School of Textiles, exploring capacity building and second-hand clothing business development through the action-based project The Life of a Dress and dreamandawake brand, where dresses are revived through redesign and photography; and Andrew Brooks, a Lecturer in Development Geography at King's College London, whose research maps connections between places of production and spaces of consumption, with a specific focus on the links between poverty in Africa and affluence in the global North.

Second-hand fashion, up-cycling and exports

Second-hand clothes are a focus for attention for many designers and researchers in the sustainable fashion sector. The burgeoning 'up-cycling' fashion movement, which takes on old clothes and transforms them into new garments, is flourishing among subcultures in London, Stockholm, New York and elsewhere. Up-cycling may reflect an environmental concern with the over-consumption of new clothing, or people may alter clothes out of necessity, for fun or as boutique businesses. Existing materials and new labour are combined to cut and tear away the old, and stitch and weave new life into dresses, skirts and shirts. Up-cyclers source their raw materials from thrift stores and charity shops and search for appealing items worthy of a second life. Apparel is adorned with buttons, pockets and zips, or reshaped to reflect contemporary fashions. These shopping, crafting and handiwork practices are all part of a broader second-hand clothing system of provision (Brooks, 2013).

In the United Kingdom and the United States, around 15 per cent of old clothing is donated for recycling (Morley *et al.*, 2006: 6). Most people are familiar with the donation of used clothes to recyclers via doorstep collections and textile banks and the local networks of sale. Although some is resold in local thrift stores, such as Value Village in the US, and charity shops, such as Oxfam in Britain, or reprocessed into new garments, this is only a relatively small proportion of the total volume collected. When clothes are resold locally in Europe and America, this is often a socially beneficial activity, helping raise funds for community projects, while reusing clothes in a sustainable way. However, few people choose to shop for second-hand clothes, and even the poor have moved away from used goods with the ready affordability of low-cost fashion from Primark, Walmart and other value retailers. The growing trends in up-cycling clothes as well as vintage fashion are interesting niche counter-culture activities that provide an alternative pathway for used clothes. Yet, in general, the market for re-wearing and recycling second-hand clothes in affluent countries is limited, especially in comparison with the near endless growth of new-clothing consumption (Brooks, 2012a).

A vast surplus of second-hand clothing is produced by the constant cycle of clothing consumption and disposal, and far greater volumes of second-hand clothing are collected than can ever be locally retailed. Our estimates indicate only 10–30 per cent of donated clothing is resold in the UK, similar to the proportion in Canada and the US (Brooks, 2012a). The vast majority of donated clothing is exported overseas and retailed in the developing world, via a trade pattern that is largely unknown among the general public. Across the globe, rich and poor people are intimately linked, as used clothes pass through networks of charitable and commercial exchange that trade second-hand clothes between continents (Rivoli, 2009). Used clothes collected by charities and clothing recyclers are overwhelmingly sold, and not distributed for free, in Africa, Asia and Latin America, in a sector worth in excess of $2 billion (Baden and Barber, 2005; Frazer, 2008; UN Comtrade, 2011). Profits are made by different charities, firms and individuals that link supplies of used clothing and markets in the developing world, such as Canada and the US to Zambia (Hansen, 2000), Japan to the Philippines (Milgram, 2005) and the UK to Benin, Kenya, Nigeria and Mozambique (Brooks and Simon, 2012). Clothing is collected, processed and sorted in industrial processing plants and baled up for export to markets around the world. African importers in Cotonou (Benin), Dar-es-Salaam (Tanzania), Maputo (Mozambique) and many other ports buy shipping containers jammed full of second-hand clothes, which go on to reach marketplaces across the continent.

Andrew has explored the political economy of the second-hand-clothing trade in previous work (see Brooks, 2013). Second-hand clothing is massively important in sub-Saharan Africa and difficult to appreciate for readers unfamiliar with the context. Countries such as Kenya, Mozambique, Uganda, Senegal and Zambia have major second-hand-clothing markets (Hansen, 2000; Baden and Barber, 2005). Second-hand-clothing imports have different impacts upon African economies and societies, which are much disputed. Charities and commercial recyclers foreground the potential benefits of imports, promoting how second-hand clothing provides affordable garments to some of the world's poorest people and offers relief from price inflation. They also celebrate the potential ecological benefits of reusing unwanted clothes over sending garments to landfill. Such an endorsement can be countered by the argument that societies in Europe and North America could address their own over-consumption of fashion and look for local patterns of reuse, rather than exporting the problem.

The economic benefits of second-hand-clothing imports also have to be critically considered. Two major problems in Africa are important to highlight. First, second-hand clothing contributes to maintaining a relationship of economic dependency between Africa and the rest of the world, and, second, imports of used clothing are one of several factors that have undermined African clothing manufacturing. A relationship of continued economic dependency is maintained, as the import of second-hand-clothing commodities represents a net out-flow of money from poor countries, contributing to balance-of-payment deficits, which are hampering economic growth in many African countries. Importers in developing countries use valuable foreign exchange on shipments of second-hand clothes; this currency goes to economies in the global North, exacerbating existing trade imbalances. This is especially so in sub-Saharan Africa, where second-hand clothes are frequently the largest consumer import by volume and account for over 50 per cent of the clothing market in many countries (Hansen, 2000; Baden and Barber, 2005: 1; Frazer, 2008). Money spent on second-hand-clothing consumption by poor Ghanaians, Mozambicans or Senegalese eventually reaches charities and companies based in America and Europe. The second significant economic issue is that imports of used clothing can out-compete and displace African clothing manufacturing, a sector that could provide an early step on the ladder of industrial development. Various African policymakers have accused second-hand-clothing importers of 'killing' local textile and garment sectors (Kandiero, 2005: 335).

The decline of African clothing industries is an outcome of economic liberalization. Second-hand-clothing imports are part of a broader process and one of the factors that made African manufactured clothing less competitive in domestic markets, but it is not simply a case that poor African consumers switched from buying more expensive, locally made goods to buying cheap, imported, second-hand clothing. Other factors also operated in concert, eroding the viability of African clothing production. In previous work, we illustrated how second-hand clothing is contributing to the erosion of African clothing industries, but also that,

> declining incomes reduced Africans' purchasing power, depressing demand; the privatization of textile firms, rentier profiteering and poor management capacity led factories to fail; and increased competition from imported Asian clothing producers, which have greater labour productivity and lower production costs and could export into liberalized African markets, were also important contributing factors.
>
> *(Brooks and Simon, 2012: 1284)*

Mozambique and second-hand clothing

Mozambique is a poor country that curves around the south-east coast of Africa. Opportunities for the poor are very limited in Maputo, the capital of this former Portuguese colony. Many women and men work in the informal sector, casually employed as labourers, working in small workshops or trading goods along the side of the downtown avenues and in the sprawling markets (Lindell, 2010). Selling second-hand clothes has become an important livelihood, and several thousand people work trading used garments imported from Australia, Canada, Europe and the United States. Traders buy 120-lb (55-kg) sealed bales of graded used clothing, such as jeans, T-shirts or dresses, from warehouses run by international importers and carry them down to markets where they open them up for retail.

There are markets across Maputo, including Fajardo and Xipamanine Markets, which contain hundreds of tightly packed stalls selling second-hand clothing. All manner of used garments hang on rails and are piled on polythene sacks and sell for different prices (see Figure 9.1). Men's office shirts average US$3.50, ladies' tops and blouses US$1.80, and children's T-shirts US$2.30.

Prices vary though: there are pristine and desirable garments, as well as unfashionable, soiled and torn waste apparel (Brooks, 2012a). Selling second-hand clothing is a difficult way to make a living, and market vendors encounter problems with the quality of stock and face risks trying to achieve profits and support their families. Selling used clothing in Maputo is a precarious way to make a living. We found that traders earn an average of US$5.38 a day, which has to support a whole family. Although this is a greater income than most Mozambicans, it still leaves traders in persistent poverty (Hanlon and Smart, 2008; Brooks, 2012b: 233). Vending used clothing allows people to move out of destitution, but they manage little more than survival. People find it difficult to profit from the trade, as many of the imported clothes are of low quality or are not appealing to local consumers.

Few African traders do much to transform and create new value in clothing, and it is unusual for garments to be cleaned, repaired or altered before being sold. Hansen's work (2000) has documented examples of people retailoring used clothing to better suit local tastes in Zambia. In the Mozambican markets, some tailors do use a mixture of second-hand clothing together with the traditional capulanas (printed sarong) to add value and produce something different for local consumers, but this was unusual. In contrast to this general pattern, we have worked with Nelly and Nelsa, who use second-hand-clothing imports as the basis to make desirable new commodities, taking old textiles and creating high-value, up-cycled, second-hand dresses. Through this process, the two women are using resources that have been discarded by other countries, put on to the global market and imported to Mozambique. Through their work, they are both questioning the way fashion is made today on a global scale, as well as contributing to the contemporary design scene in Mozambique. Nelly and Nelsa are trying to find an independent way of gaining an income through using existing trade patterns and are creating a platform of their own to play and experiment with materials and ideas.

Figure 9.1 Nelsa Guambe shopping for second-hand dresses in Maputo

Mima-te and The Life of a Dress

Our work on up-cycling in Europe and research into the African second-hand-clothing trade was connected following an invitation from the Swedish Embassy to bring the concept of The Life of a Dress to Mozambique. An exhibition and workshop were organized where materials from Xipamanine Market and sewing machines were put out for visitors to use and up-cycle clothes. The *Núcleo de Arte* (Art Nucleus) gallery was soon filled with dresses and photographs. Local art students participated, bringing with them handicraft techniques that could be applied to textiles, and visitors came to watch, talk, discuss and make. The twin sisters Nelly and Nelsa Guambe showed great interest in the up-cycling of used dresses and agreed to participate in a photo shoot and model the small collection *Queen of Africa*. When Amanda met them in November 2010, Nelly worked for a bank, and Nelsa had recently returned to Mozambique and was looking for work. Since then, they have developed their own fashion brand, *Mima-te* (spoil yourself), which is based on creating new, fashionable garments from second-hand clothes. Although the inspiration for the concept behind *Mima-te* came from their visit to The Life of a Dress exhibition, the twins had previously, just like many Mozambicans, been mending second-hand clothes for their own use. Their mother had also sold second-hand clothes at home for extra income.

After our meeting, they became frequent visitors to Fajardo and Xipamanine Markets, buying more dresses to refine and redesign, finding which stalls had the most interesting dresses, and becoming known by market vendors as 'the twins who buy what no one else wants'. The dresses are often ones from the 1960s, 1970s and 1980s, which do not match local desires for contemporary clothing. Nelly and Nelsa, however, have realized there is latent value that can be realized in these garments and are inspired to challenge the system of second-hand trade and play with the language of fashion. From the outset, they wanted to create their own fashion brand, under which they would buy, redesign and sell dresses. They asked for advice, and Amanda shared her experiences to help them develop an initial strategic plan and gave advice on sizing, price and styles. Private and monthly sales at *Núcleo de Arte* were organized. A *Mima-te* logo was developed, screen-printed and sewn on to the garments as labels. Photographers wanted to collaborate with the two attractive twins, and this gave the brand a strong visual message, as they themselves appear in promotional materials modelling the dresses (see Figure 9.2). Visual media and an online platform were used as crucial tools to communicate to a wider international market and promote their emerging brand. The twins pick out styles that suit an international and cosmopolitan audience, while drawing on their Mozambican cultural heritage for further inspiration. Names for the dresses were chosen that focused on using Mozambican and African words and phrases to relabel the dresses, and the association with place has become a key way to inscribe the dresses with greater value.[1]

The overall aim was to create something that was not just a new version of the West's old clothes, but a Mozambican creation. 'Mima-te's believe [belief] is that up-cycling what has been given to Africa as a sign of good will (but much too often ends up as waste) is an innovative way of creating a new image of Mozambican clothing' (*Mima-te* website). Technology, branding, marketing and a strong visual aesthetic have been at the heart of this successful up-cycling project. *Mima-te* dresses are priced between US$70 and US$90 and cater to a completely different type of clientele to the poor who buy second-hand T-shirts, blouses and shirts for a few dollars in the market. They sell to affluent members of the local arts community, rich and urbane young Mozambicans, as well as expats and tourists, and the limits of this business do need to be further explored.

Figure 9.2 Nelly and Nelsa Guambe modelling *Mima-te* dresses

Future research agenda

This chapter has illustrated that there is a widespread transnational trade in second-hand clothing that intimately connects people around the world, through diverse sociogeographical relationships. Although these trade patterns are often cited as examples of charitable and environmentally beneficial acts, the broader impacts of donors' good intentions can be negative for Africa's economic development. Though Hansen's pioneering work (2000), as well as Andrew's previous interventions, these topics have begun to be investigated; however, far more research is required to investigate how mass imports of second-hand clothing influence economic and cultural development. Importantly, researchers from the global North engaged in the second-hand-clothing trade have to appreciate that this sector has its greatest impacts in Africa and other poor regions of the world. We have identified three main areas where future research can provide new insights into fashion and sustainability in Africa: mapping second-hand-clothing commodity chains, exploring opportunities for design and reuse of second-hand clothes, and investigating possibilities for the sustainable development of African clothing industries.

First, one of the areas in which knowledge is lacking is detail of the commodity chains that link supplies of second-hand clothing in North America and Europe to retail markets. Further empirical work is required to understand the flows of capital that accompany the movement of different types of second-hand clothing. Mapping these connections will direct greater attention on to the networks of inequality in which clothing donors, charities, second-hand clothing merchants and African consumers are all embroiled.

Second, research can examine how Africans are not passive recipients of the West's cast-offs and investigate the potential to use fashion as a vehicle for exploring radical socio-economic change. *Mima-te* offers one case study, but it is not the first such African up-cycling initiative. In neighbouring Swaziland, fashion designer Khulekani Msweli has managed to successfully combine up-cycling with traditional handicraft under his label *Jerempaul*. Further afield in Senegal, the designer XULY.Bët's has had some success at the couture end of the market, exporting to France (Rovine, 2005). From a critical perspective, *Mima-te* and other African up-cycling projects pose two main questions that future research may address: namely, how can this type of initiative be expanded and have a greater impact? And what are the effects of developing a fashion brand based on materials left over from the northern model of fashion-as-consumption? To respond to the first question, further research is required to investigate how African business people in the clothing sector can work to build viable and sustainable fashion brands. Currently, this is an under-researched area, and examples of both success and failure from small-scale enterprises in clothing and allied creative sectors need to be identified. The role of social entrepreneurship in African development is contested, and the impacts may be limited, benefiting only a select number of savvy individuals and early adopters. Yet, some business people may be able to take advantage of recent economic growth in Mozambique and elsewhere to develop niche business opportunities that serve cosmopolitan and international clients. This leads on to the second question and the potential for broader effects. By considering the impacts that extend beyond the immediate proximate effect of buying and selling dresses, there is arguably an opportunity for fashion to be used as a creative means to challenge existing socio-economic relationships. The *Mima-te* brand functions as a vehicle for stimulating questions around consumption and production of clothing commodities, and the ability to generate media interest is something that Nelly and Nelsa have started to capitalize on. Alongside this, we have attempted to answer some of the broader questions surrounding business development.

Third, the relationship between the failure of African clothing industries and second-hand-clothing imports requires greater research. Efforts to establish a sustainable fashion as well as a mass-market clothing sector in Africa face many challenges, beyond local competition from imported second-hand clothing. One of the primary obstacles to establishing production for domestic markets is competition from cheap new clothing imports from Asia. Additionally, there are issues relating to knowledge, training, access to markets, communications, labour conditions, environmental impacts and design, where research interventions could shed light on both the constraints and possible opportunities for developing clothing production in Africa. New research could explore how existing African clothing industries could be better protected, and how they can produce new designs and products that are competitive in both domestic and international markets.

Conclusion

It should be possible to build sustainable business from remaking second-hand fashion in Africa, yet, as with the market for up-cycled fashion in Europe and North America, there will be limits as to how many refashioned second-hand dresses can be sold and who benefits from this activity. *Mima-te* has been successful because Nelly and Nelsa are, perhaps, uniquely creative and able to cultivate a striking aesthetic. In parallel, they are linked in to the international community in Maputo, are able to draw upon technology and have more capital than most Mozambicans. This project differs from American and European up-cycling interventions, as *Mima-te* is simultaneously illuminating the inequality between the global North and South, while also taking unwanted clothes and reforming value within them, drawing on a Mozambican world-view.

Fashion is used to express identity, yet, by its very nature, is effective in restricting social mobility. Affluent consumers in the global North are placed in a never-ending contest of purchasing, wearing and discarding clothes, and simultaneously fashion is one of the cornerstones of cultural and economic globalization. Equally, African dress today is partially dictated by the mass imports of discarded Western used clothes. Although well intentioned, many donation and recycling schemes that originate in the West and export to Africa have little in the way of positive effects on either environmental sustainability or poverty reduction. Indeed, some may be harming African economies through creating dependence, while legitimizing new cycles of consumption and disposal in the global North (Brooks and Simon, 2012). The lessons to be learned from Nelly and Nelsa's experiences are that creative design can be used to showcase how Africans must play a role in their own future, and should not be trapped as passive recipients of the West's cast-offs. Their business model draws upon the basic market approach of using a raw material and labour to create a new consumable good. The products are new commodities, fashion garments, but, through the concept, Nelly and Nelsa are also communicating an alternative pattern of consumption and production. We would argue that this project is ultimately most powerful as a model for economic and cultural activism that challenges the notion that Africans should be locked into relationships of dependency with the global North, rather than employ a new mode of sustainable mass production. In this sense, parallels can be drawn with the emerging 'craftivism' (craft as activism) sector found among up-cyclers and alternative designers in Europe and the US, who seek to challenge fast fashion through up-cycling and traditional handicraft techniques. Such interventions cannot alone resolve the ecological and social sustainability impasse in the clothing sector, but do make a contribution to liberating people's imaginations and allow us to think of different ways of organizing our relationships with clothes.

Acknowledgements

First and foremost, we would like to thank Nelly and Nelsa Guambe for sharing their experiences, as well as their helpful comments on a draft. Thanks also go to the Swedish Embassy (Maputo), *Núcleo de Arte* and Amanda's accompanying team on her research trip to Maputo. Andrew would like to extend his gratitude to Manuel Ngovene for his excellent work as a field assistant, as well as the traders who participated in the livelihoods research in Xipamanine Market.

Note

1   See *Mima-te* (2013): www.mimate-maputo.com

References

Baden, S. and Barber, C. (2005), *The Impact of the Second-Hand Clothing Trade on Developing Countries.* Oxford, UK: Oxfam.

Brooks, A. (2012a), *Riches from Rags or Persistent Poverty? Inequality in the Transnational Second-hand Clothing Trade in Mozambique.* Unpublished PhD thesis, Department of Geography, Royal Holloway, University of London.

Brooks, A. (2012b), Riches from rags or persistent poverty? The working lives of secondhand clothing vendors in Maputo, Mozambique, *Textile: The Journal of Cloth and Culture*, 10 (2): 222–37.

Brooks, A. (2013), Stretching global production networks: the international second-hand clothing trade, *Geoforum*, 44: 10–22.

Brooks, A. and Simon, D. (2012), Unravelling the relationships between used-clothing imports and the decline of African clothing industries, *Development and Change*, 43 (6): 1265–90.

Frazer, G. (2008), Used-clothing donations and apparel production in Africa, *Economic Journal*, 118 (532): 1764–84.

Hanlon, J. and Smart, T. (2008), *Do Bicycles Equal Development in Mozambique?* Woodbridge, UK: James Curry.

Hansen, K. T. (2000), *Salaula: The World of Secondhand Clothing and Zambia.* Chicago, IL: Chicago University Press.

Kandiero, T. (2005), Malawi in the multilateral trading system, Case Study 23, in P. Gallagher, P. Low and A. L. Stoler (eds) *Managing the Challenges of WTO Participation: 45 Case Studies.* Cambridge: Cambridge University Press: 326–36.

Lindell, I. (2010), The changing politics of informality: collective organizing, alliances and scales of engagement, in I. Lindell (ed.) *Africa's Informal Workers.* London: Zed Books: 1–32.

Milgram, L. B. (2005), *Ukay-Ukay* chic: tales of second hand clothing in the Philippine Cordillera, in A. Palmer and H. Clark (eds) *Old Clothes, New Looks: Second Hand Fashion.* Oxford: Berg: 135–53.

Morley, N., Slater, S., Russell, S., Tipper, M. and Ward, G. D. (2006), *Recycling of low grade clothing waste.* Oakdene Hollins, Salvation Army Trading Company, Nonwovens Innovation and Research: 8.

Rivoli, P. (2009), *The Travels of a T-shirt in the Global Economy: An Economist Examines the Markets, Power, and Politics of World Trade.* London: Wiley.

Rovine, V. (2005), Working the edge: XULY.Bët's recycled clothing, in A. Palmer and H. Clark (eds) *Old Clothes, New Looks: Second Hand Fashion.* Oxford, UK: Berg: 215–27.

United Nations Comtrade (2011), UN COMTRADE Database [online]. Available at: http://comtrade.un. org/db/dqQuickQuery.aspx?cc=26701&px=S1&r=826&y=2010&rg=2&so=17 (accessed 15 November 2011).

10

FASHION AND SUSTAINABILITY IN THE CONTEXT OF GENDER

Mirjam Southwell

Introduction

Sustainability and fashion are often presented as antithetical constructs, with the consumption of fashion being largely seen to be in the hands of women in much the same way as is responsibility for the environment. This chapter explores the role of gender in the context of sustainability and fashion discourse and practice. Our gender, sexuality, ethnicity, social and economic class, education etc. can all make us feel included or may emphasize our otherness. I want to encourage you to look for difference and otherness where it is not explicit and to challenge the gender neutrality of language used in the sustainability and fashion discourse. This is essential for real change, albeit providing no absolute solution.

Working in a developing country as a designer introduced me to the issues of gender and sustainability. I sought to 'unpick' the complexity and grappled with theory before committing to a pragmatic feminism that allows me to look for where women are visible and to magnify where they are not. I take an explicitly feminist perspective when reading literature, exploring and analysing discourse. A feminist perspective also ensures that 'otherness' can be explicitly sought and treated equally, although space does not permit me to address all difference in depth here.

As with feminism, much has been written about gender. I will not rehearse the arguments regarding gender equality having been achieved or not, but refer to an extensive study instigated in 2012 by the World Bank, involving over 4,000 participants in twenty countries, across rural, traditional, urban and modern communities. The researchers found embedded social and gender norms, universal in both the distinction between productive and reproductive roles and expected feminine or masculine behaviours. Although gender norms are being contested, bent and relaxed by younger generations, they are not fully broken or changed; compliance may be delayed 'to a later point in time, but the norms and the expectations around them do not change' (Munoz Boudet *et al.*, 2012: 149). These universal social and gender norms are perpetuated by, and make it easier for, patriarchy to manage femininity by endorsing a limited array of gender identities, ultimately reducing them to dichotomies, either–or/good–bad options (Crymble, 2012). Changing stereotypical male identities, for example metrosexuality and retrosexuality, arguably shifts patriarchy as the dominator to a seemingly gender-neutral capitalism (Anderson, 2008). However, the World Bank study reveals patriarchy is alive and well globally, the gendered binary is far from dissolved, and both women and men are governed by deeply embedded gender norms.

Gender and sustainability

There continue to be few sex-disaggregated statistics in relation to the environment, making it problematic to assess gender differences in managing and protecting natural resources (Warth and Koparanova, 2012). However, where there are gender disaggregated data, there is evidence that, in the home, women exhibit stronger environmental attitudes and behaviour than men (OECD, 2011; Momberg *et al.*, 2012). Women are also more likely to take action in all aspects of their daily lives than men (Stevens, 2010; Weinreb, 2013). This is evident in the study by McElhaney and Mobasseri (2012), who asked whether having women in positions of power in a company had a positive effect on the environmental and social impact of that company. They found a correlation between having at least one female corporate/board director and the company having a proactive approach to environmental and social issues. Interestingly, although acknowledging that men are disproportionally in positions of power, Wanner (2009: 98) argues that men and masculinities are essential for women's empowerment and gender equality, because both men and women 'play a critical role in [. . .] the transfer and application of knowledge, and the workings of communities and hence the realization of ecological sustainability'. There are both men and women present and in positions of power and influence in many, if not all, areas of the sustainable fashion discourse, from industry to academia, designers, producers and consumers. However, it is less clear that there is gender equality in taking responsibility for the environmental damage caused by fashion. After all, women buy more fast fashion than men, buy more clothing in general than men (Shah, 2008) and, in most households, have responsibility for laundry (Shehan and Moras, 2006). Looked at from another angle, arguably this is all happening within the dominant discourse of patriarchy, and women find themselves in a no-win situation.

Gender, consumption and fashion

Women may be key players in the fashion and clothing industry, but it is as consumers that they are most discussed. Chang *et al.* (2004) argue that men and women differ in most aspects of consumption: women actively seek out more product information than men and spend more time in shops when buying clothes, because, although both genders feel pressured by sociocultural dress norms, this is stronger for women. Noting that gender socialization influences choice, they argue that buying fashion, with its focus on newness, becomes hedonistic, compulsive consumption. More recently, Pentecost and Andrews (2010) observed that, although studies on the consumption of fashion have gathered data from both men and women, gender difference is rarely discussed, but, where it has been considered, they surmise that women are more passionate about fashion, more positive towards fashion and more likely to impulse buy fashion than men. Discussing Generation Y, those born between 1980 and 1998, Pentecost and Andrews (2010) note that women in Generation Y are 'socialised' into the consumption of fashion earlier than preceding generations. Staying with Generation Y, Joergens (2006) found that personal needs took precedence over ethical issues when purchasing fashion clothing. Catterall *et al.* (2005) argue that focusing on consumption has been at the expense of more critical analyses that explore gender assumptions in important interrelationships between production, reproduction and consumption. There was also an automatic assumption that consumers are likely to be female, so that it did not need to be researched. A feminist perspective applied to recent literature suggests that this is still the case, and gender from the fashion industry's point of view means women.

Gender and consumers

The gender-neutral 'consumer of sustainability' is assigned multiple personality traits and behaviours, including power, passivity and 'wilful ignorance' (see Ehrich and Irwin, 2005; Aspers, 2008; Fletcher, 2008; Vinz, 2009). Identify the consumer as female, and we can add hedonism to the mix (Chang *et al.*, 2004). In Shaw *et al.*'s (2006) discussion of fashion choices and the impact of fair-trade concerns, the consumer remains resolutely gender neutral. Exploring the consumption of fashion by young families, Ritch and Schröder (2012) focus on women rather than men, because of women's explicit roles as professionals, mothers and consumers of fashion. Although they do not comment on feminist theory in relation to production and reproduction, they also selected women because of a mother's central position in household purchasing. Ritch and Schröder (2012: 204) argue that this group of consumers are more likely to engage in the consumption of sustainable fashion because they are women with children, whose presence in a 'household has been recognized as heightening concern for ethical issues', and, as previously discussed, are more engaged with environmental issues than men.

Blogs and commentaries as a window on to current discourse

In trying to determine where to start looking for gender and sustainable fashion, I decided to initiate the search with the UK national daily newspaper *The Guardian* (and its Sunday publication, *The Observer*), using its website, because I was aware of articles about fashion and sustainability. This proved to be enlightening. *The Guardian* online supports a number of 'specialist' blogs and commentaries, including Sustainable Business, Fashion, Ethical Living and Comment is Free. Using the search terms fashion, sustainability, gender, women and feminism/feminists, results appeared most frequently in blogs and commentaries in Life & Style, Ethical Living, Sustainability, Fashion and Sustainable Business. I restricted the published date to 5 years, starting in 2008 and finishing in March 2013. Twenty blogs or commentaries are presented in the tables below; they are not necessarily the only ones on the site and are, therefore, not presented as definitive. However, they provide an insight into the concerns and issues over a period of time. Of the twenty pieces, fifteen are written by women, three by men, and one by a woman and a man. The gender of the authors of one interview is unclear, but the interviewee is female. The male writers appear in the sustainable-business section only.

In the years 2008–10 (Table 10.1), few blogs or commentaries came up using the search criteria, and none in sustainable business. The content ranged from optimistically asking if fast fashion had met its end and recognition that the fashion industry did its best to avoid criticism regarding green issues, to misogyny, belittling fashion and a female public figure described as a pin-up girl for eco-fashion, as evidenced by her carrying a silver clutch bag made from recycled aluminium ring pulls to a political event.

There is a significant increase in blogs and commentaries in 2011–13 (Tables 10.2–10.4). These appeared in the following sections on *The Guardian* website: Fashion, Comment is Free and Sustainable Business, which interestingly resulted in the most. Consumers and consumerism, environmental and human costs of the fashion industry are the main foci.

Table 10.1 Blogs and commentaries, 2008–10

Year	Issue/comment	Author/gender	Section in The Guardian
2008	Fast fashion has had its day, have we seen the end of our 'love affair with fast fashion'?	Siegle/female	Life & Style
	Fashion industry 'adept at avoiding green censure and criticism'		
2009	UK government's voluntary initiative, Sustainable Clothing Action Plan: can it 'address the evils lurking in the global fashion closet?'	Siegle/female	Ethical Living
	Sustainable Clothing Action Plan makes no reference or commitment to overseas producers		
2010	High-profile public figure in the UK (not a model or celebrity) described as the 'poster girl for sustainable fashion'	Fox/female	Fashion
	'an element of misogyny in this belittling of fashion. It's part of peoples' lives. People care about their looks even when they do not consciously know it'	Cartner-Morley/female	Sustainability

Table 10.2 Blogs and commentaries, 2011

Year	Issue/comment	Author/gender	Section in The Guardian
2011	British Fashion Council recognises female fashion designers	Fox/female	Fashion
	Sustainable fashion inherently oxymoronic	Aitkenhead/female	Fashion
	Designer brands prevented from being sustainable because of the 'pesky issue of conspicuous consumption'	Townsend/female	Sustainable Business
	Gucci 'could teach the world that without sustainability, fashion is doomed; and without desirability sustainability is impotent'		
	Impact of fashion industry on environmental, social and governance issues	Kaye/male	Sustainable Business
	The Sustainable Apparel Coalition and lessening the human cost of producing cheap clothes		
	The importance of the supply chain and trend for measuring water consumption, waste and emissions	Milton/male	Sustainable Business

Table 10.3 Blogs and commentaries, 2012

Year	Issue/comment	Author/gender	Section in The Guardian
2012	Fairtrade and limited data available on its impact on fashion chains but well documented that growth in fashion chains 'often comes at the expense of the workers'	Lissaman/ female	Sustainable Business
	The need for sustainable production and sustainable consumption	Goffman/male	Sustainable Business
	Consumers want 'sustainability by stealth'		
	Cynicism of consumers re. fashion industry's attempts to be seen to engage with sustainability and corporate social responsibility	Ravasio/female	Supply Chain Hub, Sustainable Business
	Consumers 'expect sustainability efforts to be integral to how companies do business'		
	Copenhagen Fashion Summit's pre-summit discussed how to engage consumers in the consumption of sustainable fashion (designers, business executives and government) and agreed that industry needs to talk to consumers about sustainability but this is not easy because of the complexity of themes	Pasquinelli/ female	Sustainable Business
	'Disruptive change must come from within the industry'		

Women are explicit in only four of the pieces, and gender as an issue is not mentioned in any. However, if we use a feminist perspective when reading the tables, the consumer becomes explicitly female, and we can ask: Do women want sustainability by stealth, or are women aware enough of the issues to be cynical about the fashion industry's attempts at environmentalism? Do women expect sustainability to be integral in the way industry does business, and is this the same as wanting sustainability by stealth? Are women incapable of understanding the complexity of the issues?

A feminist reading of the most recent discourse, in 2013, produces the following questions: If women are more concerned with the environment than men, are women's concerns being sidelined through eco-fashion being sidelined as a niche option? Will women ever be able to bridge the 'intention–behaviour' gap, if sustainable fashion remains a niche option? Is it women's responsibility to demand sustainable fashion?

Twitter

Given the increasing prominence of Twitter in expressing and shaping opinion, it seemed important to see what it had to offer. Gould's (2013) list of fifteen top influential sustainable-fashion tweets provides the next stage of the study. Thirteen of the fifteen tweets were written by women (and the remaining two might have been), and I hoped they might provide some answers to the questions raised above, and I also wondered whether, with female tweeters, gender might be mentioned. The ethnicity and age of the tweeters is harder to report, but all appeared

Table 10.4 Blogs and commentaries, January–March 2013

Year	Issue/comment	Author/gender	Section in The Guardian
2013 incl. March	Making the feminist case for fashion week	Filipovic/ female	Comment is Free
	'Hypocritical to single women out for being shallow in their wardrobe spending' when men similarly consume unnecessary products		
	Survey of 800 sustainability professionals including those from business, government, academia and NGOs – governments need to be involved for networks to have a chance of success	Buckingham & Read/ female & male	Sustainable Business
	The most effective collaborations concentrate on a single issue		
	'Collaboration is not always the answer'; competition can encourage companies to develop sustainable business models too		
	'Growing sense that "eco-fashion" has been side-lined as a niche option for shoppers with a conscience'	Payton/female	Sustainable Business
	Roundtable debate hosted by *The Guardian* newspaper and Timberland, attended by 'a host of ethical and sustainable fashion luminaries'		
	Consumers' 'intention–behaviour gap' (roundtable participant)		
	Agreement that, for fashion industry to change, there has to be widespread demand for sustainable fashion		
	Generation Y has grown up 'in a society where eco-consciousness was becoming the norm'	Rogers/female	Sustainable Business
	Generation Y expects sustainability to be integral to a product, not simply a specialist line or brand		
	Generation Y is a potential 'goldmine for sustainable products and companies'		
	Sustainability offering social currency to image-focused younger consumers, 'particularly when it is from a premium brand'		
	Celebrities wearing ethical fashion on the red carpet and T-shirts with slogans	Angel/female	Sustainable Business
	Image is 'all-important in the world of fashion'		
	If sustainable fashion is to become mainstreamed, it has to lose its worthiness and become cool, perhaps by dropping the word sustainable		
	Fifteen top influential sustainable fashion tweets	Gould/female	Sustainable Business

to be professionally involved in sustainable fashion. The female tweeters identified themselves as experts, authors and journalists. One is the owner of an ethical clothing line, and one describes herself as a tree-hugging geek in stilettos. The two Twitter feeds where the author's gender is not explicit are an online magazine about the future of sustainable fashion and 'The world's eco-fashion guide'.

A snapshot of content was taken for 1–31 March 2013, and only tweets posted by the owner of the tweet were 'counted'. The geographical locations of the tweeters were the USA and Europe. The number of followers ranged from 974 (author with two tweets) to 12,629 (online magazine with 256 tweets). The number of tweets over the month varied considerably, from 2 to more than 500. The gender, age and ethnicity of the intended audience are not explicit, neither is the economic/social class, although easy access to the Internet is required to follow and participate.

The subjects covered varied considerably from: chat to facts, local to global, personal promotion to public events. Some were specific to sustainable fashion; others were miscellaneous. The subjects lend themselves to be responses to questions that might be asked by someone wanting to find out about sustainable fashion:

- *What should I worry about most?* Chinese fur farms, my 'slavery footprint', my domestic water usage, the poverty of producers, cotton-picking in India, wasteful clothes slashing, deforestation of the Amazon, the supply chain, manufacturing water usage and wastage, human trafficking.
- *What is happening now?* Ikea's better cotton initiative, working with artisans, Fairtrade fashion label helping HIV-positive women in Cambodia, recycling carpets, recycled leather, Gucci promoting leather, sustainable design and eco vintage, Redress Eco Fashion & Textiles Conference, International Women's Month, International Women's Day, recycled plastic and wood turned into jeans, collecting environmental data from manufacturers, celebrities wearing environmentally aware designers on red carpet, celebrities wearing slogan T-shirts on stage, a dress worn at the Oscars made with recycled sweet wrappers.
- *What can I do?* Reuse prom dress, avoid big retail, buy animals in peril scarf, lease not buy jeans, recycle, reuse, wear vintage clothes. If I feel guilty about consuming fast fashion, shall I give it up for Lent? Or take a 'giveaway' bag of clothing to a local store and get 15 per cent off my next purchase? As an average UK woman I must own twenty-two garments I don't wear. Make my own cosmetics.
- *What could or should be happening?* Eco-textile labelling that doesn't confuse consumers, teach sustainability to designers, create solutions via action not finger-pointing, philanthropic business, social enterprises, laws forcing consumers to be sustainable.
- *Anything else?* Celebrities, Barbie's LED dress, 3D print dress, Syria, cluster bombs.

The multiple topics covered confirm both the complexity and confusion of fashion and sustainability. Reading about reusing prom dresses in one 'breath' and having a 'slavery' foot-print in the next is uncomfortable. And, although global, political issues are discussed, these are presented alongside celebrity and the personal. Can male readers identify with the content, or is it implicit that women are the intended audience?

Discussion

Almost overwhelmingly, I saw women, not men, and very little diversity represented in the tweets, blogs and commentaries. More questions are raised for the (female) individual wanting advice, to get involved and change behaviour than are answered. As a female or male consumer of fashion, am I more likely to react by not changing my behaviour, as it is too complex to understand, or is it too superficial to warrant more than a passing glance? Although there are hints at how we might bridge the intention–behaviour gap, it isn't easy! Through an iterative process and revisiting literature, I have identified three areas key to making some sense of gender and sustainable fashion: status and celebrity, the process of feminization and cognitive dissonance.

Frequent references are made to celebrities in the tweets, blogs and commentaries. Veblen's *Theory of the Leisure Class*, written in 1899, is a useful starting point to situate this apparent fascination, celebrities being Veblen's rich and nouveau riche. Central to Veblen's approach is a hierarchical social structure driven by competition for status and a trickle-down mechanism where high-status brands are first acquired by the wealthy and then absorbed into the buying habits of the less well off (Brown, 2000; Schor, 2007). Criticism of Veblen's model has come from intervening models of consumption, but brand loyalty and celebrity following continue, and the Gucci bag epitomizes the power of the wealthy to influence the purchasing choices of consumers, female and male. Although there is the argument that consumption now produces individual identity, the result of individual agency rather than overt social conformity (Schor, 2007), we have to acknowledge that both exist. Female consumers learn from an early age to consume fashion, and the construct of identity is integral to the fashion industry.

The literature established that women express stronger environmental concerns than men and are more likely to act on this concern than men. Women are also the main consumers of fashion and clothing, and, as the world's second largest industry, textiles and clothing have a considerable impact on the environment and natural resources (Momberg *et al.*, 2012; Joung and Park-Poaps, 2013). The vast majority of those publicly expressing concern for sustainable fashion are women, and so the feminization of sustainable fashion comes as no surprise. However, Chant's (2006) feminization of responsibility and obligation and Vinz's (2009) concept of the feminization of responsibility for the environment lay much at the door of women and are epitomized in the concerns of sustainable fashion. Chant (2006) argues that the gender differences in household inputs and outcomes for women have to be addressed in terms of environmental responsibility and obligations. Women's household inputs increase and diversify: from recycling to water and from buying cheap school uniforms to heeding calls to make do and mend. Vinz (2009: 163) asks two questions: First, whether women have to be responsible for solving our ecological problems through ecologically oriented household management, when these problems are caused by factors outside their control; and, second, whether this will lead to women experiencing 'eco-stress'. There has to be gender equality at all stages of the fashion chain for responsibility to be shared, and, if the literature is to be believed and women demonstrate stronger environmental attitudes and behaviour than men, then the answer to Vinz's second question has to be a resounding 'yes'.

Reading the blogs, commentaries and tweets, I found myself becoming increasingly conscious of my own behaviour. I recycle assiduously at home, but what's the point when I buy 'three for the price of two' cotton T-shirts every spring? This may be an example of cognitive dissonance, a valuable concept to use when exploring the way women (and men) respond to information that challenges their beliefs and behaviour. First introduced by Festinger in 1957, cognitive dissonance is the mental disharmony experienced when an individual has two, or more, conflicting beliefs, ideas or values. To avoid cognitive dissonance, the individual seeks to alter behaviour, attitudes or beliefs. As it becomes increasingly difficult to deny the environmental impact and implications for sustainability of fashion, it becomes increasingly difficult to achieve 'cognitive consistency' (Festinger, 1957). This is exemplified by women consuming fast fashion to keep up with social expectations or buying cheap school uniforms because their children grow quickly, while at the same time being shocked by, and wanting to be sensitive to, those who perished in the Rana Plaza clothing factory collapse in Bangladesh in April 2013. Siegle (2013) posits that this tragedy could be 'a tipping point', the shock that consumers need to take action. However, although dramatic events can result in ethically minded people changing their behaviour (McLeod, 2008; Hjelmar, 2011), rationalizing negates the discomfort caused by a purchasing decision that fails to reflect one's moral principles (Ritch and Schröder, 2012).

The prevailing discourses can be read in many ways, but can be summed up as predominantly being: women as consumers of fashion are wilfully ignorant (Soutar and Sweeney, 2003; Ehrich and Irwin, 2005), rationalizing the purchase of cheap clothing to avoid moral disjuncture (Ritch and Schröder, 2012), while simultaneously living with eco-stress (Vinz, 2009).

Future research

Space has not allowed me to explore all difference, diversity and 'otherness' in relation to fashion and sustainability. However, I suggest two areas of considerable importance for fashion and sustainability: the younger Generation Y, those born in the 2000s; and the globalization of emerging economies. We learn to consume fashion from an early age, and, although forming one's identity happens throughout life, it is particularly anxiety-provoking in adolescence — reformulating one's identity can be a constant pressure, promoted by ever-changing trends in fashion (Fletcher, 2008). Arguably, this is the case in all societies where, Workman and Lee (2011: 50) note, 'dress is a culturally accepted means of displaying status, power and success'. Discussing the globalization of emerging economies, and India specifically, Handa and Khare (2013: 112) argue that Indian youth want to acquire luxury brands because of the 'desire to enhance self-image in the social context', and this can be most immediately achieved and publically displayed through fashion. With a focus on globalization and both female and male youth, future research could explore McRobbie's (1997: 87) observation that,

> the energetic enthusiasm of women across the boundaries of class and ethnicity for fashion could be used to transform it into a better place of work rather than allowing it to remain a space of exploited production and guilt consumption.

Conclusion

Responsibility for the environment has become feminized, with women being both more likely to show concern and more likely to act on these concerns in a positive way than men. Much the same thing appears to be happening in the area of fashion and sustainability, where women are unquestioningly seen as the instigators and consumers of fashion, while at the same time being regarded as having responsibility for its environmental impact. Although much of the discourse appears to be 'it's not us, it's them' from consumers, female and male, and industry, the latter implicitly lays responsibility on women. Certainly within the household, at least, women find themselves in a no-win situation, struggling with cognitive and identity dissonance. The feminizing of fashion and sustainability takes hold, but the reality is that there is no such thing as a gender-neutral consumer. The task is to develop models for sustainable fashion that inspire. These models, while addressing complexity, do not have to mean confusion, but rather offer opportunities for individuality and diversity, not only in what people wear, but also in how they address their environmental concerns. In fashion and sustainability, one size does not fit all.

References

Anderson, K.N. (2008), From metrosexual to retrosexual: The importance of shifting male gender roles to feminism. Series: *Thinking Gender Papers*, Los Angeles, CA: UCLA Center for the Study of Women.

Aspers, P. (2008), Labelling fashion markets, *International Journal of Consumer Studies*, 32: 633–8.

Brown, S. (2000), The laugh of the marketing Medusa: men are from Marx, women are from Veblen, in M. Catterall, P. Maclaran and L. Stevens (eds) *Marketing and Feminism: Current issues and research*. London and New York: Routledge: 129–42.

Catterall, M., Maclaran, P. and Stevens, L. (2005), Postmodern paralysis: the critical impasse in feminist perspectives on consumers, *Journal of Marketing Management*, 21: 489–504.

Chang, E., Davis Burns, L. and Francis, S. K. (2004), Gender differences in the dimensional structure of apparel shopping satisfaction among Korean consumers: the role of hedonic shopping value, *International Textile & Apparel Association*, 22 (4): 185–99.

Chant, S. (2006), Re-thinking the 'feminization of poverty' in relation to aggregate gender indices, *Journal of Human Development*, 7 (2): 201–20.

Crymble, S. B. (2012), Contradiction sells: feminine complexity and gender identity dissonance in magazine advertising, *Journal of Communication Inquiry*, 36 (1): 62–84.

Ehrich, K. R. and Irwin, J. R. (2005), Wilful ignorance in the request for product attribute information, *Journal of Marketing Research*, 42: 266–77.

Festinger, L. (1957), *A Theory of Cognitive Dissonance*. Stanford, CA: Stanford University Press.

Fletcher, K. (2008), *Sustainable Fashion & Textiles: Design Journeys*. London and Sterling, VA: Earthscan.

Gould, H. (2013), Sustainable fashion top tweeters list [online]. Available at: www.guardian.co.uk/sustainable-business/sustainable-eco-fashion-twitter-list (accessed 4 October 2013).

Handa, M. and Khare, A. (2013), Gender as a moderator of the relationship between materialism and fashion clothing involvement among Indian youth, *International Journal of Consumer Studies*, 37: 112–20.

Hjelmar, U. (2011), Consumers' purchase of organic food products. A matter of convenience and reflexive practices, *Appetite*, 56: 336–44.

Joergens, C. (2006), Ethical fashion: myth or future trend? *Journal of Fashion Marketing and Management*, 10 (3): 360–71.

Joung, H.-M. and Park-Poaps, H. (2013), Factors motivating and influencing clothing disposal behaviours, *International Journal of Consumer Studies*, 37: 105–11.

McElhaney, K. A. and Mobasseri, S. (2012), Women create a sustainable future. Berkeley, CA: UC Berkeley Haas School of Business.

McLeod, S. A. (2008), Cognitive dissonance theory [online]. Available at: www.simplypsychology.org/cognitive-dissonance.html (accessed 5 May 2013).

McRobbie, A. (1997), Bridging the gap: feminism, fashion and consumption, *Feminist Review*, 55 (Spring): 73–89.

Momberg, D., Jacobs, B. and Sonnenberg, N. (2012), The role of environmental knowledge in young female consumers' evaluation and selection of apparel in South Africa, *International Journal of Consumer Studies*, 36: 408–15.

Munoz Boudet, A. M., Petesch, P. and Turk, C. with Thumala, A. (2012), On norms and agency: conversations about gender equality with women and men in 20 countries. Washington, DC: The World Bank.

OECD (2011), *Greening Household Behaviour: The Role of Public Policy*. OECD Publishing.

Pentecost, R. and Andrews, L. (2010), Fashion retailing and the bottom line: the effects of generational cohorts, gender, fashion fanship, attitudes and impulse buying on fashion expenditure, *Journal of Retailing and Consumer Services*, 17: 43–52.

Ritch, E. L. and Schröder, M. J. (2012), Accessing and affording sustainability: the experience of fashion consumption within young families, *International Journal of Consumer Studies*, 36: 203–10.

Schor, J. (2007), In defense of consumer critique: revisiting the consumption debates of the twentieth century, *Annals of the American Academy of Political Social Science*, 611 (May): 16–30.

Shah, D. (2008), View, *Textile View Magazine*, 82: 10–11.

Shaw, D., Hogg, G., Wilson, E., Shui, E. and Hassan, L. (2006), Fashion victim: the impact of fair trade concerns on clothing choice, *Journal of Strategic Marketing*, 14: 427–40.

Shehan, C. L. and Moras, A. B. (2006), Deconstructing laundry: gendered technologies and the reluctant redesign of household labour, *Michigan Family Review*, 11: 39–54.

Siegle, L. (2013), Fashion still doesn't give a damn about the deaths of garment workers [online]. Available at: www.guardian.co.uk/commentisfree/2013/may/05/dhaka-disaster-fashion-must-react (accessed 5 May 2013).

Soutar, G. and Sweeney, J.C. (2003), Are there cognitive dissonance segments? *Australian Journal of Management*, 28 (3): 227–50.

Stevens, C. (2010), Are women the key to sustainable development? Sustainable Development Insights, Boston University, 3 April.

Veblen, T. (1899), *The Theory of the Leisure Class* (reprinted in 2009). Oxford World's Classics. Oxford, UK: Oxford University Press.

Vinz, D. (2009), Gender and sustainable consumption: a German environmental perspective, *European Journal of Women's Studies*, 16 (2): 159–79.

Wanner, T. (2009), Men-streaming food security: gender, biodiversity and ecological sustainability, *The International Journal of Environmental, Cultural, Economic and Social Sustainability*, 5 (3): 97–109.

Warth, L. and Koparanova, M. (2012), Empowering women for sustainable development. Discussion paper series, no. 2012.1, United Nations Economic Commission for Europe, Geneva, Switzerland.

Weinreb, E. (2013), At work, do women care more than men about sustainability? [online]. Available at: www.GreenBiz.com (accessed 4 October 2013).

Workman, J. E. and Lee, S.-H. (2011), Materialism, fashion consumers and gender: a cross-cultural study, *International Journal of Consumer Studies*, 35: 50–7.

11

SPIRITUALITY AND ETHICS

Theopraxy[1] in the future of sustainability within the supply chain

Sue Thomas

Introduction

Sustainability as a locus of innovation and practice is maturing, expanding and diversifying. It has always been a broad church of ideas, an opportunity for radical positivity and a licence to care. It is opportune to dig into our psyches and look beyond 'I' and 'my' in philosophy and industrial endeavour, and ask questions. As a design academic, I have asked questions and advocated internationally for ethics and sustainability in education, design practice and the supply chain. Furthermore, working in Australia – geographically and politically close to South East Asia, the location of a high percentage of global offshore production – I am keenly aware of the lack of understanding of the potential of applied ethics. Consequently, the personal and professional ethical decisions made by industry practitioners will change fashion manufacture and disposal in the next 20 years, but also the viability of the planet and its inhabitants, because, in spite of changes in practice and consumer awareness within the supply chain, they are too little and too late. Long-term, permanent damage is being done because of our practice and industry.

It is proposed here that the driver for sustainability practice is a desire to be fair, to preserve, to share, to reinstate an equality, to 'do the right thing', to behave ethically (Thomas, 2011). Ethics are fundamental to sustainability. Practitioners engaging with the status quo will find some jobs in production are badly paid, or deny human rights, or processes are poisoning the earth, or companies are perpetuating corporate neo-colonialism by enforcing their processes and compliance requirements, and they may experience cognitive dissonance. This response has been explained as: 'the feeling of discomfort that results from holding two conflicting beliefs. When there is a discrepancy between beliefs and behaviors, something must change in order to eliminate or reduce the dissonance' (Cherry, 2013).

Cognitive dissonance (see also Chapter 10) is the disquiet that occurs when one has two conflicting beliefs; thus, it can be a powerful driver for change, when personal ethics do not reconcile with professional ethics. Yet, is the industry considering what ethics are, or where the ethics are 'sourced'? If industry participants urgently need to act ethically for the long-term common good, then spirituality-based ethics should be considered as a driver for decision-making and practice. Why this has not happened, or why religion has not been included in sustainability practice, are issues that warrant further examination and reflection. Furthermore, to achieve inclusive sustainable outcomes, it is necessary to be understood.

This chapter is a speculative examination of how spirituality and ethics could aid future sustainability practitioners within the industry and facilitate a shift from orthopraxy to theopraxy; that is, from orthodox or normal practice and behaviours, to practice informed by theology or spirituality. The chapter will start with reflection on our motivations, followed by the definitions of spirituality and ethics for the advocated argument. The notion of spirituality being the 'last taboo' or prohibition in design practice or supply-chain management will be explored. The inherent fear of loss of reason and rationality in practising spirituality will be examined, and the notion of spirituality or religion in practice in the supply chain, past and present, will be addressed. An argument will be made for spirituality both in design and, more importantly, within the industry. The chapter will conclude with a speculation on spirituality in the future of sustainability, the potential limitations and the many possible benefits.

Self-reflection

Before broaching definitions, there needs to be self-reflection, to analyse why fashion industry professionals are motivated to make decisions or carry out actions. This is undertaken to identify the tension between our individual beliefs and our professional behaviour. Our ethics may be conflicted in our practice. As humans, when we witness inequity or disadvantage, we empathise with the other responding, trying to restore, or compensate, or find a less harmful action. As Simon Baron-Cohen, in his book *Zero Degree of Empathy – A New Theory of Human Cruelty*, wrote, 'If they are suffering to any degree, you just know to offer comfort and sympathy' (2011: 11). In addition, he observed that empathy has two parts: '*recognition and response*' (2011: 11), having earlier clarified in the book: 'Empathy occurs when we suspend our single-minded focus of attention, and instead adopt a double-minded focus of attention' (Baron-Cohen, 2011: 10). Thus, Baron-Cohen delineates the move from self-involvement to acknowledgement and comprehension of another perspective and set of needs. By considering the other – their feelings, their experience of life and their current and future well-being – we are empathising, adopting the '*double-minded focus*'.

Reflection on the long-term common good is essential for ethical behaviour. Were we to ask where the ethics come from, the answer might be a religion, a faith or a belief system – that is, spirituality. Thus, design and manufacture in developed countries might be considered to be contextualised or culturally informed by Abrahamic[2] (Christian, Jewish or Muslim) faiths and ethics. Would there be a different outcome if sustainability practice was theopraxy – that is, a practical enactment of spirituality, as architect Michael Benedikt (2007) wrote in his book *God is the Good We Do*: our positive actions (industrial practice) are an enactment of God?

Definitions

The argument for spirituality in practice is contentious, and so, to pursue this, it is essential to establish definitions; in this case, those in the *Concise Oxford English Dictionary* work well. First, the definition of 'spiritual', '1 of or concerning the spirit as opposed to matter. 2 concerned with sacred and religious things holy; divine; inspired', works in this argument (Thompson, 1995: 1342). Second, the definition of 'religion' is useful: '1 the belief in a superhuman controlling power, esp. in a personal God or gods entitled to obedience and worship. 2 the expression of this in worship. 3 a particular system of faith and worship' (Thompson, 1995: 1161). Definitions

2 and 3 are applicable in this instance. In addition, I should note that, in the chapter, 'spirituality' and 'religion' will be interchangeable. The term 'ethics' needs to be made clear: the *Concise Oxford English Dictionary* again: '1 (usu. treated as sing.) the science of morals in human conduct; moral philosophy. 2 a (treated as pl.) moral principles; rules of conduct' (Thompson, 1995: 463). For this argument, the second definition – 'moral principles; rules of conduct' – has the most relevance, relating as it does to practice. Benedikt contextualised 'ethical actions' when he explained his definition of 'morals' and 'ethics':

> A note about the words 'moral' and 'ethical'. The boundary between them is fuzzy. In the tendency, however, moral actions are (good) things done for whatever reason: and the subject matter of 'morality' tends to be interpersonal (e.g. sexual behaviour, aid, decency). Ethical actions are good things done on the account of the principles behind them and in our knowledge of our freedom to do otherwise. The subject matter of 'ethics' thus tends to be institution – and business related. (Hence 'business ethics' or 'medical ethics'.) Very roughly: religion cares more about morals, and law and moral philosophy about ethics.
>
> *(2007: 26)*

With better comprehension of the terms, it is possible to proceed further with the argument of spirituality in practice being the last prohibition or taboo.

The last taboo in sustainability practice: the loss of reason to religion?

Perhaps unexpectedly, sustainability offers a dynamic locus for spirituality, the last taboo in (contemporary Western) industrial practice. Taboo is an odd term perhaps, but spirituality is faith based; consequently, in the empirically proven domain of consumer goods industries – think industrial design and architecture – it represents the last prohibited area of theory and practice. I speculate that this is fear driven. Designers and industry practitioners are afraid to declare spirituality or faith as a source of motivation. Fear is in two parts: first, as an apparent loss of reasoning or reason; and second, in discarding reason, fear of becoming vulnerable to proselytising via adopting spirituality as both sustainability practitioners and consumers. The argument may seem odd situated in the fashion industry, not famed for logic or reason. Yet international labels are entirely pragmatic and logical in their risk analysis, planning and sourcing of production months in advance. Beyond sound bites and celebrity-driven media, it is an industry driven by the rationality of cost and time, affecting lives and livelihoods. Spirituality, in the light of global planning and manufacture, could be perceived as a refuge of sentiment, with no place in the rigour of rational design and production. This is particularly likely, as there is a wave of public intellectuals and commentators such as Richard Dawkins and the late Christopher Hitchins championing atheism in the secularised West. History would support this surmise.

Spirituality or religious belief within the design process in the last 300 years has been untenable, as it appears to be the rejection of rationality. Such a rejection would mean goodbye Age of Enlightenment, cheerio Bauhaus; all the hard-won achievements of rational designers, across the disciplines, erased in pursuit of spirituality? For the argument, the term rationality is taken from the *Concise Oxford English Dictionary* definition of 'rational': '1 of or based on reasoning or reason. 2 sensible, sane moderate; not foolish or absurd or extreme. 3 endowed with reason, reasoning. 4 rejecting what is unreasonable or cannot be tested by reason in religion or custom' (Thompson, 1995: 1139).

Yet where does fashion fit in Thompson's rigour-driven, 'reasoning or reason . . . sensible, sane', rational industrial activity? Within the sector, there is a polarity of thinking: reason is lauded, and yet creativity, whimsy and originality are desired and sought. Fashion is seen as trivial, frivolous and disposable. As Barbara Vinken wrote: 'Glittering and blinding, fashion draws attention away from the substance of things. It is the very personification of the individual alienated in the rush of consumption, of self lost in the brilliant worlds of commodities' (Vinken, 2005: 3).

Indeed the industry and the mainstream media have been complicit in constructing the impression, colluding for nonsensical sound bites, video clips, 'reality' and runway shows. Contemporarily fashion is a spectacle, a divertissement, entertainment, a performance, a palliative for the general public. However, the trivialisation masks a multi-million-pound industry that is of both emotional and psychological worth to its customers, and a vital source of employment locally and internationally to thousands of women workers (see Chapter 2, by Joanne Entwistle). Employment of one worker can mean food, housing, some education and health provision for an extended family. Sourcing and buying decisions, made within what is portrayed as an 'irrational' industry, can start (or stop) the production of tens of thousands of garments. It is an industry that can rationalise (and often reduce) a price point, a shipping time, a delivery date and the seconds it takes to make a pair of jeans. Yet, with its well-publicised problems – environmental impact, sizeism, sexism, racism, sentient and labour rights, child-labour infringements and speciesism – it is an industry in dire need of a radical change of paradigm. Consumers are ready to be part of the solution, as BBMG, GlobeScan and SustainAbility, found in The Regeneration Consumer Study (2012):

> Respondents across all markets are also eager to participate by taking action on the issues they care about. Indeed, seven in ten consumers (72%) globally 'believe in voting and advocating for issues important to me,' a belief shared by consumers in both developing (77%) and developed (67%) markets. Interestingly, Chinese consumers (80%) are the most likely to say so.

If fear is stopping the change, then it needs to be confronted, to better understand the impetus of the argument being made.

Fear of spirituality

Does fear occur, for example, if it's a non-local or non-predominate faith? Therefore, are we more alarmed by a faith with which we are unfamiliar, than by one we know? Accordingly, we may find faith and practice changes hard to assimilate. If it is permissible, for example, for a Roman Catholic to design a church, could a Jew design a church to glorify God? Where is the cause for concern? Architecture of the past was built as an expression of belief and faith; consider the cathedrals at Chartres, Ely, the Taj Mahal mausoleum and the Hagia Sofia mosque. Is there any doubt of their searing beauty, professionalism and spirituality? Could industrial practices be both an enactment and a dedication to contemporary beliefs and global faiths? This does not have to be an 'either/or' solution, as more organisations seek/gain kudos from their international ventures. Projects, for example, in the economically expanding Gulf States would require more than a passing knowledge of Islam and how it affects client expectations, provision and use. Thus, to be able to reference knowledge, and design and production sensibilities sympathetic to Islam, is an employable skill.

There are a series of questions that arise when contemplating this possibility: what if, within sustainability practice, there was a religious intent: to honour a (or several) god(s), and/or celebrate and protect sentient life? Following on, would the religious intention be perceived as a taint to the other intended good that sustainability practice could do? Or would it fast-track the simplicity and holistic generosity, core to the understanding of sustainability subscribed to here? Might faith be an alternative method of fast accessing responsibility and ethics – 'what would Jesus do'? That is the enactment of ethics in our practice, our supply chain: serving the common good, behaving fairly, acknowledging the other. Perhaps even more radical: acknowledging the lack of the other, that we are indeed one? If we are all one, as Thich Nhat Hanh,[3] Buddhist leader and peace advocate, said, then 'we inter are'. He argues for 'interbeing'; thus, there can be no separate other. Consequently, when we help others, we are helping ourselves.

Spirituality in design (past and present)

History reveals a variety of examples of faith- (and culture-) based design. In the eighteenth century, the Amish, Mennonites and Shakers, Protestant sects, migrated to North America. Based on their religious principles, they made artefacts that are renowned for their beauty, simplicity and skilled utilisation of materials. A twentieth-century example of faith in practice is David Fletcher Jones,[4] who, returning from the First World War to regional Australia, started a company, Fletcher Jones & Staff. As the name implies, the company (manufacturing and retailing tailored garments) had a radical business and ownership structure that included staff. Fletcher Jones was inspired by Toyohiko Kagawa,[5] a Japanese Christian Pacifist, social reformer and advocate of Christian cooperatives. Fletcher Jones supported Kagawa's plan to visit Australia – an unorthodox decision in 1930s, with the infamous White Australia Policy still in place.

Again in Australia, in 2003, a Lebanese-born woman, Aheda Zanetti, started a company, Ahiida,[6] designing and making modest swimwear for Muslim women. The company is known for the burquini®: a two piece of tight-knit trousers and A-line (thigh-length) top with long sleeves, usually worn with a knitted hijab, or hijood® (Figure 11.1). It has proven successful locally and internationally for women of many cultures, who wish to visit the beach, but not to expose skin, for reasons of modesty, size, age and health.

Contemporarily, the business style of Galahad Clark (sixth generation of the Clark UK footwear family) aligns with the ethics of his Quaker antecedents: 'We are directly inspired by these principles' (personal communication, 12 July 2013). Clark is managing director of Vivobarefoot, working with his cousin Asher Clark, head designer, having pioneered upcycling of materials in his earlier company, Terra Plana (Figure 11.2). Vivobarefoot advocates and educates for healthy movement through the new shoe type. Social reform runs through the Quaker family, including Galahad's father, Lancelot Clark. He started the Soul of Africa social enterprise, to help women learn the skills of shoemaking and fund support for AIDs orphans. Vivobarefoot and Soul of Africa are collaborating on a new line of shoes that are made in local African communities through the Aid Through Trade scheme.

Spirituality in fashion production

I would argue that, within spirituality, it is ethics that are of key interest for practitioners; that is, it is not how practitioners pray, or what their deity looks like, but what codes of conduct they follow, if you believe, as Paul Gilding (2012) former global CEO of Greenpeace wrote, 'The earth is full. In fact our human society and economy is now so large we have passed the limit of our planet's capacity to support us and it is now overflowing' (Gilding, 2012: 1). Here is our Earth's saving incentive to search for a new way of engaging! Fashion industry practitioners need a set of ethics to utilise that is more broadly inclusive of all supply-chain participants.

Figure 11.1 Burquini by Ahiida

Spirituality offers additional and alternative ways of perceiving situations, of being with the situation and all participants. Different and more authentic ways of engaging with sustainability practice are provided, enabling more participants in the supply chain. Accordingly, core ethics and methodologies can be about empowerment and exchange, rather than corporate imposition of 'my multinational company' ethics and 'my multinational company' sustainability, via 'tick the boxes' compliance rules.

Figure 11.2 Vivobarefoot shoe

Ethics are inner, practised awareness and understanding, a responsibility, a respect for our self and the other – if there is an other. If 'we inter are', then it is a losing, a surrendering of self. As a driver of fashion practice, it is a surprising concept, but perhaps not for a sustainability practitioner. To dedicate oneself as a person and a sustainability practitioner, in service of a faith or the other, is, in the developed world, strange. Realistically, is this what would happen, or, typical of sustainability practice, would several alternatives need to be considered? Within the supply chain, there could be participants following a particular faith, and but also some coordinators or managers cognisant of several faith-based beliefs. Therefore, the outcome could be faith-based response as a personal enactment for the common good, or a management method of inclusion and empowering.

In the past, I have proposed utilising Socially Engaged Buddhism ethics as a pilot model (Thomas, 2011), but, for our future, there needs to be a breadth of approaches, including other spirituality sources. Surveying the spirituality or religions among the supply-chain participants would include a breadth of ethics we do not consider: Muslims, Hindi and Sikhs. Imagine the diversity of approach to ethics and, thus, sustainability this would expose. We could consider the merits of a collaborative interfaith coexistence, as in eighth-to-twelfth-century Cordoba in Spain (Abdul Rauf, 2004: 2).

Conclusion: spirituality in the future of sustainability

Perhaps referencing the Cordoba Caliphate in a speculative examination of how spirituality and ethics would help future fashion practitioners engage with sustainability may be fanciful. But we are looking broadly for drivers and motivation for a new ethical paradigm: 'Fostering this new way of seeing is the on-going biggest challenge of sustainability for fashion and textile sector – to build a convincing, reflective and ethical paradigm that is sustainable by design' (Fletcher, 2008: 23).

Surely, the search for a new ethical paradigm has to be audacious, and brave, as well as fanciful! Still, there are concerns and limitations about how the idea would be realised. Believing we are looking for an either/or solution is a mistake, and that it would be a rejection of reason or rationality is not true. *One* solution is not being recommended for a designer, company or the industry; ethics in spirituality could be pluralistic. Sustainability practitioners need more than one driver or source of motivation for the supply chain. Just as consumers come from many cultures and follow many forms of spirituality, so do the workers in the supply chain. We are looking for a fruitful, generous coexistence and collaboration, maybe with several spiritualities, and rationality, because His Holiness the Dalai Lama sees the problems of entirely religion-based *ethics*: 'ethics based on any one religion would only appeal to some of us; it would not be meaningful for all' (2011: xiii). Spirituality links numerous peoples, but also separates some; there are many embedded prejudices, fears of the unknown and of the other. Yet, at the grass-roots level, in war-torn neighbourhoods, the interfaith movement and faith-based reconciliation groups have brought disparate families and communities together. Fear is a barrier, fear of fundamentalists, of evangelists and of proselytising, which sometimes occur. Understandably, within the supply chain, participants usually wish to choose for themselves and don't appreciate any form of pressurising. The prospect of 'resting' traditional (Judeo-Christian), developed-country business ethics and engaging with others in the charged political environments where production takes place is an ethical, a philosophical and an economic risk. But the alternative, of perpetuating the current status quo, has been established as unsustainable (Fletcher, 2008; Gilding, 2012). The prospect of trying something new is scary, but support is not far. Jeremy Till writes, in his book *Architecture Depends*, 'Imperfect ethics is not a contradiction in terms but an aspiration, because right at the heart of that term is a responsibility for the other and the appreciation of the differences of the other' (Till, 2009: 186).

It is possible to question if either or both the consumer and the worker would be happy that a garment was made in a supply chain with faith-based ethics? In terms of marketing and consumption, ethics are 'the new black'; the market for values-based purchases is growing. As noted in the 'Implications and opportunities for action' in The Regeneration Consumer Study in 2012:

> Aspirational consumers crave what we call 'total value': products that deliver practical benefits like price and quality but that also negate buyer's remorse by providing societal and environmental good and provide 'tribal benefits' that help them feel connected to a larger community that shares their values. Brands that hit on all three categories – and effectively communicate as much – will be rewarded with the loyalty of these consumers, particularly in emerging markets like Brazil, India and China.

Thus, in established markets, the current demand for authenticity[7] could be addressed by theopraxy. It is possible to question if the practice of faith-based design functions as a predictor of outcome, or a selector of projects? That would likely depend on the industry professional and their company. Realistically, the outcomes will not be products covered in religious symbols or script. More likely, it finds expression in those practices through the supply chain that embody the ethics of the religion(s), addressing key issues according to their perception of importance: labour rights – child labour, sweatshops – animal rights, environmental impact, sizeism, ageism, sexism, speciesism, racism, intellectual and cultural copyright (Thomas, 2011).

Ethics have been perceived in the past as a developed-world, middle-class response. However, along with the luxury brands, ethics have become an import. With the international purchases come the connected ideas, perceptions of the culture of origin. Animal rights are a growing concern for the young Chinese urban middle class (O'Dwyer, 2012). There is a growth in activism and commitment to the rights of both domestic pets – 'friend, not food' – and wild animals identified by the Animals Asia Foundation (O'Dwyer, 2012: 17). What is apparently an intriguing anomaly is also a tipping point and indicator that a culture previously pigeonholed as only interested in luxury products and branded goods is also interested in ideas and sensibilities. In their empathy, they have become activists, using flash mobs and Weibo to stop the dog-meat trade and the moon bears being farmed for bile (O'Dwyer, 2012).

If adopting a new set of ethics within the supply chain were not possible, the process of reflection on spirituality-based ethics opens our minds to what could be. Looking at a scenario or an inequity from a different perspective releases the imagination, enhances problem-solving and engages empathy. Therefore, it is proposed that ethics hasten the pursuit of sustainability. Confronted by an industry still perpetuating poorly paid employment in dangerous work environments, as evidenced in the deaths of 1,129 people when the Rana Plaza collapsed in Bangladesh in 2013 (see also Chapter 21), and poisoning waterways, according to Greenpeace in its Toxic Threads reports,[8] where participants urgently need to act responsibly for the benefit of others, spirituality has not been considered as a driver for decision-making and practice.

Without doubt, sustainability practice and the incumbent ethics are needed within the industry. Owing to the extreme geographical, cultural and religious diversity of participants in the fashion supply chain, it is ripe for alternative paradigms. Fashion could be an industry where reason and spirituality are already occurring together, if not actually practised. But, in the very near future, it could be the industry that pilots new ways of practice. Thus, theopraxy in sustainability practice could be a model paradigm. Worthy of revisiting, sustainability practice is transparent in its intention to preserve the planet and its occupants for the future, and potentially restoring what has been lost. With such an intention, it snugly fits the notion of faith, a deeply held belief that the common good must be served by all.

Notes

1   Benedikt's premise is that god is manifested by the good that humans do, specifically designers; therefore, design becomes theopraxy, the practical enactment of god. Although Jewish by birth, the god Benedikt references appears to be non-denominational (Thomas, 2011: 15).
2   Iman Feisal Abdul Rauf has written about the shared ethics of the Abrahamic faiths in his book (2004: 16–20).
3   Thich Nhat Hanh, who founded the Order of Interbeing between 1964 and 1966, wrote about 'interbeing' in his short poem Interrelationship (see the extract below) in 1989, where he writes 'we inter-are':

> You are me, and I am you.
> Isn't it obvious that we 'inter-are'?
> You cultivate the flower in yourself,
> so that I will be beautiful.

4   The story of Sir David Fletcher Jones (1895–1977) and his company Fletcher Jones and Staff Pty Ltd is related in the *Australian Dictionary of Biography* article, 1996, available at: http://adb.anu.edu.au/biography/jones-sir-david-fletcher-10638 (accessed 6 July 2013).
5   For those wanting to find out more about Toyohiko Kagawa, there are a variety of sources, including: Morimoto, A. (2007), The forgotten prophet: rediscovering Toyohiko Kagawa (p. 293) in *The Princeton Seminary Bulletin*.
6   The webpage shows the garments and their characteristics. Available at: http://ahiida.com/ (accessed 6 July 2013).

7   Consumers expect transparency and authenticity. Brands can build credibility by sharing the good, acknowledging the bad and inviting new ideas and solutions to tackle challenges together. See: http://ahiida.com/ (viewed 14 July 2013).

8   Greenpeace's report *Toxic Threads Putting Pollution on Parade* (December 2012), part of their ongoing investigation, identified how textile factories in China were polluting the rivers with chemical residue from manufacture. Available at: www.greenpeace.org/international/en/publications/Campaign-reports/Toxics-reports/Putting-Pollution-on-Parade (accessed 7 July 2013).

References

Abdul Rauf, F. (2004), *What's Right with Islam – A New Vision for Muslims and the West*, New York: HarperSanFrancisco.

Baron-Cohen, S. (2011), *Zero Degrees of Empathy: A New Theory of Human Cruelty*, London: Allen Lane.

Benedikt, M. (2007), *God is the Good We Do – Theology of Theopraxy*, New York: Bottino Books.

Cherry, K. (2013), About.com Guide: Psychology: What Is Cognitive Dissonance? [online]. Available at: http://psychology.about.com/od/cognitivepsychology/f/dissonance.htm (accessed 6 July 2013).

Clark, G. (2013), Discussion on the influence of Quaker ethics [telephone conversation]. (Personal communication, 12 July).

Dalai Lama (2011), *Beyond Religion – Ethics for a Whole World*, New York: Houghton Miffler Harcourt.

Fletcher, K. (2008), *Sustainable Fashion and Textiles: Design Journeys*, London: Routledge.

Gilding, P. (2012), *The Great Disruption: Why the Climate Crisis Will Bring On the End of Shopping and the Birth of a New World*, London: Bloomsbury.

O'Dwyer, E. (2012), The animal kingdom, good weekend, *The Age*, 10 November: 16–19.

The Regeneration Consumer Study (2012), *Rethinking Consumption: Consumers and the Future of Sustainability*, BBMG, GlobeScan and SustainAbility [online]. Available at: http://theregeneration roadmap.com/files/reports/TRR_Rethinking_Consumption.pdf (accessed 6 July 2013).

Thomas, S. (2011), *Situated Empathy – Constructed theoretical discourse addressing the empathetic motivations shared by fashion design for sustainability, and the potential of Socially Engaged Buddhist Ethics to inform design practice*, Doctorate thesis, RMIT University [online]. Available at: http://researchbank.rmit.edu.au/eserv/rmit:15885/Thomas.pdf (accessed 6 July 2013).

Thompson, D. (ed.) (1995), *The Concise Oxford English Dictionary*, Oxford, UK: Clarendon Press.

Till, J. (2009), *Architecture Depends*, Cambridge, MA: The MIT Press.

Vinken, B. (2005), *Fashion Zeitgeist: Trends and Cycles in the Fashion System*, Oxford and New York: Berg.

12

CONSUMPTION STUDIES

The force of the ordinary

Ingun Grimstad Klepp and Kirsi Laitala

Consumer research deals with the acquisition, use and disposal of goods and services. Our workplace, SIFO, the National Institute for Consumer Research in Norway, dates back to the 1930s, when home economics and testing of products were predominant. The work aimed at guiding consumers, at that time called housewives, through the 'jungle' of novel consumer goods. More recently, SIFO's work combines social science and textile technology to study the social and technical aspects of consumption. In this chapter, we ask: *how can knowledge of clothing consumption contribute to the work on sustainable fashion?* We will answer the question through examples from interdisciplinary projects on textiles at SIFO, as well as from consumer research. However, we will not give an overview of consumer research on clothes and sustainability. But first, an admission: fashion – the topic of this book – operates according to a different logic from our field of work. We would have posed the question differently: how can consumer research – and all the other fields of expertise covered in this book – contribute to more sustainable patterns of clothes production and consumption? Therefore, we also have to include a discussion of the concept of fashion.

The contribution of consumer research

Research on consumption and the environment has studied the relationship between consumer knowledge, attitudes and the choice of more or less environmentally friendly goods, such as products with environmental labels. However, consumer research can also challenge the way we think about society, politics and the consumer's role. In his book, *Acknowledging Consumption* (1995), anthropologist and consumer researcher Daniel Miller summarizes the fundamental challenges and basic premises for the understanding of consumption in four myths. The first is that mass consumption causes global homogenization. This includes a belief that the world of commodities has destroyed significant differences. This notion is connected to the idea of Americanization and the erosion of culture. In terms of clothing, the belief in global uniformity is widespread and closely linked to the main idea associated with fashion, i.e. that clothes change rapidly owing to global 'fashions'.

The second myth is that consumption is opposed to sociality and premised on materialism and desire for goods instead of concern for people. This myth is closely related to the dualism between person and object. We recognize this belief in the assumption that a beautiful exterior hides a shallow interior (Klepp, 2009; Rhode, 2010), but also in the perception that research on clothes and appearance in itself is unnecessary and superficial.

The third myth is closely related to the idea that consumption is in opposition to authenticity. One aspect of this is the belief that consumption is more superficial than production and, at the same time, an act of free choice. It also includes the notion of a dualistic relationship between production and consumption. In recent years, this myth has increasingly been challenged, among other things through the use of Alvin Toffler's term *prosumer* (1980), which emphasizes the transitions between production and consumption, and in various forms of user participation in the field of design (Lofthouse and Lilley, 2006). This critical perspective is important in clothing research that studies how clothes are adapted and repaired, but, perhaps even more radically, taken into use – as a case of co-production, as discussed in the chapters by Kate Fletcher and Amy Twigger Holroyd.

The fourth myth claims that consumption creates a particular kind of social being. Among other things, this involves the idea that consumers naturally tend to compete over status as their main mode of social relation. Conspicuous consumption and display, therefore, become important. Clothing is often studied as a way to impress, rather than as an expression of the subjects' wish to spread joy, care and safety, or their anxiety and caution (Clarke and Miller, 2002), or their desire for physical well-being and safety, e.g. being dry, warm and unconstrained.

Miller's four myths apply to consumption in general, but are also reflected in the understanding of clothes. Our problem with the term *fashion* is that it incorporates some of these myths. As defined by clothes researcher Elisabeth Wilson, fashion is: 'dress in which the key feature is rapid and continual changing of styles. Fashion, in a sense *is* change, and in modern Western societies no clothes are outside fashion' (Wilson, 1985: 3). In this definition, we see that fashion can be understood both as a cultural process that contributes to change and as clothes that are particularly affected by this process. However, a central principle in research is not to accept things at face value. Whether something is stable or changing should be an empirical question, and not part of the definition of the phenomenon. To the extent that we have conducted studies of consumption in different countries, we find significant differences, e.g. the use of wool in Norway and Great Britain (Hebrok and Klepp, 2013). The new reference work on world dress indeed shows regional variations (Eicher, 2010). Clothes consumption consists of both stable and changing features. The term fashion contributes to the fact that slow changes are not identified and studied. Frequently, slow changes may be more significant than rapid and more superficial changes.

Fashion as a mechanism applies to almost all areas of life, e.g. the names people give to their children. However, whereas researchers in other areas of consumption can choose to discuss fashion, its relevance is taken for granted in clothes research. The confusion created by the concept itself, together with the dominant position of marketing in understanding of clothes, may help to explain why research on everyday clothes consumption has been marginal (Buckley and Clark, 2012).

Miller argues that consumption is often understood as merely the act of purchase, which is understandable, as this is the only act that benefits businesses (1995). Buying something is not the same as using it. In our studies, every fifth garment was either never used or only used once or twice by the current owner, whereas other clothes are used hundreds of times before they are discarded. In research on consumption, it is important to study consumption on its own terms, and not through the concepts and limitations that originate in market-oriented research. This is the reason why we cannot accept the term *fashion* without reservations. The term implies a perspective on clothes that has markets and not consumption as its frame of reference.

Sources of ordinary consumption of clothing

Contrary to the understanding of consumption as individual choice driven by desire for status and superficial commodity fetishism, we emphasize consumption mainly as collective and normatively regulated practices in everyday life (Warde, 2005). This understanding builds on practice theory, which is explained in Sophie Woodward's chapter (Chapter 13).

Tools are essential to every craft, and research is no exception. Tools make a difference (Latour, 2005). We know that the average consumer does not know why some things feel right or wrong, or how many items of clothing they have in their closet. We need methods that enable us and our informants to grasp practices – and not just conventional ways of understanding them. We have, therefore, developed methods of clothes research that are not completely dependent on language.

An important method in this work is the *wardrobe study* (Skov, 2011; Klepp and Bjerck, 2012). A wardrobe study consists of an inventory of clothes in a wardrobe. This inventory involves cataloguing the garments, combined with a tape recording of what the owner, user or caretaker has to say about the individual garment and its history of use. The material frames of practices – the clothes, the wardrobes and laundry baskets – are studied. The goal is to look at the relationship between the individual item of clothing and the larger material totalities. A first-rate ski boot is useless without its twin, just as a suit jacket is of less value without matching trousers. Even the use of clothes without such 'steady companions' becomes difficult if the wardrobe does not contain anything that 'matches'.

Another example of a method that combines interviews with concrete textile examples is a *sample test*. We ask the consumers to touch and describe different textile samples and guess which material they are made of (Hebrok and Klepp, in press). *Laboratory tests* of textiles are used to measure physical and chemical characteristics. By combining tests with what the users say about specific clothes, we get a chance to compare different people's perception of terms such as 'worn', 'worn out' or 'pilling', and how such evaluations vary from one type of clothes to another (Laitala and Boks, 2012). Another method that we have developed to connect linguistic descriptions of clothes to physical and material conditions is odour testing (Laitala *et al.*, 2012), in addition to more common methods, such as fieldwork and diaries of purchases.

Life span and use time

Most of the life-cycle assessment studies on clothing show that the use phase is the most energy-demanding stage (Madsen *et al.*, 2007). The use phase also has significant environmental impacts, because it determines how long the garments are used, and how they are disposed of. A short lifetime increases the need for products to be replaced, hence, increasing the environmental load from the production and disposal phases. One of the possibilities for increasing sustainability in the field of textiles and clothing is to prolong the use period (Klepp, 2001; Fletcher, 2008).

We have conducted a wardrobe study of 620 discarded items of clothing. The informants got to talk freely about their perceptions of the garments and the reasons why they stopped using or, in some cases, never started using them. Figure 12.1 gives the distribution of the main reasons for disposal among children and teens and among adult men and women. Material properties of the clothes dominate the informants' descriptions. Nearly half of the clothing for adults had changed appearance, e.g. items had holes or were torn or looked worn. The second largest group was related to problems with sizes and fit: either that the owners had grown out of their clothes, or that the clothes never fitted well. The third biggest group was different taste

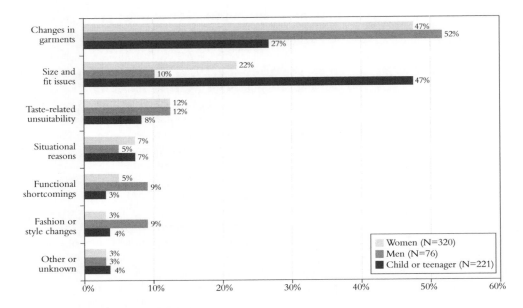

Figure 12.1 Clothing disposal (N refers to number of clothing items in each category)

preferences, e.g. that the user has never liked the colour or style of the clothes. The fourth group includes different situational reasons, e.g. that the owner has several similar or better garments, or that their life situation has changed. The fifth group is called functional short-comings. It includes garments that are described as impractical, uncomfortable, itchy or not warm or waterproof enough for the intended use. Fashion does not come up until the sixth group, which shows that only 4 per cent of garments are disposed of because they are out of fashion or otherwise outdated. The same main group includes changes in own style (3 per cent). This change is often related to cultural aspects such as fashion, even though the owner might not be aware of it.

One concrete example is 31-year-old Fiona's explanation of why she is going to dispose of a pair of jeans (see Figure 12.2):

> These are also old Acne jeans that I have used a lot and have repaired myself. They have become too tight (laughs). I think I've used them a couple of years. And all my jeans get damaged here (shows patching between the thighs). It is a common place for girls, as they have a bit more thighs than men. I used them last year a couple of times, I think. I had probably found someone to give them to. Most of my friends are a bit smaller than me. I thought that since they have been patched, I don't want to sell them. Had they been flawless, I would have sold them, but since they are mended . . .

This garment was registered as blue denim jeans of woven material, 98 per cent cotton and 2 per cent elastane. The jeans were evaluated to be in quite good condition, but with noticeable signs of wear. Apart from the patched areas between the legs, no holes or broken seams were found.

Figure 12.2 Fiona's patched jeans (model Sara Almgren)

The jeans were disposed of because Fiona had grown out of them. She used them for two years and, during that time, she had patched them neatly. The trousers got too tight about a year ago, after which they have been waiting for potential weight loss or a new user (Figure 12.3). Even though the trousers were expensive, and Fiona often sells her clothing, she did not want to sell these jeans, owing to the visible mending. She would have liked to give them to a friend, or charity.

Knowledge of how and why clothes are discarded can be used both to improve textile waste management and to design clothes with potentially longer lifespan. For example, discarded clothing can be used to identify exposed areas where abrasion resistance could be increased through the use of more durable materials, reinforcements or finishing that reduces the friction, thus increasing the potential for longer lifespans and reuse.

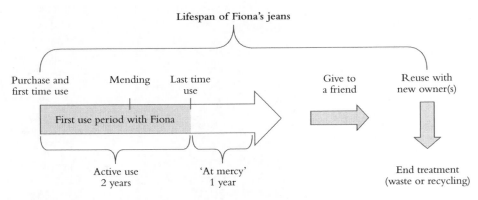

Figure 12.3 Illustration of the different stages that occurred during the use phase of Fiona's jeans

Active users

Repair, altering and redesign are alternatives available to users to prolong the use period of clothes. These activities give consumers an option to actively take part in shaping the products and an opportunity to change the way they are used. Prosumers have always been a reality as an empirical phenomenon, but recent social changes increase their importance in modern society (Ritzer and Jurgenson, 2010). Today, information computer technology tools and networks make it possible to co-operate and share in new ways.

It is commonly assumed that consumers do not mend their clothing any more, but about 35 per cent of respondents in a survey in Norway said they repaired damaged clothing often, 51 per cent sometimes, and only 14 per cent said they never did it (Laitala and Boks, 2012). The performed repairs are usually easy tasks, such as sewing on a button or repairing a seam, followed by mending holes or tears in clothing, either by patching or darning. Amending size of clothing was not that common, as it was often found to be too difficult. Women are more active in all mending and altering activities. The elderly are more active in repair, whereas younger people are more likely to make something new of old clothing. More mending occurs in lower–income families.

Both the techniques and reasons for mending changed during the twentieth century, from very specialized, time–consuming and invisible mending methods to far simpler techniques, where the potential for unique aesthetic expression became more important (Klepp, 2000). Creativity has become a more important reason for home sewing, compared with economic reasons (Johnson, 1960). The trend of participating in crafts seems to be growing in the UK, as evident in the market of craft activities in festivals, workshops and make-your-own kits developed by craft-makers (McIntyre, 2010: 50). Home production continued for longer in Norway than in the UK, and we assume that it has been on a higher level up until today, but we have few comparative studies of clothing consumption and, therefore, no firm basis for this assumption.

Different considerations play a role when deciding whether to repair an item of clothing or not. The value of a garment is considered important. Value includes, not only the purchase value, but also functional, symbolic, aesthetic and exchange value. Favourite items are more likely to be repaired if damaged. The type of clothing and its use areas are important as well. Holes in sportswear or children's wear are more often repaired than holes in more formal clothing (Laitala and Boks, 2012).

In the wardrobe studies, we see what kinds of clothes people mend or make themselves, and how. In a wardrobe study in three Norwegian families, 20 per cent of the woollen clothes were homemade, and a study of discarded clothes showed that 7 per cent of them were repaired or altered, although not always successfully. Less than 2 per cent were handmade (see Amy Twigger Holroyd's chapter, Chapter 25). There is a need for better analysis of the knowledge and motivations behind making, repairing and altering different kinds of clothes, in different countries.

Owners – and users

Clothing consumption is often understood as something personal. However, as we have stated earlier, we base our research emphasis on the way in which consumption is collectively and normatively regulated (Warde, 2005). The collective comprises not only norms, but also the actual use of clothes. An item of clothing can have a number of users. This takes different forms, such as inheritance, renting and second-hand sales and different kinds of shared ownership. It has been shown that the greatest environmental savings are achieved through direct, private reuse, followed by reuse through organizations, which gives more than five times higher CO_2 equivalent savings compared with material recycling, such as using textiles as rags. (Farrant, 2008; Fisher *et al.*, 2011). Still, material recycling is more important in the public debate, at least in Scandinavia. To the extent that reuse is discussed, it is usually in terms of the commercial forms, but the scope of private reuse is much bigger. Almost twice as many Norwegian consumers say they have received clothes from friends and family (33 per cent) as those who have bought second-hand clothing (18 per cent) in the last year (Laitala and Klepp, forthcoming).

Knowledge of the different kinds of shared ownership might help us to understand how clothes can be produced to enable such use, and how we can build on the good practices that already exist. Unfortunately, there is a lack of studies of the relationship between ownership and use of clothes in the household. In a study of sports clothing, we found, for instance, that sharing took many different shapes: inheritance between siblings, of course, but also from bigger children to mothers. For some of the pieces of clothing, ownership was more indeterminate, and they were used by those who needed them (Klepp and Skuland, 2013). Also, in the other wardrobe studies we have conducted, there are clothes that are used by all household members. Here is an example involving socks:

> These are our communal socks. Big woollen socks. Which we share . . . who knitted them . . . it was actually my sister's husband's grandmother . . . who is blind . . . but who can knit like on autopilot . . . they get like five pairs each Christmas . . . and sometimes guests borrow them if their feet are cold . . . so we've pretty much always had one or two pairs lying around.

In the study on clothes disposal, we found that 19 per cent of all discarded clothes were either inherited or bought second hand. This was mainly children's clothing. We also noticed that the owners had more emotional connection with clothing that they had inherited than they had with other clothing, often based on their relationship with the previous owner. These connections can be positive and contribute to more use and repairs, as the following shows (see Figure 12.4).

> My mother knit [*sic*] this a long time ago. I think it was in the 70s. Our dog has chewed on the wooden buttons leaving marks. I will always keep this. I think it is

Figure 12.4 Home-made woollen cardigan

gorgeous. Great colour, nice pattern, just the right size for me, and really warm. I use it quite often, and I have since my mother gave it to me about six years ago. It is like wearing history, it's very nice.

The relationship between homemade clothes, inheritance and repairs is thus an area that is potentially important to investigate, also because it represents different experiences from the marketing perspective that equates new with nice.

The emperor's new clothes

The awareness of the environmental impact of clothes and the responsibility put on consumers increase. But, in this connection, it is important to ask whether consumers have enough information to make informed choices, and if environmental challenges can be solved through choices in a market. Our answer to both these questions is no. In this article, we have emphasized that acquiring knowledge about consumption can contribute to a different way of understanding, thereby also potentially solving the problems, rather than placing blame.

In the Danish fairy tale *The Emperor's New Clothes*, by H. C. Andersen, the king's nakedness was completely acceptable, as long as everyone just thought it was their own fault that they could not see his clothes. The little boy made a difference because he described what he saw:

'The emperor is stark naked!'. Such is the power of fashion, too. Only when everyone believes it is powerful, does it become powerful. To be unable to wear a suit or a dress you like because it is no longer 'in fashion' is a question of what you think others will think. If you think clothes quickly go out of fashion and, therefore, become unwearable, it will not be economical to buy expensive clothes. It will not be profitable, either, to produce durable clothes, or advertise the technical longevity of clothes. Thus, the belief in fashion is important for the disposal of clothes and contributes to their short lifespan.

Improvements in the production of clothes are necessary, both to reduce environmental impact and improve the lives of those who work in the clothing industry. But, to enable more radical changes, we must change the way we think about production and consumption. This touches on more fundamental questions of how clothes are understood and discussed. There are major challenges in the ordinary consumption of clothes, such as too-frequent washing, purchasing too many clothes and clothes of low technical and aesthetic quality. But there are also experiences and practices that are worth bringing to the fore, because they break with the dominant understanding of fashion. Fashion is not an important reason why clothes are discarded. And age might just as well increase the value of clothes for the owner as decrease it. There are two reasons why this may be important knowledge.

First, a focus on clothes consumption will help us distance ourselves from the marketing perspective on clothes, and thereby also make it possible to criticize the lines of thought that characterize, not only marketing, but also journalism and public opinion, often verbalized as how everyone 'else' is and thinks. Research on everyday practices will potentially create other images and show, for example, that there are, in fact, many alternatives.

Second, more knowledge about the factors that help to promote longevity or swapping or sharing arrangements and many other aspects of clothes consumption will potentially be very useful in the work on clothes design. By starting from how clothes are used, and not just what contributes to sales, we will have clothes that are better, both for the environment and for the users.

The combination of the market and its terms, perspectives and projects, on the one hand, and consumption, on the other, provides little room for change. As long as everyone thinks that today's way of organizing production and consumption of clothes is the only way possible, that is how it will remain. At best, consumer research can be the little boy in the fairy tale who so aptly pointed out what the others did not see, because they did not think it was true.

Consumer research can contribute to sustainable development within clothing consumption, but a lot remains undone. First and foremost, we lack knowledge about the actual clothing consumption – that is, what people *do* – such as comparisons between countries, gender and clothing, or consumers with different social and physical abilities, in the following areas:

- how much and what kind of clothing consumers have, and when, where and why it is used;
- the scope of traditional and new forms of sharing, as well as prosumption (repair, alteration, adjustment, home production etc.);
- how the various stages of consumption (acquisition, use and disposal) influence each other;
- how knowledge about the use could be used systematically in the manufacture of clothing;
- how consumers could be informed about the use properties of clothing in acquisition situations (such as expected lifespan);
- how the use could be incorporated as a criterion in comparisons between products' environmental impacts.

References

Buckley, C. and Clark, H. (2012), Conceptualizing fashion in everyday lives. *Design Issues*, 28: 18–28.

Clarke, A. and Miller, D. (2002), Fashion and anxiety. *Fashion Theory: The Journal of Dress, Body & Culture*, 6: 191–213.

Eicher, J. B. (ed.) (2010), *Berg Encyclopedia of World Dress and Fashion*, Oxford, UK: Berg.

Farrant, L. (2008) *Environmental Benefits From Reusing Clothes*. Kgs Lyngby, Denmark: Technical University of Denmark.

Fisher, K., James, K. and Maddox, P. (2011), *Benefits of Reuse Case Study: Clothing*. Banbury, UK: WRAP.

Fletcher, K. (2008), *Sustainable Fashion & Textiles: Design Journeys*, London: Earthscan.

Hebrok, M. and Klepp, I. G. (in press), Wool is a knitted fabric that itches, isn't it? *Critical Studies in Fashion and Beauty*.

Johnson, D. (1960), A new direction in clothing construction. *Journal of Home Economics*, 52: 752–3.

Klepp, I. G. (2000), Fra eggvendte laken til festlig lapp på baken – Råd og teknikker for å økonomisere med tekstiler 1900–2000. Arbeidsrapport nr. 3–2000. Lysaker, Norway: SIFO.

Klepp, I. G. (2001), Why are clothes no longer used? Clothes disposal in relationship to women's clothing habits (English summary). Report no. 3–2001. Oslo: SIFO.

Klepp, I. G. (2009), Does beauty come from within? Beauty and well-being in Norwegian spas. *Medische Antropologie*, 21: 39–51.

Klepp, I. G. and Bjerck, M. (2012), A methodological approach to the materiality of clothing: wardrobe studies. *International Journal of Social Research Methodology*, 'Online First' published 30 October 2012, DOI 10.1080/13645579.2012.737148.

Klepp, I. G. and Skuland, S. (2013), 'The rationalisation of consumption reasons for purchasing outdoor recreational outfits', in Vaccarella, M. and Foltyn, J. L. (eds), *Fashion Wise*. Witney, UK: Inter-Disciplinary Press.

Laitala, K. and Boks, C. (2012), Sustainable clothing design: Use matters. *Journal of Design Research*, 10: 121–39.

Laitala, K. and Klepp, I. G. (forthcoming), Consumers' Clothing Reuse: Potential in Informal Exchange.

Laitala, K., Kjeldsberg, M. and Klepp, I. G. (2012), Trouble with the solution: Fabric softeners and odour properties. *Tenside Surfactants Detergents*, 49: 362–8.

Latour, B. (2005), *Reassembling the Social. An Introduction to Actor-Network-Theory*, Oxford, UK: Oxford University Press.

Lofthouse, V. A. and Lilley, D. (2006), What they really, really want: user centred research methods for design. *International Design Conference – Design 2006*. Dubrovnik.

McIntyre, M. H. (2010), *Consuming Craft: The Contemporary Craft Market in a Changing Economy*. London: Crafts Council.

Madsen, J., Hartlin, B., Perumalpillai, S., Selby, S. and Aumônier, S. (2007), Mapping of evidence on sustainable development impacts that occur in life cycles of clothing: a report to Defra. London: ERM.

Miller, D. (ed.) (1995), *Acknowledging Consumption: A Review of New Studies*, London: Routledge.

Rhode, D. L. (2010), *The Beauty Bias: The Injustice of Appearance in Life and Law*, New York: Oxford University Press.

Ritzer, G. and Jurgenson, N. (2010), Production, consumption, prosumption. *Journal of Consumer Culture*, 10: 13–36.

Skov, L. (2011), Entering the Space of the wardrobe. *Creative Encounters Working Papers Series*.

Toffler, A. (1980), *The Third Wave*, New York: Bantam Books.

Warde, A. (2005), Consumption and the theory of practice. *Journal of Consumer Culture*, 5: 131–54.

Wilson, E. (1985), *Adorned in Dreams: Fashion and Modernity*, London: Virago Press.

13

ACCIDENTALLY SUSTAINABLE?

Ethnographic approaches to clothing practices

Sophie Woodward

Introduction

I would like to start this chapter in a slightly unconventional manner, with a confession: I don't usually write about, nor carry out research 'into', sustainable fashion. My research predominantly centres upon clothing as a form of material culture that is embedded within, and emerges from, everyday life, relationships and wider consumption patterns. The approach I adopt is that of an in-depth, and long-term, ethnographic approach to fashion, wherein clothing is contextualised within people's lives and relationships more broadly. It would not be categorised by others as research into sustainability. However, I was asked in 2012 to write an article for *The Ecologist* about jeans and sustainable consumption, as I had recently carried out an ethnography into why ordinary people wear jeans in north London (along with Daniel Miller; see Miller and Woodward, 2012, for more details). As I reflected on the data through the lens of the article I was writing, I started to realise that this ethnographic approach to understanding clothing practices in a holistic and contextualised manner actually offered important insights into sustainable consumption practices. Specifically in relationship to jeans, people were found to have highly personalised and long-term relationships with particular pairs, therefore not always falling in synch with the rhythms of rapidly changing fashions. Similarly, people tended not to wash their jeans as often as other garments, through perceptions of how jeans look and feel best on the wearer. When clothing is investigated as a set of ordinary consumption practices, through the long-term approach of ethnography, it is possible to challenge assumptions of consumers as fickle or that fashion is always 'fast'.

This chapter will explore how these initial observations can be developed to suggest an approach to sustainable consumption in relationship to the different temporalities of clothing, which dovetails with Fletcher's idea that items of clothing can be 'accidentally durable' (Fletcher, 2012). This will be developed here through considering the potentialities of a practice-theory approach (Warde, 2005) to clothing and fashion, which has so far been developed predominantly in terms of sustainable food consumption (e.g. Evans, 2012). Practice theory entails focusing upon consumption as the use of things in the service of enacting social practices (Warde, 2005). The approach of practice theory to consumption studies within sociology has gained momentum since Warde's exploration of the possibilities of this framework (Warde, 2005); it has, however, thus far remained underdeveloped in relationship to clothing (although see Klepp and Bjerk, 2012 for some consideration of this as an approach).

This chapter argues that research into everyday clothing practices can be usefully developed as an approach to understanding sustainable fashion. It will first consider current research into everyday clothing practices from the anthropological and sociological literature. This work does not tend to be 'into' sustainable fashion, but, as I will argue, offers important insights into how we understand and define fashion, as fashion is not understood as a separate or isolated phenomenon, but is embedded in wider cultural practices. Sustainability is not seen as a separate 'add-on', but rather as something that *emerges from* everyday practices. Second, the chapter will then consider this in light of the framework of practice theory that has been developed within sociology to consider ordinary consumption and sustainability (Warde and Southerton, 2012). It will briefly outline the approach and how this could be usefully developed within the arena of clothing. Rather than see everyday clothing practices as inherently problematic, as consumers are 'blamed' or assumed to be fickle (Cooper, 2010), the chapter will suggest that it is important to understand in what ways people's already-existing clothing practices can be seen to be sustainable, and how this can be enhanced or enabled through design practices (see also Chapter 1). Adoption of this approach, which is not moralistic in terms of what people 'should' do, nor assumes practices to be negative or problematic, offers more optimistic possibilities for future developments. The chapter will adopt an unconventional approach to the literature: although it aims to develop an approach to understand sustainable fashion, it will not focus upon the rich anthropological literature on issues pertinent to sustainable fashion such as recycling (e.g. Norris, 2005). Instead, the chapter aims to be provocative in suggesting that new understandings of fashion and sustainability can be developed through looking at everyday clothing practices.

Fashion as practices of assemblage

In this section, I will consider accounts of *clothing practices* to outline how fashion is defined and the potentialities these approaches have to understanding sustainable fashion. Broadly speaking, they all adopt an ethnographic methodology, which entails attempting to embed the phenomenon in question within wider cultural contexts over a period of time. So, even if clothing or fashion is the foregrounded research topic, this is always understood as contextualised within, and emerging from, wider cultural values and categories such as gender, identity and social relationships. In a practical sense, this involves living with (or at least carrying out in-depth participant-observation with) a particular group of people or community, in order to see the phenomenon from the inside out, as it matters to people themselves. This involves not only a focus upon what is said, but also observations of what is done, which has obvious implications for sustainable fashion in terms of accessing what has been termed the values–action gap (Yates, 2008). Yet specifically here, I will discuss its significance in how it focuses upon what Hansen has termed 'clothing practices' (2005) – broadly defined here as how people select and wear clothing on a daily basis. Fashion is seen as both knowledges that inform the selection and wearing of clothing and also as something that emerges through novel or repeated clothing assemblages. Fashion here is, therefore, understood as everyday practices of wearing and selection of clothing, rather than as externally defined or imposed. The importance of looking at the daily act of women selecting clothing as they get dressed was explored in Tarlo's (1996) account of the act of choosing what to wear in the context of an Indian village. Through looking at how clothing is selected, she highlights how clothing identities are not prescribed by social categories such as caste, but are in fact contested and negotiated. This ethnographic approach to looking at how women select clothing every day and focusing upon clothing practices was developed by myself in the context of the UK (see Woodward, 2007) through an ethnography of women's wardrobes. The focus here was more explicitly on fashion itself as a framing context and as a practice of assemblage, rather than as determined by magazines or by designers. Even 'new' looks or innovations were not necessarily bought wholesale from the shops, but, in fact, were created through novel combinations of what people already owned (such as by breaking the fashion rules), or as old items are recombined with newly purchased ones. Fashion, therefore, always connects with what is already owned.

This raises important issues related to sustainable practices in terms of the relationships between novelty, fashion and temporality. We are assumed to live in an era of 'fast fashion', which can be understood from multiple entry points of the fashion system: the capacities of production, design, how people consume and magazine and media promotions. Fletcher (2010) discusses it, in terms of business practices, as being fundamentally driven by economic growth, defined by core features such as mass production, being cheap and items being regularly replaced. Importantly, although 'speed' is a facet of 'fast fashion' in terms of the replacement of items, it is not the only defining feature; as Fletcher suggests, this needs to be situated within an understanding of the broader *values* that are driving it. This is as true at the level of production and design as it is at the level of consumption. Clothing is not seen as disposable but as a dynamic relationship that develops between wearers and garments, and as a relationship between garments in the wardrobe as they are combined in different ways. One of the core problems that is assumed to exist in relationship to fashion and sustainability is that the two cannot co-exist when fashion is defined through novelty. However, when we consider the ways in which people recombine things that they already own, it is apparent that novelty and innovation are not just the sole preserve of the manufacture of new clothing that is then discarded, if it is no longer of the moment. Fashion is not, therefore, in contradiction to the long-term relationships that people have to clothing. I have discussed elsewhere (Woodward, 2009) how the notion of fast fashion is problematic when seen through the lens of what people actually wear. New items that are purchased are often combined with things people already own, and the frequent shifts in fashion are often shifts such as the lowering of hemlines rather than complete shifts in types of clothing. Similarly, there are 'slow burners' – that is, items such as skinny jeans or denim skirts that, in a long-term observation of street style, were seen to persist over time (Woodward, 2009). By understanding fashion as practices of assemblage that includes items people already have in their wardrobes, then it becomes apparent that there are elements and strategies of current consumption practices that are already commensurate with sustainable fashion practices. This echoes the observations mentioned in the introduction regarding denim and the long-term relationships that people have to jeans, which makes them 'accidentally' sustainable. The durability of jeans emerges here through what people do with them, as an exemplar of what Fletcher defines durability to be: not being an 'aim of what people do with stuff but an "outcome"' (Fletcher, 2012: 233). Items of clothing that are worn for long periods are sustainable when replacement items are not rebought. The long-term relationships people have to clothing and the multiple temporalities of clothing (incorporating both swift changes and 'slow burners') emerge through in-depth ethnographic observations over time.

The ways in which clothing is selected do not, of course, just take place in front of wardrobes, and considerations of how people purchase clothing as a set of embedded practices are similarly instructive. The most significant example of this can be found in Karen Tranberg Hansen's work on the second-hand clothing markets in Zambia (2000, 2005). She focuses upon *salaula* – translated as the practice of rummaging through and selecting clothing from the second-hand-clothing bundles that are delivered there from discarded Western clothing. As her work focuses upon clothing that has been discarded, it has obvious implications for sustainable fashion in terms of how we look at the wider systems of fashion and how it operates, in terms of production, but also, significantly, the redistribution of clothing. There is a great deal of material in Hansen's work that is instructive for considerations of sustainability, yet here, specifically, I would like to focus upon the emphasis in her ethnography of how the clothing people select in these street markets is not reduced to its position in a global structure – as off-casts from Western excess. Rather, by looking at how selections take place, she attributes agency to people, as they actively select and reject items as a means through which to construct gendered sensibilities and personal and social identities, through the construction of particular styles and looks. People make these selections in light of the clothes they already own and their participation in clothing practices, which are embedded within wider cultural practices and values.

Understanding clothing ethnographically entails seeing fashion and clothing from the perspective of the people wearing and selecting clothing, which is important in showing that the meanings of clothing cannot be reduced to an externally defined fashion system or, in the case of the Zambian material, to global structures of clothing provisioning. A long-term, contextualised understanding of fashion allows a reconfiguration of how we understand fashion, as it is not assumed to all be moving in fast cycles of complete replacement. People's participation in clothing and fashion practices is always embedded in specific personal, relational and social contexts. If we adopt such an approach, how fashion can indeed be sustainable starts to be imaginable. It is important to understand local contexts of fashion practices and how local meanings are articulated and worked out through clothing selections. This matters in addressing questions of fashion sustainability, as the values attributed to clothing are never just the values of fashion; they are the values of individuals, social context, communities and cultural categories such as age, gender and ethnicity.

I would like to end this section by addressing what such microstudies can offer in answering the big questions, such as how to make fashion more sustainable. It would be very easy to dismiss detailed empirical work on clothing practices as being so context specific that they cannot help us address the big issues. However, I would like to challenge such propositions by arguing that fashion does not only exist in the abstract, but is also composed precisely of a series of localised practices and interactions at the level of consumption, production, distribution and design. By building up a comparative picture of micro-practices, this is when we can start to develop answers to the pressing questions of our times, such as how fashion can become more environmentally sustainable. A precedent of such an attempt in which I have been involved is the Global Denim Project (Miller and Woodward, 2011). The project was developed to understand why denim jeans are one of the most globally ubiquitous items of clothing, which we attempted to address through a series of ethnographies in several global locations exploring the wearing and consumption of denim jeans. Rather than the micro being seen as a poor relation to meta-theories or the meta-narratives of commodity histories such as jeans, building up a comparative picture of ethnographic work, true to an anthropological tradition, becomes fertile grounds for the generation of new theoretical positions.

Practice theory and sustainability

In this section, I will outline how the approach of practice theory has been applied to understand everyday consumption, and how, in turn, this understanding has been used to inform debates over the development of more sustainable lifestyles. It is not explicitly formulated as an approach in the work discussed in the previous section, but resonates with some of the findings and orientations. Practice theory is not a unified theoretical field, and yet each perspective entails focusing upon social practices as the core unit of social analysis (Schatzki, 1996). When applied to the field of consumption, consumption is no longer defined in terms of differentiation and self-identity construction, but instead as the use of goods and services in the enactment of particular social practices (Warde, 2005). Consumption is understood as embedded within other social practices, rather than as a stand-alone sphere. This is evident in some of the findings from the research into denim, where, rather than being interested in jeans in terms of brands or as fashionable, many of our participants wore jeans as a medium through which to be ordinary (Miller and Woodward, 2012).

How we understand consumption has direct implications for the possibilities of how fashion is consumed, designed and produced through more sustainable processes. There has been a dominance of approaches that see consumption in terms of purchasing decisions, which presume an individual consumer who makes free 'choices' (critiqued by for example, Warde and Southerton, 2012). This has been extended to attempts to reduce the amount of clothing consumed, or the types of thing that people buy, through, for example, the provision of more information at the point of sale. However, the relationships people have to clothing cannot be reduced to 'information' about fashion or even sustainability. For example, within the ethnography into denim jeans, very few people were aware of, or purchased, 'ethical' denim. However, most people owned jeans that they had worn for a long time and with which, as such, they had a long-lasting relationship (which often stopped them buying replacement jeans). This suggests that a more instructive way of understanding sustainable fashion practices emerges from a focus upon what people do with clothes they already own. The ineffectiveness of policy initiatives to provide more 'information' about sustainable fashion comes from a misunderstanding of what the consumption of clothing is. Instead, as Warde and Southerton suggest, how we consume arises more out of routinized or repetitive actions than individual deliberations. So far, this approach has not been fully applied to clothing, as an emphasis upon habit and repetitive decisions seems anathema to our understandings of how fashion operates. However, if we see fashion as emerging from what people do, and that many clothing decisions over what to wear arise from 'habitual' selections from the wardrobe (Woodward, 2007), rather than a self-conscious engagement with questions of identity, then the approach is far more compatible.

An emphasis upon what people do with clothing they already own is one that has been explored by Fletcher as the 'craft of use' (discussed in Fletcher, 2012) – understood as what people do with clothing post-purchase, in terms of mending, wearing and storing, being pivotal to understanding satisfying relationships people have to clothing. The implication is that we cannot reduce our understanding of the durability of items of clothing to the materials and how they are designed, but we also need to pay more attention to how people wear things or keep them in their wardrobes (also discussed in Woodward, 2007), rather than just how to make new things. This approach suggests that what people do with what is already in their wardrobes is central to understanding and developing more sustainable consumption practices. Continuations of and changes in clothing practices do not just emerge from external changes in fashion or policy decisions, but instead also need to be understood as emerging from how everyday life is enacted. These approaches have been developed in relation to food, as Evans (2012) has explored how the organisation of everyday life in the home results in a surplus of food. Rather than being assumed to be a consequence of the wastefulness of individuals, eating is seen as a social practice embedded in everyday life. When extended to clothing, it is evident that developing more sustainable clothing practices is a question of understanding, not only what people do with their clothes, but also how this relates to other social practices within the home.

For too long, fashion consumption has been seen in the popular imagination and in policy discourses to be the domain of fickle individuals who participate in fast fashion as they buy new clothes, constantly dependent upon what is in fashion or what identity an individual wishes to construct. As the previous section on clothing practices makes clear, this is not borne out by in-depth ethnographic analysis. People participate in fashion cultures as embedded individuals, and how people make choices regarding what to wear and buy relates to the organisation of relationships and the social and material contexts of the domestic as much as the retail environments. Practice-theory approaches to sustainable consumption critique the assumptions of the 'throwaway society' (e.g. Cooper, 2010) that consumers are the problem in their fickle desires for new things. However, blaming individuals in this manner does not constitute effective sociological analysis, which, as this chapter argues, needs to pay attention to the ways in which people's everyday lives are organised. This carries particular resonance when applied to clothing, as it is often taken as the cipher of the throwaway society. As research into clothing practices highlights, decisions over clothing emerge from the relationships people have to others and wider social contexts. People have items they love and cherish and wish would last longer (see Woodward, 2007) and often express a desire not to replace things. The relationship between what people do with their clothes and the material properties of the clothes (in terms of both the materials of which they are made and also the way in which items have been constructed) is a pivotal one to understanding everyday clothing practices. The materiality of clothing (one of the core elements of social practices) is one that emerges from both the properties of clothing (the fabric and how it is sewn together, for instance) and also how these items are stored by people, washed and also worn. The life of the clothing does not always fit with the desired life of the clothing, as people may wish to discard an item they no longer like, or wish to extend the life of one that has fallen apart.

Overall, this section has outlined practice-theory approaches and how these can usefully be applied to understanding sustainable fashion practices. The core issues for developing a research agenda for ethnographic research into sustainable fashion practices centre upon: moving analysis away from just 'individuals', seeing fashion and clothing as forms of consumption embedded in everyday life, to consider habitual practices as much as those that change and to understand *what people do with things* as much as what they say about them. Overall, this can be developed to challenge the moralistic positions that blame consumers for unsustainable facets of fashion. In particular, as the denim research mentioned in the introduction highlights, this can allow a more optimistic view of people's clothing practices to explore that which is 'accidentally' sustainable, or, as Park (2010) terms it, the 'unintentional' durability of things. Durability is important as a facet of sustainable fashion practices, in terms of both things that last, as this may inhibit the purchase of replacements, and also in terms of durable relationships that people have with their things. As Fletcher notes (2012), material durability is not just as a result of design, but also of what people do with their clothing. Understanding why certain things are slow burners, and where innovations can come that do not involve purchasing new outfits in their entirety, can have implications for sustainable design and the fashion system more broadly. The relationship between fashion practices and sustainable design processes is one that is explored through the *Local Wisdom* project (Chapter 1), which explores the links between the craft of use and design practices. The approaches suggested in this chapter point in a similar direction. Shove *et al.* (2012) have suggested how practice theory-led research can impact upon product design, by seeing design in terms of how products relate to each other and shared norms and habits. This is a different orientation to design that attempts to change individuals' behaviours or is directive in solving particular problems, as it is exploratory in its approach (true to the ethnographic traditions already outlined) to the practices of everyday life. Looking at clothing practices that persist and also practices that are accidentally sustainable could allow for important synergies between design innovations and consumer practices. This applies as much to the design of garments as to innovations in materials and production.

Future research directions

Although there is a wealth of research into both sustainable fashion and also clothing practices, there is a lack of research that considers the fields together. This chapter has outlined the possibilities of adopting an ethnographic, qualitative approach to clothing and fashion practices; such research can carry important implications for how we understand ways in which consumers' choices are already sustainable and the ways in which these can be enhanced. However, this agenda needs to be developed more explicitly, rather than as just an accidental by-product. The challenge remains to allow the approach to retain its exploratory stance, which is what characterises the research into fashion practices; this is essential, given that the possibilities for more sustainable modes of consumption are embedded in everyday life and ways of living, rather than as a separate 'add-on'. My own personal research agenda will involve considering this approach to clothing in relationship to other genres of material culture within the home, through things that are no longer used, but are kept within the homes as formerly used, or never-used products that accumulate within the spaces of the home – including the wardrobe.

One thing that characterises this research is that it involves long-term, fine-grained observations of what people do with clothes, although the particular sites of these observations are far from prescriptive. Research can usefully take place in a series of microsites, including bedrooms, streets, social locations and streets, markets and retail sites. Although the practice-theory approach that connects what people do to sustainability focuses predominantly upon what happens in the domestic sphere, given that clothing is worn in multiple locations, research can similarly be multi-sited. What is important is that it is not then reduced to questions of identity. The long-term facet of the research is also important, as this can allow an understanding of the persistence of fashion and also practices over time.

As the Global Denim Project exemplifies, in order for ethnography to be able to address the 'big' issues, it needs to develop a series of comparative projects. This is particularly important in the field of consumption, to allow an understanding of what people do in different locations, both in terms of cross-cultural comparisons, and also in terms of different points within the flows of fashion. Cross-cultural comparisons can allow an understanding of the global positioning of fashion practices in terms of global structures of clothing provision. It is important to ensure that these microstudies understand the interconnectedness of people and clothes within the fields of fashion. As the final part suggested, this will entail looking at the links between design and consumption, which will involve a dialogue between ethnographers of consumption and practitioners (of fashion design). The novelty of this approach is that it is one that sees the potentials in people's already existing practices to be sustainable rather than inherently problematic, and seeks to enhance these possibilities.

References

Cooper, T. (2010), *Longer Lasting Products*, Farnham, UK: Gower Publishing.

Evans, D. (2012), Beyond the throwaway society: ordinary domestic practice and a sociological approach to household food waste, *Sociology*, 46, 1: 41–56.

Fletcher, K. (2010), Slow fashion: an invitation for systems change, *Fashion Practice*, 2, 2: 259–66.

Fletcher, K. (2012), Durability, fashion, sustainability: the processes and practices of use, *Fashion Practice*, 4, 2: 221–38.

Hansen, K. T. (2000), *Salaula: The World of Second-hand Clothing and Zambia*, Chicago, IL: University of Chicago Press.

Hansen, K. T. (2005), From thrift to fashion: materiality and aesthetics in dress practices in Zambia, in Kuchler, S. and Miller, D. (eds) *Clothing as Material Culture*, Oxford, UK: Berg.

Klepp, I. and Bjerk, M. (2012), A methodological approach to the materiality of clothing: wardrobe studies, *International Journal of Social Research Methodology*. [Published online] DOI: 10.1080/13645579.2012. 737148.

Miller, D. and Woodward, S. (eds) (2011), *Global Denim*, Oxford, UK: Berg.

Miller, D. and Woodward, S. (2012), *Blue Jeans: The Art of Being Ordinary*, Berkeley, CA: University of California Press.

Norris, L. (2005), Cloth that lies: the secrets of recycling in India, in Kuchler, S. and Miller, D. (eds) *Clothing as Material Culture*, Oxford, UK: Berg.

Park, M. (2010), Defying obsolescence, in Cooper, T. (ed.) *Longer Lasting Products: Alternatives to the Throwaway Society*, Farnham, UK: Gower: 77–106.

Schatzki, T. (1996), *Social Practices: A Wittgensteinian Approach to Human Activity and the Social*, Cambridge, UK: Cambridge University Press.

Shove, E., Pantzar, M. and Watson, M. (2012), *The Dynamics of Social Practice. Everyday Life and How it Changes*, London: Sage.

Tarlo, E. (1996), *Clothing Matters*, Chicago, IL: University of Chicago Press.

Warde, A, (2005), Consumption and theories of practice, *Journal of Consumer Culture*, 5, 2: 131–53.

Warde, A. and Southerton, D. (eds) (2012), The habits of consumption, *COLLeGIUM of Studies Across Disciplines in the Humanities and Social Sciences*, 12.

Woodward, S. (2007), *Why Women Wear What They Wear*, Oxford, UK: Berg.

Woodward, S. (2009), The myth of street style, *Fashion Theory*, 13, 1: 83–102.

Yates, L. (2008), Sustainable consumption: the consumer perspective, *Consumer Policy Review*, 18, 4: 96–101.

14

THE WORLD IN A WARDROBE

Expressing notions of care in the economy and everyday life

Joe Smith

Introduction

This chapter tells a brief history, politics and geography of consumption, told through garments. It explores some changing meanings of notions of 'care' (for things, for people, for the environment). It achieves this through the story of one woman's century-long lifetime of buying, making, wearing and caring for clothes. The woman in question happens to be my grandmother, Betty Howard Smith. She was born in 1910, at the tail end of the British Edwardian summer, and died in 2010, a couple of years into the worst economic recession since the 1930s. She really had seen it all before. Her changing wardrobe guides the story, helping to pick out themes of contemporary relevance from some of the key events in her life. The story is organised around four sections, the last being a discussion of what can be learnt from the story about the pursuit of a more environmentally and socially sustainable system of fashion and clothing.

Paris match: consumption is identity

Betty Smith's family had sweated their way into the Edwardian middle classes through making and selling stuff to their fellow strivers (tailoring in one branch of the family; paint and wallpaper in another). Once they had made it into the middle classes, they were quick to fill their wardrobes with objects that clearly signalled their progress in society. Fashion magazines and department stores would guide the development of the taste of uncertain new arrivals.

The first years of the twentieth century in Britain saw the embedding of mass consumer culture, particularly among the newly affluent and fast-growing urban middle class that Betty's family were now firmly embedded in. Increasingly fast-paced cycles of taste were provided for in department stores that were supplied by increasingly global networks of production and consumption. There was nothing new in the principle of international trade over distances – particularly in textiles. But the scale of flows of goods increased dramatically. This increase was made possible by developments in a range of technologies, from agricultural, to freight, to specialised large-scale industrial production through to steel-framed building construction that could house vast selections of goods sold with new forms of marketing. Developments in print and communications supported the symbiotic expansion of advertising, publication and consumer goods' industries.

Thorstein Veblen (1857–1929), author of *The Theory of the Leisure Class* and the first social theorist of consumption, argued that the practice was valuable to people as a form of display that permitted subtle public rankings of power and wealth. Veblen is a satirist as well as theorist, and, writing more than a century ago, intended to disrupt as well as describe the consumer society that was growing at such a pace. He offered up a stock of phrases that could make sense of the meaning of material consumption that are still circulating today, including 'the leisure class' and 'conspicuous consumption'. The emergence of this leisure class was built on international networks and flows of resource exploitation, trade, labour and innovation. These networks were welded together by the institutions of imperial, corporate and political power.

The display of power was not restricted to the purchase or wearing of the clothes, but also to their maintenance. Betty's family's clothes were cared for by an extravagant infrastructure. Specifically, it required a large portion of society to be employed in service, with much of its time dedicated to cleaning, pressing, mending and carefully storing these high-value and high-status goods. The wardrobe was one significant substructure within the clearly delineated class system. Upward shifts in status were possible, but hard. Once achieved, the promotion would be signalled above all by the cut of your coat, the quality of the cloth and the level of care invested in its maintenance by employees.

Betty's education was completed with a trip to Paris. My grandmother lodged with others in a genteel Madame's home, in order to receive a robust training in French language, food and fashion. This was the home of the most renowned department stores, such as Le Bon Marché, Printemps and Samaritaine. These were innovating in their forms of presentation and marketing in ways that would support the increasing pace of middle-class acquisition, including fixed pricing of goods and department managers with high autonomy. This allowed attention to shifting tastes and individual customers' needs within a larger corporate machine. This combination could both catalyse and respond to changes in taste at pace and scale.

Her wedding photograph, just a few years on from her Paris trip, is a beautiful thing: two people surrounded by well-wishers on the steps of All Saints Church, Derby. She had gone for the sweet-natured but economically modest clockmaker, rather than one of the millionaire twins or her other well-heeled suitors that her training, wits and well-considered wardrobe had presented her with. One of the ways of reading the image is to consider the economy of care surrounding her outfit: hours of craft skill, expensive and difficult-to-maintain fabrics, exclusivity.

However, even by the time of her wedding, it was clear that the wardrobe was due for a clear out. The Great War had contributed to a transformation of relations of class and labour, and of Britain's relative economic status. The Edwardian middle-class wardrobe had required a service class that could support elaborate and varied costumes at the household scale. At the widest scale, it also required a global colonial system of human and resource exploitation. Class and colonial relations, and the household economy of service, had started to be unpicked by the economic and social changes brought by the war. In the 1930s, the newly titled Mrs Betty Smith enjoyed some home help, but the notion of a maid became a quaint childhood memory. Was this felt as a loss? More likely, these changes brought a sense of liberation for the served as well as the servant, with greater privacy, more manageable family finances and a loosening of the social codes surrounding dress.

Making do and mending: skill and care

The second global war of her life arrived in Betty's twenty-ninth year and had its own impact on her wardrobe. The consumer economy of global flows of goods was suppressed, and the resources were diverted into the war effort. The phrase 'making do and mending' has the status

Figure 14.1 Betty Smith on her wedding day

of simple virtue in our present period of economic and ecological crisis. But the connection between global events and the practice of household skills was very direct in her mind, and not simply driven by the necessities of wartime austerity. With freight shipping being torpedoed and goods rationed, this making do and mending was also motivated by a desire to express patriotism, to put on the best show possible and, perhaps also, the need to keep one's hands busy in the evenings, at a time when her industrial home town was a target for bombing. Her wardrobe was augmented with some ingenious reworkings of found materials. Redundant parachute silk (early nylon) was refashioned into underwear, with the offcuts being used to stuff a sagging sofa. The demonstration of skills of self-reliance and prudence, but also imagination and self-expression, in presenting herself to the world must have marked a startling contrast with the middle-class Edwardian household of her childhood, just a couple of decades earlier.

One of the items that entered the wardrobe at this time was a grey-green stiff tweed suit – the uniform of the Women's Voluntary Service. This saw a cohort of mostly middle-class women serving tea, delivering meals and, in myriad other ways, aiding bombed-out families from other towns and cities and also overseas refugees. The social changes wrought by the war in Britain and elsewhere, and particularly much more direct experience of the everyday life of the working class by the middle class, were to have profound effects on politics. 'Democratisation' of experiences of threat, hardship, risk and limitation, the latter enforced by universal state rationing of food and other goods, would form one of the foundations of post-war consensus around the welfare state.

Figure 14.2 Betty Smith's Singer – wedding present? Last serviced 17 March 2000 by Arthur Middleton and Sons Ltd. Estd. 1917

One nation – one wardrobe

Although portrayals of 'one nation' pulling together are exaggerated, it is clear that, during and after the war, some significant markers of social differentiation were being rolled back. As rationing lifted, Betty would often find herself shopping for the same clothes in the same department stores as working-class women. The shift to more widely shared tastes and consumption patterns was felt in many fields, but was particularly evident in clothing.

The reasons for holding obligations to others, specifically those between the middle and working class, were changing. Where Betty's self-made grandfather felt compelled by his non-conformist religion to give much of his new-found, late-Victorian wealth to charity, and much of his time to internationalist causes, by the middle of the twentieth century, direct personal experience of the suffering and insecurity of others' lives supported a more directly empathetic politics. Experiences of the war also made it even more difficult to justify (or economically and politically sustain) the British Empire.

These political changes at home and abroad brought consequences for the makers as well as the wearers of garments. By the late 1940s onwards, organised labour in the UK and other developed countries had won substantial improvements in conditions, and, over time, the women's movement battled to ensure that women experienced these to the same degree as men. There were varied reasons for the acceptance of this new, substantial revision of the Western political economy among capitalists. Investors and company owners, with an eye on the expansive state socialist system of Eastern Europe, viewed this novel social contract as the only viable way of maintaining social cohesion and a political system that would ultimately protect their interests. It also became clear that future economic competitiveness would depend on a well-educated, healthy workforce.

By the late 1960s, the number of items of clothing in most people's wardrobes went up, as costs came down. Innovations and relative price-drops in domestic technologies – washing machines, dryers, electric irons – as well as in the fabrics themselves, also prompted changes. The value to the owner of individual items of clothing went down as they became cheap to replace, more easily worn or damaged. Some items were more difficult to mend, but also skills were progressively lost. Perhaps more influential than any of these changes was the increasing pace in fashion cycles. Photography, printing, fabric and dye technologies splashed colour across the high street.

The woman in the blue suit – technology for good and ill

Technology and entrepreneurship had always been central to fashion. In the mid twentieth century, with its context of a low price on fossil fuels and a high social value placed on widespread access to choice, this resulted in a dramatic leap in material production and consumption. Betty would have shared a table as a young woman with the risk-takers who, in parallel with the innovations in her father's paintworks, were experimenting with new chemical processes that delivered easy-to-wear and easy-to-care-for fabrics. She grew up in a region that had good claim to being the birthplace of the industrial revolution – and textiles had lain at the heart of it all.

Certainly, she was thrilled at hearing of the invention of American nylons – chemical giant Dupont's most celebrated achievement. This was a topic that would light up her eyes many decades after her first pair came out of the box. At the same time, the pollution generated by these new forms of industrial production and material consumption did begin to cause pause for thought. Treasured landscapes that had begun to recover from the coal-fired industrial revolution were now expected to dilute mystery cocktails of effluent. Roads laid out to take shoppers and delivery vans to the department stores started to brutally remodel much-loved street scenes in the centres of towns.

One of my grandmother's most favoured items of clothing was a pale blue trouser suit, probably in Rayon. Produced and purchased at some point in the late 1960s, it proved to be very long-lasting indeed. I recall picnics as a pre-schooler at which it featured. Indeed, I can't easily recall much else she wore throughout the 1970s and 1980s. In echoes of the 1951 Ealing comedy *The Man in The White Suit*, it appeared almost luminous, and it carried virtually no blemish or apparent wear across decades. The eponymous hero of the film, played by Alec Guinness, was an English version of Wallace Carothers, the American industrial chemist who discovered nylon. Guinness's character hadn't fully absorbed the consequences of his invention of a material that was durable, stain resistant and easily dyed: it threatened the very industry he appeared to have saved by never needing to be replaced. He need not have worried: the garment industry resolved this threat by coaxing consumers into ever-faster cycling of fashion, such that the durability or otherwise of clothing had become irrelevant. The low (subsidised) cost of fossil fuels within the economies of the second half of the twentieth century meant that the disposal of clothing carried more value to the economy than its preservation.

It took a self-confident person with a sense of their own style to wear the same trouser suit across several decades. It was usually set off with the same pair of trusty white-patent leather shoes with a sensible heel, and perhaps a gold-effect chain. I can only guess that the suit represented several forms of liberation achieved across a lifetime. The wearers were freed from the corsets, layers and, not least, convention faced by their immediate forbears. They no longer required a supporting service economy to care for its preservation and maintenance. It is more likely than not that the suit was made during the last days of British mass textile production. The labour that produced it was probably decently paid and supported by a robust and reliable new collective system of welfare. On account of her very independent sense of style, and perhaps also her thrifty nature, she put the garment to work long after most of her fellow shoppers had sent theirs to the fast-growing mounds of landfill waste. She might have bought it at the dress shop in a pretty and lively street, just next to the church she was married in. It was, in all senses, a good piece of clothing. One of the last of its kind?

Over the same period that tastes and patterns of use, care and disposal were becoming more universalised, the post-colonial settlement had revised the terms of trade with and production in the developing world. A series of factors fed what became dubbed globalization in the textiles and garment trade. Greater sovereignty over natural resources, lower wage rates, fewer regulatory obligations, gradual liberalization of trade globally, including more fluid capital and the extension and expansion of transnational companies, and advances in communications technologies came together to see textile and clothing production in the global South overhaul the first centres of industrial production of clothing in, among other places, the mills of Derbyshire's Derwent Valley. Despite vigorous tending and mending of her clothes, Made in China, Made in the Philippines, Made in Bangladesh steadily displaced familiar British trade names in labels on the clothes in the laundry basket.

Taking care of things

What the clothes went through once they got to the laundry basket changed enormously across her lifetime also. After leaving her well-staffed Edwardian childhood home, the rest of Betty's life would see her doing at least a portion of the laundry and the mending herself. She had a perhaps unusual level of enthusiasm for these tasks for a woman of her class, and the kit that they required. She also found it very difficult to throw anything away, hoping that items might be repaired some day and be put to good use.

Hence, when she left her large family home in later years she had accumulated what must have been an internationally important collection of white goods, from electrically powered mangles of the 1920s to washing machines bought from the nationalised Electricity Board shops in the 1970s. The pace of redundancy and difficulty of repair accelerated through the latter years of the twentieth century. The pre-war galvanised-steel washtub, operated by hand, could be put into service at any time. I imagine it was handy during the 1970s power cuts. She could still plug in and use the 1960s top loader if there was a big backlog of laundry. However, a salesman today would frankly admit that you would be lucky to get 6 years out of a decent brand of washing machine. New machines can gauge the weight of the load, attend to a range of fabrics and levels of dirt and include programmable 'eco options'. Special programmes allow for freshening of an individual item after a single use, a goal that Betty would have achieved with a short spell on a hanger in the breeze on a clothesline. The new model has more computing power than the Apollo mission that put human beings on the moon. It is precisely this complexity that guarantees its short-term obsolescence.

Conclusion: good value

In the last years of her life, Betty lived mostly in a small room on the top floor of a residential care home, with a view across a valley towards the village in which I grew up. She took naughty delight in the fact that this vast Edwardian mansion had once belonged to the family of the super-rich twins who had competed for her hand in marriage. She had everything she needed within easy reach, in what would originally have been a maid's room. Others laundered her clothing again now, but she kept up the mending habit. It was a good place to go and sit and share thoughts. I wish she were still there to get advice from and do some fact checking for this chapter. One phrase used to describe her was that she was always 'good value' – that is – someone who is very enjoyable and useful company. But she was also intensely interested in good value in the financial sense, and her Christian faith also dictated that values of justice and compassion should always inform the individual's and the community's actions.

What good value would she have contributed to a 'handbook of sustainability and fashion'? The events and experiences of Betty's century have a good deal to tell. They suggest that we may be making a mistake in implying that there is a need to move 'from' unsustainability 'to' a new, unimaginably distant and radically different state. The composition of and care for the garments in Betty's wardrobe over a century can be patched together into an account of a more sustainable life with clothing. Many of these elements are covered in far more detail in other contributions to this book, but they can be shoehorned into a paragraph.

Investing in some pieces of long-lasting quality rewards the maker and the owner. These are heritage items, where the expertise and skill of the designers and makers need to be well rewarded, but the garments carry and communicate value for many years. Learning and practising skills of mending, maintaining and refreshing clothes are satisfying things to do that increase self-respect and independence and that benefit the rest of life. If time and enthusiasm are short, people can spend small amounts of money rewarding someone else's skill in order to keep good clothes going. Consideration for the well-being of the makers of textiles and garments is an obligation upon the wearer. Awareness of the realities of their lives is within easy reach (though eyes are easily averted). The business of buying clothes can be done within a fairer economic system that supports the welfare and striving of people near and far, as the British post-war settlement demonstrated. The price paid for 'good' clothes should permit decent and secure lives all the way along the supply chain, whether it stretches across a few miles or a few continents. Innovation should be treasured just as much as the classic piece. New developments can result in pleasure and surprise, but also less environmental and social cost, if the right priorities are set in design and manufacturing training and practice. Researching the whole life cycle of a product, and stripping out waste and harm with the rigour that economic globalization has previously only applied to cost, will result in dramatic reductions in resource consumption in the production, use and disposal of garments. Price signals that reflect or are driven by changing social pressures and values can be a powerful and rapid way of expressing ethical commitments and a shared vision of the future. Assigning adequate prices to the value of labour and of material inputs, including water, crops and fossil fuels, provides intuitive ways of delivering change at pace and scale throughout a system.

Can we really imagine all of these things happening? To do so, it is necessary to look away from the static political imaginary of the present – one concerned solely with the idea that salvation lies in another burst of impact-blind consumption and GDP figures going up. Rather, it helps to look back and reflect upon the scale and pace of technological, economic and political system changes across the last century. Human beings need to remind themselves that the devices and systems we live with aren't mysterious natural forces to be endured, but rather human artefacts that we can drive towards deliberate purposes. The Edwardian household economy of service, the colonial economy of resource exploitation and the stark class divide in life chances of 1930s Britain were all transformed in the course of only the first half of Betty's lifetime. At the time these changes were going on, some if not all of them would have been met with some trepidation, if not opposition, by people of Betty's class and background, but it is now difficult to imagine that the world could be otherwise.

Looking into a lifetime of wearing and caring for clothes has demonstrated a whole set of practices and experiences that are present today or within easy reach, from care for clothing to care for others through modifications to the economy. This century-long life story confirms that system changes are possible and can be determined by positive goals. It includes the development of personal and professional skills, the responsible judgements of consumers, rigorous environmental protection and guaranteed reward of workers, as well as changes to the regulation and pricing of global commodities. These are ways in which we can, across the space of just one generation, choose to ensure that what we wear is, in all senses, 'good value'.

Bibliography and suggested reading

This chapter has been written as an unreferenced essay, but the following suggested readings are drawn from human and environmental geography and science and technology studies. They have informed the argument and would support any exploration of notions of geographies of care around fashion.

Barnett, C., Cloke, P., Clarke, N. and Malpass, A. (2011), *Globalizing Responsibility: The Political Rationalities of Ethical Consumption*, Chichester, UK: Wiley-Blackwell.
Cook, I. (2004), Follow the thing: papaya. *Antipode*, 36(4): 642–64.
Latour, M. and Weibel, P. (eds) (2005), *Making Things Public: Atmospheres of Democracy*, Cambridge, MA: MIT Press.
Massey, D. (2004), Geographies of responsibility. *Geografiska Annaler*, 86(B): 5–18.
Veblen, T. (2009), *The Theory of the Leisure Class*, Oxford: Oxford University Press.

PART III

Perspectives on refining fashion from within

The previous part of this book presented views on fashion and sustainability from scholars outside the immediate remit of fashion. In contrast, Part III comprises contributions from scholars and practitioners working inside the fashion system, using their rich experience and knowledge as a magnifying glass to scrutinize and suggest ways to reform and revise practices in the field. As a whole, these chapters highlight and celebrate work of a maturing realm of study, presenting an association of frameworks, models, standards, terminology – as well as jargon, specialisms and practices. Simultaneously, the chapters show the shortcomings of these – along with new problems and dilemmas arising from the very strategies and practices implemented. These include the rebound effect, which describes how behavioural or other systemic responses tend to offset the beneficial effects of new measures that increase the efficiency of resource use per garment.

Part III also highlights a discrepancy between the state of practice in industry and the knowledge and ideas familiar to, and now well rehearsed by, the fashion and sustainability research community and among some specialized practitioners. This raises important questions about the efficacy of dissemination of new knowledge and practice to the industry audience; shines a spotlight on the high walls that act to inhibit more radical change (and even that which is sometimes less than radical) that a commercial framework represents; and is an unremitting reminder that, in order to effect change, knowledge needs to be accompanied by creativity, courage and confidence.

A recurrent theme in this part is how fashion, which thrives upon change and novelty, is, ironically, also conservative and unyielding. Alongside a commercial framework, with its associated profit and reporting structure, sit organizing principles based on seasons and professional hierarchies that present effective barriers to advancing cognitive and practical action around sustainability, regardless of the desires of many individuals working within them. Yet what is clear from many of the contributions in this part is that a new generation of action and understanding in fashion and sustainability must not only reside in the pockets of an organization, but must also permeate its whole. Several of the authors call for or hint at a new generation of approaches to fashion and sustainability that live more deeply inside the questions. They do so each with different characters, variously calling for reframing as a new way of understanding the field, or exploration and development of novel and emerging scientific methods, technologies and tools. All draw our attention to a series of complex relationships in the fashion sector and make suggestions for important realignments. These comprise different scales and directions, from the gentle – but important – investigation of past practices hitherto regarded as largely unremarkable; to difficult, disruptive technological innovation complete with attendant risks; to compassionate engagement with workers; among others.

No volume on futures of fashion and sustainability could be healthy or complete without an exploration of the past. **Sasha Rabin Wallinger** (Chapter 15) presents us with a snapshot of the work in fashion and sustainability as a moment in a long trajectory of actions of resourceful production and use of clothes through history. These, until very recently not termed or understood as 'sustainable', can offer inspirations to advance work today and onwards. Her piece also points to a series of historical moments where, in the face of different challenges, such as war, communities have mobilized creativity and skills to make do. This can prompt us to ask ourselves what it takes for such mobilization today. She also highlights how often single individuals (such as Lynda Grose, also a contributor to this book), through their tenacity, insights and inventions, have propelled leaps in the advancement of fashion and sustainability. Yet another poignant reminder of this piece constitutes the persistent interest through all times in beautiful and interesting clothing. This is an important reminder when we nostalgically (and sloppily) hark back to times free of frivolity, or imagine times ahead free of fashion.

From the perspectives of brand and design management, **Simonetta Carbonaro and David Goldsmith** (Chapter 16) offer a sharp critique of superficial sustainability work and green fashion consumerism and challenge us to a shift beyond 'change-as-usual' towards '*sustainability-driven strategic brand direction* and *sustainability-driven brand management*'. Drawing on a range of current industry examples of both stagnant and forward-looking practices, they point to what they see as both a necessary and omni-beneficial conceptual and practical realignment of companies that positions sustainability at the heart of a brand, from which a multitude of manifestations of genuine care can sprout. Pivotally, such realignment can inspire new business models, for example enabling temporary use instead of permanent ownership.

From the world of branding and marketing, **Else Skjold** – a contributor to fashion magazines and current scholar of fashion and dress – takes us to the adjacent remit of fashion media, in Chapter 17. She argues that dominant fashion media, because of a dependency on advertising revenues, cannot critically engage with, for example, body ideals, diversity and over-consumption. She calls for fashion media to represent better the rich experiential dimensions evident in the real and actual use of fashion and clothing, as well as the wide demographic and psychographic spectrum of users. Powerfully, she draws our attention to commercial fashion's 'other', which constitutes the majority of clothing users in the world, yet is invisible in dominant fashion media. She proposes 'style' as a more embracing term than fashion, which 'can work as an overall understanding of what it is people do when they dress, no matter to what age group or part of the world they belong, and no matter what grouping they see themselves as part of'. Yet an important theme of this text is how the low status of fashion (as capitalism's child and assumed female pursuit) in both academia and the arts has isolated it from critical intellectual enquiry, and how this also has contributed to a slow engagement with sustainability.

Two chapters in this section present views on technological advances to support fashion and sustainability. **Greg Peters**, **Hjalmar Granberg** and **Susanne Sweet** (Chapter 18) contribute with a broad outlook on scientific and technological initiatives throughout the clothing life-cycle stages, drawing on findings from a comprehensive research project, Mistra Future Fashion. This offers an impression across a range of fields – from fibre innovation to digital empowerment of users. In accordance with some other chapters in this volume, this one points out the lateness of the fashion industry's engagement with sustainability (here exemplified by late adoption of life-cycle assessment), remarkable considering clothing's prominence in human culture. In contrast to Peters' and his co-authors' broad overview, **Carole Collet's** chapter, Chapter 19, homes in on one particular possibility for fashion and sustainability – that of biological engineering/synthetic biology. A science in its infancy, the controlled and contained growing of fibres, and their properties, harbours potential for minimizing resource use as well as a sophisticated fit with demand. However, imagined new risks include intellectual property ownership, bio-terrorism or hacking, as well as intricate ethical issues. This prompts the author to call for a new skillset in designers and their colleagues: to engage with living systems. Both chapters examining advances in science and technology should prompt us to explore the very role of this field for the future of fashion and sustainability, as well as the ethical, environmental and financial implications of specific inventions and approaches. They also highlight the rich spectrum of proposals presented in this volume – from the paradigmatic to the pragmatic, and from the holistic to the technical.

Timo Rissanen's chapter (Chapter 20) brings us to the remit of one specific aspect (we may assume) of fashion production, the pattern cut. He explores the emerging field of zero-waste-fashion design and reflects on the tensions of working to eradicate waste from one part of the fashion production process (the cutting room) and not others – while perhaps implying it does. With self-awarness and clarity, Rissanen yields important insights, not only into a new efficiency of design and pattern cutting, but also into a new creative dependency between design and pattern cutting. Perhaps most profoundly, this text shows how zero-waste-fashion design can challenge current hierarchies and organization in the fashion industry, exposing and revealing the extent to which unsustainability is an intrinsic feature of the current system, often shaped by historical behaviours; an insight that he also explores as significant for fashion education.

Part III ends with a contribution by **Liz Parker** (Chapter 21), drawing on her long and rich experience of labour rights work in fashion. In this chapter, dense with insights and facts and set against the appalling tragedy that unfolded as the Rana Plaza factory building collapsed in Bangladesh, with the loss of 1,129 lives, she examines the work fashion companies are currently undertaking to address workers' rights in the supply chain. Citing recent research, she highlights the failure of the common code+audit model to bring about significant change, a failure she argues is systemic and strongly linked to financial pressures on factories. Parker envisions a framework, beyond the code+audit model, that seeks to address the root causes of workers' violations and be in service of real well-being for makers.

15

A HISTORY OF
SUSTAINABILITY IN FASHION

Sasha Rabin Wallinger

Introduction

In *Gone with the Wind*, Scarlet O'Hara's green velvet dress, made from converted window dressings, is iconic, but not as an early representation of sustainability in fashion (Gable *et al.*, 1993). Yet, its construction from previously used materials, resourceful design and interpretation of then current styles are contributing ideas in ethical and environmental responsibility in fashion today. One could argue that a reason this dress is not frequently mentioned in contemporary sustainability in fashion is that there is not currently a defined area of research where historic moments in fashion would be juxtaposed with similar milestones in environmental history. Although the two areas of study have been well documented independently, there is very little research that has been conducted in the intersections between these two fields. This chapter argues that the ability to strategically connect past behaviors that influence the contemporary movement of sustainability in fashion is one method that empowers action for change in sustainability. I identified the need for this type of approach during my Masters research, where I recognized the potential of uncovering hidden historical connections and practices that are the foundations of what we call sustainability in fashion, to better understand the dynamics of the field.

The language of sustainability in fashion

Uncovering missing historical connections associated with sustainability in fashion can create a foundation for present and future movements in both fields. This is accomplished by identifying previously unexplored relationships and patterns that ignite new ways of understanding the field. The need for this approach becomes apparent when gaps between the well-documented environmental and fashion histories are brought to light.

One result of a missing historical account of the intersections between environmental and ethical responsibility in fashion is the absence of a shared language for key ideas and terminology (Niinimaki, 2010: 150–162). This has become increasingly problematic when identifying themes and assembling patterns to establish a more cohesive understanding of the field of sustainability in fashion. Therefore, before investigating history's impact on environmental and ethical responsibility in fashion, it is helpful to establish working definitions of these terms.

In short, "sustainability" is used in this chapter as a model for "living lightly on the Earth" in the present, to enable future generations to have the opportunity to do the same (Snyder, 1974: 99). "Fashion" is an act and visual language of self-expression that includes the creation and appropriation of stylish clothing, footwear and accessories to construct reflection of contemporary trends (Cosgrave, 2000: 7). Although these terms have broad interpretations, employing them consistently throughout the chapter will begin to establish a model for creating a cohesive method to link environmental and fashion histories.

Drawing on past tools and technologies to understand the history of sustainability in fashion

Fashion historians estimate that the first documented clothing was constructed in 500,000–100,000 BCE from naturally occurring materials, including hides and furs, selected to offer early humans protection from the elements (Brown, 2012: 12). Although these materials are still widely used in contemporary fashion collections, prehistoric fashions have decomposed. In lieu of these garments, the tools used to develop the early foundations of the fashion system can aid in establishing the ways that past technologies connect to present and future values of ethical and environmental responsibility in the industry. Indeed, museums, historical societies and virtual collections house a wealth of hidden historical patterns that are relevant to present-day sustainability in fashion. One example of these resources is the American Textile History Museum (ATHM), in Lowell, Massachusetts.

Located in one of the epicenters of nineteenth-century American textile production, the ATHM houses a vast collection of tools from the Industrial Revolution (1760–1840), a historical period that prompted radical changes in production and consumption patterns in the US, the UK and beyond. The working spinning wheels, looms, carding machines and pre-industrial artifacts at ATHM simulate technologies used in early American textile and fiber manufacturing (American Textile History Museum, 2011: 1). By tracing the evolution of tools that contributed to developing early fashion systems, ranging from 1810 to 1970, "an appreciation of the roles of the people involved, from inventor and builder to owner and operator, and ultimately to the significance of these machines to the larger society" is established (American Textile History Museum, 2011: 3). This experiential model is one way to establish how past technologies, developed to increase the speed and scale of supply-chain operations, connect to present and future values of ethical and environmental responsibility in the industry.

Through interacting with tools used during the Industrial Revolution, the researcher can also establish a direct connection to what deep ecologist Joanna Macy refers to as a time when "the whole basis of society was transformed, including people's relationship with one another and with Earth" (Macy and Johnstone, 2012: 26). Environmental historians have identified the increased speed of production and the technological innovations developed during the Industrial Revolution as critical milestones that instigated an intensified impact on natural resources (Weart, 2008: 1).

The dominant culture of the late nineteenth century did not express an overwhelming interest in slowing down the technological innovations brought about by the Industrial Revolution. In the early 1850s, fashion became popularized in magazines. At the same time, the sewing machine, invented in the late 1700s, became more widely used in households, both increasing the speed with which garments were created and enabling innovative interpretations of fashions at home

(Brown, 2012: 166, 200). In 1858, British born Charles Fredrick Worth orchestrated a shift from traditional dressmaking by making custom-fitting, luxurious clothing available to clients in his atelier in Paris. This marked the birth of "haute couture" and the world of artistic fashion design (see also Chapter 17) (Brown, 2012: 198–199). Although behaviors of opulence and waste that helped to shape the haute couture ethos are antithetical to the current system of sustainability in fashion, an examination of the history of how the movement became popularized can illuminate key values that are relevant to contemporary production and consumption patterns. One trademark of Worth's fashions was his exclusive and sought-after label, a precursor to the luxury lifestyle brands' emphasis on logos, which peaked in the 1980s and continues to flourish today.

Evidence of missing historical accounts of the overlaps between environmental and ethical responsibility in fashion is demonstrated in the British film, *The Man in the White Suit* (MacKendrick *et al.*, 1951). The comedic story chronicles the plight of Sidney Stratton, a chemist in an English textile mill, who invents a fabric that repels dirt and can last forever. Upon learning of Stratton's innovation, the textile industry fears that consumers will eventually stop purchasing cloth and, therefore, put it out of business. This leads the heads of the mills to persecute Stratton, who represents the ultimate threat to their secure and lucrative industry. Although the hero of *The Man in the White Suit* uses a highly toxic substance to create his ever-lasting suit, the film does hint at issues of consumer care and optimized durability—relevant topics in contemporary sustainability in fashion. Revisiting these fictitious stories from past popular culture can inspire collaborative new ways of reframing technologies and tools to work across industries that may have been otherwise ignored. Film is an excellent medium for tracing the past, because it provides both visual and social snapshots of the time period it was made in and the moment it was seeking to portray.

Tracing the history of sustainability in fashion through popular culture examples

Connectivity between the histories of sustainability and fashion can also be witnessed in artistic movements that influenced both fields. As Biomimicry Institute's Janine Benyus explains: "the first artists were practicing mimics, re-presenting the natural world in painting, song, and dance" (Benyus, 1997: 296). It is, therefore, hard to dispute that, from prehistory to date, nature has inspired designers and performing and visual artists to explore their creativity. During World War I (1914–1918), the Bloomsbury Group, made up of artists and authors including Virginia Woolf, E. M. Forster and John Maynard Keynes, flourished in the UK. This collective, largely descended from upper-class families, prided themselves in challenging their parents' Victorian values. They sought to experience "the dailyness of life" by doing their own laundry, mending their own clothing and making the items they used (Rosenbaum, 1993: 301). The group's experiment of living life outside the expectations of their class system included an appropriation of less ornate clothing, as a reaction against the formal dress of their parents. The group took pleasure in their counter-cultural, free-spirited values with which they self-identified (Koppen, 2011: 19). Although not exclusively focused on environmental activism, the Bloomsbury group members were inspired by their natural surroundings and chose to display this relationship in part through their counter-cultural dress and overtly simplistic communal living.

Designing a lifestyle that voluntarily embraced an ethos of consuming and producing less without the sacrifice of style can be found in contemporary issues of sustainability in fashion.

The Bloomsbury Group's practices indirectly paved the way for another type of open culture rebelling against sociocultural norms, popularized in countercultural 1960s and 1970s America, where there was a "celebration of simplicity, back-to-the-land sloganeering, and endorsement of savvy consumerism" (Morozov, 2014: 1). Inspired by politics, art, and music created in opposition to dominant cultural norms, "hippies" used naturally occurring materials to produce handmade garments, with guidance from do-it-yourself books, including Alicia Bay Laurel's *Living on the Earth* (1971) and Stewart Brand's *Whole Earth Catalog* (1968–1972). These texts provided resources for independent solutions to developing a practical making lifestyle. Both the hippies and the Bloomsbury Group's counter-cultural activism can be examined as precursors to contemporary making and open-culture models.

Another example of popular culture's influence on the history of sustainability in fashion is the American silent film *It* (Bow *et al.*, 1927). *It* chronicled the journey of a department-store shop girl, Betty Lou, who modified her clothing to rise out of her class bracket. Betty Lou could not afford a new gown; however, she understood the societal need to wear something stylish to an important date at the Ritz. As she couldn't afford a new dress, Betty Lou converted her long-sleeve frock into a sleeveless evening gown with just a pair of scissors and ingenuity. Betty Lou's dress modification exhibited cultural values of social mobility, conspicuous consumption and aspirational fashion, popularized in the media during the twentieth and twenty-first centuries. Mending, resourcefulness and re-appropriation of garments, including those found in thrift stores, became tools of power that can also be seen within sustainability movements in fashion today.

Using remaking skills to achieve social conformity and social mobility through fashion is also demonstrated in the American movie *Pretty in Pink* (Ringwald *et al.*, 1986). Released in 1986, it explored class differences through the main, working-class character, Andie Walsh, contrasted with her wealthy love interest, Blane McDonough. The clothing that they each wore told the story of their class differences—Andie appeared in carefully put together outfits she created from thrift-store and borrowed clothing, whereas Blane was only seen in generic, "preppie" clothing, which lacked the personalization that gave Andie her style. Like heroines Scarlet O'Hara and Betty Lou in the 1920s and 1930s, Andie prevailed by making a dress that enabled her to go to the prom, and get the guy.

However popular *Pretty in Pink* was at the box office, it did not represent the tone of the decade's voracious appetite for consuming fashion. The dominant rule of fashion in the 1980s can be summarized in one word—excess. The decade was represented by a full spectrum of styles, but voluminous hair, multiple layers of gaudy jewelry and power suits with shoulder pads shaped the popular silhouette, which proclaimed that bigger was better. Madonna preached that it was a "material world" (1984) and promoted luxury labels, and lifestyle brands such as Ralph Lauren and Calvin Klein drove the emergence of supermodels, leading to a rise in aspirational purchases during this decade (Brown, 2012: 386–387). Although not the prevailing aesthetic, vintage and recycled clothes made their way into counter-cultural fashion movements as a response to luxury brands' call for over-consumption in popular culture during the 1980s, and perhaps it was the contrast to these values that laid the groundwork for a revival of interest in sustainability in the decades that followed.

Socially driven milestones in the history of sustainability in fashion

Historic milestones in popular culture can illuminate contemporary ideas of ethical and environmental responsibility in fashion; however, there are other areas that made an impact.

Humanitarians developed institutions that would later be considered integral to key elements of sustainability in fashion. One example was Goodwill Industries (1902), founded in the US by Methodist minister Reverend Edgar J. Helms (Goodwill Industries, 2009: 1). This thrift store collected used garments to sell back into the supply chain as low-cost alternatives for resourceful or needy consumers. A similar organization, Oxfam Industries (1942), was founded in the UK by a group of Quakers and social activists who also assisted their customers with the growing need for social services (Oxfam, 2013:1). However, historical social milestones in sustainability in fashion were not confined to consumers donating and purchasing recycled and reused clothing. Collaborations between social activism, art and fashion became popularized in the 1990s and impacted the evolution of cross-industry partnerships in contemporary sustainability in fashion.

Artist Lucy Orta noted that her work in the 1990s was inspired in part by "the economic recession, resulting from the repercussions of the first Gulf War and the stock market crash" (Pinto *et al.*, 2003: 38). Orta's *Refuge Wear* shelters were a contemporary interpretation of past camping and military tools that connected to present values of what she called a freedom of movement or "*homo mobilis.*" Orta explained that she took inspiration from "rampant unemployment, [where] you could feel the effects of such instability sweeping the streets" (Pinto *et al.* 2003: 8). Orta's *Refuge Wear* combined fashion and social activism to envision clothing as emergency structures for nomadic populations, for the homeless and for crisis situations such as earthquake zones (Virilio, 1995: 1). This gave a voice to the homeless, unemployed people in need of emergency structures, which referenced the tribulations and uncertainty of the historic US Great Depression.

During this same time period, forward-thinking fashion designer Lynda Grose designed the Ecollection at Esprit, which challenged designers to "look beyond the surface of fashion and discover the social and environmental impacts of apparel manufacturing" (Esprit, 2011: 1). The Ecollection launched in 1992, the same year the United Nations Conference on Environment and Development, known as The Earth Summit, was held in Rio de Janerio. This was a momentous event in the contemporary history of environmental awareness, largely owing to the ripple effects it created in future political, social and economic innovations, including instigating working groups on climate change and biological diversity (United Nations, 1992: 1).

Another pivotal social milestone influencing sustainability in fashion occurred in 1999, when anti-globalization NGOs, labor unions and concerned citizens showcased their protests against multinational corporations at the World Trade Organization's meeting in Seattle, Washington. Opposed to the establishment of trade agreements that compromised the health and safety of global workers, protestors called for fair-trade, sustainable development and attention to human-rights issues (World Trade Organization, 2011). This marked a confluence of ethical responsibility with sustainability in fashion. Professor Marsha Dickson summarized that, "sustainability is the ultimate goal of successful socially responsible practices. It improves the lives of workers, and the health of the environment in which they live for the future" (Dickson *et al.*, 2009: 36–37).

In the late 1990s and early 2000s, amid artistic collaborations and political protests, sustainability in fashion was popularized on the runway, in some cases garnering attention owing to its social causes. While designers adopted key elements of sustainability in fashion, which included selecting less environmentally harmful materials and production methods, they also advocated for socially responsible practices throughout their supply-chain operations. Natalie Chanin's Project Alabama (2001) established regional sewing circles to produce fashion collections that created work for local artisans, a nod to the Mountain Artisans Co-Op sewing circles, established in Appalachia to fight poverty and preserve heritage crafts during the 1970s (Rabin Wallinger, 2011: 14–15).

From past to present: the emergence of contemporary sustainability in fashion

In 2007, Julie Gilhart, Barneys's fashion director, proclaimed in *Women's Wear Daily* that sustainability in fashion was a movement, not a trend (deMay, 2009: 1). In 2008, the London College of Fashion's Centre for Sustainable Fashion opened, and an outpouring of publications on sustainability in fashion also helped to back up Gilhart's statement. These included: Kate Fletcher's *Sustainable Fashion and Textiles* (2008*)*, Sandy Black's *Eco-Chic: The Fashion Paradox* (2008), Regina Root's *Special Issue on Ecofashion* in *The Journal of Dress, Body & Culture* (*Fashion Theory*, 2008) and Janet Hethorn and Connie Ulasewicz's, *Sustainable Fashion: Why Now* (2008).

In 2010, US fashion-design-competition television show, *Project Runway*, awarded Seth Aaron Henderson and Gretchen Jones top honors for their designs, which demonstrated sustainability. That same year, the Fashion Institute of Technology's exhibit, *Eco-fashion: Going Green*, displayed examples of fashionable garments, shoes and accessories from 1760 to 2010 (Farley and Hill, 2010: 1). The exhibit highlighted past technical practices to strategically connect behaviors that influenced the contemporary movement of sustainability in fashion. It did so by organizing the exhibit through six areas of technical adjustments relevant to sustainability in fashion throughout time: (1.) repurposing and recycling of materials; (2.) material origins (natural or synthetic); (3.) textile dyeing and production; (4.) quality of craftsmanship; (5.) labor practices; and (6.) the treatment of animals (Farley and Hill, 2010: 6).

A vital environmental issue that impacts sustainability in fashion today is climate change. The accumulation of greenhouse gases and the resulting global warming have historical ties that pre-date the Industrial Revolution (Weart, 2008: 1). Examining environmental and fashion histories side by side can identify how and when the fashion industry became unable to offset its environmental footprint, in order to create solutions for present environmental concerns. There is also a great deal of information that can be understood from these two histories about slowing down the process of global warming. In the film *An Inconvenient Truth* (Gore and Guggenheim 2006), Al Gore states that, although there is a shared legacy contributing to global warming, there is a shared opportunity to make consumption and lifestyle shifts that can promote a decrease in carbon emissions. This call to action involves a variety of methods to solve the massive problems facing both the environment and fashion industries and it requires collaboration from a wide range of unexpected partners.

The future

Coverage of the Spring/Summer 2014 London Fashion Week ethical showcase *Estethica* (www. britishfashioncouncil.co.uk/content/1146/Estethica) claimed that, with an industry worth of over $237.5 million, sustainability in fashion was "far from being a fad" (Kharpal, 2013). Macklemore and Lewis's song "Thrift Shop" (2012), rejecting designer clothes in favor of thrift-store fashions, reached the top of the US Billboard chart in 2013, bringing the practice of reuse and upcycling to mainstream popular-music audiences. Although these events showed signs of a mainstream awareness of key issues of sustainability in fashion, *The Guardian's*

Sustainable Business editor, Jo Confino, reported that, "until [the sustainability movement] is able to showcase a plausible paradigm shift, then no-one is going to feel safe letting go of the current system that is driving us towards the edge of an environmental and social abyss" (Confino, 2013: 1). Historically, engaging cutting-edge technologies to develop future-facing solutions has a persistent allure. However, this approach may produce only temporary solutions to current issues of over-consumption and dwindling environmental resources. However, it is this knee-jerk reaction to fast-forward to future solutions that has created the contemporary need for investigating overlaps between past environmental and ethical responsibility in fashion and across industries.

Media theorist Douglas Rushkoff referred to the cultural obsession with the future as having "robbed the present of its ability to contribute to value and meaning" (Rushkoff, 2013: 17). Although the aim of this chapter is to argue the importance of developing a historical account of sustainability in fashion, the goal is not to simply call for an archive of past information merely for the sake of chronicling it. Potential applications of tracing key historical values and behaviors exhibited in contemporary sustainability in fashion can be used to bring participants in the current fashion system new approaches and incentives to collaborate, while practicing environmental and ethical responsibility across their global supply-chain operations. More incidents of historic parallels of sustainability in fashion design, production and consumption patterns are evident with each passing year. Courses in sustainable fashion design, materials and communications are becoming more commonly taught around the world.

The ancient Japanese term *mottainai*, meaning "do not waste," and its contemporary resurgence is an example of history informing future trends in sustainability and fashion. *Mottainai* gained international popularity in the early twenty-first century when Kenyan environmental activist and Nobel Peace Prize recipient Dr. Wangari Maathai developed the *Mottainai* campaign in Japan and Kenya to reduce the effects of plastic waste on the environment. The campaign was a success, and the term and praxis of *mottainai* became reused in Japanese culture and was distributed globally through children's books, television programs and exhibitions that showcased the ancient art of Japanese patchwork quilted garments, called *boro* or *saki-ori* (Rabin Wallinger, 2012: 338). The contemporary appropriation of ancient *mottainai* ideas and practices is an example of how a lesson from the past can be applied to contemporary practices of sustainability in fashion, shared with new audiences and built upon to unleash previously unexplored potential. It is in that light that, after reading this chapter, I encourage you to explore the channel of the history of sustainability in fashion that most interests you and share that knowledge with others, to begin to add to the developing history of sustainability in fashion.

Conclusion

Historical examples drawn from across industries and geographies illustrate the many points of intersections between sustainability and fashion. In addition to the examples mentioned in this chapter, there are an infinite amount of areas that can be traced in the past, present and future of ethical and environmental responsibility in fashion. However, one goal of using history in this field is to promote the understanding of the patterns and connections that exist between environmental and fashion histories and potentially develop this new field of study. Therefore, the aim of this chapter is to introduce and begin to explore the position that through an examination of the many historical foundations of sustainability and fashion there is room for new methods and collaborations to be uncovered.

References

American Textile History Museum (2011), Information card. Lowell, MA: American Textile History Museum.

Benyus, J. (1997), *Biomimicry: Innovation Inspired by Nature*. New York: Morrow.

Black, S. (2008), *Eco-Chic: The Fashion Paradox*. London: Black Dog.

Bow, C., Moreno, A., Gadsden, J., Austin, W. and Badger, C. (1927), *It*. New York: Distributed by Paramount Pictures.

Brown, S. (2012), *Fashion: The Definitive History of Costume and Style*. New York: DK Publishing.

Chanin, N. (2001), Project Alabama [online]. Available at: www.alabamachanin.com/about-alabama-chanin (accessed May 6, 2014).

Confino, J. (2013), Sustainability movement will fail unless it creates a compelling future vision. *The Guardian Sustainable Business* [online]. Available at: www.theguardian.com/sustainable-business/sustainability-movement-fail-future?CMP=twt_gu (accessed November 28, 2013).

Cosgrave, B. (2000), *The Complete History of Costume and Fashion: From Ancient Egypt to the Present Day*. New York: Checkmark Books.

deMay, A. (2009), Turning points: Eco fashion. *Vogue Magazine* [online]. Available at: www.vogue.com/voguepedia/Eco_Fashion (accessed April 17, 2011).

Dickson, M. A., Eckman, M. J. and Loker, S. (2009), *Social Responsibility in the Global Apparel Industry*. New York: Fairchild Books.

Esprit, (2011), What we stand for [online]. Available at: www.esprit.com/sos/esprit/what.php?WYSESSID=rpwxnxsg (accessed April 28, 2011).

Farley, J. and Hill, C. (2010), *Eco-Fashion Going Green*, Fashion and Textile History Gallery, May 26–November 13, 2010. New York: The Museum at Fashion Institute of Technology.

Fashion Theory (2008), Special Issue on Ecofashion, edited by Regina Root, 12(4).

Fletcher, K. (2008), *Sustainable Fashion and Textiles*. London: Earthscan.

Gable, C., Leigh, V., Howard, L., De Havilland, O., Fleming, V., Selznick, D. O. and Mitchell, M. (1993), *Gone With the Wind*. Culver City, CA: Distributed by MGM/UA Home Video.

Goodwill Industries (2009), Goodwill's history [online]. Available at: www.goodwill.org/about-us/goodwills-history (accessed July 17, 2013).

Gore, A. and Guggenheim, D. (2006), *An Inconvenient Truth*. Hollywood, CA: Paramount Classics.

Hethorn, J. and Ulasewicz, C. (2008), *Sustainable Fashion: Why Now*. New York: Fairchild Books.

Kharpal, A. (2013), London Fashion Week: Is sustainability on trend? *CNBC Business News* [online]. Available at: www.cnbc.com/id/101032638 (accessed October 18, 2013).

Koppen, R. S. (2011), *Virginia Woolf, Fashion and Literary Modernity*. Edinburgh: Edinburgh University Press.

MacKendrick, A., Guinness, A., Greenwood, J. and Parker, C. (1951), *The Man in the White Suit*. London: Ealing Studio.

Macklemore and Lewis (2012), Thrift shop, on *The Heist*. Seattle, WA: Macklemore LLC.

Macy, J. and Johnstone, C. (2012), *Active Hope: How to Face the Mess We're In Without Going Crazy*. Novato, CA: New World Library.

Madonna (1984), Material girl. Burbank, CA: Warner Bros. Bottom of Form.

Morozov, E. (2014), Making it. *The New Yorker Magazine* [online]. Available at: www.newyorker.com/arts/critics/atlarge/2014/01/13/140113crat_atlarge_morozov?currentPage=all (accessed January 5, 2014).

Niinimaki, K. (2010), Eco-clothing, consumer identity and ideology. *Sustainable Development*, 18, 3: 150–162.

Oxfam Industries (2013), History of Oxfam [online]. Available at: www.oxfam.org.uk/what-we-do/about-us/history-of-oxfam (accessed July 17, 2013).

Pinto, R., Orta, L., Bourriaud, N. and Damianovic, M. (2003), *Lucy Orta*. London: Phaidon.

Rabin Wallinger, S. (2011), *From the Garden to the Atelier: The History of Eco Fashion in America, 1960–2010*. Portland, OR: Reed College.

Rabin Wallinger, S. (2012), *Mottainai*: The fabric of life, lessons in frugality from traditional Japan. *Textile: The Journal of Cloth & Culture*, 10: 336–344.

Ringwald, M., Stanton, H. D., Cryer, J. and Deutch, H. (1986), *Pretty in Pink*. Hollywood, CA: Paramount.

Rosenbaum, S. P. (1993), *A Bloomsbury Group Reader*. Oxford, UK: Blackwell.

Rushkoff, D. (2013), *Present Shock: When Everything Happens Now*. New York: Current.

Snyder, G. (1974), *Turtle Island*. New York: New Directions.

United Nations (1992), UN Conference on *Environment and Development* [online]. Available at: www. un.org/geninfo/bp/enviro.html (accessed June 20, 2013).

Virilio, P. (1995), *Refuge Wear Editions*. Paris: Jean-Michel Place.

Weart, S. R. (2008), *The Discovery of Global Warming*. Cambridge, MA: Harvard University Press [online]. Available at: www.aip.org/history/climate/timeline.htm (accessed October 18, 2013).

World Trade Organization (2011), *Aid For Trade and Value Chains in Textiles and Apparel: Executive Summary* [online]. Available at: www.wto.org/english/tratop_e/devel_e/a4t_e/aid4trade_e.htm (accessed October 19, 2013).

16

BRANDING SUSTAINABILITY

Business models in search of clarity

Simonetta Carbonaro and David Goldsmith

Hope against hope

Many are the reasons to be pessimistic in these times. A bleak black is the color of our future, if we accept the message supported by authoritative studies—for example, the one from the Stockholm Resilience Centre (Rockström and Klum, 2012), which tells us that three of the nine planet boundaries that guarantee the survival of our biosphere—climate change, biological diversity, and nitrogen input—have already been transgressed. Change analyses by governmental agencies, such as the U.S. National Intelligence Council's 2010 report (2012), also point out that, by 2030, severe weather patterns will intensify climate instability, further diminish already scarce water supplies, cause dramatic food scarcities, and contribute to major economic and political systemic changes. These two forecasts, along with countless others, indicate that we are heading toward an imminent economic, sociocultural systemic and environmental breakdown.

From our positions, however, as a strategic business consultant and professor of humanistic marketing and as a PhD candidate researching design management for sustainable fashion, we don't think that this grave and grim scenario is the end of opportunity for prosperity. We prefer, instead, to optimistically consider this evolution-challenging moment in time as the beginning of a transformational process toward new cultural, social, economic, and environmental models of living sustainably. The apparel and fashion industry is not only a part of this transformation, but is increasingly taking on a more relevant, active, and sometimes even a leading role, in embracing and creating the changes that are required to move through and beyond today's challenges.

Changes, ongoing and emerging

The list of established and incipient changes taking place in our societies is long and, we suggest, significant enough to nurture hope. The positive changes taking place within the apparel sectors, and business in general, begin with the fact that a majority of global businesses have recognized that the dysfunctional dimensions of doing "business as usual" have economic risks for their own activities. They are thus engaging in a process of change that, even if sometime motivated by pure self-interest, nonetheless has positive implications for society. Indeed, environmental impact mitigation, corporate social responsibility, socially responsible investment, and charitable support are now *change-as-usual* practices that have more or less become adopted standards, not only by worldwide brands, but also by companies of all sizes.

Coalitions of international brands are openly innovating and concretely cooperating to set global standards to mitigate environmental damage and avoid human exploitation. By pre-competitively developing and sharing indexes and metrics for risk management practices and clean, fair supply-chain strategies, these partnerships, such as the Sustainability Consortium, and the Sustainable Apparel Coalition (SAC), are fostering consensus and, therefore, a critical mass that can produce change. SAC, for example, is comprised of brands, retailers, manufacturers, non-governmental organizations, and academic institutions, whose commercial members represent more than a third of the global apparel and footwear industry business. SAC's focus is developing and collaboratively utilizing the Higg Index, an assessment tool "that standardizes the measurement of the environmental and social impacts of apparel and footwear products across the product lifecycle and throughout the value chain" (Sustainable Apparel Coalition, 2013).

Similarly, legislation is emerging that is likely to impact assessment policy worldwide. The European Commission, for example, is proposing EU-wide methods to measure, to rank the environmental performance of products and organizations, and to inform consumers about that via products' labelling. One motivation for that action is the fact that, "According to the latest Eurobarometer report on Green Products, forty-eight percent of European consumers are confused by the stream of environmental information they receive," but industrial federations are also calling for one single-market, pan-European approach, built on EU-wide, science-based assessments and life cycle analysis (European Commission, 2013).

A continuously growing number of people are rethinking their roles as consumers and starting to declare their readiness to change their purchasing behavior (see Nielsen Company, 2012). After too many scandals and tragedies in the food and apparel sector (see also Chapter 21), consumers want brands to be transparent and responsible, so that they can shop in ways that don't make them feel co-responsible for the indignities of *low cost at any cost*. Peter Drucker's prescient statement that marketing is the whole business, seen from its final side, that is the customer's point of view (Drucker, 1973), has become a reality. People want to make decisions about their purchases with a full understanding of the brands' backstage policies and directions regarding the supply chain and value creation.

Entrepreneurialism in the field of sustainability is rapidly growing, as innovators are experimenting with new business models and alternative product offers that may also be based on access to new forms of financing formulas (i.e. crowd funding, ethical banking).

The engagement with new business models and alternative product offers that potentially reduce the number of new garment units or reduce environmental impact is taking place at various scales.

As the Internet and social media have rapidly increased the transparency of businesses' models and practices, they have also facilitated a number of consumer-to-consumer trading formulas that allow people to auction (e.g. ebay.com) or to freely give away or swap (e.g. freecycle.org) all kinds of item, including garments that they no longer want or need. Likewise, small enterprises' business-to-consumer (B2C) portals now offer rental services for new, second-hand, vintage, or soon to be multi-hand garments (e.g. rentarunaway.com, Mädchenflohmarkt.com, preloved.co.uk, thredup.com, BuffaloExchange.com), which is a response to a new consumer pattern based on temporary use of goods rather than permanent ownership.

Also interesting is the way the Internet and social media are enabling the long-tail economy (Anderson, 2008) via various formulas of e-commerce and web portals that allow a mass of niche producers to directly reach a globally distributed mass of customers who are interested in products that are, for example, unusual or unique, eco-friendly or artisanal, or allow a direct producer–consumer relationship (e.g. etsy.org). B2C portals are also responding to people's demand for unique-of-a-kind garments by creatively up-cycling worn-out garments (e.g. upcycling-fashion.de, globehope.com) and, by doing so, stretching the life cycle of clothing material otherwise predestined to increase discharges to landfills. These alternatives to large-scale, industrial, mass-market logic have the potential to be a new engine of prosperity in post-industrial as well as developing economies.

The challenge of branding sustainability

Although these are hopeful developments, in order for fashion and apparel businesses to potentially become effective agencies for change toward sustainability, they must, just as all other businesses must, confront and resolve complex challenges, including those of branding in today's hyper-saturated markets.

At the beginning of this reflection on sustainability branding, the tenet of today's conventional marketing practice that we would like to put under scrutiny is the notion of branding as the need for the creation, in the consumers' minds, of a unique name and for a company's offer. This belief mainly and merely assimilates branding as one of the tactical communicational tools of strategic marketing. However, prioritizing the strategic dimension of marketing over what one considers just the tactical goal of branding is, however, based on a conception that can no longer be understood as successfully scoped, given that even the "pope" of marketing, Philip Kotler (2005), admits that, "The haunting truth is that traditional marketing is not working."

Furthermore, during the three decades that Carbonaro has been a consultant for leading international brands of the consumer-goods industry, she has collected evidence that most of the companies, independent of their size, do not understand the difference between branding and marketing. Her definition, built upon her practical experience, is that, "a brand is everything a company is"; that is to say, a brand starts from its brand idea, values, mission, purpose, and extends into the promise it makes to its customers, employees, and stakeholders. All this has to be translated and manifested in each and every step of the company's value creation process. Whereas the strategic role of a brand is to keep the promise made, the tactical purpose of marketing is, in essence, to deliver the company's brand promise. Marketing, then, should be considered as the *longa manus*, the far-reaching hand, of a brand, not vice versa.

Today's fuzziness about the scope and relationship between branding and marketing is one of the reasons why brand communication is, for change-as-usual fashion businesses, still following the rules of the persuasive, marketing-as-usual language that is itself based on a consumerist ideology whose profit model revolves around ever-increasing throughput and consumption of material goods. This approach has been used also by many "green" fashion businesses in recent years. This "me too" marketing approach is driven by attempts to reach customers via lifestyle and experiential marketing techniques. The implicit message, an example of which will be discussed later, does not question (hyper)consumerism, as, for example, the slow food movement did and does in the food sector. It simply proposes "green fashion" as a trendy, premium purchasing option designed to meet the wants and wishes of the relatively upscale and well-educated population segment often defined as the LOHAS (lifestyles of health and sustainability) target group.

However, for fashion brands that are innovatively and more paradigmatically aiming at sustainability, including via the power and the role of brand communication as a cultural trans-formational change driver of today's consumerism, the essential challenges are to escape, not only the vicious circle of fashion business-as-usual, but also branding-as-usual communication.

Branding sustainability

Only a minority of fashion and apparel brands, even if they are driven by a foundational aim of achieving sustainability, are today using radical approaches that we refer to as *sustainability-driven strategic brand direction* and *sustainability-driven brand management*. The former starts with, and always refers to, the initial visionary business and brand idea that translates a brand's values, principles, and mission into business rules. This business model is inseparably linked to the responsible ecological position and social awareness of its founding entrepreneurs, as well as their capability to respond to or anticipate market demand for sustainability. Sustainability-driven brand direction is not only important in terms of aligning coworkers and stakeholders within a platform of business rules, but it is also essential for igniting the imagination and sense of responsibility to a company's community, so that old presumptions can be substituted with innovative management methodologies and intrapreneurship (the use of entrepreneurial approaches within a large business), which foster the continuous changes that characterize the never-ending process of understanding, and perhaps one day capturing, the always-moving target of sustainability (Chouinard and Stanley, 2012). As a consequence, sustainability-driven brand management, the implementation of a sustainability-driven brand direction, is understood and run as a way to lead the range strategy, the product design and development, the company's policies and partnerships towards employees, suppliers, and stakeholders, relationship with shareholders, and, last but not least, as the competence that will run the design management of the whole brand communication.

With the above frames of reference in mind, questions arise: Can today's sustainable business models communicate (both inwardly, throughout the company, and outwardly to its customers) their alternative business model and brand by using the same marketing approach, the same design esthetics, language, grammar, and syntax as those of business-as-usual brands? Must they instead go for a paradigm shift in their internal and external communication that represents— *starting from, and at one with*—their alternative brand idea, values, principles? What, in the latter cases, are the exploratory means and routes that give substance to their image and mission? What are the new esthetics of this new generation of branding ethos and ethics?

Established businesses' branding sustainability

Let's observe examples of how established businesses/brand ideas are using the language of branding to communicate their relationship with sustainability by analyzing and decoding some of their messages, and let's extract a few of their most revealing signs from their brand experience offer.

Diesel: cynical branding

Let's begin in the devil's den, with the trendy, street-style-driven fashion business/brand, here represented by mythmaker Diesel. Diesel's business/brand idea is cultish, street-style fashion. Its brand name, evoking engines, oil, and burning rubber, unabashedly proclaims the opposite significance of what one would associate with any green cultural sign. Diesel's brand image was designed, from the beginning, as the emanation of its business founder Renzo Rosso's character, one well known for constantly attempting to generate shock, laughter and disbelief, cynicism, irony, provocation, and sex appeal. This brand character was coherently translated into the 2007 advertisement "Global warming ready," which showed, for example, two vamping women, one lurking, steamy hunk in a black suit, and a flock of vividly multicolored Brazilian parrots in Venice's Piazza San Marco. Diesel's brand communication was a perfect illustration of its business/branding idea: Who cares if climate changes? Cool people will continue to buy fashionable clothing, even in a world affected by climatic disaster. Prosecco! Cin cin!

H&M: fast-fashion branding

We see H&M as the originator of an innovative, disruptive, and democratic business/brand idea to bring *"peu coûteux prêt-à-porter"* fashion to the many people for whom it would otherwise be unaffordable. (See also other views on fashion and democracy in this volume, including von Busch, Chapter 27). The "chic and cheap" business model has contributed to the fast-fashion sociocultural and economic phenomenon. One can argue that the H&M business model is innately unsustainable, because it relies on ever-increasing volumes of material throughput, triggered by brand communication that incentivizes voracious consumption addiction.

Yet, like all global fashion brands today, H&M presents its concern for sustainability and highlights the concrete actions it is taking to mitigate environmental harm and promote social-labor compliance. Its website's sustainability link, though hard to find, provides information about its harm-mitigating initiatives, for example, relating that it is the biggest user of organic cotton, has educated hundreds of workers about their rights, and saves thousands of liters of water. In fact, its *Conscious Actions Sustainability Report* (H&M, 2013) would give any reader confidence that H&M truly values sustainability and is working hard toward achieving it, especially through its dedicated stream of clothing called the Conscious Collection.

Yet, if we look at H&M's brand image and communication, what we see doesn't differ from any other trends-driven or celebrity-driven branding communication. H&M's business-as-usual brand communication, when it is linked to sustainability messages, is often duplicitous and oxymoronic. Its brand image-making is confused and confusing; for example, in the campaign from Spring 2013 that uses Vanessa Paradis, singer, actor, and former spokes-model for Chanel, as a testimonial celebrity shows her in a grand old European drawing room. While off-camera fans blow wind through her postmodern/pre-Raphaelite dress and hair, she is shown swinging on artificial tree branches. In this image, nature is not more than a theatrical prop, and the ambiguity of the total impact is the image and promotion of a celebrity-consumption-driven culture. This ambiguity is reinforced by the tagline of the campaign: "more sustainable fashion." Does that mean that, at H&M, sustainable fashion already exists, and that the brand is harmlessly offering more of it? Or does H&M intend to mean, with the words "more sustainable," that its fast fashion offer is "less harmful" than its other offerings? Or is H&M, simply and conventionally, encouraging *more* consumption?

Patagonia: don't buy branding

In contrast, let us consider the well-known case of sustainability-pioneering Patagonia. Starting in the 1960s, Patagonia's brand direction has been evolving into a systemic business model approach achieving sustainability as a process that requires constant reassessment, evolution of practices, and, perhaps most importantly, commitment to "build the best product and cause no unnecessary harm." Patagonia increasingly evolves its business/sustainability mission by, for example, opening venues that sell second-hand Patagonia clothing; by providing a consistent and reliable repair service; and by creating partnerships with small companies that fit Patagonia's "re-imagination" program, which offers new products made with old or irreparable Patagonia clothes. Similarly, downloadable handbooks for customers' DIY repairing and amending will soon be online.

Figure 16.1 "Don't buy this jacket": Patagonia's 2011 Black Friday advertisement
Source: Property of Patagonia, Inc. Used with permission

Patagonia's concern for today's "environmental bankruptcy," as it calls it, also addresses consumerism in a paradigmatic way: for example, in its 2011 advertising campaign, "Don't buy this jacket" (Figure 16.1), in which a Patagonia jacket was pictured and accompanied by the message, "We ask you to buy less and to reflect before you spend a dime on this jacket or anything else" (Patagonia, 2011). The brand is, in this case, questioning the very nature of consumerism and nudging people to shop in a considered way and only for what they really need.

Looking at Patagonia's website, it is easy to decode its brand scope and message: the attempt to detox people from compulsive shopping addiction by presenting—instead of images of its products—dramatic wide-screen images, of, for example, snowy, craggy peaks, sparsely populated with real sportspeople enjoying self-generated endorphins, while exploring our hopefully never-to-be-tamed planet.

Emerging businesses' branding of sustainability

Let's turn now to what we are calling emerging businesses, those that have more recently come into being in our contemporary environmentally, socially, culturally, and economically crisis-riddled era. The examples we have chosen to discuss are, like Patagonia, approaching the idea of sustainable fashion from a foundation that is formed by brand ideas and business models that are themselves based on achieving sustainability.

Honest by: branding transparency

Honest by is a new fashion brand that is interesting because of its radical model of transparency. Its web-based business/branding entry is a platform for new, quality-driven fashion, from and curated by the fashion designer Bruno Pieters, whose professional history has been with European high-end labels, including Maison Martin Margiela and Hugo Boss. Honest by's spare, predominantly white website is running messages in a friendly looking, sans serif black typeface across the center of a white screen. The brand messages, moving at reading pace, include: "the business of truth"; "being human in my relationships, being human in my diet, being human in my consumption, being human in my work"; "money is a tool for change"; and "everyone matters."

The brand image is based on collections modeled by brightly lit, lightly made-up individuals who seem slightly alien or perhaps on the threshold of a new reality (Figure 16.2). But what makes Pieters *et al.*'s brand communication unique is its extreme transparency. Each product is, in fact, linked to a digital dossier about its materials, manufacturing details, and carbon footprint, such as how much sewing thread was used in a dress. Even more interesting, and perhaps for the first time in fashion history, a transparent calculation of manufacturing costs is given. This rational and open accounting of monetary costs is a bold move: it communicates the honesty of the business promised in the label; justifies the higher than low-priced high-street prices; and gives customer-citizens an additional point of view from which to reassess the material and immaterial value of fashion and potentially apply that knowledge to their fashion decision-making vis-à-vis sustainability.

IOU Project: branding empathy

The IOU Project is an exciting new business idea that stands for a new way to deliver a fairly traded apparel offer via an emotional and affective form of transparency, as well as via an inclusion of customers into the business's value creation. IOU's founder, Kavita Parmar, by understanding that more than 4.3 million workers in India depend on traditional hand weaving as a means for their livelihood (Government of India, 2011), made it her mission to connect Indian handloom weavers, garment-makers, consumers, and her social business into the same value chain. Not only are the customers enabled, through the use of the e-shop, QR codes, and products' tags, to purchase an IOU garment and learn the stories of the artisans working on it at each step along the supply chain, but they are also given the chance, thanks to digital media and social networking, to at the same time act as testimonial-givers and traders for the company. IOU consumers are, in fact, able, through the use of smartphone apps, to also earn commissions on sales generated through their own virtual trunk, shown over their social networks.

WomenWeave: in search of branding

The charitable organization WomenWeave's social enterprises, Gudi Mudi and Khatkhata enterprises, aim to make the world a better place by (co)developing, making, and marketing what could be called fashion-relevant, artisanal, textile products, made by craftspeople living in artisan-rich locations such as Columbia, Guatemala, Thailand, or, in this case, India.

Figure 16.2 Honest by

In connection with sustainable fashion, handcrafted products symbolize alternative choices, but may also provide tangible benefits, such as low energy use during production, manageable production systems, and the "emotional durability" that Chapman (2005) suggests would help consumers form longer-lasting (less promiscuous) relationships with their garments. The brand mission is to make handloom a "profitable, fulfilling, sustainable and dignified income-earning activity particularly for women in rural areas of India" (WomenWeave, 2012), and it does so by training people to produce and sell what Goldsmith, in his research practice, refers to as *naya khadi*: modern, color-rich, and playful versions of the plain homespun khadi that Gandhi promoted and Indians used as a tool to achieve India's independence.

WomenWeave's website's splash page shows lush close-ups of its product and process: handwoven cottons dyed with madder, pomegranate, eucalyptus, indigo, and iron; a pair of elegant female hands at the loom, tying a broken cotton warp thread. These views and others feel on the pulse of a new, slow fashion esthetic of the sort that might be viewed in tomorrow's Trend Union presentation. Positioned on the *de rigueur* white background, the images are surrounded by simple and generic grey links to Products, About us, Events, and Media. Beside a handful of mechanical issues and navigation inconsistencies, the site is straightforward and clear. However, the website underserves WomenWeave's known sustainability-driven vision and new enterprise model by not yet having developed a powerful visual or verbal design grammar that would clarify its means and message, as have related new handloom enterprises, such as IOU Project, which presents its story and style quickly, cleanly, and with humor, or LemLem, whose garments are easily recognized by their striped patterns, neon accents, and simple shapes.

Merci: thank you for caring branding

Merci is a charity concept store in Paris whose brand image is perceived as "lovely, lovable, and loving" (My Little Paris, n.d.). Its business profits support an endowment for women's and children's education in Madagascar (Merci, 2013) and offers an eclectic range of clothing, home furnishings, flowers, food, and more, including a quota of items that brands, designers, and celebrities are donating. Merci's brand communication, from its in-store visual merchandising to its website, is enlivening and artful. The architecture and displays are nothing like the shambled interiors of yesterday's charity shops, such as the Salvation Army or Goodwill. They are on a par esthetically with upscale concept stores, such as Colette, also in Paris, 10 Corso Como, in Milan, or Dover Street Market, in London, New York, and Tokyo.

Merci's brand message is the upscalization of the esthetics of consumption linked with philanthropy. It is, in fact, through the contributions of artists, designers, and "avant-crafter", that the company is addressing the values of sentiment-driven consumers, who are, today more than ever, striving to find the Ariadne thread that will enable them to contribute to the restoration of our environment and fraying social fabric. This new esthetics of philanthropy is what lets shopper-donors feel part of the cultural–creative community, described by Ray and Anderson (2001) as those who strive for beauty, want to be involved in creating a new and better way of life, but also want to feel good while doing good.

Researching sustainability-driven business and branding

The quick sketches above—of Patagonia's strive toward purity; H&M's attempts toward mitigation; Honest by's faith in transparency; IOU's belief in the power of affective and effective relationship; WomenWeave's social activism; and Merci's new esthetics of altruism—represent some of the most coherent and/or transformative approaches that fashion enterprises are taking toward sustainability, business, and branding. Each case illustrates seemingly valid brand directions and practices that simultaneously show that extensive research is needed, in both the deductive/measurable and inductive/unquantifiable realms, to understand what effects these innovations are having and what could be done to take them further.

We suggest three areas to prioritize in order to establish a fundamental platform of knowledge. First, we must work to fill the gap between the macro level of sustainability-marketing theory and the micro level of sustainability-driven fashion business and branding. How has what has been speculated upon been implemented in practice? How can what is known from experience be infused into research? Second, there is a lack of basic interdisciplinary research investigating if and how the emerging sustainability-driven businesses are changing, via their brand idea and communication, our notions of fashion and fashion consumerism. Little is clear about how they are, or are not, shifting social values, building a new esthetics of ethics, and changing consumer patterns toward the sustainable. Finally, we must engage in semiotic research, such as we have merely rudimentally begun with our examples, to interpret, then beneficially utilize and develop, the signifiers/forms and the signified/meanings that are being expressed by the new wave of sustainability-driven brand communication cases.

Practical advice

With regard to the above-mentioned needed directions for marketing research, we refer to an orientative contribution made by Belz and Peattie (2009). Their categorization of the fundamental eight tenets of sustainability branding provides a consistent direction for both theorists and practitioners. Their "eight Cs" start with the sustainability of companies' *core business*, which must be based on *cooperative* formulas that define their supply- and value-chain creation. They have to be *credible* and substantiate real *consumer benefits*. Their branding communication should not be monological, but must be *conversational*, that is, based on two-way interactions. Finally, it must have *consistency* in its ways of demonstrating *commitment* and *continuity*.

The complexity deriving from the interplay among these sustainability-branding tenets compels us to add to Belz and Peattie's eight Cs still another "C", for *clarity*, because sustainable businesses, in order to move forward, need to become crystal clear in their branding and marketing approach. That implies being certain about the fact that we must free ourselves from the confusing sophistication of postmodern communication that is obsessed with the most extravagant latest lifestyle or eccentric experiential marketing trend, but has no clue about the grammar and syntax of a new and pure language that simply expresses what really matters. Sustainability-driven businesses/brands must scrape off all the encrustations of conventional marketing language that has blanketed us in signifiers that don't clothe our bodies, but rather engage us in an endless game of deconstruction and reconstruction of the same rhetorical questions—a dead end game that Benjamin, in *The Arcades Project* (2002), described as the endless return of apparent novelty.

References

Anderson, C. (2008), *The Longer Long Tail: The Revised and Updated Edition: Why the Future of Business Is Selling Less of More*. New York: Hyperion.

Belz, F.-M. and Peattie, K. (2009), *Sustainablity Marketing: A Global Perspective*. New York: Wiley.

Benjamin, W. (2002), *The Arcades Project*. Trans. Eiland, H. Cambridge, MA: Belknap Press.

Chapman, J. (2005), *Emotionally Durable Design: Objects, Experiences and Empathy*. London: Routledge.

Chouinard, Y. and Stanley, V. (2012), *The Responsible Company: What We've Learned from Patagonia's First 40 Years*. Ventura, CA: Patagonia Books.

Drucker, P. (1973), *Top Management*. London: Heinemann.

European Commission (2013), *Environment: Helping Companies and Consumers Navigate the Green Maze*. European Union.

Government of India (2011), *Annual Report 2011–2012*. Delhi: Ministry of Textiles.

H&M (2013), *Conscious Action Sustainability Report 2012*. Stockholm: H&M.

Kotler, P. (2005) Preface, in Tybout, A. M. and Calkins, T. (eds) *Kellogg on Branding*. New Jersey: John Wiley: ix.

Merci (2013), The Company [online]. Available at: www.merci-merci.com/en/the-company.html (accessed July 7, 2013).

My Little Paris (n.d.), Merci, yes, but who? [online]. Available at: www.mylittle.fr/mylittleparis/en/concept-store-paris.html (accessed July 7, 2013).

National Intelligence Council (2012), *Global Trends 2030: Alternative Worlds*. Washington, DC: Government of the USA, Office of the Director of National Intelligence.

Nielsen Company (2012), *The Global Socially-Conscious Consumer*. New York: Nielsen.

Patagonia (2011), Don't buy this jacket. [online]. Available at: www.patagonia.com/email/11/112811.html (accessed July 7, 2013).

Ray, P. H. and Anderson, S. R. (2001), *The Cultural Creatives: How 50 Million People Are Changing the World*. New York: Broadway Books.

Rockström, J. and Klum, M. (2012), *The Human Quest: Prospering Within Planetary Boundaries*. Stockholm: Langenskiölds.

Sustainable Apparel Coalition (2013), The Higg Index [online]. Available at: www.apparelcoalition.org/higgindex/ (accessed December 16, 2013).

WomenWeave (2012) About us [online]. WomenWeave Charitable Trust. Available at: www.women weave.org/# (accessed July 7, 2013).

17

TOWARDS FASHION MEDIA
FOR SUSTAINABILITY

Else Skjold

This chapter presents an outline of the history and development of fashion media as cultural product, emphasising how cultural and economic currents in Western society have shaped the format. Furthermore, fashion media are perceived as cultural production from a systemic perspective, highlighting how institutionalised practices that have been developed around fashion media are inherently counter-productive in terms of sustainability. On the basis of this, I will argue how fashion media can be powerful formats for developing more sustainable role models and practices in the future, if the formats are pushed in new directions within the existing framework.

I write this as a former contributor to fashion magazines and as a scholar of fashion and dress. My research is positioned between cultural studies, consumer anthropology and design research, where I focus on the everyday interaction between people and dress objects through the so-called 'wardrobe method' (Skjold, 2014). Looking into this, I find how there is a discrepancy between people's rich and multifaceted experiences of dressing, and the consumerist logic represented in fashion media as they exist today. I therefore suggest developing new typologies of fashion media that embrace people's actual sensory and experiential levels of dressing, by pushing the envelope of media from within.

To highlight how the current practices around fashion media production represent a barrier to sustainability issues, I will follow the argument of Moeran that: 'we need to take account, as best we can, of the *total* social processes surrounding the representation, distribution (circulation) and reception (consumption) of such cultural products [the fashion media], as of the products themselves' (Moeran, 2003: 2).

The development of fashion media – a historic outline

It is not possible to separate the history of fashion media from that of fashion.

As widely agreed among scholars, the development of European fashion saw its beginning in the Burgundian courts in the fourteenth century (Lönnqvist, 2010). Over the centuries, the dissemination of new fashions between the various European courts increased (Breward, 2007). As stated by Simmel, it became inherent in the nature of fashion that it is disseminated from fashion leaders and emanates outwards – hence, his 'trickle-down theory' (Carter, 2003: 69). The production and consumption of fashion were already, at this point, markers of status, not only for the individual, but also for regions, their governmental institutions and respective industries. Still today, regardless of whether new fashions and trends 'trickle down', 'bubble up' (Polhemus, 1994) or 'trickle across' (Blumer, 1969), they always have a centre and a periphery. Some wearers take the lead, and others follow. This explains how an important element in fashion media is embodied in the *style icon*, as this figure represents shifting structures of dominance; whereas fashion once conveyed the supposed 'civilized' West, it now displays the 'fashion capital' of individuals in powerful regions of the world, and shifting style icons have reflected this, from members of the courts, to the models and celebrities of our time.

The first fashion journals emerged in France in the late eighteenth century. Their appearance marked a widening of fashion's audience, from the aristocracy to the rising class of the bourgeoisie. Women of the new powerful class of the dawning industrialism read about new styles and trends in journals such as *Buissons Cabinet des Modes* (1758–91), *Le Journal des Dames et des Modes* (1797–1837), *La Mode* (1829–62), *Le Follet* (1829–82) or *Le Petit Courrier des Dames* (1821–69) (Nørgaard, 2002: 252; Best, 2010). Already at this point, a hierarchy of fashion was established, which made France, and particularly Paris, the epicentre of fashion activity. The emergence of these journals reflected how the French began promoting their textile and cloth industry as part of political power games in Europe during the eighteenth century (Parmal, 2006). However, in the aftermath of the French Revolution, Britain took over the lead of menswear production, leaving the French to dominate the production of women's garments (Hollander, 1994).

In this division of the European fashion industry, fashion became culturally embedded in our ideas of femininity, as it reflected the strong dichotomisation that took place between genders in the period: while menswear was perceived as 'rational' and measurable, celebrating core values in the technological rise of the century, fashion and women were perceived as strangely irrational, yet seductive creatures (Hollander, 1994). The style icons of the time were courtisanes, *grand dames* of high society (Davis, 1994: 146), and later the mysterious *la passante* in the new urban life (Baudelaire, 1860, in Rocamora, 2009), embodying a 'to-be-looked-at-ness', as later phrased by Mulvey (2003: 52). Moeran highlights how fashion magazines are still, to a great extent, produced according to the sociological divide between genders emerging in this period. He states how fashion magazines are, on the one hand, commodities, a publishing site for advertising, sales and hard business, typically taken care of by men. On the other hand, they are cultural products, whose editorial content on fashion, beauty and health is produced mostly by women, to circulate in the cultural economy (Moeran, 2003: 3).

Throughout the twentieth century, this legacy still influenced both the development of the format itself and the practices and institutions creating it. The naturalisation of Paris as the centre of fashion was continued, even if the cities of Milan, London and New York evolved as other dominant 'clusters' of fashion during the twentieth century (Kawamura, 2005; Best, 2010; Skov, 2011a). Rocamora has shown how both the imagery and rhetoric of fashion magazines are still deeply influenced by the legacy of Paris, as all fashion media inscribe themselves in an inherently French 'fashion discourse', consisting of fashion commodities, practices, agencies and the physical space and history of Paris itself (Rocamora, 2009). Even with the current plurality of media, they all still seem to adopt the same discourse and French *esprit*, although with adjustments and variations. Yet, the American launch of *Harper's Bazaar* (1867) and *Vogue* (1892) represented a challenge to the dominance of Paris as fashion capital. In this shift, the fashion media linked the legacy of the powerful textile and fashion industry of the 'old world', in Paris, and the epicentre of all that was modern, the 'new world', America. This happened as movie stars of Babel, later Hollywood, were promoted as style icons in magazines such as *Vanity Fair* (1913), *La Gazette du Bon Ton* (1915), or *Jardin des Modes* (1922). The glamour of these magazines was counterweighted by later magazines such as *Marie Claire* (1937), labelled 'the poor woman's *Vogue*' (Best, 2010: 148). The format continued to produce new sub-typologies, placing themselves between an art-like approach for the well off and a more pragmatic approach for the less affluent. General distinctions are 'domestic weeklies', 'young women's weeklies', 'glossies' or 'gossip magazines' (Rocamora, 2009: 61; Moeran, 2010). Regardless of the type of magazine concerned, celebrity culture and fashion media entered a close liaison in the early twentieth century that is still hard to separate. Hence, the emerging beauty industry, the advertising and, later, trend industry, the movie industry and the fashion industry, with all their agencies, institutionalised rituals, gate-keepers and power centres, started co-operating. The reputation of fashion as being 'capitalism's child' was cemented here, because it became really difficult to distinguish between what was actually editorial content and what were advertisements of products (Moeran, 2003).

In the era of post-industrialism, the production and consumption of fashion magazines have been widened once again, causing new sub-typologies to evolve. First of all, men's fashion magazines have developed throughout the twentieth century. From being, originally, journals on male etiquette and immaculate dressing, such as the British *The Gentleman's Magazine* (1731–1914), they entered the 'fashion discourse' described by Rocamora (2009). As this is highly delicate, because of fashion's strong female connotations, men's fashion magazines often 'cover up' traditional magazine contents, such as fashion, beauty and health, with overly masculine issues, such as soft pornographic material, sports or mechanical gadgets. In this respect, the development of men's fashion magazines mirrors the development of masculine ideals throughout the late twentieth century (Gauntlett, 2002). In early-twentieth-century magazines such as *Esquire* (1933) or *Gentleman's Quarterly* (1957, later *GQ*, 1983), male models would embody the more traditionally masculine, 'international style' of dressing and behaving, whereas an increasing variation of male types and masculinities would be represented throughout the boom of magazines that emerged during the 1980s and 1990s, with 'lad' magazines such as *Arena* (1980), *Loaded* (1994), *FHM* (1996) or *Maxim* (1995), and, later, more fashion-oriented ones such as *V Man* (2003), *Men's Vogue* (2005) or *AnOther Man* (2005) (Skjold, 2010).

Another important development in the production and consumption of fashion magazines has happened as fashion is increasingly entering the realms of art, which has produced what Lynge-Jorlén calls 'niche fashion magazines', where art and fashion overlap (Lynge-Jorlén, 2012). These magazines developed from the British 'youth quake' in the 1960s and continued with the punk and DIY scene of the 1980s and the techno scene of the 1990s. Emerging out of subculture's 'guerilla warfare' on mainstream culture (Hebdige, 1979; Hodkinson, 2002), magazines such as *i-D* (1980), *the Face* (1980) or *Dazed & Confused* (1991) draw on anti-fashion's virtues of subversion, avant-garde ideas and opposition. These magazines oppose dominant ideas about power, ethnicity and gender, as they display alternative beauty ideals, dress styles and approaches to life to what is to be seen in mainstream fashion magazines. Closely connected with these magazines are 'art fashion magazines' (Lynge-Jorlén, 2012), such as *Visionaire* (1991), *Purple* (1996), *Self Service* (1993) or *AnOther Magazine* (2001), which are produced 'for and by industry creatives' (Breward, 2007: 281).

Last but not least, the blogging explosion of the twenty-first century has produced new formats for the production and consumption of fashion media. However, they continue to be 'a kinetic, continuous sequence of textual and pictorial information', like magazines on print (Breward, 2007: 279). But, as pointed out by Rocamora, the sequence is no longer linear; it is hypertextual, wild growing and works by mediating links to other websites in a continuing, rhizomic process (Rocamora, 2011). In spite of the immense democratic potential of the web, fashion blogs are often surprisingly conservative in their content, mimicking the established 'fashion discourse'.

Still, the wild-growing 'bloggersphere' has shaken up the power structures of fashion media severely, but hitherto only to replace known and experienced fashion editors with young and less experienced ones. Perhaps the one real change that has occurred seems to be that now, as opposed to earlier, information about new trends is disseminated with more feverish haste than before.

This reflects fashion's inherent logics, shaped by industrialism and modernity, and, hereby, also logics of economic growth at all costs, which must be questioned in a sustainability context (Baudrillard, 1999 [1970]; Cooper, 2005). Furthermore, there have been surprisingly few examples of democratic development in fashion media, in spite of the technological possibilities the web offers. Fashion might have become more polycentric (Davis, 1994), but it is still industrialist, and Parisian at heart. This is why fashion media are still mainly promoting Western standards, over-consumption, non-equality of gender and ethnicity, and power imbalance. And this is also why it is time to start looking for typologies that could push the format in other directions.

Learning from art magazines

As perfectly tuned vehicles of modernity, fashion images have shown us how to look, move and think about life throughout the last centuries. They have *adorned us in dreams*, as so precisely formulated by Wilson (1986). Photographers, stylists, beauty and fashion editors have created this imagery in collaboration with contemporary artists; from Dali, Cocteau and Schiaparelli from the early European avant-garde, to glamorous movie stars of Hollywood or pop and rock artists, over to new realists such as Corinne Day and Wolfgang Tillmanns, the elite of art and pop culture have worked in close liaisons with fashion media. What I wish to address here is how fashion media might be turned into vehicles for sustainable approaches to fashion and dressing, providing that new typologies are developed that carry with them an inherent arm's-length distance from the industry. It is my argument that a possible template for such typologies might be found in the format of the art magazine, with its inherent critical approach to commercial agendas. In other words, fashion media might win more critical potential by approaching the practices of the art world.

It was Barthes (1983, 2006) who defined fashion journalism as 'written fashion' – how language works as a semiological 'shifter' that turns a given dress object into a fashionable object of desire. I will argue here how this kind of journalism, as it is widely practised in current fashion media today, represents a barrier to sustainability. As much of the production of fashion magazines is financed through advertisements, it becomes very difficult indeed for a given editorial staff to take a stand and produce a kind of journalism in these media that can really criticise behaviours such as over-consumption. Hence, matters of sustainability, for example, are treated as add-on value or 'greenwashing' of doing business as usual (Black, 2013). It is this schism that Moeran refers to using the term 'service journalism': a type of journalism that is non-critical of the industry, and its inherent logics of growth, which produces fashion clothing, as Baudrillard phrases it, 'with an eye to its death', not for its 'use value or its possible durability' (1999 [1970]: 46). Hence, the main aim of much fashion journalism seems to be a critiqueless presentation of the 'moods' and trends of the season, in the shape of new stuff to buy.

One important explanation for this journalistic practice is that fashion has been isolated from critical intellectual enquiry, because of its low status in both academia and the hierarchy of the arts (Taylor, 2002; Skov, 2010). Hence, fashion journalism simply corresponds very little with overall public debates on the connection between objects, experiences and culture. It seems to have developed in a kind of cultural vacuum, where a particular language, structure and self-understanding have been nurtured that do not correspond very well with general critical debates on, for example, sustainability issues. Therefore, an important step to develop more critical journalism in the area of fashion is to increase education and knowledge in the field, and to appreciate fashion as an aesthetic field in the line of art, films, literature, music and other design forms. This is starting to happen with the academisation of design schools and the emergence of educational programmes at universities and business schools, all over the world (Skjold, 2008; Kawamura, 2011), just as the scholarly areas of fashion studies (McRobbie, 1998) and 'new museology' (Anderson, 2000) argue how fashion is rising in the hierarchies of the arts, positioning itself as an important contemporary art form.

In many respects, a parallel can be drawn with the public debate on films, once this topic became a 'serious' object of research. With the rising popularity of film and media studies at universities 20–25 years ago, films went from lowbrow to highbrow culture, which is why it is generally debated in a broader intellectual, technical and societal perspective. Scholarly approaches to the topic are manifold and continue to bring new insights to the production and consumption of films. The development of film's intellectual, cultural and creative position in society continues, however, to co-exist with an obsession with celebrity, appearance and mono-logical beauty ideals, as evidenced by red-carpet performances at film festivals. But, even if the film industry is heavily commercialised, it is still generally referred to as an important art form in contemporary culture. Could this level of public debate be developed with regard to fashion, and what would it take to move the media in this direction?

As mentioned before, niche fashion magazines such as the art fashion magazine could help push the envelope for a kind of critical fashion journalism that would correspond to the writing in art, film and design magazines. An attempt on this can be seen in the Norwegian *Personae*, a biannual magazine based on the template of the film or art magazine, covering issues such as 'religion and rituals' (December 2011) (see Figure 17.1). According to its website, its aim is as follows: 'to put into perspective the relation between clothes, body and culture both philosophically, aesthetically and socially, and to open up the field for a more reflected dialogue than the one we have today'.[1] As such, templates such as *Personae* have the potential for taking the topic of fashion and dress to another level of enquiry than what is most often practised.

Learning from user experience

Within most research into fashion and dress, there is a tendency to distinguish between 'fashion', 'anti-fashion' and 'the unfashionable' (Church-Gibson, 2000:80; Lipovetsky, 1994). The last category thus represents the majority of the world's population, who, after all, get dressed every day. Thus, just like Simone de Beauvoir's distinction between 'man' and his female 'other' (de Beauvoir, 1989 [1952]), all the people in the world who do not re-enact the skills, codes and practices of 'Parisian chic', as outlined above, become 'wrong'. I therefore argue that there is a huge discrepancy between most current fashion imagery and the self-image of the majority of people in the world.

Following a call for more focus on the 'ordinary' from consumer studies (Shove, 2004, 2007), as well as design research (Fry, 2011), which has its focus on how it might be possible to produce more durable design that reflects a sustainable balance between people's needs and desires, I claim that the daily dress practices and routines of ordinary people provide an extraordinary lens on to individual, embodied negotiations of societal practices, cultural structures, economic currents or other overall ideological frameworks. Therefore, research into ordinary people's interaction with their wardrobes represents a powerful approach to the connection between fashion and sustainability that could spill over to new and more diverse typologies of fashion media built on actual user experience.

Figure 17.1 Norwegian magazine *Personae – Klær, Kropp, Kultur* (Dress, Body, Culture), 3/4, 2011.
Theme: religion and rituals

In my own research, I work with the so-called 'wardrobe method', which has been developed in a network of Scandinavian and British scholars in the last decade (Klepp, 2001; Hansen, 2003; Woodward, 2007; Skov, 2011b). The wardrobe method takes its departure from user-anthropological studies of individual dress practices, with a particular interest in the dress objects that are stored in the space of the wardrobe. In my own research, I understand dress objects as both sensory and experiential aspects of self, following the development of 'emotional design' within the field of design research (Jordan, 2000; Norman, 2004; Mättelmäkki, 2007). This understanding provides a view on the discrepancy between fashion logics and user behaviour that calls for a widened perspective of what it is that we do when we dress, because it becomes obvious that people do not act on fashion's logics, but on other parameters, when they build up their wardrobes throughout their lives. What I suggest is to look at the skills, codes and practices of fashion as quite limited, in terms of user behaviour. I suggest, instead, looking deeper into the concept of style, as it has been defined by cultural-studies scholars such as Hodkinson (2002; Hodkinson and Bennet, 2012). In his study of the Goth scene and of ageing members of subcultural groupings, Hodkinson introduces a view on sartorial style that is about the way people build their idea about themselves throughout their lives, centred around social 'tribes' or scenes of shared ideas, ideologies and taste. Thus, I believe that the concept of style can work as an overall understanding of what it is people do when they dress, no matter to what age group or part of the world they belong, and no matter what grouping they see themselves as part of. Seeing the concept of style this way opens up an opportunity to form new typologies of fashion media that build on generally ignored users of dress, such as elderly people, or dress users with other values and ethics than Western/European ones. In other words, such typologies could provide a framework for fashion's 'other'.

Actually, there are templates to be found that indicate a way forward through this perspective. First, there is *ILikeMyStyle Quarterly* (2010), which marketed itself as 'the first ever user-generated fashion magazine'.[2] It emerged from a blog of the same name, where people could upload photos of themselves and their style. Second, there is advancedstyleblogspot.com (2008), a fashion blog with pictures of elderly and old people – women in particular – as 'proof from the wise and silver-haired set that personal style advances with age'[3] (see Figure 17.2).

What these two media promote is not the frantic and 'restless' haste of *fashion*, but the calmer and slower pace of *style* (see also Chapter 12): people being 'adorned in dreams', and yet at the same time in balance with themselves and how they look.

Conclusion

New practices in fashion journalism must be encouraged that embrace a critical stance to issues such as over-consumption and lack of diversity. Such practices could be developed through adopting the tone and level of debate in art magazines and, hence, adopting the autonomy and arm's-length distance from the industry represented here. This development is supported by the heavy build-up of research, education and museological approaches to the area of fashion and dress taking place the world over.

Research on dress practice is currently underdeveloped, but bears the potential to move the public and scholarly debate from fashion to style, embracing hereby both fashion and its 'other'. Typologies built on actual user experience could establish new types of fashion medium that continue to celebrate the disturbing, beautiful and spectacular imagery that the fashion media have always provided their readers with, but at the same time promote a better balance between who we are, what we do and what we wear.

Figure 17.2 101-year-old Rose posted at advancedstyleblogspot.com, 28 November 2012

Notes

1   See personae.no, as read March 2013.
2   As seen on the Facebook profile of 'ILikeMyStyle', 29 July 2013: www.facebook.com/ilikemystyle?
    fref=ts
3   As seen on advancedstyleblogspot.com, 29 July 2012: http://advancedstyle.blogspot.dk/p/about.html

References

Anderson, F. (2000), Museums as fashion media, in Bruzzi, S. and Church Gibson, P. (eds) *Fashion Cultures. Theories, explorations and analysis.* London and New York: Routledge/Taylor & Francis Group: 371–89.
Barthes, R. (1983), *The Fashion System.* Berkeley, CA: University of California Press.
Barthes, R. (2006), *The Language of Fashion.* Oxford, UK: Berg.
Baudrillard, J. (1999 [1970]), *The Consumer Society.* London: Sage.
de Beauvoir, S. (1989 [1952]), *The Second Sex.* New York: Vintage Books/Random House.
Best, K. N. (2010), The fashion journalism in West Europe, in Skov, L. (ed.) *Berg Encyclopedia of World Dress and Fashion: West Europe,* Vol. 8. Oxford, UK: Berg: 143–50.
Black, S. (2013), Interrogating fashion: Introduction, in Black, S. (ed.) *The Sustainable Fashion Handbook.* China: Thames & Hudson: 8–11.
Blumer, H. (1969), Fashion: from class differentiation to collective selection, *Sociological Quarterly,* 10: 275–91.
Breward, C. (2007), Fashion on the page, in *The Fashion Reader.* Oxford, UK: Berg: Chap. 35: 279–81.
Carter, M. (2003) Thorstein Veblen's leisure class, in *Fashion Classics: From Carlyle to Barthes.* Oxford, UK: Berg: 41–59.
Church-Gibson, P. (2000), No-one expects me anywhere. Invisible women, ageing and the fashion industry, in Bruzzi, S. and Church Gibson, P. (eds) *Fashion Cultures. Theories, explorations and analysis.* London and New York: Routledge/Taylor & Francis Group: 79–89.
Cooper, T. (2005), Slower consumption: reflections of product life spans and the 'throwaway society', *Journal of Industrial Ecology,* 9, 1–2: 51–67.
Davis, F. (1994), *Fashion, Culture and Identity.* Chicago, IL: University of Chicago Press.
Fry, T. (2011), Design, politics and defuturing (Chaps 1–2), in *Design as Politics.* London: Berg: 17–46.
Gauntlett, D. (2002), *Media, Gender and Identity. An Introduction.* Trowbridge, UK: Cromwell Press/Routledge.
Hansen, K. T. (2003), Fashioning: Zambian moments, *Journal of Material Culture,* 8, 3: 301–9.
Hebdige, D. (1979), *Subculture, the Meaning of Style.* London: Routledge.
Hodkinson, P. (2002), *Goth. Identity, Style and Subculture.* Oxford, UK: Berg.
Hodkinson, P. and Bennet, A. (eds) (2012), *Ageing and Youth Culture. Music, Style and Identity.* Oxford, UK: Berg.
Hollander, A. (1994), *Sex and Suits. The Evolution of Modern Dress.* New York: Alfred A. Knopf.
Jordan, P. (2000), *Designing Pleasurable Products. An introduction to the new human factors.* London: Taylor & Francis.
Kawamura, Y. (2005), *Fashion-ology: An introduction to fashion studies.* Oxford, UK: Berg.
Kawamura, Y. (2011), *Doing Research in Fashion and Dress. An Introduction to Qualitative Methods.* Oxford, UK: Berg.
Klepp, I. G. (2001), *Hvorfor går klær ut av bruk? Avhending sett i forhold til kvinners klesvaner,* Lysaker, SIFO Rapport nr. 3–2001.
Lipovetsky, G. (1994), *The Empire of Fashion. Dressing Modern Democracy.* Princeton, NJ: Princeton University Press.
Lönnqvist, B. (2010), Overview of dress and fashion in west Europe, in Skov, L. (ed.) *Berg Encyclopedia of World Dress and Fashion: West Europe,* Vol. 8. Oxford, UK: Berg: 24–32.
Lynge-Jorlén, A. (2012), Between frivolity and art: contemporary niche fashion magazines, *Fashion Theory,* 16 (1): 7–28.
McRobbie, A. (1998), *British Fashion Design: Rag Trade or Image Industry?* Oxford, UK: Berg.
Mättelmäkki, T. (2007), *Design Probes.* Helsinki: UIAH, Helsinki University.
Moeran, B. (2003), International Fashion Magazines. Paper for the 6th Conference of the European Sociological Association, 23–6 September, Murcia, Spain.
Moeran, B. (2010), Fashion magazines, in Eicher, J. B. (ed.) *Berg Encyclopedia of World Dress and Fashion: West Europe,* Vol. 10: 207–15.

Mulvey, L. (2003), Visual pleasure and narrative cinema, in Jones, E. (ed.) *The Feminism and Cultural Reader.* London: Routledge: 44–53.

Norman, D. A. (2004), *Emotional Design, Why We Love (or Hate) Everyday Things.* New York: Basic Books.

Nørgaard, M. (ed.) (2002), *Modeleksikon. Fra couture til kaos.* Narayana: Politiken: 251–2.

Parmal, P. (2006), La Mode: Paris and the development of the French fashion industry, in Parmal, P. and Grumbach, D. (eds) *Fashion Show: Paris Style.* Hamburg, Germany: Gingko Press: 13–85.

Polhemus, T. (1994), *Streetstyle. From Sidewalk to Catwalk.* London: Thames and Hudson.

Rocamora, A. (2009), *Fashioning the City: Paris, Fashion and the Media.* London: I. B. Tauris.

Rocamora, A. (2011), Hypertextuality and remediation in the fashion media, *Journalism Practice*, 6, 1: 92–106.

Shove, E. (2004), *Comfort, Cleanliness and Convenience.* Oxford, UK: Berg.

Shove, E. (2007), *Design of Everyday Life.* Oxford, UK: Berg.

Skjold, E. (2008), *Fashion Research at Design Schools*, monographic report commisioned by Designskolen Kolding, funded by Danish Centre for Design Research (DCDR), in collaboration with MOKO.

Skjold, E. (2010), Men's fashion magazines, in Eicher, J. B. (ed.) *Berg Encyclopedia of World Dress and Fashion: West Europe*, Vol. 10.

Skjold, E. (2014), *The Daily Selection.* PhD thesis, to be finished Spring 2014. ©Kolding School of Design/Copenhagen Business School.

Skov, L. (2010), The study of dress and fashion in West Europe, in Skov, L. (ed.) *Berg Encyclopedia of World Dress and Fashion: West Europe*, Vol. 8. Oxford: Berg: 3–6.

Skov, L. (2011a), Dreams of small nations in a polycentric fashion world, *Fashion Theory*, 15, 2: 137–56.

Skov L. (2011b), *Entering the space of the wardrobe.* Creative Encounters working paper, Copenhagen Business School.

Taylor, L. (2002), *The Study of Dress History.* Manchester, UK: Manchester University Press

Wilson, E. (1986), *Adorned in Dreams: Fashion and Modernity.* London: Virago.

Woodward, S. (2007), *Why Women Wear What They Wear.* Oxford, UK: Berg.

18

THE ROLE OF SCIENCE AND TECHNOLOGY IN SUSTAINABLE FASHION

Greg Peters, Hjalmar Granberg and Susanne Sweet

Introduction

Fashion embodies human pleasure, creativity, social codes and technologies that have enabled societies to prosper, laid burdens on the environment and caused competition for arable land. No single actor, action or technology is sufficient to shift us away from the environmental and social challenges embedded in the fashion industry – nor to meet the demands for sustainable development of society at large. However, scientific and technological developments are important for progress towards sustainable fashion. 'Technology is indeed a queen: it does change the world' (Braudel, 1981), but it is also socially constructed and embedded in society (Hughes, 1987).

An important role of technological innovation is to deal with the limits placed on industry by nature's limited resource base and the need to prevent pollution, reduce negative social impacts and keep products affordable. Scientific developments play the role of suggesting where technological innovation can go and assessing whether the innovations actually improve matters.

We are three of the dozens of people engaged in the Mistra Future Fashion programme, an ongoing, cross-disciplinary research programme investigating significant sustainability challenges linked to the production and consumption of fashion and textiles. Greg Peters is a chemical engineer and Associate Professor at Chalmers University of Technology. He brings a perspective built on the application of sustainability assessment tools in the water, chemicals and agricultural industries. Hjalmar Granberg has a PhD in physics and works as a senior research associate at Innventia AB. His research focuses on designing new materials based on wood, including cellulose electronics and mechano-active materials that respond to the environment. Susanne Sweet is Associate Professor of Business Administration at Stockholm School of Economics. Her research explores the interconnections in a global world that provide inspiration but also unsustainable economic, technological and behavioural lock-ins.

This chapter aims to shed light on the role of science and technology in fashion and sustainability, by drawing on a few of the scientific and technological parts of Mistra Future

Fashion. A life-cycle perspective is adopted. After describing what this means, this chapter steps through the clothing life cycle, from the origins of the materials and new fibres, to the manufacturing processes and how we assess them, to the use phase and the possibilities of tagging technology, and finally the technological possibilities of transforming garment end-of-life.

The life-cycle perspective of fashion and textiles

What is the life-cycle perspective?

The *life-cycle perspective* is an approach to the management of products and processes that aims to intervene in the design process to avoid end-of-pipe solutions for polluting industries. It includes a range of methods, from relatively qualitative *life-cycle thinking* to formalised, quantitative disciplines such as *life-cycle assessment* (LCA). From an original focus on energy conservation, LCA has broadened to a technique that can potentially consider environmental, social and financial elements of sustainability, though the latter is usually termed *life-cycle costing*. The best-known LCA indicator is the *carbon footprint* – used in international climate negotiations and product labels. Another is the *water footprint*, an indicator particularly relevant to the cotton-based fashion industry (Sandin *et al.*, 2013).

The broader church of *life-cycle thinking* has too many elements to mention here, but some key approaches used by the fashion industry and other manufacturing industries include Cradle to Cradle and The Natural Step (Robèrt, 2002). Many approaches do not require the use of any particular quantitative assessment method in product design, but rely on considerations such as product recyclability and checklists regarding aspects of the provenance of raw materials. This makes them quicker and cheaper to apply, at some cost to accuracy and precision. A common element is the need to consider the fashion product itself as environmentally relevant material, with a use phase and end-of-life, rather than focusing exclusively on sustainable management of fields and factories.

How has LCA of textiles grown

An indication of the growth in LCA in the textile industry can be obtained using statistics derived from bibliographic databases. A search of the Scopus database for all publications including the phrases 'life-cycle assessment', 'life-cycle analysis', 'carbon footprint' or 'water footprint' and product types 'textile', 'garment' or 'clothing' identified 168 articles published over the last 20 years. This is astonishingly few, considering the ubiquity of clothing in human culture. If one posits that clothing is one of our primary physical needs, along with food, water and shelter, and compares the results for these products, it seems the fashion industry is late to 'get with the trend' – see Figure 18.1. Several aspects of Figure 18.1 are noteworthy. It shows that the current publication rate for studies of textiles is lower than the other three application areas (tens per year versus hundreds). Another sign of belated interest is offered by curve fitting. The curves graphed on the log scale suggest that the use of LCA in the fashion industry is currently growing exponentially, but it started to do this a decade after the food, water and building industries (see also Introduction and Chapter 2 for a discussion about how fashion is viewed). The late symbiosis between LCA research and the fashion industry means that there is less reliable information to inform policy-making and sustainable textile product development than would otherwise be the case.

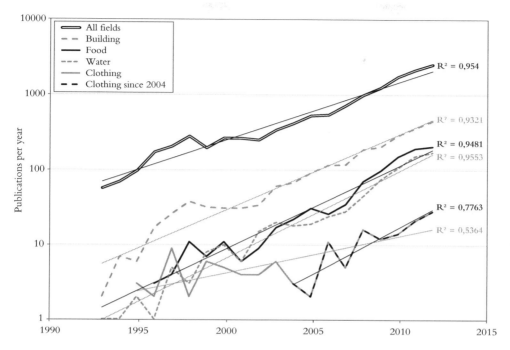

Figure 18.1 Growth in LCA activities in different fields from 1993 to 2012. 'Building' includes housing and construction. 'Food' includes drink and beverages. 'Water' includes sewage and waste-water treatment. This search was performed in November 2013. Maximum correlation (R^2) between the publication rate for clothing and the exponential line of best fit occurs when curve fitting starts in 2004

Fibre production

Some technological developments in fibre production

Sustainability means considering the environmental, social and economic performance of a product. Although new fibres may have better performance, current mainstays of the fashion industry such as polyester and cotton will be part of our future, and the pressure is on to make them more sustainable.

Cotton

Cotton consumption has been falling since 2007, as the Organisation for Economic Cooperation and Development (OECD) data in Figure 18.2 show. Chinese production has experienced rising labour costs, and Chinese demographic trends are expected to keep them high. Cotton production is also affected by competition with food production for water and irrigable land. Food production is expanding to cope with our increasing global population and increasing demand for meat. Considering these pressures, the OECD predicts that cotton prices will prevent consumption from exceeding its 2007 peak until at least 2022 (OECD, 2013).

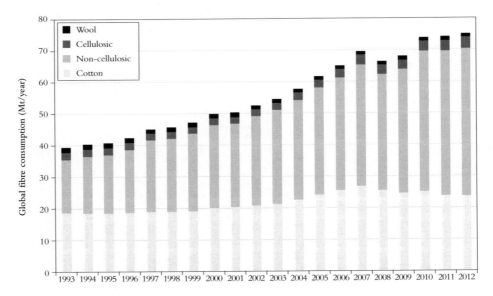

Figure 18.2 Fibre consumption by type, 1993–2012
Source: OECD, 2013

The main technological development confronting the price of cotton is the improved yield achieved using genetically modified organisms (GMOs). The implantation of genes from the bacterium *Bacillus thuringiensis* into the 'Bt cotton' makes it toxic to the cotton bollworm caterpillar (*Pectinophora gossypiella*). A recent study of Indian farmers suggested that this innovation has led to 24 per cent higher yields, even after correcting for the increased use of water and fertilisers that often accompanies the investment in the GMO cotton (Vaidyanathan, 2012). Many people believe that using GMOs represents the release of exotic DNA into the environment, akin to the introduction of the cane toad *(Bufo marinus)* to Australia for crop protection. (The toad escaped agriculture and is killing native species in national parks.) Nevertheless, Indian production has increased thanks to Bt cotton, partly compensating for reduced Chinese supplies, and Indian and Pakistani production can be raised further in this way.

Synthetics (non-cellulosic)

Fashion consumers may not imagine themselves stepping into petrochemical-industry outlets when they go shopping, but, as Figure 18.2 indicates, synthetic fibres represent the majority and the fastest-growing segment of global fibre consumption. Therefore, technical developments in the petrochemical industry are significant for the future of fashion.

Rising consumer demand underlies attempts to extract oil from environments previously considered too technologically challenging, such as Arctic regions (Alaska and Siberia), where the climate presents extreme safety engineering challenges, and deep reservoirs in the Gulf of Mexico. However, one of the most dramatic technological innovations to affect the petro-chemical fashion industry has been implemented in comfortable terrestrial regions: hydraulic fracturing or 'fracking'. The technology involves pumping water, sand and chemicals under high pressure into gas- or oil-bearing strata. The water splits deep rocks, and the chemicals help push the sand into the cracks to release the hydrocarbons (gas or oil). Fracking is controversial and is banned in some jurisdictions, owing to concerns about groundwater depletion and physical damage to aquifers, but political support for it is strong in the USA, where fracking has reduced the cost of hydrocarbons. This is keeping the cost of nylon and polyester down and is predicted to enable the USA to overtake Saudi Arabia as the world's largest oil producer by 2017 (Jansen, 2013). Some may argue about one element of sustainability (economics) being allowed to triumph over intergenerational equity and the environment, but, if the short-term alternative is more irrigated cotton, or oil produced from Canadian oil sands or Chinese coal, a lively debate is feasible.

New fibres

Curiosity and the desire to avoid the impacts of producing cotton and current synthetics drive the development of new fibres. Recent ideas include *CelluNova* (a cellulosic fibre intended to be a more environmentally friendly version of viscose – TPP, 2013), *Qmilk*, and the radical-sounding, biomimetic option of *hagfish slime* (Negishi *et al.*, 2012). The latter two, protein-based fibres have the advantage of strength compared with cellulosics and are easier to make than the old holy grail of spider silk, owing to the smaller size of the proteins. Heeding the debate around biofuels, the German Qmilch company claims to make *Qmilk* from *waste* milk, so that fibre production does not compete with food production. *Qmilk* has attractive properties, including being compostable and hypoallergenic. Another new fibre is DuPont's Sorona, which is poly (trimethylene terephthalate) – chemically similar to polyester. What makes it different is the use of 1,3-propanediol produced from corn-derived glucose by recombinant *Escherichia coli* bacteria. When this reacts with petrochemical terephthalic acid, 37 per cent of the resulting fibre mass is bio-based, so that the carbon footprint of this fibre is smaller than 100 per cent petrochemical synthetics.

Some scientific developments in the assessment of fibre production

Two major flaws in product environmental impact assessments have been the lack of methods to assess the transformation of biodiverse ecosystems and the use of water. Taking the latter example for illustration, wildly different numbers have been published regarding the amount of water required to produce agricultural products. For the textile industry, which uses wool, cotton and (increasingly) wood pulp, this is problematic. How much water is actually needed for a T-shirt? It is relatively easy to find the volume of water going into a dyeing factory – typically, the manager sees it on the bill. However, agricultural water use has to be estimated by systems that may be non-existent. Then the question arises: does extracting a litre of water from a Swedish river to wash a cotton T-shirt cause the same amount of environmental damage as extracting a litre of water from an exotic river in Uzbekistan to grow the cotton? Most people would answer 'no', as there is rain aplenty in Scandinavia, but there is no consensus on how to calculate a meaningful aggregation of the water use over the whole life cycle. This is a topic of current research (Kounina *et al.*, 2013; Sandin *et al.*, 2013), a global effort towards methodological synthesis under the auspices of the United Nations Environment Program, and a draft ISO standard (ISO14046).

From fibre to garment

Some technological developments

Evaluating whether production processes are sustainable means understanding processes such as spinning, weaving and wet treatment. These processes are diverse; for example, the latter can involve many chemicals, including those that bleach, dye or provide functions such as waterproofing or softness.

As with the provision of new fibres, technical developments in the chemical industry play a major role in the development of new textiles. An example of this is the development of new 'durable water repellent' (DWR) chemicals. Traditional oilskins were impregnated with linseed oil, but waterproofing changed fundamentally with the patenting of Goretex™ membrane in 1976, enabling outdoor garments to be both breathable *and* waterproof. People often assume the membrane *or* the DWR chemical on the outer fabric is responsible for the breathable water-proofness, but it is actually the membrane that makes the garment waterproof, and the DWR that keeps the outer fabric dry, enabling the membrane to 'breathe'.

Most DWRs are based on fluoropolymers. They are attractive from an engineering per-spective, because the fluorine–carbon bonds are very stable. Unfortunately, from an environ-mental perspective, this stability makes them highly resistant to all the methods the Earth uses to clean up pollution. Fluoropolymers have been found in increasing amounts in the bodies of polar bears and seals in remote Arctic locations. In humans, they are associated with kidney disease, depressed immune systems and cancer. So, substitution of the worst fluoropolymers in textiles with safer chemicals or waterproofing systems is an important goal of researchers in the Mistra Future Fashion consortium based at Chalmers University of Technology and Swerea IVF, who have joined with Stockholm University, Vrije University Amsterdam, outdoor retailer Haglöfs and the Käppala waste-water district in Stockholm to pursue the goal of evaluating substitutes for current fluoropolymers (www.supfes.eu). This involves thinking about the technical function of the chemicals and laboratory analysis of the toxicological properties of the alternatives.

The scientific challenge of assessing the production process

Many alternative textile chemicals are not yet applied to any particular garment, preventing empirical testing during its use. There are also gaps in the scientific data necessary to make precise estimates of the fate of chemicals in the environment. Scientists have been working on this problem for years and steadily refining the available tools. One of them is the *group contribution method*, where one imagines cutting the chemical up into pieces and adding up the contribution that each of the pieces (groups) makes to (for example) the water solubility of the chemical. We can estimate what each group contributes by looking at other known chemicals that contain this group and comparing their water solubility. Methods for the prediction of many properties of chemicals have been developed, from boiling point to the propensity to bioaccumulate, and they continue to be improved. What is especially exciting about this scientific idea is that it means that, in principle, analysts can estimate the properties of textile chemicals that do not even exist yet!

This kind of ability is important when it comes to running models such as UseTox, an Excel-based tool built on scientific consensus for characterising human and ecotoxicological impacts of chemicals in LCA (www.usetox.org). Readers familiar with the idea that methane is a more potent greenhouse gas than carbon dioxide will be familiar with the idea of 'global warming potential' factors, which bring these two gases and others on to a common scale of 'kilograms of carbon dioxide equivalent' emissions. UseTox does the same job for chemicals by bringing their carcinogenic and non-carcinogenic toxic effects on human health and ecosystems on to a common scale. By 2013, UseTox had been used to generate characterisation factors for over 3,000 chemicals, and the list is being extended continuously.

The fashion use phase

Technological developments in tagging

One of the current technological trends that has the capacity to significantly change the fashion industry is 'The Internet of Things'. This expression has been used for about 15 years to describe a world in which objects are connected to the Internet using tagging technologies. The most common are radio frequency identification and traditional one-dimensional (1D) optical bar-codes. Tags can also be coupled to sensors that read, for example, ambient temperature or moisture, position, time, speed or mechanical stress – almost anything can be read, stored and communicated by a sensor-tag–Internet system.

Technological power to the people

Recent smartphones allow reading of advanced, low-cost tags by consumers. Traditional 1D barcodes and new 2D barcodes containing unique IDs can be scanned by cameras in most smartphones. Newer models allow for simpler reading by holding the phone close to battery-free, 'near field communication' (NFC) tags. These technologies empower the consumer by providing the means to read tags that were previously limited to dedicated readers within the supply chain. As the smartphone has a unique ID that is strongly connected to its user, the tags allow the possibility of exploring links between personal preferences and objects.

One benefit of this digital empowerment is the potential for consumers to easily access different data channels (e.g. WiFi, Bluetooth, 4G) and materials such as film, music, games and literature. Placing the textile tag in the right context makes it possible to associate a specific textile with positive experiences obtained when the textile is worn. It could connect with interactive games for socialising, or interesting information at the right time and place. Clothing could also interact with other persons' clothing and give feedback to social networks or Internet games; different fashions could trigger different media to play at a museum; and so forth.

Technology for new business models

Today, the most common fashion business model is based on people buying clothes, but other models are possible – such as treating clothes as a service rather than a product. This model is being tried out at a small scale – consumers pay a subscription to access clean clothes on a weekly basis (e.g. Gothenburg's 'Clothing Library' – see www.kladbiblioteket.se/lanekort). This is supported by the emerging trend of pooling services powered by Internet-based social networks. Today, smartphone applications are being developed that support reuse of clothes via social networks, e.g. the *Walk In My Closet* iPhone application. In this space, tags and sensors can be used to automate the handling of the large amounts of different textiles needed to obtain a good textile-pool service. Information such as fitting measurements, previously accepted clothing and number of previous uses and washes can be important to monitor for business management.

Scientific data for people and experts

Beyond the entertainment and business benefits described above, tags read by smartphones could be used to access Internet media that give sustainability information about a textile: for example, a video showing how the material was produced, or data on the number of times it has been recycled. It can also help consumers keep track of the scale of their wardrobes. That knowledge could empower individuals to reduce the impact of their participation in fashion, such as helping them avoid unnecessary washing activities and accumulation of excess garments.

Beyond the consumer, there are important roles that tagging can play for the improvement of our understanding of the impacts of fashion. The use phase of garments is relatively poorly understood by analysts (see also Chapters 1, 12 and 13). Currently, self-reporting is widely used for studying consumers' behaviour. These reports are not fun for the consumer, and feedback to the consumer is rarely possible until the end of a study. By giving test groups clothing equipped with sensors and tags, it becomes possible to automatically measure different wearing and washing behaviour, give immediate feedback that can change behaviour and provide scientists with better data. This reality is not far away, as washing-machine producers such as Dai Nippon and NXP have recently started to add NFC readers on their washing machines. In summary, it is possible to create new functionality, combining modern textiles with tags, sensors and the digital world. The examples given above represent just a subset of the possibilities, and it is up to the combined efforts of the industry and research organisations to unlock the full potential of tagging for sustainability.

End of life

The fashion industry is moving towards 'fast fashion': faster production with lower quality and shorter fashion cycles (see also Chapters 1 and 7). This trend decreases the fraction of clothing that can be reused, because garments are less robust, driving the waste down the waste hierarchy (Figure 18.3). For a more sustainable future, this trend must reverse. Alternatively, for successful closed-loop recycling, the materials must be equally good, better or cheaper after recycling (Bartl *et al.*, 2005: 351). The only large-scale recycling processes available today for mixed textile waste are mechanical methods based on shredding. This is unfortunate, because the fibre quality of the output material is lower and generally only useful for applications such as stuffing, automotive components, carpet underlays or low-grade blankets. In Mistra Future Fashion, we are working on alternatives higher up in the waste hierarchy. One is chemical recycling of low-grade fashion textile waste.

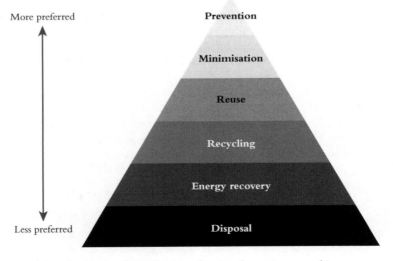

Figure 18.3 The waste hierarchy: a general classification of options by environmental impact

Technological challenges for recycling

For textiles to be recycled, technical challenges need to be overcome. Two key challenges are the degradation and blending of fibres. During garment use, fibres are slowly degraded, primarily by washing but also by friction and wear. The degradation, which reduces fibre and polymer chain lengths, is further intensified by mechanical recycling. Shorter fibre lengths mean lower strength and quality – a major problem for efficient closed-loop recycling.

Another major challenge is the blending of fibres. It is not just that garments use yarns of different types – individual yarns are often cellulosic/synthetic blends. Three problems arise here. First: sorting is currently impossible, because there is, to date, no commercial online analytical technique for identification of the fibre content in garments. Second: mechanical recycling becomes difficult, because (for example) polyurethane fibres get tangled up in the shredder, and polyester fibres are strong – tearing them demands energy. Finally: chemical dissolution and separation are difficult, because it is hard to tune the chemical process to any particular mixed fibre in a stream of mixed fibres.

Better science for chemical recycling

Chemical recycling of garments is interesting, because it could potentially re-establish fibre quality. One frequently hears claims that someone has developed a chemical recycling process, but practical demonstration is elusive. As a consequence, there are research activities on this topic all around the world. In the Mistra Future Fashion programme, we are concentrating on cotton and polyester fibres, trying to provide data to enable dissolution of old garments to replace virgin materials. Our assessment suggests that chemical recycling of these fibres offers significant environmental benefits over energy recovery (Zamani *et al.*, 2013). Our focus is to understand how these fibres are affected by use, and what technologies can be used to convert used fibres into new, high-quality fibres.

To ensure adequate understanding and control of the textile materials, we emphasise the importance of characterisation methods covering all levels of the textile fibres: the molecular level (molecule scale), the macromolecular level (polymer scale) and the morphological level (fibre scale). One part of the work is a laundering study of post-consumer garments. This study investigates impacts of controlled use and laundering on textile quality, to understand the degradation mechanisms and the expected properties of fibres intended for different chemical-recycling processes. We believe that this knowledge will be important when determining the chemistry needed to restore the quality of post-consumer textile fibres.

To restore the quality of post-consumer cellulosic fibres, such as cotton, we are investigating dissolution of used cotton fibres. Dissolution of cotton using systems such as the viscose process, which is optimised to dissolve cellulosic fibres, will overcome the degradation problem, as new, comparable fibres can be spun from the polymeric solution (Negulescu *et al.*, 1998: 31).

In the Mistra Future Fashion project, we believe that a wide chemical and polymeric knowledge of post-consumer textile fibres will provide answers on how to better recycle both natural and man-made fibres. We also believe that, with increased fibre knowledge, environmental impacts caused by the use of chemicals and energy in contemporary systems can be reduced.

Conclusion

Science and technology have important roles to play in the future of fashion. To fulfil them, more research is needed on how to:

1   keep the feedstocks for cotton and polyester material affordable;
2   produce cellulosic alternatives to cotton that provide the same or better functionality;
3   keep track of clothes in use; and
4   make sustainable use of waste clothes.

As with the political and economic drivers of change, technology-driven change can create new impacts, ethical dilemmas, winners and losers. Developing the life-cycle science will help us understand the consequences of technological change and inform evaluation of the best means to manage it. This means more research to:

5   model the impacts of resource use on biodiversity and water systems;
6   make assessment of chemicals in product design more inclusive and practical; and
7   evaluate the sustainability of innovations for delivering 1–4 above.

There are many other domains of human intellectual endeavour, such as sociology and business management, that have a major role to play in making the life cycle of clothing more sustainable, because there are so many different facets of each life-cycle phase to consider. It is hoped that interdisciplinary research and development projects such as Mistra Future Fashion will enable researchers and industry players with a wide variety of expertise to interact and create the changes that are necessary.

References

Bartl, A., Hackl, A., Mihalyi, B., Wistuba, M. and Marini, I. (2005), Recycling of fibre materials, *Process Safety and Environmental Protection*, 83 (4): 351–8.

Braudel, F. (1981), *Civilization and Capitalism 15th–18th Century. Vol. 1, The Structures of Everyday Life.* London: William Collins Sons.

Hughes, T. P. (1987), The evolution of large technological systems. In Bijker, W. B., Hughes, T. P. and Pinch, T. J. (eds), *The Social Construction of Technological Systems*. Cambridge, MA: MIT Press: 51–82.

Jansen, R. (2013), Oil & gas: the shale revolution, *The Chemical Engineer*, 863: 34–6.

Kounina, A., Margni, M., Bayart, J.-B., Boulay, A.-M., Berger, M., Bulle, C., Frischknecht, R., Koehler, A., Milà, I., Canals, L., Motoshita, M., Núñez, M., Peters, G., Pfister, S., Ridoutt, B., van Zelm, R., Verones, F. and Humbert, S. (2013), Review of methods addressing freshwater use in life cycle inventory and impact assessment, *International Journal of LCA*, 18: 707–21.

Negishi, A., Armstrong, C. L., Kreplak, L., Rheinstadter, M. C., Lim, L.-T., Gillis, T. E. and Fudge, D. S. (2012), The production of fibers and films from solubilized hagfish slime thread proteins, *Biomacromolecules*, 13 (11): 3475–82.

Negulescu, I. I., Kwon, H., Collier, B. J., Collier, J. R. and Pendse, A. (1998), Recycling cotton from cotton/polyester fabrics, *Textile Chemist and Colorist*, 30 (6): 31–5.

OECD (2013), Cotton. In *OECD–FAO Agricultural Outlook 2013*. OECD Publishing. DOI: DOI:10.1787/agr_outlook-2013-13-en (accessed 26 November 2013).

Robèrt, K.-H. (2002), Strategic sustainable development – selection, design and synergies of applied tools, *Journal of Cleaner Production*, 10: 197–214.

Sandin, G., Peters, G. M. and Svanström, M. (2013), Moving down the cause–effect chain of water and land use impacts: an LCA case study of textile fibres, *Resources, Conservation and Recycling*, 73: 104–13.

TPP (2013), *Ny bioekonomiskt textil av cellulosa ska konkurrera med bomull. The Paper Province*, 21 November [online]. Available at: www.mynewsdesk.com/se/paperprovince/pressreleases/ny-bioekonomiskt-textil-av-cellulosa-ska-konkurrera-med-bomull-931472 (accessed 26 November 2013).

Vaidyanathan G. (2012), Genetically modified cotton gets high marks in India, *Nature*, 3 July, DOI:10.1038/nature.2012.10927 (accessed 26 November 2013).

Zamani, B., Svanström, M. and Peters, G. (2013), End-of-life management: LCA of textile waste recycling. *Proceedings of the 6th International Conference on Life Cycle Management*, 25–8 August, Gothenburg, Sweden.

19

THE NEW SYNTHETICS

Could synthetic biology lead to sustainable textile manufacturing?

Carole Collet

Introduction

This chapter investigates a radically bold future for fashion inscribed within a new era of biological engineering, where fabrics can be produced by bacteria, and the supply chains of fashion brands are genetically programmed. This is not science fiction. Today, biologists have developed the tools to reprogramme bacteria for the production of silk, biofuel and medicine. Our future factories could be genetically engineered living cells, designed to custom-make materials to suit our needs. Synthetic biology, the science responsible for this cutting-edge technology, is portrayed by some leading public organizations as a potential means to achieve a more sustainable future. As a Reader in Textile Futures, I investigate the role of new technologies for future sustainable textiles, horizon 2050. In this chapter, I will explore the foreseeable impact of synthetic biology on the textiles and fashion industry and will question the controversial claims that this new and uprising biotechnology could foster a more sustainable future. And, rather than endorsing the inevitability of a 'bio-technopolis', I will end by proposing a new framework for designing with the living: from biomimicry to 'biofacture'.

Horizon 2050: transformational technologies for a paradigm shift

From climate change to resource depletion and population increase, we are not short of drivers to instigate change. More than 9 billion people will need to clothe and feed themselves in a little more than 30 years time (United Nations, 2013: 15). Oil, a key raw material at the core of textile production is running out. Water resources are stretched, and agricultural production is beginning to suffer from the effect of climate change (Ackerman and Stanton, 2013: 8). The mainstream textile and fashion industry is linked to resource pressures and thus faces a future shaped by providing for a growing population, at the same time as reducing ecological impact.

Although the past 20 years have seen improvements in terms of environmental production and legislation of fashion and textile products (European Commission, 2011; Nuthall, 2011), there is a risk that these measures are not fast or efficient enough to meet the demands of an expanding global population living on a finite planet. No matter how fast we get into a more eco-efficient economy, incremental change will not suffice. We are exploiting our natural systems and resources faster than they can actually regenerate and are in 'overshoot' mode by as much as 50 per cent (Moore and Rees, 2013: 42). To readjust the balance, not only do we need to acknowledge the issue, but I believe that we should begin to develop truly transformational technologies to help make a radical leap forward. Referring to seventeenth-century Easter Island as an example of a society that destroyed itself by over-exploiting its natural resources, evolutionary biologist Jarred Diamond argues that all the signs that can lead to a societal collapse are already here today (Diamond, 2006: 495). He suggests that, even if societies have the means and technologies to prevent such a collapse, they may act too late to remedy the situation. In order to prevent reaching a critical point of no return, we need to engage with the quest for a paradigm shift. One aspect of my research is to explore emerging and so-called 'disruptive' technologies that could make a radical step-change for a positively sustainable model of manufacturing, horizon 2050. A technology is qualified as disruptive when it challenges and interrupts a sector or market and has a fundamental impact on innovation and business models (Christensen and Bower, 1995). Synthetic biology is a strong candidate that is beginning to generate new and innovative models for industrial production. It involves the genetic re-engineering of living organisms, a biotechnology that allows us to create purpose-built organisms designed to fulfil specific functions. Al Gore, co-recipient of the Nobel Peace Prize in 2007, states that the future to come will be radically different from what we know. He refers to the emergence of revolutionary biotechnologies that will 'cross the ancient lines dividing species, and invent entirely new ones never imagined in nature' (Gore, 2013: 14). I argue that, if it stays on its current trajectory, synthetic biology could have the same impact on our society that the Internet has had on our everyday experience in the past decade. The questions I pose are:

- Could synthetic biology be a transformational technology able to pave the way to a new, greener society?
- How will the creation of genetically engineered organisms designed to fulfil our material needs impact on our fashion and textiles production methods and design tools?
- Can we consider synthetic biology, a form of extreme genetic engineering, to be a sustainable technology?
- What are the ethical implications related to synthetic biology?

The section below will examine how and when synthetic biology has arisen and how it is beginning to reshape our future materiality.

Horizon 2010: biology has become a digital technology

If, in the twentieth century, we became masters of chemistry and physics, it seems that, in the twenty-first century, we will become masters of biology. In 2010, scientist Craig Venter announced the creation of the first synthetic bacteria, nicknamed '*Synthia*'. This was the first living organism whose DNA had been computer generated. The bacteria survived and self-replicated. Up until then, scientists had been able to genetically modify a species, but, with Synthia, Venter and his team proved it was possible to rewrite an entire genome. Today, we can recode DNA sequences in the same way that we can programme a computer. We can insert this so-called 'synthetic' DNA inside a living bacterium and 'reboot' it, as we would install a new operating system on a laptop.

Synthetic biology is rapidly gaining the ability to reprogramme a range of living organisms to create new ones that have never before existed on planet Earth. This includes programming bacteria to produce biofuel, artemisinine (a malaria drug treatment) or yeast to produce vanilla. In terms of textile-specific genetically engineered species, silk seems to be the focus.

> As silk is a protein, its chemical composition is encoded in the genes of the organisms that make it. Researchers have unraveled this composition, but it is too complicated to put silk together 'by hand' using industrial methods. A better approach is to turn organisms into living silk factories.
>
> *(Ball, 2001)*

There are a number of recent scientific publications that record attempts to re-engineer bacteria, potatoes, tobacco plants or even worms to produce silk, some more successful than others. The speed at which synthetic biology is now being developed is tremendous. Last year (only 2 years after the first synthetic organism was created), UK Chancellor George Osborne announced that synthetic biology was one of eight key technologies that would expect greater investment, as part of a broader research strategy aimed at boosting the stuttering economy (Osborne, 2012). The value of the global synthetic biology market is projected to reach $10.8 billion by 2016, as reported by the Technology Strategy Board (UK Synthetic Biology Roadmap Coordination Group, 2012: 8). As the research intensifies and accelerates, greater and even bolder industrial applications for synthetic biology can be predicted. Below, I explore its potential impact on the textile and fashion industry.

How will the creations of genetically engineered organisms impact on our production methods and design tools?

When it comes to textiles and fashion, there are no specific direct applications derived from synthetic biology yet, except for bacterial silk, such as produced by Professor Kaplan of Tuft University (although the primary focus there is medical applications for silk protein). However, the use of synthetic biology for chemical waste treatments, or the production of biodegradable plastics (see also Chapter 3) and the replacement of petroleum-based polyester would be fully relevant to the sector. Here, we are looking at medium-to-long-term futures in terms of technology transfer and mainstream accessibility to manufacturing with synthetic biology. At its most basic, synthetic biology will reframe our fibre and fabric classification and will enable us to bypass finishing processes that will, instead, be integrated in the genetic core of the fibre. For instance, one could develop bacteria programmed to produce a waterproof silk that changes colour in response to humidity levels. Today, we look to nanotechnology to augment our fabrics with such 'intelligent' characteristics and improve the performance of materials. Nanotechnologies relate to the non-biological engineering of matter at the nano (10^{-9}) scale by controlling the realignment or reorganization of atoms and molecules. However, with synthetic biology, biological living matter can be controlled as well. Textile finishes could, therefore, be biologically programmed in the DNA, at the start of the process, at the heart of the 'living factory'. A key future research agenda is to investigate how synthetic biology could fundamentally redesign, not just our manufacturing systems, but also our taxonomy of materials, and even our sector-specific vocabulary. Table 19.1 illustrates what might be available in a textile handbook in 2050.

If synthetic biology enables us to bypass production processes that currently require high volumes of water and energy, as well as generating toxic waste-water effluents, then we begin to understand how tantalizing that technology could be for a manufacturing industry that is trying to 'clean up its act'. And, although none of these new bio-fibres are commercially available yet, a growing number of innovators are beginning to explore the realms of this upcoming

Table 19.1 Textile classification horizon 2050

Natural fibres (agriculture)	Vegetal (cotton, linen, hemp, ramie, nettle etc.) and animal (wool, silk etc.) fibres
Regenerated fibres (manufacture)	Fibres made from cellulose – plant-based material – (such as wood pulp) and then chemically processed. They include rayon, acetate, viscose
Synthetic fibres (manufacture)	Fibres made from petroleum derivatives. They include nylon, acrylic, polyester
Synthetic bio-fibres (biofacture)	Any fibre from the previous three categories, but made by genetically engineered living organisms, such as bacteria, yeast, algae and plants. These fibres are usually programmed with enhanced characteristics (such as antibacterial, anti-crease, colour changing, waterproof, fireproof)
Synthetic bio-fabrics (biofacture)	Fabrics directly grown into constructed structures by synthetic living organisms, such as bacteria, yeast, algae, plants. These living organisms are programmed to produce knitted, woven or non-woven structures. They can also grow fabrics with smart characteristics and behaviours, such as shape-change or climate-control fabrics

Source: ©Carole Collet 2013

synthetic world. Some are engaged with laboratory-based scientific experiments and actively bridge the design and science communities. Others anticipate products and manufacturing processes that could result from synthetic biology by developing speculative design proposals. Some of these groups use design as a tool to promote a broader public debate about the risks and ethics of using a self-replicating technology. Here, we will examine two examples that are concerned with fashion, textiles and sustainability.

Natsai Chieza is a textile designer and researcher who is investigating bacteria as living factories to generate textile dyes. With her project 'Faber Futures' and in collaboration with Professor John Ward from UCL, she has developed a process by which she can induce bacteria to produce specific colour schemes. She can then extract the biodegradable dyes and use them to dye or print textile samples: 'By growing bacteria as an ink factory and using traditional textile screen print techniques, "Faber Futures" presents the first collection of textiles produced by traditional screen printing but using dyes produced by bacteria' (Chieza, 2013: 37). Her next step is to investigate how synthetic bacteria could be programmed to generate a wide range of colours in high quantities, and if synthetic biology could help produce fully biodegradable and colour-fast dyes that could replace the current chemical finishes derived from the petroleum industry (Figure 19.1).

From this experimental project, it is easy to extrapolate how fashion trends would influence the programming of new living species designed to 'biofacture' next season's colours. But it can go much further than that. Fashion houses could design and own the patent of unique, genetically engineered species that would produce fibres, colours and fabrics intrinsic to their brands. Designer DNA would take precedence over natural DNA. What would a bacterium working for Chanel produce? What would a yeast designed by Marc Jacobs do? What if Dolce & Gabbana were to employ plants to spin lace? The fashion system as we know it today would be a very different landscape. It would require a full integration of biological design with textile and fashion design. This is echoed in Biolace, a speculative design proposal that refers to current research into the genetic control of plant morphogenesis. The 'Strawberry Noir' in Figure 19.2

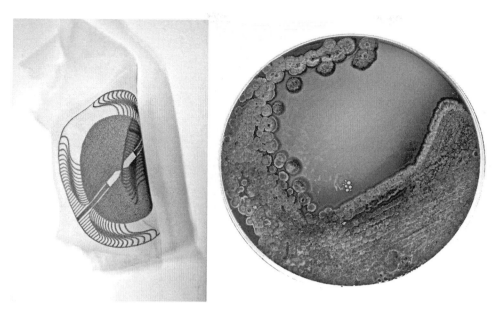

Figure 19.1 Silk screen print on habotai silk using a pink pigment produced by *Streptomyces coelicolor.* Commonly found in soil, S. *coelicolor* can produce a range of blues, pinks, purples and reds under varied growth conditions

Source: ©Natsai Chieza 2014

is a fictional plant that would produce black strawberries, augmented in anti-oxidants and vitamin C, together with a black lace for the fashion market (Collet, 2013: 36).

Grown in hydroponic greenhouses, located near large urban centres, these hyper-engineered and multifunctional plants would cater for both the food and the textile industry. The lace would be ready for harvest at the same time as the strawberry. In this context, manufacturing becomes farming. Biologists have argued that this 'Strawberry Noir' would be possible to make in 20 years' time from now, but here, as in the examples suggested above, the most overriding questions are those of ethics. Should we turn to such extreme genetic engineering to provide for the forecasted 9 billion people living on the planet in 2050? Will we have a choice?

Have we reached a point of no return, where even synthetic biology, a form of extreme genetic engineering can be considered a sustainable technology?

If we agree that 'the most disruptive force on the planet resides in DNA' (Wohlsen, 2011: 3), then we can consider that synthetic biology is perhaps the most disruptive technology at play today. Most public organizations and government agencies claim that this biotechnology can provide a new toolkit for sustainability. 'Synthetic biology can help us address key challenges facing the planet and its population, such as food security, sustainable energy and health' (OECD and The Royal Society, 2010: 8). But how can an extreme genetic-engineering science be portrayed as an ecological champion? It seems that it is not because of the engineering process itself (i.e. the genetic reprogramming of living organisms), but because of what novel substances can be produced by these living factories. Potential future industrial applications range from

Figure 19.2 Strawberry Noir *(Fragaria Fusca Tenebris)*
Source: ©Carole Collet 2013

bioremediation, such as waste-water treatments, to the production of biofuel, bioplastics, biosensors, medicine, food or even carbon-capture biological devices (UK Synthetic Biology Roadmap Coordination Group, 2012: 25–6). All these applications relate to environmental challenges we will need to tackle in the short-, medium- and long-term futures. Hence why an imaginary of synthetic biology is often associated with sustainable goals. However, the science is still in its infancy. It has not reached large-scale, mainstream-manufacturing capacity yet, and, therefore, it is still too early to conduct any kind of robust and rigorous assessment of any claims in terms of sustainability. All there is for now is a series of policies and governance strategies that have put in place protocols to deal with ethics and risks of containment. The main challenge is identified as being our ability to control these living factories – technologies that can self-replicate – and prevent them from escaping or impacting on our natural biological habitats. If we were to fail, what is put forward rather ambiguously as a sustainable technology would become an environmental and health hazard. Craig Venter argues that, although we have robust safeguards in place, inherited from the past 30 years of molecular biological science, we should not 'drop our guard', as we operate in uncharted territories (Venter, 2013: 154), a point that supports the consensus expressed by scientific communities around upholding the precautionary principle, i.e. the social responsibility to protect the public from exposure to harm, when scientific investigation has found a plausible risk. Issues of intellectual property also arise: can we, and should we, patent the living? (Baldwin *et al.*, 2012: 136). A more perverse use of this technology by bio-terrorists or bio-hackers is also a critical concern (ETC Group, 2007). Despite the promise of synthetic biology, remaining in command of this technology must be a top priority, alongside a critical questioning about whom this technology benefits, and an ethical framework should be developed to guide the transfer to any industrial applications.

A growing community of genetic designers

Despite the moral and ethical implications of hacking living systems, billions of dollars of government funding is currently injected into the science and engineering communities dedicated to synthetic biology around the world. The objective is to take it to market and 'to invest to accelerate technology responsibly to market' (UK Synthetic Biology Roadmap Coordination Group, 2012: 5). A fast-growing community of biological engineers is emerging thanks to iGEM, an international competition targeted at students from high school to PhD level. Every year, teams compete to develop new biological systems. They are given access to registered biological parts provided by the BioBricks Foundation, an organization dedicated to developing an open-source registry of biological parts, so as to facilitate the design and engineering of new species. Software such as 'Gene Designer 2.0' enables biologists to cut and paste biological devices to create new organisms. Three-dimensional printing of DNA is now an option. The large-scale deployment of such a transformational, cutting-edge technology will revolutionize how and what we design. Projects such as Faber Futures and Biolace may become mundane design contributions.

As we are moving towards a digitization of biology, I believe that the fusion between our current digital manufacturing systems will merge with biological systems. What kind of fashion education will be necessary to address the growth of biology as a technology? Where will designers stand, when creating textiles will be a matter of engineering living organisms? Could and should design become a cultural tool, through which we can emulate informed ethical debates related to extreme genetic engineering?

In the next section, I will propose a new strategy for biodesign that allows designers to position their design practice in the context of a newly emerging synthetic nature.

From biomimicry to biofacture: a new hierarchy for designing with the living

Our current manufacturing models are based on the use of natural resources, be they pumped out of Earth, like petrol, or grown in massive monoculture agricultural landscapes, like cotton. With the emergence of synthetic biology as a technology, we are slowly creating a new 'synthetic nature' that can be programmed, localized and customized. We are beginning to construct relationships with different kinds of 'nature'. This will impact on how we design and manufacture in the near and far future. However, rather than endorsing a future bio-technopolis where synthetic biology replaces conventional manufacturing, I argue that we can sustain a variety of different design strategies, and I suggest a series of design transitions, from biomimicry to 'biofacture', to reach sustainable goals, horizon 2050. In the recent exhibition 'Alive, New Design Frontiers' at the EDF Foundation in Paris, several examples of design, from architecture to products, jewellery, textiles and fashion, were showcased according to these five strategies (see Figure 19.3).

The basis of this new hierarchy promotes biomimicry (the imitation of natural systems and behaviour) as a starting point to develop sustainable design and manufacturing strategies. The field of biomimicry emerged in the 1960s and has since become ever more prominent as a potential model for sustainability. Benyus advocates that we need to produce as nature does, at ambient temperature, without emitting toxic gas, poisoning our water stores and depleting our energy resources (Benyus, 1997: 97).

Starting from biomimicry, the diagram in Figure 19.3 encourages designers to explore new relationships to nature and 'to navigate on a sliding scale between "natural nature", and "re-programmable nature" in the quest for new ecological models' (Collet, 2013: 6). This framework allows designers to develop a critical perspective on how their design practice relates to production methods, be they the result of a natural or a synthetic nature.

The hierarchy I propose revolves around five different relationships to nature:

1   'Nature as a model': Here, designers imitate nature but still rely on conventional and current production processes. For instance, a product such as Velcro is designed to imitate how seed pods (from the burdock plant) hook on to foreign materials, thus providing a means to 'glue' and 'unglue' at will, without the use of chemicals. Yet Velcro is made of polymer-based synthetic fibres, dependent on finite oil resources. 'Nature as a model' is a first step to gain a better understanding of natural systems and to learn from Mother Nature.

2   'Nature as a co-worker' proposes to integrate natural biological systems to achieve the production of a material or a structure. Here, we can refer to the Biocouture project (biocouture.co.uk), where bacteria naturally produce cellulose, which can then be harvested as a non-woven cellulosic material. The bacterium is a co-worker, which needs to be nurtured and fed to produce the cellulose. Manufacturing becomes farming.

3   'Reprogrammed nature' is the realm of synthetic biology. This is where new natural organisms can be genetically engineered to produce custom-made materials and synthetic ecosystems.

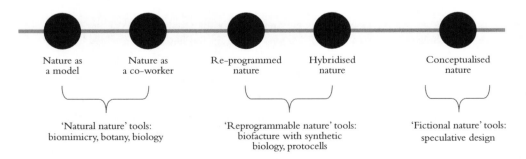

Figure 19.3 Diagram illustrating designing with living systems
Source: ©Carole Collet 2013

With synthetic biology, we can now go beyond imitating the process of nature, we can actually design biological factories ourselves, not arising from billions of years of evolution, but emerging after a few days in a lab.

4   '*Hybridised nature*': Here, designers may investigate the fusion of nanotechnology with synthetic biology to explore sustainable goals. For instance, researchers have now managed to attach gold nano-particles to DNA strands, which could lead to the development of nano-bio electrical living materials. These techniques could be used to develop bio-degradable, wearable technologies.

5   '*Conceptualised nature*': Here, designers use speculative design tools to explore and provoke future ideas, as well as to facilitate a much broader public engagement.

The framework 'From biomimicry to biofacture' enables designers to explore multifarious design perspectives, all related to working with the living, but without relying on one prominent strategy. The advantage of working with living systems is that they are responsive and have the capacity to adapt. As such, they present resilient characteristics currently absent in our technology-driven manufacturing systems. In this framework, 'reprogrammed nature' is a very new possibility that very few designers have encountered or considered to date. But it is this new addition that provokes the need to rethink the way we use natural resources. Despite claims that synthetic biology could lead to sustainable manufacturing, it is of paramount importance that designers, who set out design specifications for products, begin to understand and explore the pros and cons of manufacture versus 'biofacture'. Engaging with this critical framework will allow fashion and textile designers to assess the ethical implications of their design proposals, whether they wish to embrace or rebel against upcoming extreme biotechnologies. What is crucial at this stage is to develop both an understanding and an informed critique of emerging twenty-first-century 'biofacturing' technologies.

Conclusion

The road to sustainability is not linear, and we know that, to address key future environmental challenges, we need to explore step-change drivers. In this chapter, we have focused on the emergence of synthetic biology as a potential candidate to help solve key sustainable challenges, horizon 2050. But, despite claims of sustainability, synthetic biology remains a new, emerging genetic-engineering technology, associated with critical risks and complex ethical issues. In the absence of reliable and rigorous assessments related to such radical biotechnological solutions, it is vital that designers chart new ways to engage with living systems. If we have to learn from nature, the framework 'From biomimicry to biofacture' provides a starting point from which one can engage with sustainable principles, yet critically explore different strategies for manu-facturing with the living. Above all, responsible fashion and textile designers should join the quest for ecologically positive manufacturing, and this includes exploring unprecedented solutions such as synthetic biology, while also remaining critical of the promises of such emerging biotechnologies.

Acknowledgements

With thanks to Central Saint Martins and TFRC, University of the Arts London, for supporting this research project.

References

Ackerman, F. and Stanton, E. A. (2013), *Climate Impacts on Agriculture: A Challenge to Complacency?* Global Development and Environment Institute. Working Paper No. 13–01. Medford, MA: Tufts University.

Baldwin G., Bayer, T., Dickinson, R., Ellis, T., Freemont, P. S., Kitney, B. I., Polizzi, K. and Stan, G.-B. (2012), *Synthetic Biology, A Primer*, London: Imperial College Press.

Ball, P. (2001), Silk and chips. *Nature News*, Nature Publishing Group [online]. Available at: www.nature.com/news/2001/010531/full/news010531-11.html (accessed October 2013).

Benyus, J. (1997), *Biomimicry: Innovation Inspired by Nature*, New York: Harper Collins.

Chieza, N. (2013), *Alive, New Design Frontiers – En Vie, Aux Frontières de Design*. Exhibition Catalogue, Collet, C. (ed.). EDF Foundation.

Christensen, M. C. and Bower, J. (1995), Disruptive technologies: Catching the wave. *Harvard Business Review*, January.

Collet, C. (ed.) (2013), *Alive, New Design Frontiers – En Vie, Aux Frontières de Design*. Exhibition Catalogue. EDF Foundation.

Diamond, J. (2006), *Collapse, How Societies Choose to Fail or Survive*, New York: Penguin Books.

ETC Group (2007), *Extreme Genetic Engineering – An Introduction to Synthetic Biology* [online]. Available at: www.etcgroup.org/issues/synthetic-biology (accessed 24 January 2014).

European Commission (2011), *Green Public Procurement Textiles Technical Background Report*. Brussels: DG-Environment by BRE, European Commission.

Gore, A (2013), *The Future*, New York: WH Allen.

Moore, J. and Rees, E. W. (2013), *State of the World 2013. Is Sustainability Still Possible?* Washington, DC: The Worldwatch Institute, Island Press.

Nuthall, K. (2011), *Regulations Drive Sustainability* [online]. Available at: www.just-style.com/management-briefing/regulations-drive-sustainability_id110457.aspx (accessed October 2013).

OECD and The Royal Society (2010), *Symposium on Opportunities and Challenges in the Emerging Field of Synthetic Biology*, Synthesis Report [online]. Available at: www.oecd-ilibrary.org/science-and-technology/symposium-on-opportunities-and-challenges-in-the-emerging-field-of-synthetic-biology_9789264086265-en;jsessionid=1kwxknihjtlmr.delta (accessed 24 January 2014).

Osborne, G. (2012), Speech by the Chancellor of the Exchequer, Rt Hon George Osborne MP, to the Royal Society, 9 November 2012 [online]. Available at: www.gov.uk/government/speeches/speech-by-the-chancellor-of-the-exchequer-rt-hon-george-osborne-mp-to-the-royal-society (accessed October 2013).

UK Synthetic Biology Roadmap Coordination Group (2012), *A Synthetic Biology Roadmap for the UK*. Technology Strategy Board [online]. Available at: www.rcuk.ac.uk/publications/reports/synthetic biologyroadmap (accessed October 2013).

United Nations, Department of Economic and Social Affairs, Population Division (2013), *World Population Prospects: The 2012 Revision, Highlights and Advance Tables*. Working Paper No. ESA/P/WP.228.

Venter, C. (2013), *Life at the Speed of Light*, New York: Little, Brown.

Wohlsen, M. (2011), *Biopunk. DIY Scientists Hack the Software of Life*, New York: Penguin.

20

THE FASHION SYSTEM THROUGH A LENS OF ZERO-WASTE FASHION DESIGN

Timo Rissanen

Introduction

Since 2008, 'zero-waste fashion design' (ZWFD) has received considerable attention and interest from fashion media, industry and education. In the broad context of fashion and sustainability, at times the attention has been disproportionate relative to the issue it addresses. Often, that larger context is understood poorly, or is overlooked or avoided. Unless we examine the interrelatedness of the different stakeholders within this complex system, any proposed solution risks not having significant long-term impact. Nonetheless, ZWFD provides a useful lens through which we can examine the fashion system and the relationships between and within the fashion industry and fashion users. ZWFD was the topic of my PhD, which I completed in 2013. Since 2010, I have taught an undergraduate elective course on ZWFD at Parsons in New York, as well as supporting students who approach their final collections through ZWFD.

ZWFD in this chapter refers to the activities and processes that lead to garments, the making processes associated with which do not result in any fabric waste. A garment designed through such a process contains all of the fabric that was used to create it, with pre-consumer fabric waste eliminated through design. This waste eradication is achieved through integrating pattern cutting in fashion design, where previously they have been differentiated and linearly consecutive activities. The average fabric wastage created through designing conventional garments is approximately 15 per cent (Cooklin, 1997: 9). There is an inherent risk in the term ZWFD: resolving the issue of pre-consumer fabric waste does not address any other problem of waste in fashion – and there are many – while perhaps implying it does so.

Although each designer may approach ZWFD differently, a generalisation of the process is possible. In broad terms, ZWFD is an approach over time with a concern for fabric wastage. Early in the process, appearance and fit are the main focus, with pattern cutting being integrated alongside any other design ideation tools. Appropriate early decisions – for example, choosing to maintain certain edges of certain pattern pieces at matching angles – can facilitate later tessellation of pattern pieces on a fabric width. Once the main pattern pieces result in satisfactory appearance and fit, they can be examined on actual fabric width. Through repeated trial and reiteration, garment details (designed through pattern cutting) and full interlocking of all pattern pieces on the fabric width are resolved. Throughout the process, the designer and pattern cutter ought to ensure that the cost of manufacturing the garment is kept within the company's target range.

In this chapter, I examine a number of relationships in the fashion system through a lens of ZWFD, as this lens sheds light on relationships and practices that could work better or more efficiently, regardless of whether fabric waste ultimately is a consideration. First, I consider the relationship between fashion design and pattern cutting, questioning the conventional separation of the two roles, and opportunities for new kinds of interaction between these roles to emerge through the lens of zero waste. I then go on to examine the relationship between fashion design and fashion manufacture: in order to create a zero-waste garment, two activities conventionally situated within fashion manufacture, marker making and grading, must shift to be concurrent with fashion design instead of consequent to it. Marker making refers to the placing of the garment pattern pieces on a fabric width. Grading refers to the sizing up or down of pattern pieces to create a size range of garments. As with pattern cutting, it is not suggested that fashion design subsume these activities; rather, opportunities for new modes of interaction may exist, to which the zero-waste lens points. Furthermore, this lens points to deep engagement with cloth, the primary material of fashion, and this can occur at most, perhaps all, points of the fashion system, from fashion design to manufacture to garment use. Finally, the chapter identifies some opportunities for reimagining fashion design education directed at sustainability. Although zero-waste fashion design may seem an unachievable aspiration in the context of the existing fashion system, and is but one of many approaches to one of countless challenges, it nonetheless points to the most urgent shared concern for us: to shift from a conversation shaped by historical behaviours focused on fixing parts of the system, to a holistic look at the system and what is possible. Although ZWFD is a small part of the whole, its reliance on many other parts of the whole points to this interconnectedness.

Fashion design and pattern cutting

Early during my PhD project on ZWFD, I realised that how I had previously designed – mainly through sketching – was not working towards creating garments without creating fabric waste. Pattern cutting became part of the design process. The function of a garment pattern is to help realise the designer's idea aesthetically and produce a garment of appropriate appearance and fit at an appropriate cost. All of these are specific to the company employing the designer. Furthermore, the pattern should facilitate efficient construction time during manufacture and be efficient in terms of fabric use. Whether or not fabric waste is a criterion, the garment pattern impacts on the other three criteria. The garment appearance and fit are entirely inseparable from the garment pattern and, depending partially on how the garment pattern is designed, impact on the cost of the garment. Pattern cutting is, therefore, in effect fashion design. Pye (1968: 1–3) argues that design proposes, workmanship disposes, and, for conventional fashion design, this is true. The pattern cutter is the first of several 'workmen' realising the designer's proposition. ZWFD, however, ruptures this divisive hierarchy. The pattern cutter is as much a designer as the designer. Within conventional practice, problem-solving the garment appearance is almost solely the designer's responsibility and the activity for which the designer is often publicly lauded. ZWFD raises the question: what space is there for sharing this responsibility, and its rewards, with the pattern cutter?

Fashion design tends to focus on the garment appearance and fit and the cost of producing it. How the pattern pieces of the garment place on a fabric width is ordinarily not a concern for fashion designers. During a lecture in 2011, Holly McQuillan stated that she is not satisfied with a garment unless the pattern is also visually as pleasing to her as the garment (Figure 20.1). In her work, the pattern diagrams are as essential to the aesthetic whole as the garments, and a concern for eliminating fabric wastage is part of that whole, rather than solely a technical endeavour. McQuillan is not alone in this. Yeohlee Teng has regularly exhibited the garment patterns alongside her garments (Teng and Major, 2003). They are inseparable from the complete work. Similarly, in displaying his work in print, Yoshiki Hishinuma (1986) includes diagrams demonstrating the cuts of some garments. These are no technical illustrations; they are integral to presenting the ideas. The three designers uncover the usual invisibility of the pattern. ZWFD points to a question: is the final garment somehow more valuable than the pattern that was used to cut it?

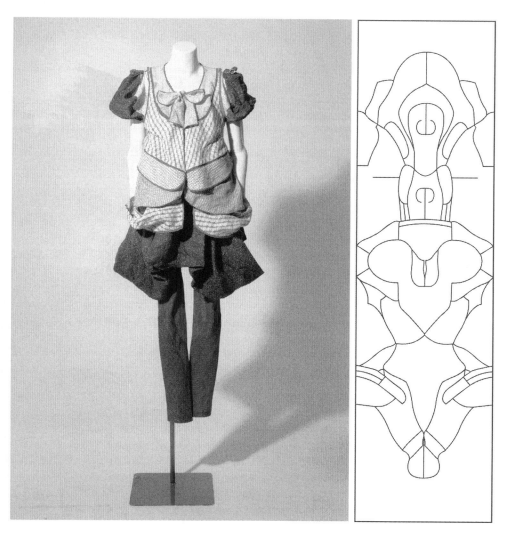

Figure 20.1 A zero-waste fashion design garment and pattern by Holly McQuillan, with textile by Genevieve Packer

Pattern cutting is a skilled activity that makes ZWFD possible. Although pattern cutting is usually taught as part of fashion design, in industry practice the two tend to be separate roles. In a company that manufactures its garments in another country, the roles may also be geographically separate. In such a situation, ZWFD may become unfeasible, unless new approaches to communication between the fashion designer and pattern cutter are imagined. Perhaps the primary change in these communications, however, is irrespective of geographic location. I would argue that communication between the fashion designer and pattern cutter is mainly a 'top–down' conversation. For ZWFD to work, non-hierarchical, reciprocal communication is crucial. Opportunities for such collaborations ought to be researched further.

Patternmaking (USA, Australia) and pattern cutting (UK) are often presented and used as interchangeable terms, depending on location. In the context of ZWFD, pattern cutting seems more descriptive of a fashion design practice of the future. Its creative scope is broad, and it suggests action rather than reaction. Patternmaking is most commonly a response to an idea by the designer. However, Shingo Sato, Julian Roberts, Holly McQuillan, Yoshiki Hishinuma and others have demonstrated that pattern cutting can be as powerful a design ideation tool as sketching (Rissanen, 2013: 38–42). Pattern cutting can initiate the design process. My aim is not to pose pattern cutting and sketching as opposites; each has its advantages, and the two are complementary. The significance of cutting cloth is reflected in the title Roberts, McQuillan and I chose for a joint research project, 'The Cutting Circle' (McQuillan *et al.*, 2013). We see cutting as essential to design practice, and we recognise that the cut has implications beyond our initial intentions as designers. To cut is to take a risk, whether an aesthetic, economic or ecological risk. It is also, however, liberating. In a now–unavailable blog post from 2010 (Rissanen, 2013: 144), the designer Tara St James notes that the fear of failure disappears with the first cut: 'Once the fabric is cut it's no longer perfect, no longer pristine, no longer untouched, and can both mentally and literally be transformed'.

In my PhD study on ZWFD, I proposed fashion design activity to negotiate four criteria during designing: appearance, fit, cost and sustainability. I regard the four criteria of equal importance; fashion design is a process of finding a balance between them. The criterion of sustainability is unfolding as we engage with it, and, as Fletcher notes (2008: 166–9, 175), appropriateness is key: different garments are used in different ways and at different intensities, and this variability needs to be accounted for during design. Therefore, different issues under the broad criterion of sustainability will bear different weights, depending on the garment being designed.

Fashion design and manufacture

If it were deemed desirable for ZWFD to be widely adopted, a demolishing of traditional hierarchies within the industry would be required. Traditionally, fashion design has dominated the way in which the industry is presented to the public through media. For example, the website style.com almost always includes a photograph of the designer to complete a suite of runway photographs, implying the collection, almost always the work of a team, is created by this one individual. Alternative examples exist. Kirke (1998) and Golbin (2009), in their respective books on Madeleine Vionnet, highlight in rich detail the crucial roles that various employees, named in the books, played within Vionnet's company, contributing to her success. More recently, McRobbie (1998) has called for the gap between fashion design and manufacture in fashion education to be bridged, albeit for different reasons. McRobbie noted the financial difficulties that fashion designers in the UK ran into, when, upon graduation, they were encouraged to set up businesses without sufficient knowledge of manufacturing or business practices. A new reason can now be added to the overall rationale for introducing manufacture and business into fashion design education in a richer way: sustainability.

ZWFD does not function well within conventional fashion industry hierarchies. In ZWFD, marker making and grading are necessarily design as well as manufacturing activities. Both activities have direct impacts on whether fabric waste will be created or not, and, therefore, these are inherently part of ZWFD. Fashion designers possess a capacity for spatial reasoning in shaping cloth over a human body, and it would seem a natural extension of this to negotiate the garment within the space of the cloth, with the pattern cutter where necessary.

In ZWFD, pattern grading is a design as well as manufacturing activity. In my PhD study, I speculated that hybrid approaches were required in grading the patterns of zero-waste garments (Rissanen, 2013: 131–2). The identification of the most appropriate approach to grading a garment on a case-by-case basis is not typical of the conventional industry approach to grading. Grading is hardly a perfect 'science', and, even when fabric waste is not a consideration, some dynamism in a conventionally rigid aspect of fashion manufacture could result in efficiencies of time and cost.

The cut and construction of some zero-waste garments I have created, notably the Endurance Shirt of 2009 and its follow-up, Endurance Shirt II of 2011, have been described as complex and, as a result, costly to make (Figure 20.2). These shirts would not be appropriate in terms of cost or manufacturability for a lower-priced product line. However, future repair and alteration were criteria during the design of these garments, resulting in a number of additional seams that might seem unnecessary, but that in fact facilitate later garment alteration. I argue that a larger initial investment made in the construction of these garments, with a resulting higher cost, can be offset by later repair and alteration, resulting in a prolonged usable life for the garments and, hypothetically, a lower cost per wear.

Conversations about the cost of fashion, real and perceived, are required. The human aspect of sustainability, including the right to a living wage and safe working conditions for every person along the chain of manufacture, has been absent from much mainstream economic

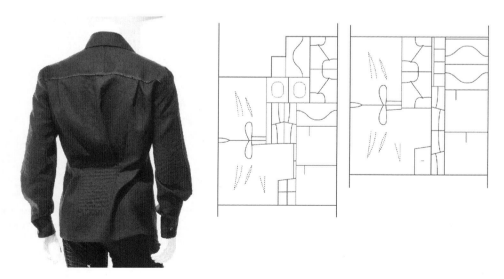

Figure 20.2 Endurance Shirt by Timo Rissanen

discourse in fashion. The garment factory fires in Pakistan and Bangladesh in 2012, followed by the collapse of the Rana Plaza garment factory complex in Bangladesh in April 2013, have made the real human cost of inexpensive fashion visible in a tragic way. It might be difficult to see what, if any, connection there is between these catastrophes and the perceived added cost, via increased time in design and manufacture, of ZWFD. The link is simple: these wastes, of fabric and of human life, are rarely considered such within the dominant economic structures that govern how the fashion system operates. Yet, in conversation, we agree that not wasting fabric is a good idea, and that even a single avoidable death within fashion is unacceptable.

Fashion in use and in time

Fashion has a particular relationship with time. Fast fashion speaks to both the speed at which new styles are manufactured and sold, and the relationships we have with our clothes. The speed is present in fashion design: to be able to design fast is an asset in designer employability. What then of ZWFD, which, at least in the context of my PhD study, was a slow way to design when I compared it with my previous, conventional approach to design? Part of the slowness was due to being a novice. However, the artificial context was also an opportunity to reflect on one's process extensively during designing; this is apparent in the journals produced during that project (Rissanen, 2013: Appendix C). The reflection inevitably extended from fabric waste to garment use and transformative practices situated in a hypothetical yet plausible future, such as repair and alteration. These in turn informed design: certain garment details were specifically designed to facilitate future repair and alteration. This additional time during designing was reflected in how the garment was considered within an expanded life span. Given that up to 80 per cent of a garment's energy consumption occurs during use (Fletcher, 2008: 78), allowing more time during designing for considering the garment use phase would seem common sense. However, within the current economic value systems of most fashion companies, design time to consider use might be difficult to justify.

Some fashion designers speak of speed and time in ways that perhaps do not fit the dominant norm. Issey Miyake is frank: 'To change every six months . . . is crazy. It's designer suicide' (Frankel, 2001: 48). ZWFD reinforces the notion that good ideas are worth revisiting. The 2-year gap between the two Endurance Shirts was an opportunity to identify possibilities for improvement, and, at the time of writing, another 2 years later, that process has not ended. Granted, this work is not part of the dominant industry system. However, Maison Martin Margiela speaks to the advantages of reflecting on ideas:

> We have always had garments that we continue to propose for many seasons in a row (in some instances twelve!). It remains more important for us that someone finds their way of dressing as opposed to a way of dressing as prescribed by anyone else or an over-riding trend.
>
> *(Frankel, 2001: 35)*

Furthermore, Margiela touches on the seemingly intangible relationship that fashion design has with garment use. Just as future repair and alteration can be speculated on in fashion design, so too can richer patterns of garment use and disposal. Although fashion changes as society does, the pace of real fashion change – that is, the change in what most of us wear – is not as fast as the fashion media and many companies would have us believe. With practice, any designer is likely to become more adept and faster at ZWFD, and yet one should wish that the opportunities for reflection on garment use are always allowed for.

Fashion design education

Since 2010, I have taught an elective course titled Zero Waste Garment at Parsons. I developed the course from the findings of my PhD research. Although, overall, students find the course useful, it sometimes sits uncomfortably within the overall curriculum students take. A broad challenge for fashion design education is that, for a long time, sustainability-focused or -related courses have been mainly offered as electives. In such an approach, sustainability may seem optional, an added extra. This has been the case with the ZWFD course at Parsons until recently. There are now degrees focusing on sustainability in fashion, such as the MA in Fashion and the Environment offered by the London College of Fashion, established in 2008, and a Masters programme in Sustainability in Fashion offered by ESMOD Berlin, established in 2011. Although the increased presence of sustainability issues in fashion design education is to be commended, the challenge is to incorporate it into core courses at undergraduate and postgraduate levels. Presenting 'sustainability' as somehow separate from 'conventional' fashion design is risky, in that it can marginalise the complex, inevitable problems that the industry and humanity are facing, while potentially doing a disservice to students' learning.

After a near decade of planning, Parsons launched a new undergraduate curriculum in August 2013. The new first year of a 4-year degree includes a required course titled Sustainable Systems. All undergraduate students at Parsons, including fashion design students, will take this course in their first year of study. Using water, air and climate change as access points, the course teaches systems thinking to students. The curricula for the 3 years that follow will build on this learning. Implementing such a shift in a relatively large institution comes with challenges, including faculty development. Different yet parallel developments at California College of the Arts suggest that these challenges can, through shared commitment, be effectively overcome (Grose, 2013: 146).

Weekly reflective journal entries are a requirement of the course at Parsons, to provide a space for the students to reflect on and recognise their own learning about ZWFD in the context of their overall studies. In my experience of teaching the course, the most significant challenge for students is to understand that they could not design the garment in its entirety through sketching; each student realises this at a different point in the course. This is a broader challenge for sustainability as well. In 2011, a committee at Parsons attempted to measure the ecological literacy (level of understanding of sustainability) of graduating students, using their graduating work for this assessment. For fashion students, the assessed work was a set of photographs of the 'final' collection. Very quickly, we realised that, with no written statement to accompany the photographs, such an assessment was impossible: sustainability, or zero waste, is not evident in how a garment appears. ZWFD, in that sense, becomes an access for students to understand that design is also, and primarily, a thinking rather than solely a drawing activity. Student C. Ca. reflected, at the conclusion of the course: '[Zero-waste] garments are not just about creating a product to sell. They are about exposing the design process, and invoking curiosity about how and where a garment is made' (Rissanen, 2013: 265).

A key challenge for including ZWFD in fashion design education is that pattern cutting is often taught as separate from, or supportive of, fashion design, whereas fashion design is presented as a process of inspiration and market research, fabric and colour selection, and extensive sketching. Pattern cutting tends to be presented as subsequent rather than concurrent to fashion design. Furthermore, pattern cutting courses, as well as texts, tend to present pattern cutting as a somewhat closed, rule- or convention-bound and technical process, rather than the open, creative and *creating* process that it can be. These factors might risk conditioning students and, thus, future fashion designers to perceive pattern cutting as a primarily technical endeavour – which it also can be – potentially preventing them from seeing the creative potential of pattern cutting in fashion design. I argue that pattern cutting and making garments are inseparable from, and integral to, fashion design, because the garment pattern is inseparable from the attributes of garment appearance, fit and cost, as well as sustainability. During undergraduate study, I received a robust, yet limited and limiting, education in pattern cutting. We were assessed on how accurately our patterns reflected the sketch. Such a narrow approach denies the opportunity to use pattern cutting as a dynamic design ideation tool. In my experience as a teacher, students tend to sketch what they already know. It is more challenging to draw the unknown. Pattern cutting combined with sketching can enrich the exploratory ideation phase in a design project, particularly the enquiry into form.

For future courses on ZWFD, two key issues to address are presenting it within its larger context, the interconnected fashion system, and the relationship between fashion design and fashion manufacture. Certain challenges for ZWFD arise from manufacture. Education can foster close collaboration between fashion design and manufacture. If the two reside within different departments or institutions, collaborative projects between them should be fostered. There are areas of expertise unique to each, but the goals are common, and these goals rely on the specific fields of expertise.

Conclusion

ZWFD needs examining in its broader context of fashion and sustainability. A zero-waste garment is not inherently 'good'; the context is decisive. For example, a zero-waste garment produced within a fast-fashion business model, worn a few times after purchase and then discarded, is hardly a model of best practice. This chapter, together with all in this book, demonstrates that the context is complex and situation-specific, and yet that need not prevent us from examining it.

A fashion designer with an understanding of pattern cutting and garment manufacturing practices, particularly pattern grading and marker making, is able to design garments while greatly reducing or eliminating the amount of fabric waste generated in the production of the garment. ZWFD may differ from design processes that are currently being taught within fashion design courses worldwide, but the skills learned during fashion design education, as well as through working in the fashion industry, can be harnessed for an approach that eliminates or dramatically reduces the amount of fabric wasted. ZWFD demonstrates that existing skills and practices can have value added to them by utilising them in new ways.

In an essay titled 'To cut is to think', Germano Celant (1997: 22) states: 'The cut is the soul of clothing'. It is partially the cut that transforms cloth into clothing, but can we accept most clothing today to have a vital, vibrant soul? The essay title, however, rings true for ZWFD, and could for all fashion design: we ought to think with every cut we make into cloth. Cutting and making garments are fashion design. As a practice, fashion design could be seen as an interplay between various crafts and critical thinking, and could be framed as such in fashion education. Within that context, ZWFD can be a metaphor for deep engagement with materials, processes and garment use, by the fashion industry and fashion users.

Is zero-waste fashion a utopian idea? Although ZWFD may seem difficult in the context of the current fashion system, it is not impossible to imagine a reorganisation of its hierarchies that would facilitate the creation of garments without the creation of fabric waste. I encourage further research on ZWFD, conducted in partnership with companies of varying sizes. What are the opportunities and barriers to ZWFD? If a company (or part of one) reorganizes itself to facilitate ZWFD, how does that manifest in the overall operations of a company? The involvement of industry partners is crucial to provide an accurate sense of the opportunities and barriers. The involvement of industry partners may also be one of the main challenges, as business has a propensity towards promoting solely positive outcomes. Traditional research reporting of successes, failures and everything in between may perhaps seem risky to business. How do we create a culture within fashion where competing companies mutually share information for the benefit of all?

Design is problem-solving. In the case of fashion, the primary problem that we have set for fashion design is to create profit for the company employing the designer. What becomes possible if we articulate a whole new set of problems for fashion design to solve? Through inter-disciplinary collaborations, imagination is the limit. Our focus ought to shift from conversations about fixing part of the system, to conversations about what is possible, and what we want our shared future to be.

References

Celant, G. (1997), To cut is to think, in G. Celant (ed.) *Art/Fashion*, New York: Guggenheim Museum: 21–7.

Cooklin, G. (1997), *Garment Technology for Fashion Designers*, Oxford, UK: Blackwell Science.

Fletcher, K. (2008), *Sustainable Fashion and Textiles. Design Journeys*, London and Sterling, VA: Earthscan.

Frankel, S. (2001), *Visionaries. Interviews With Fashion Designers*, London: V&A.

Golbin, P. (ed.) (2009), *Madeleine Vionnet*, New York: Rizzoli International.

Grose, L. (2013), Fashion design education for sustainability practice. Reflections on undergraduate level teaching, in M. A. Gardetti and A. L. Torres (eds) *Sustainability in Fashion and Textiles. Values, Design, Production and Consumption*, Sheffield, UK: Greenfield Publishing: 134–47.

Hishinuma, Y. (ed.) (1986), *Clothes by Yoshiki Hishinuma*, Tokyo: Yobisha.

Kirke, B. (1998), *Madeleine Vionnet*, San Francisco, CA: Chronicle Books.

McQuillan, H., Rissanen, T. and Roberts, J. (2013), 'The cutting circle: how making challenges design', *Research Journal of Textiles And Apparel*, 17, 1: 39–49.

McRobbie, A. (1998), *British Fashion Design: Rag Trade or Image Industry?* London and New York: Routledge.

Pye, D. (1968), *The Nature and Art of Workmanship*, Cambridge, UK: Cambridge University Press.

Rissanen, T. (2013), *Zero-waste fashion design. A study at the intersection of cloth, fashion design and pattern cutting.* PhD thesis. Sydney: University of Technology Sydney.

Teng, Y. and Major, J. S. (eds) (2003), *Yeohlee: Work. Material Architecture*, Mulgrave, Australia: Peleus Press.

21

FASHION BRANDS AND WORKERS' RIGHTS

Liz Parker

Introduction

The collapse of the Rana Plaza building in Bangladesh, in April 2013, added the names of more than 1,000 men and women to the list of men and women who have been killed in fashion supply chains in the last 10 years. The tragedy focused the world's attention on working conditions in global fashion supply chains. On a daily basis, workers in global fashion supply chains face pernicious violations of their rights to a living wage, reasonable working hours, a safe working environment free of harassment and abuse and a secure employment relationship, among many others.

The focus of this chapter is on the work being undertaken by fashion brands to address these violations of workers' rights in mass-manufacture supply chains. This is not to suggest that these industry initiatives hold the key to enhanced well-being for workers, nor that the work of the fair-trade or artisanal movement holds no potential for respecting the rights of the people who make clothes. Instead, it is a reflection on the work that major brands and retailers are doing in relation to the greatest proportion of export fashion production.

In this chapter, I draw on existing research, as well as 14 years' experience working as an activist, educator and project manager in relation to workers' rights in consumer product supply chains. I open the chapter with an overview of workers' rights in the garment industry, before reviewing brand initiatives to address them in a context of weak government protection of workers' rights and limited opportunities for holding companies accountable. Many brands and retailers have adopted a 'code+audit' model, and some are experimenting with ways to empower workers and build capacity of suppliers, yet few have taken significant steps to address their commercial practices. Most recently, more than 100 brands have signed the Accord on Fire and Building Safety in Bangladesh, a form of joint liability agreement, which holds signs of promise as a new form of corporate accountability. I conclude with reflections on additional areas for future research in relation to empathy, trade unions, worker well-being and the relationship between production and consumption.

Workers' rights

Research by academics such as Stephanie Barrientos, NGOs such as the Clean Clothes Campaign, governmental institutions such as the International Labour Organisation (ILO), brands such as H&M and trade union federation IndustriALL Global Union provides extensive evidence of violations of a range of workers' rights in fashion supply chains across garment exporting countries in Asia, Africa, the Americas, and west, central and east Europe. Women (who account for around 75 per cent of the estimated 25 million garment workers globally), migrant workers and home-based workers are particularly affected by the fashion production system. Not all working environments where violations of workers' rights occur will be dark, dirty sweatshops. A number, though certainly not all, of contemporary factories are of modern industrial factory design, with high ceilings, space, good lighting and sufficient ventilation. However, although particular health and safety standards may be met, this does not mean that workers have their rights respected.

The most common reference points for workers' rights in national labour law and corporate codes of conduct are the conventions of the ILO, a United Nations agency. ILO conventions are legally binding international treaties for ratification by Member States. They represent minimum, rather than highest, standards of human welfare, even if many remain aspirational. Drawing on a small number of ILO conventions, the following areas are commonly regarded as key to workers' rights in consumer product supply chains:

1 freedom of association and collective bargaining;
2 forced or compulsory labour;
3 child labour;

Figure 21.1 'Graffiti for garment workers' by Clean Clothes Ireland, in collaboration with MArk FiTZ Art for Living Wage Campaign 2013

Source: MArk FiTZ; see www.markfitzart.com

4   discrimination;
5   wages and remuneration;
6   health and safety;
7   working hours;
8   employment relationship;
9   harassment and abuse.

From a rights-based perspective, trade union rights, including freedom of association and collective bargaining, are central to a decent workplace. These process rights provide an opportunity for workers to collectively have a voice and negotiate terms and conditions of employment, such as wages and hours (Barrientos and Smith, 2007: 714). Fulfilment of trade union rights should ensure, theoretically at least, that conditions in the workplace can be monitored and should establish a system of workplace governance whereby workers are supported to bring cases against employers. Workplace unions may federate to national trade unions or to a global union federation that deals with labour rights relevant to the sector on an international level, such as international campaigns and negotiating agreements with multinational companies (McMullen and Maher, 2011).

There are no recent statistics on union density in the garment industry, but industry commentator Doug Miller estimates that between 5 and 10 per cent of workers are unionised in independent trade unions. In part, these low figures are due to repression, which can range from union members being given the worse jobs in a workplace to dismissal, blacklisting and verbal or physical abuse. In some garment exporting countries, such as Vietnam and China, the right to freedom of association is denied by law, and, in other countries, this right is restricted in free-trade zones. Other factors including gender, insecure employment contracts, migrant status and sourcing practices, such as frequent relocation of production by buyers, restrict the ability of workers to join unions (McMullen and Maher, 2011).

Governments

The extent of violations of workers' rights suggests that governments are failing in their responsibility to protect workers. This can be viewed in terms of the content, monitoring and enforcement of laws. In theory, ratified ILO conventions should be embedded in state legislation, but, in practice, this is not always the case, and, in many garment-exporting countries, the conventions are not even ratified. Labour inspectors are employed by states to check standards in factories, but these can be grossly under-resourced. Human Rights Watch, for example, reports how, in 2013, the Bangladesh Ministry of Labour had just eighteen inspectors and assistant inspectors to monitor an estimated 100,000 factories in Dhaka (Human Rights Watch, 2013). Labour courts provide a mechanism for enforcement of laws and provide workers with a means of redress in relation to their employers, but these may not exist, as in Cambodia, which has no labour court to pass legally binding judgements (Worrell and David, 2013), and, where they do, protracted legal processes, lack of resources (International Labour Organisation, 2003), corruption and intimidation prevent workers from achieving redress.

Strengthening and improving state protection of labour rights are challenged by the fact that national governments may be fearful of driving away sources of economic development, job creation or taxation by enforcing laws and regulation. In addition, the overlap between garment manufacturers and government, such as in Bangladesh, where more than thirty garment industrialists are members of parliament (approx 10 per cent) and where many others have strong political ties, is a further potential hindrance (Chalmers, 2013).

There is pressure and support from intergovernmental organizations such as the ILO for governments to protect workers' rights, but none has sufficiently strong enforcement mechanisms. A number of international trade agreements include monitoring and supervision mechanisms, such as the European Union's GSP+ system. Countries that sign these trade agreements are expected to protect labour rights or face the withdrawal of trade preferences. In practice, this rarely happens, although the EU withdrew GSP+ trade preferences from Sri Lanka and Burma/Myanmar, and the US government withdrew GSP preferences from Bangladesh after the Rana Plaza disaster.

Corporate accountability

There are a number of mechanisms for holding brands accountable for human-rights violations: legal options to hold a company liable for violations committed abroad, mediation mechanisms that have the potential to directly address the responsibility of companies, and mechanisms linked to the financial support, such as investment, that companies receive (International Federation for Human Rights, 2012). Nevertheless, holding brands accountable is extremely difficult.

Corruption, the unwillingness or inability of states to ensure foreign companies respect workers' rights, absence of adequate judicial systems allowing victims to seek justice where the brand is based, and legal obstacles due to the complex structure of multinationals are just some of the barriers to using them to seek justice (International Federation for Human Rights, 2012).

In this context of failed governance and lack of mechanisms to hold brands to account, and facing mounting criticism of violations of labour rights in supply chains, in the 1990s global fashion brands began undertaking voluntary initiatives to address workers' rights violations. Today, the majority of UK high-street clothing companies are engaging in voluntary corporate social responsibility initiatives in some shape or form, to address workers' rights in their supply chains. As voluntary, brand-driven initiatives, they lack mechanisms to hold companies accountable.

Code + audit model

A common approach by brands and retailers to address workers' rights violations is the code+audit model. This entails adopting a code of conduct outlining the expectations the brand has of employers in manufacturing units in relation to working conditions, and then carrying out social audits, a form of factory inspection, during which the workplace is assessed against the code.

What happens if violations of the code are found varies from company to company. Some brands take a zero tolerance approach to particular violations such as forced child labour and will cease a relationship with a factory if these are uncovered. Where the violations are not regarded to be of such serious nature, a set of remedial or corrective actions are typically put into place, and the factory will be given time to make improvements. Some brands use audit findings to rate their suppliers' compliance with the code and introduce incentive schemes for their staff to place more orders with better factories and fewer orders with worse-performing suppliers.

The limitations of this code+audit approach for ensuring decent workplaces have been extensively researched (see, for example, Oxfam, 2010, or Pruett, 2005). A study of eleven companies, twenty-three supplier sites and 418 workers, plus interviews with eighty key informants across different industrial sectors, by Barrientos and Smith (2007), found this approach has brought about limited change. The researchers found that change generally benefitted directly employed, permanent workers and was related to 'outcome' standards, in particular health and safety and working hours. Less change took place in relation to non-permanent workers, or in relation to 'process' rights, such as freedom of association. Workers in manufacturers subcontracted by top-tier suppliers tend not to be included in audits, because the brand is not aware of the subcontracting – or chooses not to be aware.

Some of the limitations of the code+audit approach relate to the fact that best practice in auditing is not implemented, such as ensuring the gender of the auditor is the same as the interviewee. The research shows, however, that the limitations are more systemic, meaning social audits can even have negative consequences. As a system, the code+audit model encourages secrecy and cover-ups, such as coaching workers on what to say to auditors, as the key incentive for factories is to secure the next order and meet brand demands, rather than to bring about long-term change and well-being of workers. The code+audit model is a useful data-gathering tool as a snapshot of factory conditions, but the risk of pushing violations further out of sight limits its efficacy.

Beyond the code+audit model

Recognising the limitations of the code+audit model, many brands are experimenting, typically through projects, with different ways to address workers' rights in their supply chains, broadly grouped around the following themes:

- addressing buying practices;
- capacity building;
- empowering workers;
- joint liability agreements.

Addressing commercial practices

Nova and Kline (2013) argue that it is the very business model that undermines all corporate efforts to address workers' rights, and they place particular emphasis on pricing strategies. As You Sow (Galland and Jurewicz, 2010), quoting research by the MFA Forum, highlights six key factors in brand–manufacturer relationships that have a direct impact on working conditions: unstable relationships, downward pressure on prices, increased quality demands, shorter time pressures, changes to orders and cancellation of orders. Other research finds similar issues and demonstrates how these practices are linked to workers' rights violations, including low wages, insecure employment relationships, long working hours, worker stress and health and safety issues (see, for example, Ethical Trading Initiative, n.d.; Gap Inc., n.d.; Acona Ltd, 2004; Raworth, 2004; Gooch *et al.*, 2008).

In contrast, responsible commercial practices could include staggering orders throughout the year to enable continuous employment, sticking to the critical path to prevent bottlenecks in production and consequent pressure on workers to meet deadlines, and, critically, paying a price to suppliers that can enable a living wage to be paid and other reforms to be made. Gooch *et al.* (2008) propose brands should establish a set of operational principles that define the ground rules for purchasing relationships and develop an enabling environment where brand staff and manufacturers are incentivised on performance against both commercial and ethical trading targets. No high-street fashion brand can claim to have aligned its commercial practices with its ethical responsibilities, and few appear to have even partially addressed commercial practices.

Responsible purchasing will not necessarily lead to improved working conditions: increasing prices paid to suppliers does not guarantee that workers will be paid more; managing the critical path better will not necessarily mean that factory management will manage working hours any better, and so on. Nevertheless, reform of commercial practices is necessary to make it feasible for factory owners to address workers' rights, although this needs to be coupled with effective accountability mechanisms, such as as unions and genuinely independent monitoring of factories (Nova and Kline, 2013).

Capacity building

Another common response by brands to the failure of the code+audit model to improve working conditions has been to develop capacity-building projects to address a perceived lack of resources, technical expertise and management systems in factories, based on the idea that failings in these areas are part of the root causes of labour rights violations (Locke, 2013: 78). Brands, as well as other actors such as donors, are experimenting with a number of different capacity-building projects that typically aim to improve working conditions through improvements in the skills, technology and organisational systems within the workplace, particularly in relation to factory productivity and efficiency, human resources management, communication systems and information sharing. A number of projects are aiming for a win–win–win for suppliers, workers and brands: increase supplier efficiency and productivity, so that workers' wages increase while hours decrease, meaning brands can benefit from better-quality, lower-priced goods.

There are a number of concerns about capacity-building projects. Fundamentally, Nova and Kline (2013) argue that these largely or completely ignore brand pricing practices, 'the primary obstacle' to progress in workers' rights, arguing that better communications or trust building cannot address this. In other words, they suggest that the analysis on which capacity-building projects are based is fundamentally flawed.

Even where wages are raised or hours reduced, they can be proportionately low compared with gains to the factory and, in real terms, do not indicate significant change. For example, a British government-funded project in Bangladesh, involving UK high-street brands, achieved daily productivity increases of 17.07 per cent in the factories involved, and yet average monthly take-home pay increased by an average of just 7.63 per cent (491 taka) (DFID Bangladesh, 2013), leaving wages significantly under a living wage. In addition, there is some evidence to suggest that there may be unforeseen consequences of productivity-related changes, such as increased stress and pressure and risks to health and safety (Brown and O'Rourke, 2008). The specific impact on job losses and vulnerable workers such as home-based or migrant workers and gender-related impacts appear to be seldom considered, even though there is potential for there to be negative consequences in these areas (Parker, 2011).

Empowering workers

Some brands are exploring how to empower workers in an attempt to enable workers to express concerns about their workplace and to act on these concerns. This can involve training for workers to better understand rights, raise grievances and build worker representation (see, for example, Social Accountability International, 2012; Ethical Trading Initiative, 2013). One project supporting home-based workers in India includes a mechanism to inform home-based workers how much they should be paid for a piece and allows them to report when they do not receive this rate (Ethical Trading Initiative, 2010).

From a rights-based perspective, worker empowerment can be understood to refer to the ability of workers to join trade unions to achieve their rights, but there is a lack of evidence to date to demonstrate that external interventions can actually facilitate the formation of trade unions, and few brand-led projects directly focus on unionisation. In addition, and critically, for as long as brand commercial practices have an impact on freedom of association, the impact of worker empowerment projects is likely to be limited. For example, the flexible production that brands desire requires a flexible workforce, which in turn leads to job insecurity and short-term contracts, and workers without permanent jobs face more challenges joining a union.

Joint liability agreements

By the beginning of 2014, the Accord on Fire and Building Safety in Bangladesh had been signed by over 150 brands, international trade unions for garment workers and retail workers and Bangladeshi trade unions and witnessed by NGOs. The legally binding nature of the Accord on brand signatories, the central role for workers and their representatives, the fact that aspects of brands' commercial practices are addressed and the alliance of civil society actors involved, as well as the number of brand signatories, make the Accord distinctive.

Anner *et al.* (2013) argue that the Accord represents a new model in corporate accountability, in which brands are held jointly responsible with employers for workers' rights violations in subcontracted supply chains. They suggest that the Accord holds promise for addressing workers' rights, because it reflects core elements of 'jobbers agreements', the most successful effort to systematically eradicate sweatshop conditions to their knowledge, while cautioning that the historical context is also relevant. The jobbers agreements were signed by workers, contractors (suppliers) and, critically, lead firms (brands), in the middle of the twentieth century in the United States, and led to fair prices and stable orders, increased wages and other benefits and reduced working hours for garment workers (Anner *et al.*, 2013). The authors describe four key ways that the Accord reflects core principles of the jobbers agreements: regulation of brand buying practices; workers' representatives as fully equal and empowered participants; binding, contractually enforceable obligations on brands; and coverage of a broad portion of the industry.

As an emerging body of work, the theoretical underpinning and nomenclature, as well as the impact of such agreements, are yet to be established, but 'joint liability' agreements such as the Accord appear to hold potential for change.

Reflections

The initiatives described above show the range of work fashion brands are undertaking to address workers' rights issues in the garment industry. However, no major high-street brand or retailer claims it is meeting minimum labour rights standards across its entire supply chain. Although improvements are being made, low wages, long working hours and fear of repression for joining a trade union remain, and basic health and safety are compromised for many workers. A number of areas for future research have been outlined throughout the chapter. In this section, some additional points are considered that may provide further insights.

First, workers do not seem to be treated by consumers or fashion mediators (people working in brands, agents and manufacturers) as human beings with lives, dreams and aspirations, and their voices, or those of their advocates, are rarely heard. I suggest these are significant factors for the way in which workers are treated. Anecdotes suggest empathy for workers could be a tool for change in this regard, such as one shared with me by a designer: she left mass manufacture when she realised that the sense of frustration she felt positioning each and every sequin to create a cat motif on a jumper, on a computer, would be multiplied for the person who would have to physically stitch each of the sequins on. A question that then emerges is

Figure 21.2 Shahnaz Akter works as a sewing-machine operator in a factory in Bangladesh, where she sews 100 collars to shirts an hour. She lives close to the factory, so she walks to work every morning with her best friend. She set up a worker committee in 2006, which she now leads

Source: Schone Kleren Campagne, ©Marieke van der Velden/Hollandse Hoogte

how can empathy be facilitated that takes into account attitudes towards class, age, gender and race (Entwistle, 2000) (as the people who make clothes for export are mainly young Asian women from low-income backgrounds)? Could direct encounters between workers and consumers and mediators, virtually or face to face, be one way to do this?

Second, as described above, the right to join a trade union is an enabling right, in the sense that it has the potential to lead to other rights being respected. It puts workers in control of deciding what is important for them and monitoring conditions in their own workplaces: a long-term, sustainable approach. If brands address their commercial practices, trade unions, in theory, should be able to ensure that benefits are passed on to workers. Yet, the ways in which the right to freedom of association is violated are manifold. The conditions in which trade unions develop and grow and the kinds of intervention that can encourage their formation, particularly in a woman-dominated workforce, are grossly underrepresented in the academic literature on workers' rights in the garment industry.

Third, I would like to see robust and comparable research into the well-being of workers done 'with' rather than 'to' workers. A fashion system that supports well-being incorporates the idea of seeing people beyond 'workers', seeing them as people with lives outside the workplace. This research would take into account gender, the environment in which people live and work, and people's own sense of well-being, so that we shift from a top–down-dominated model to one that values and acts on people's own views of what is important and relevant to them. Although there are flaws in the approach, perhaps the OECD's dimensions of well-being, building on the work of Stiglitz, Sen and Fitoussi, are a starting point: health, education and skills, housing, social connections, civic engagement and governance, environmental quality, personal security and subjective well-being (OECD, 2011).

The fourth area is the relationship between production and consumption, neither of which is the primary agent in determining fashion (Entwistle, 2000). How can the relationship between consumption and production be calibrated to promote decent working conditions? If responsible buying practices are taken to their full conclusion, and the key objectives for buyers – speed, price and quality – are fundamentally addressed, can fashion business and consumption continue to operate as usual? From the consumer side, will slowing down purchases of fashion items, buying less, exchanging, making or gifting clothes negatively or positively impact on the well-being of the people making clothes? What is the impact of 'ethical' consumer shopping behaviour, for example in relation to fair trade or organic, on brand practices? Can it influence change, or are initiatives in this area always destined to be co-opted by brands? Will environmental imperatives mean that consumption patterns have to change and, thus, production too?

Conclusion

In this chapter, initiatives undertaken by fashion brands and retailers to address workers' rights violations have been identified and critiqued. The failure of social auditing and the need to address commercial practices, particularly low prices, short deadlines and unstable relationships with suppliers, is reasonably well established in theory, but practice is yet to catch up. Projects to support the capacity of workplaces to deliver workers' rights and to empower workers are yet to provide concrete evidence of their success, and there are suggestions they are based on flawed analysis. Joint liability agreements, where brands are held jointly responsible for workers' rights, alongside suppliers, are a newly emerging area, reflected in the Accord on Fire and Building Safety in Bangladesh. Its impact has yet to be determined, but the signs are promising. Gaps in research have been identified, and areas for future research have been presented, suggesting further attention needs to be paid to empathy between workers, consumers and mediators, worker well-being, the factors that could encourage the formation of trade unions and the relationship between production and consumption.

References

Acona Ltd (2004), *Buying Your Way into Trouble? The challenge of responsible supply chain management*. Insight Investment Management Ltd.

Anner, M., Bair, J. and Blasi, J. (2013), 'Toward joint liability in global supply chains: addressing the root causes of labor violations in international subcontracting networks', *Comparative Labor Law and Policy Journal*, 35 (1).

Barrientos, S. and Smith, S. (2007), 'Do workers benefit from ethical trade? Assessing codes of labour practice in global production system', *Third World Quarterly*, 28 (7), 713–29.

Brown, G. and O'Rourke, D. (2008), 'Lean manufacturing comes to China: a case study of its impact on workplace health and safety', *International Journal of Occupational and Environmental Health*, (13), 249–57.

Chalmers, J. (2013, 2 May), *Special report: How textile kings weave a hold on Bangladesh*. Reuters. Available at: www.reuters.com/article/2013/05/02/us-bangladesh-garments-special-report-idUSBRE9411CX 20130502 (accessed 17 November 2013).

Clean Clothes Campaign (2011), *Freedom of Association Protocol in Indonesia*. Available at: www.clean clothes.org/resources/recommended-reading/freedom-of-association-protocol-indonesia/view (accessed 6 November 2013).

Clean Clothes Campaign (n.d.), *Improving working conditions in the global garment industry: resources*. Available at: www.cleanclothes.org (accessed 6 December 2013).

DFID Bangladesh (2013), *Creating jobs and improving conditions in the Bangladesh's garment industry*. Available at: www.gov.uk/government/world-location-news/creating-jobs-and-improving-working-conditions-in-bangladeshs-garment-industry (accessed 18 November 2013).

Entwistle, J. (2000), *The Fashioned Body*. Cambridge, UK: Polity Press.

Ethical Trading Initiative (2010), *Indian National Homeworker Group: Programmes*. Available at: www.ethical trade.org/in-action/programmes/the-indian-national-homeworker-group (accessed 18 November 2013).

Ethical Trading Initiative (2013), *Freedom of Association in Company Supply Chains: A Practical Guide*. London: The Ethical Trading Initiative.

Ethical Trading Initiative (n.d.), *Company purchasing practices*. Available at: www.ethicaltrade.org/in-action/issues/changing-company-purchasing-practices (accessed 9 November 2013).

Galland, A. and Jurewicz, P. (2010), *Best Current Practices in Purchasing: The Apparel Industry*. Oakland, CA: As You Sow.

Gap Inc. (n.d.), *Purchasing practices*. Available at: www.gapinc.com/content/csr/html/human–rights/purchasing-practices.html (accessed 17 November 2013).

Gooch, F., Hurst, R. and Napier, L. (2008), *Material Concerns: How responsible sourcing can deliver the goods for business and workers in the garment industry*. London: Traidcraft and Impactt.

Human Rights Watch (2013), 'Bangladesh tragedy shows urgency of worker protections', *News, analysis and resources from human rights perspective*: Available at: www.hrw.org/news/2013/04/25/bangladesh-tragedy-shows-urgency-worker-protections (accessed 17 November 2013).

International Federation for Human Rights (2012), *Corporate Accountability for Human Rights Abuses: A guide for victims and NGOs on recourse mechanisms*. International Federation for Human Rights.

International Labour Organisation (2003), *Report V: The scope of the employment relationship*. Fifth item on the agenda. International Labour Conference 91st Session, International Labour Office, Geneva.

Locke, R. (2013), *The Promise and Limits of Private Power: Promoting labour standards in the global economy*. New York: Cambridge University Press.

McMullen, A. and Maher, S. (2011), *Let's Clean Up Fashion: The state of pay behind the UK high street*. Bristol, UK: Labour Behind the Label.

Nova, S. and Kline, J. M. (2013), 'Social labeling and supply chain reform: The designated supplier program and the Alta Gracia label' in Bair, J., Dickson, M.A. and Miller, D. (eds) (2013), *Worker's Rights and Labour Compliance in Global Supply Chains: Is a social label the answer?* New York and Abingdon, UK: Taylor and Francis (Routledge): 262–81.

OECD (2011), *How's Life? Measuring well-being*. OECD Publishing.

Oxfam (2010), *Oxfam Business Briefing: Better jobs in better supply chains*. Oxford, UK: Oxfam.

Parker, E. (2011), 'Win win win? Productivity, garment workers' wages and working conditions', *Women Working Worldwide Newsletter*. Women Working Worldwide.

Pruett, D. (2005), *Looking for a Quick Fix: How weak social auditing is keeping workers in sweatshops*. Amsterdam: Clean Clothes Campaign.

Raworth, K. (2004), *Trading Away Our Rights: Women working in global supply chains*. Oxford, UK: Oxfam International.

Social Accountability International (2012), *Brazil: Worker Engagement Program to improve health and safety issues*. SAI: Advancing the human rights of workers around the world. Available at: www.sa-intl.org/index.cfm?fuseaction=Page.ViewPage&pageId=1366#.Uop_j-JKRkE (accessed 18 November 2013).

Worrell, S. and David, S. (2013), 'A non-binding justice', *Phnom Penh Post*. Available at: www.phnompenhpost.com/national/non-binding-justice (accessed 17 November 2013).

PART IV

Visions of sustainability from within the fashion space

Just like the previous part of this book, Part IV comprises perspectives from within fashion. Whereas the contributors in Part III used their rich experience and knowledge to realign our understanding of, and to reconfigure current practices to better serve futures of sustainability, the scholars and practitioners in this part look far and beyond, opening up new conceptual and practical possibilities. They do so by also drawing on a range of influences from outside the remit of fashion, as well as the deeply personal. Common to this group of contributors is that they have designed a new direction for their own practice, which, in different ways, sits at the edges or margins of a fashion system – a place they find most auspicious for the advancement of fashion and sustainability, picking up themes introduced in Part I of this book. Again, in different ways, they purposefully situate themselves as agents of change and also propose new interpretations of, and possibilities for, the designer role – and that of the fashion user – to support futures of sustainability. Yet another recurrent theme is the notion of how insights and embodied experiences at the level of the garment and the individual craftsperson can yield understandings for systems and paradigms and vice versa.

The part starts with two very experienced fashion designers turned educators (and more). **Lynda Grose** (Chapter 22) treats us to her incredible command of the complex area of material flow and its many nested levels, from the details of a fibre and the mastery of the weaver, to global markets. A core theme of this chapter comprises the shortcomings of the growth framework and visions for fibre flows for fashion in a post-growth era, including the mooting of a challenging and far-sighted idea, that of linking and limiting garment consumption to the sustainability of the land. **Dilys Williams** (Chapter 23) also speaks with insight and empathy of flows, here focusing on those percolating the practice of fashion design. A core theme of her chapter is how investment in good relationships at the micro level, such as between designer and maker (investments often regarded as a 'cost and impracticability'), and respect for the experience of meaningfulness can seed positive resonance across the layers of the fashion system and industry. Williams encourages an understanding of the designer as the 'host' (an affiliated idea to that of designer as facilitator) of relationships and the inclusion of 'multi-voicedness' as a source of diversity and opportunity. She also foresees that a 'participatory ecosystem of design creates artefacts that emerge through a more dynamic bringing together of parts'.

Drawing on her personal experience of starting and running (and, in one case, setting free) community-based fashion initiatives in Leeds, UK, **Lizzie Harrison** (Chapter 24) offers

221

vigorous insights into the role fashion can have in fostering cohesive and prosperous communities. She calls for more support for these initiatives, which can, she argues, contribute both to sustainability, in the immediate sense of providing tools, skills and motivations for practices such as repair and remaking, and in building resilience and diversity. This text – like some others – points to manifestations of democracy in fashion far from the rhetoric of this as an issue of *availability* and *access* to consumption of fashion clothes made possible by low prices, which is sometimes used to defend the practices of the current system.

Like the previous contributor, **Amy Twigger Holroyd** (Chapter 25) shares insights from her own fashion initiative and celebrates the inclusion of amateurs in fashion practice. She explores the commons, specifically the fashion commons and the related notion of *openness*, commanding metaphors that help catalyse a changed vision for the fashion system in the light of environmental and human impoverishments of prevailing practices. Indeed, the value of metaphors to invite us into new places of understanding is a central theme running through this part, and also this volume more generally. By 'opening garments', Twigger Holroyd also opens up her practice as a designer–maker, as well as opening up a wider fashion system, which brings with it opportunities for *eudaimonia* in fashion.

Mending activist **Jonnet Middleton** (Chapter 26) similarly draws us to the personal and domestic manifestations of fashion practice. According to her, in its unobtrusiveness and female guise, mending (and repair, her professionalized, male cousin) is a Trojan horse that can outsmart such hard, cynical fashion frameworks as obsolescence. The personal stitch to the garment emancipates us; we become involved and active. Resources are saved. Fashion becomes radicalized by the thought that we can 'allow things to get old'. Middelton's personal, vivacious contribution draws together threads of ecological necessity, superabundance and political power, describing mending as commodity activities and leadership, to 'mend to show the way'.

Another self-declared fashion activist, **Otto von Busch** (Chapter 27), in his powerful piece on fashion supremacy, argues that, as fashion consumers, we are complicit in deeply disturbing and ubiquitous manifestations of exploitation. The path to independence he denotes, evoking the work and thought of Ghandi, is by building self-sufficiency. In a manifesto for 'fashion-ability', von Busch encourages us to 'shift the focus from the objects, or commodities, and their meanings to the strategic and social value of the capabilities produced through the engagements'.

In a circular fashion, the last chapter of this volume, Chapter 28 by **Mathilda Tham**, evokes the sentiment of hope and many possibilities offered in the opening chapter by Kate Fletcher. Tham understands fashion as the result of co-creativity and positions all collaborators of fashion as lucky spokespeople of diverse and shared futures. Drawing on a framework for sustainable peace building, she offers up the concepts of truth, mercy, justice and peace as key pillars towards a new forecasting practice that can afford an agile dance between products, systems and paradigm understandings of fashion, and integrate intra- and interpersonal value systems.

22

FASHION AS MATERIAL

Lynda Grose

Fashion as material

Materials both shape the world we make and reflect the way we view that world. All materials are inextricably linked—to each other and to the natural, social and cultural domains—through a complex of deep patterns, networks, balances and cycles. Designing with the artisan co-operative *Sna Jolobil* in Chiapas, Mexico, it was evident that the weavers understood these relationships tacitly—the rhythm and speed of back-strap-loom technology, the fabric width, symbols and ornament, the people themselves, have all co-evolved through a profound sense of place and being-in-the-world (Morris and Foxx, 1988). However, in our modern, global economic system, we experience materials quite differently, as inert substances extracted from the earth in kilograms and barrels, swiftly transformed into units for sale. More complex interrelationships are glimpsed only sometimes—usually when shocks in the system occur.

Some of these interrelationships came to light in 2010–2011, when worldwide flooding and drought devastated global cotton yields, sending fiber prices skyrocketing. Cotton fabrics became subject to bi-weekly price corrections, and apparel business projections were thrown into turmoil. To reduce costs, brands rushed to blend cotton with polyester, causing synthetic-fiber prices also to shoot upward (Nash, 2011).

Cross-sector disruptions such as these help us to see the systems in which we are embedded and to realize that our industry, our economy and we as fashion professionals are utterly dependent upon natural resources that are finite. They also present opportunities to reflect and reconnect in new ways.

Virgin material flows in a growth economy

Material flows are a proxy indicator for environmental impact—the more economic activity, the greater the tonnage of virgin materials extracted, processed and consumed, and the greater the economy's environmental footprint. Though material use in industrialized economies tends to greater efficiencies over time, consuming about 30 percent fewer resources per one unit GDP, say, in 2010 than in 1980 (Worldwatch Institute, 2011: 82), global resource use rises continuously. Population growth and prosperity drive demand upward, but the imperative of exponential growth, where a proportion of each year's output is invested to generate more the next, is most potent. Global material use between 1900 and 2006 increased from 7 billion tons to 60 billion tons, and per person from 4.6 tons to 8–9 tons (Worldwatch Institute, 2011: 81).

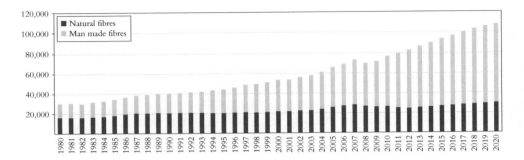

Figure 22.1 Global textile fiber outputs more than doubled between 1977 and 2007 and are projected to reach 130 million tons by 2025. This gain is due to the increased use of man-made fibers and in particular polyester

Global textile fiber outputs parallel this compound growth, more than doubling between 1977 and 2007 (Turley *et al.*, 2009: 8) and projected to reach 130 million tons by 2025. This precipitous gain in output has been made possible through the imperative of exponential growth and technological advancements, production capacity and use of fibers (man-made fibers – MMF)[1] (see Figure 22.1) directed to support that imperative. In particular, polyester production grew more than 300 percent in 20 years (from 19 million tons in 1997 to over 60 million tons in 2007)[2] (PCI Fibers, 2013) and is expected to claim 72 percent of all MMF fiber production by 2020, its success attributed to declining material costs and technical improvements to hand feel and performance (PCI Fibers, 2013).

Textile fiber flows

Asia dominates MMF production. By 2020, China is projected to take 52 percent of market share of all MMF and 72 percent of polyester. China, India and Southeast Asia account for 90 percent of global polyester production (PCI Fibers, 2013), creating a massive upwelling that then flows in fabric and product form across the globe to multiple destinations in the industrialized world.

Cotton is the most important natural fiber, accounting for 78 percent of the global natural fiber market (Turley *et al.*, 2009: 9) and 50 percent of the global apparel market. Cotton consumption is increasing on average 2.5 percent annually—from 27 million tons in 2012 to a projected 34 million tons by 2025. However, cotton's overall share of the world textile fiber market is in decline, from 31 percent in 2012 to 26 percent in 2025 (Plastina, 2013), owing to competition from other fibers (International Cotton Advisory Committee, 2013b) and volatility in cotton-fiber price. Cotton cultivation girdles the globe between the latitudes of 25–42° north and 25–35° south, with 75 percent of production concentrated in five countries: India, China, United States, Brazil and Pakistan (Turley *et al.*, 2009: 13).

Growth in all other plant fibers besides cotton is static or declining, owing to the high cost of small-scale production (flax, silk, ramie and soybean fiber) and/or technical and infrastructure issues. Wool use in textiles is in long-term decline, representing barely 1.5 percent of global fiber production in 2010 (PCI Fibers, 2013). Regenerated cellulosic fibers show prospects for growth in all forms. Lyocell, which currently represents a small percentage of total viscose production (approximately 10 percent), is favored to increase in importance owing to reduced environmental impacts in its advanced chemical pulping process (Turley *et al.*, 2009: 24).

Bio-based polylactic acid (PLA) has been slow to develop as a textile fiber, as most PLA fiber flows into the biodegradable packaging market (Turley *et al.*, 2009: 44). Teijin's chemically recyclable product (Eco Circle) represents less than 0.025 percent global polyester production (Miyatake, 2013). Persuading consumers to return items after use[3] and the expense of shipping used garments long distances to reprocessing plants are the main challenges. Recycled PET is more solidly established, accounting for 10 percent of the global polyester production in 2012 (Carmichael, 2013).

Influences affecting material flows

Polyester is independently owned and managed by the private sector, and its processing is thoroughly industrialized—the metabolism of polyester manufacturing facilities can be slowed and sped up at will, in response to, or irrespective of, external political and climactic conditions (Carmichael, 2013). In contrast, the global flow of natural fibers is diminished and redirected by a broad range of economic, natural and political factors.

The long-term static average world price for cotton fiber, for example, represents a real drop in returns for growers when inflation for inputs and equipment costs are accounted for. Consequently, farmers in industrialized nations have shifted their acreage into higher-value crops (to almonds, in California, for example), and cotton cultivation in general has migrated from capital-intensive to labor-rich regions (from the US to China and India).

Seed fibers in particular are susceptible to increasingly unpredictable precipitation patterns, influenced by climate change causing more frequent disruptions to crop yields. For wool, effects are felt indirectly, as drought reduces feed-crop yields, which in turn increase feed prices, forcing ranchers to offload their flocks. All natural fibers will suffer further as land allocation is preferenced for food production to feed a growing human population.

However, it is government policies and direct interventions in the global natural fiber market that cause the most dramatic price fluctuations, particularly for cotton (International Cotton Advisory Committee, 2013a: 2). The Chinese national reserve, for example, holds cotton stocks as large as 10 million tons (International Cotton Advisory Committee, 2013a: 2) and periodically drops these into the global market to drive the commodity price down and incentivize Chinese farmers to grow food crops. Traders wagering on global material supply and demand compound these uncertain conditions even further, while the fashion industry and its fiber producers remain at the mercy of market and speculator whims—fiber prices bear little, if any, relationship to the cost of production.

Material flow values in a growth economy

The standard response to potential disruptions in material flows is to ramp up production, with technical and "science-based" advances most favored by the fiber industries. However, this approach, according to Tony Fry (2012:25), provides an incomplete and insufficiently relational lens, for sustainability problems are also sociocultural, moral and ethical and, as such, demand that we look more broadly for solutions at what directs and motivates the bigger systems. Having worked with the Sustainable Cotton Project and California cotton farmers for more than a decade, I've witnessed the inadequacies of conventional material supply strategies first hand.

California leads the US in innovation and economic activity and is the eighth largest economy in the world (Burd-Sharps and Lewis, 2011: 16). California's cotton farmers have had access to state-of-the-art technologies for decades[4] and achieve yields as high as 3.5 bales or 1,680 lb per acre (1,883 kilos per hectare), almost 2.5 times the global average (Turley *et al.*, 2009: 23). Yet, despite their superlative productivity, many farmers still struggle financially, and rural communities in California's cotton-growing regions remain impoverished. In the congressional district of Fresno, for example, California's most productive agricultural county, median personal income is $18,000, 40 percent of children live in poverty (Burd-Sharps and Lewis, 2011: 37), and unemployment is upward of 25 percent.

The social problems in rural California are emblematic of those facing agricultural communities across the US and could be taken as a miner's canary in the mineshaft of farming regions worldwide. However, the narrative that "state of the art technologies, increased yields and exponential growth create prosperity" is nonetheless exported to developing nations, without first asking: Why is the most productive agricultural county—in the world's eighth largest economy—also one of the most socially degraded regions in the US?

This chapter, then, questions the nature of the growth economy, whom it serves and whom it benefits. Yet, it does not demand a wholesale rejection of commerce. Rather it calls for a weakening of the growth economy's dominance and the displacement of its centrality in the design of global fibre flows and, by extension, our land, our worlds and our lives.

Post-consumer material flows

Waste of all kinds increases with economic expansion, with the greatest waste occurring in the most industrialized (capitalist) economies (Worldwatch Institute, 2011: 75). Charity shops have evolved to advantage this waste by reselling discarded goods and directing revenue gained into community programs. Goodwill Industries San Francisco, for example, provides training to individuals facing a range of difficulties, from physical disabilities and homelessness to histories of incarceration and long-term dependency upon welfare (Grellman: 2013).

Although charity shops are clearly dependent upon the excessive metabolism of consumer wardrobes (Fletcher and Grose, 2012: 89), as a board member of Goodwill San Francisco, I've come to appreciate these organizations as beacons for emergent "post growth" values—that is to say, values that "consciously promote . . . social structures and activities that actually improve individual and community well-being" (Hamilton, 2004: 209), even as they operate within limited material flows. Their central operating logic generates multi-beneficial effects—the more the business grows, the greater the benefits to people (programs/training), the environment (reduced landfill) and society (reduced welfare/unemployment benefits/municipal landfill costs). Neither nature nor community is sacrificed to the priority of economic growth (Speth, 2008: 9); rather, they are integrated as one (see Figure 22.2).

Material flow values

As the fashion industry reconfigures its sustainability scope beyond incremental improvements, scaled closed-loop garment recycling systems are being prioritized. Yet, focusing on materials alone fails to fully advantage the multidimensional values of a post-growth era.

These shortcomings were recently played out in the partnerships between Soex Group, I:Collect and a number of fashion brands, which encouraged consumers to return used garments for a percentage discount on their next purchase. The initiative was met with alarm from charity shops in Europe and US alike, for it diverted *incoming* material donations to Soex's large-scale recycling facilities and, with a resale value of $7–40 per piece, threatened significant funding losses for charity social programs. Moreover, the program failed to fully actualize a hierarchy

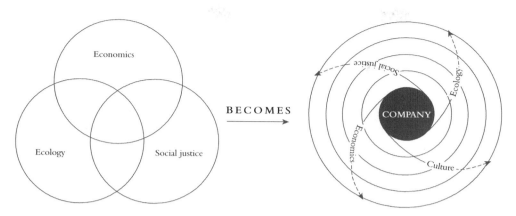

Figure 22.2 Left: In the late growth economy, the conceptual framework of the "triple bottom line" was adopted to bring sustainability into business. However, ecology and social justice were sacrificed to the priority of economic growth. Right: In a post-growth/post-dualist era, business structures change, and economics, ecology and social justice are integrated into one: as the business grows, so the ecological and social benefits also grow

of sustainability strategies—reuse/resale as is, reconditioning/repair, *then* recycling—that optimizes economic, embodied energy and business value many times over (Fletcher and Grose, 2012: 63–73).

Well-intentioned misalignments such as these are likely to persist into the early post-growth economy, for we are so unpracticed at seeing things in relationship that we lack the ability to actualize multi-system-wide solutions. Fritjof Capra describes this phenomenon as "a fragmented intellect" and Ashish Nandy names it, "sanitized cognition" (Nandy, cited in Escobar, 2012: 29). Several commentators, noting this type of disembodied state of being, call for "relational embeddedness" (Fry, 2012)—an iterative sustainability practice that builds tacit knowledge, enabling us to operate at increasingly complex levels over time.

Imagining multidimensional values of a post-growth economy

An active partnership between the fashion industry, charity shops and large-scale recyclers is now in full effect. Charity shops function as industry-wide drop-off stations, where *all* first-level value extraction occurs through garment resale. These stations also sort *outgoing* material flows into a range of fashion industry-prescribed categories. One such initiative employs hundreds of social-program participants to sort polyester and nylon apparel for chemical recycling. This tapped into already-established consumer donation habits and enabled rapid advances in closed-loop synthetic recycling infrastructure and logistics. Advantaging *outgoing* product flows also provided a larger, steadier material flow than the brand-limited return initiatives, and, as post-resale products trade at a significantly lower price (22c per pound) (Grellman, 2013), delivered a far greater opportunity to capture and optimize monetary as well as embodied energy value.

Another joint venture extracts value from jeans and chinos, two of the highest-volume categories identified in outgoing bales (Grellman, 2013), by shredding them into fibers suitable for 5–10 percent blends with extra-long staple virgin pima cotton. The resulting high-quality, heather-blue and heather-grey yarns, available in multiple counts and plied variations, are sold across a range of markets. Profits are distributed equally between the private and non-profit partners.

Besides these business partnerships, the value of charities in the private sector has been further elevated by their long-established cultural embeddedness in local communities. They provide "one stop shopping" for entrepreneurs stepping into the "fourth sector"—where social enterprises undertake businesses to support specific social missions (Alperovitz and Dubb, 2013). "Economies of collaboration" and "economies of community" thus foster richly symbiotic conditions that "up cycle the economy (so that) ecological and ethical benefits (continuously) accrue" (McDonnaugh and Braungart, 2013: 189).

Multiple bridges to a post-growth era

As environmental trends[5] unfold, the notion of a "material constrained" world moves solidly to the center of public and business zeitgeist, and the fashion industry's focus shifts from mitigating impacts in the supply chain to *building* long-term material supply and business resilience.

For the MMF sector, with its relatively self-contained production, actions initially remain within the synthetic realm, to include:

• non-toxic laminates and technologies making recycling outerwear products a reality;
• single-polymer garments designed to feed readily into closed-loop recycling systems;
• replacing traditional content labels with RFID tags to indicate precise content, eliminating cross-contamination of recyclable, biodegradable, degradable and non-degradable polymer reprocessing streams.

Work on biopolymers, however, is stalled by the effect of global climactic conditions on cultivated crops and turns instead to bio-synthetics (Conti, 2013), created in protected lab environments.

For natural fibers, more susceptible to adverse economic, climate-related and political conditions, companies develop much wider-ranging strategies, such as:

• establishing long-term contracts with cotton cultivators located close to retail markets (known as "geographical smoothing");
• converting from cotton to more "climate-resilient" fibers with a wide latitudinal range of cultivation;
• cross-sector partnerships to secure infrastructure, processing and market uptake of regenerated bast fibers (Textile World, 2012);
• developing technologies to regenerate post-consumer cotton products into new cellulosic fibers.

These combined strategies reduce the fashion industry's dependency on virgin fiber flows, easing the pressure that unbridled growth exerted upon the land. Most critically, however, they displace the central tenet of "economies of scale" (fiber), to create space for "economies of iterative sales," "economies of multi and extended use" (garments) and "economies of collaboration" (people), opening up "vast social terrains" (Escobar, 2012) and opportunities for agency. Although polyester production persists for some time as a massive commodity stream, centralized in Asia, natural fiber flows, by necessity, become more quickly dispersed and localized.

Structural (institutional) change and material flows

As the faulty logic of the growth mindset comes under scrutiny, it is evident that political agency is required to take on the structural changes necessary to ensure long-term sustainability. Gus Speth's call to "locate real possibilities for change at vulnerable locations in the political economy" (Speth, 2008: 185) sees "dissenting imaginations" (Escobar, 2012: 21) taking tangible political form within a broad framework in the post-growth era, for long and brittle global supply chains, depleted communities and tenuous farm and ranch finances offer many opportunities for creative intervention.

In natural fiber flows, for example, a number of mechanisms are applied to resituate social agency into the structure of business itself:

- Pre-planting fiber commitments reduce financial risks for growers/ranchers and secure supply for manufacturers.
- Mutually agreeable fiber prices with high and low caps normalize volatile global fluctuations.
- Payment on delivery of fiber at the warehouse, as against upon sale of fiber to the spinning mill, smooths farm/ranch cash flows.
- Spinning-mill co-ownership options for farmers/ranchers level out seasonal cash flow, as low fiber prices are offset by high returns on yarn, and vice versa.
- Integrated NGO functions strengthen chronically underfunded support for transitioning farmers/ranchers to biological practices.
- Membership options (such as food production-oriented Community Supported Agriculture) for local entities/wearers secure the market.

Structural changes, such as these, work at the small scale and are, therefore, manageable. Yet they also selectively de-link from what McDonnaugh and Braungart call the "remote tyranny of big (commodity) systems" (McDonnaugh and Braungart, 2013: 97) and strategically re-link to local needs and capacities.

Most critically, by deviating from total acceptance of market forces, they demonstrate distributaries from the mainstream (growth) narrative, create bridges to multiple "world(s) within the world" (Fry, 2012: 37) and inspire further structural change (see Figure 22.3).

Widely diverse ways of de-linking and re-linking are prompted as a result, from farmers cultivating their own non-genetically modified cottonseed, to modern-day artisan-makers accessing markets and manufacturing via web-based platforms (Anderson, 2012). "Trailing edge" technologies (second-generation tools, made widely accessible through decreased cost) further speed this de- and re-coupling process. Galya Rosenfeld and Dana Farber's concept, *Copification* (Duggan and Fox, 2010: unpaginated), for example, sees everyday people digitally scanning, remixing, sharing and producing clothes at personal 3D desktop printers. Besides reimagining fashion manufacturing and delivery systems, Rosenfeld and Farber also depart sharply from the hard resin materials typical of early 3D printing. The pliable material developed for *Copification* items inspires speculative links to small-scale local synthetic fiber production,[6] to material innovations such as bioplastics manufactured from agricultural waste (TIME IS, 2012) and multi-generation cellulose fiber technologies (such as lyocell), utilizing the feedstock of post-consumer cotton garments. Thus citizens across all sectors, from seed to final garment, work to disperse the power of large companies and champion the democracy of small-scale, distributed production.

Social patterns of organization co-evolve with this diversification of material flows, forming organically out of shared experiences. Some regions form co-operatives;[7] others form

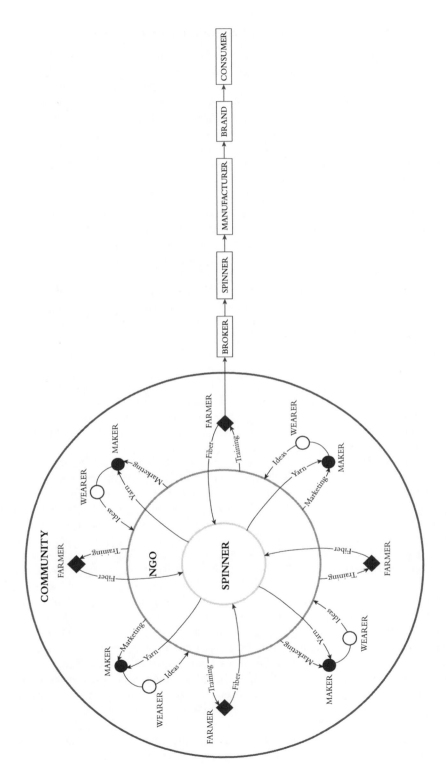

Figure 22.3 In a post-growth era (left), new forms and patterns of social order emerge, in stark contrast to the brittle linear pattern of the growth era (right), opening up vast terrains of relational learning and synergies

Table 22.1 Recent planning for a Fresno county-based spinning mill processing Cleaner Cotton™. The needs and capacities of the community and the land inform and direct product development and business planning

Land capacity	Average 3 bales per acre (1,500 lb per acre)
Mill capacity	49,000 lb yarn/week (50 weeks/year)
Annual fiber need from mill	4,050,000 lb cotton (incl. waste)
Number of acres converted to Cleaner Cotton™ to meet need	Approx. 2,5000 acres
10 farmers growing 250 acres Cleaner Cotton™	
or	
20 farmers growing 125 acres Cleaner Cotton™	
Amount of cotton fiber in average T-shirt (including waste)	0.75 lb
Amount of fiber in average queen sheet set (including waste)	3.25 lb
Number of products possible	65,000 T-shirts/week
	or
	15,000 sheet sets/week

What other products at what volumes could convert 2,500 thousand acres to Cleaner Cotton™?

farmer-/worker-owned entities; some function as food-and-fiber commons;[8] others form private–NGO–public structures, or remain as private enterprises with social missions. These community "logics" collectively form a kind of "social solidarity," paving the way for new terrains for fashion practice. Professionals engage as designers, scientists, researchers, anthropologists and new economists and, together with the public, act and interact with ideas, materials, technology and culture—to shape new social norms and unfreeze authorized narratives. This relational engagement informs a circularity of knowledge, where direct experience, responses and feedback shape further social learning. It's a process deeply familiar to designers as creative ideation and development, but, now applied to expanded scales and dimensions, it re-orients fashion practice itself to "designing the culture" of a post-growth era (Escobar, 2012: 29).

Land capacity, farm security, community resilience and restoration of air, soil and water quality are now the central tenets of human activity and being-in-the-world. Material flows, product development, business and ideas are resituated as enablers of, and in service to, this central purpose (see Table 22.1). Global-scale flows still exist, but no longer as monopolies and with a much more diminished capacity. The accepted inevitability and violence of massive shifts in material flows, isolated economic risk, inequitable income accumulation, depleted land and people, typified by the growth-above-all era now seem quite peculiar.

Research recommendations

The lingering persistence of the growth mindset and the slow uptake of "ways of being and knowledges otherwise" (Escobar, 2012: 34) have prompted several commentators to call for more "tenacious transformations". Amory Lovins encourages us to "take on projects that are important and impossible" (Lovins, 2013), and Gus Speth calls for "impractical answers" (Speth, 2008: Introduction). In this context, my recommendations for further research are to focus on projects that specifically explore and test ways to de-link from old systems and re-link to new structures. One such project, outlined below, fuses fashion industry knowledge with non-profit purpose and brings farmers together in a new relationship with the public to actively engage in social change.

Towards a cotton commons

Rather than constantly driving the land to yield more fiber per acre, farmers are asked to reduce the volume of inputs applied to crops by, say, 50 percent and to work with the land's new yield threshold. Collaborating with an agricultural economist to calculate a fiber price based on the adjusted yield and stable farm finances, yarn and fabric costs are then recalibrated to reset the price of the final product. A significant correction may or may not occur, as fiber is just one line item in costing a product. However, let's assume the garment doubles in price.

The field research is then linked to volunteer members of the public, who are already practicing post-growth values (banking with local credit unions, sharing products etc.), adding a socio-cultural dimension missed in typical fashion market studies. These participants are asked, not: "would you pay 20 percent more for an eco T-shirt?" but: "if you had the same annual clothing budget, could you accept one fewer new garment (based on pricing recalibrations) flowing into your closet per year?"

This line of inquiry opens the potential for clothing to be shaped by the capacities of the land and the regional community, as against the land being shaped by a distantly manufactured product, driven to the lowest cost. It creates white space, where the basic human needs of wearers—"I want to feel refreshed"—and farmers—"I like to watch things grow"—can be acknowledged, linked and responded to. It also creates white noise: the polarized discourse between companies and activists trapped in the market economy, the need for complicated indices and the imperative to monetize all actions for change simply melt away.

Perhaps most importantly, rather than consumers being considered as instruments for increasing and speeding the flow of material goods through the fashion system and, as such, viewed by activists as a burden (McDonnaugh and Braungart, 2013: 151), here they are recast as co-facilitators to bring the values of a post-growth era to the surface, so that society can recognize the "old story" and self-reflect; people and farmers are replaced as cultural creators and contributors; material flows are resituated in co-existence with local economy, place and people. All are partnered in a system that reconnects our common(s) sense(s) (Valero, 2010) to create "real wealth" (Korten, 2010: 14).

Notes

1 MMF includes synthetics and regenerated cellulose fibers.
2 Total polyester production, including but not limited to uses in apparel.
3 Patagonia reported only 56.6 tons of garments returned for recycling since 2005. See: www.patagonia.com/us/common-threads/, "Recycle" (accessed July 15, 2013).
4 For example: spray rigs, crop dusters, mechanical harvesters, global positioning satellite systems, genetically modified seed, laser-leveled land.
5 Failing states; food security; spikes in oil prices; peak water; peak food and fiber yields etc. (Brown, 2009: 3–75).
6 Such as Sarlaflex, SC: http://sccommerce.com/news/press-releases/sarla-performance-fibers-establishing-operations-colleton-county
7 See: http://texasorganic.com and www.calcot.com
8 See: www.thefoodcommons.org/summary

References

Alperovitz, G. and Dubb, S. (2013), *Six Economic Steps to a Better Life and Real Prosperity for All* [online]. Available at: www.alternet.org/economy/6-economic-steps-better-life-and-real-prosperity-all (accessed July 7, 2013).
Anderson, C. (2012), *Makers: The New Industrial Revolution*, New York: Random House.

Brown, L. R. (2009), *Plan B 4.0; Mobilizing to Save Civilization*, London: W. W. Norton.

Burd-Sharps, S. and Lewis, K. (2011), *A Portrait of California, California Human Development Report, 2011*, Brooklyn, NY: Social Science Research Council.

Carmichael, A. (2013), President—Americas, PCI Fibers, email correspondence, July 5–16, 2013.

Conti, M. (2013), Director, Strategic Innovation, Autodesk, Muir Beach: in conversation, August 25, 2013.

Duggan, G. and Fox, J. (Curators) (2010), "Designing machines" in *Mechanical Couture*, Design Museum Holon [online]. Available at: www.dmh.org.il/pages/default.aspx?PageId=125&catid=-1 (accessed June 30, 2013).

Escobar, A. (2012), *Notes on the Ontology of Design*, Chapel Hill University of North Carolina, Chapel Hill: draft, available at: http://aescobar.web.unc.edu/ (accessed June 18, 2013).

Fletcher, K. and Grose, L. (2012), *Fashion and Sustainability: Design for Change*, London: Laurence King.

Fry, T. (2012), *Becoming Human by Design*, London: Berg.

Grellman, G. (2013), Acting CEO, Goodwill Industries, San Francisco, San Mateo, Marin counties, San Francisco: meeting, June 12, 2013.

Hamilton, C. (2004), *Growth Fetish*, London: Pluto Press.

International Cotton Advisory Committee (2013a), *Meeting Cotton's Competitive Challenges*, Washington, DC. Report on the seminar on Competitive Challenges; pdf available at: www.icac.org/mtgs/Seminar/Cotton-s-Competitive-Challenges (accessed July 6, 2013).

International Cotton Advisory Committee (2013b), *World Cotton Situation, Outlook for 2012/13 and 2013/14*, April 18, Standing Committee SC-N-523, Washington, DC: ICAC.

Korten, D. C. (2010), *Agenda for a New Economy: From Phantom Wealth to Real Wealth*, San Francisco, CA: Berrett-Koehler.

Lovins, A. (2013), "Reinventing fire," plenary at Bioneers Conference, San Rafael, USA, October 15.

McDonnaugh, W. and Braungart M. (2013), *Upcycle: Beyond Sustainability, Designing for Abundance*, New York: North Point Press.

Miyatake, R. (2013), Teijin Frontier Co., Ltd, email correspondence, July 1–20, 2013.

Morris, W. F. Jr. and Foxx, J. J. (1988), *Living Maya*, New York: Harry N. Abrams.

Nash, J. (2011), Director of Materials, North Face Inc., Oakland, CA: in conversation.

PCI Fibers (2013), *Man Made Fibers in Apparel: Shifting Sources*. Available at: www.pcifibres.com, emailed document, July 15, Muir Beach.

Plastina, A. (2013), *Recent Cotton Demand Destruction*, Cotton Africa 7 [online]. Available at: http://magazine.cottonafrica.com/magazine/?p=1124 (accessed June 28, 2013).

Speth, G. (2008), *The Bridge at the Edge of the World: Capitalism, the Environment and Crossing from Crisis to Sustainability*, New Haven, CT: Yale University Press.

Textile World (2012), *FTC Issues Staff Opinion for Crailar "Flax" Designation on Products*, Fiber World [online]. Available at: www.textileworld.com/Articles/2012/July/FTC_Issues_Staff_Opinion_For_Crailar_Flax_Designation_On_Products.html (accessed June 5, 2013).

TIME IS (Technology Innovation Management and Entrepreneurship Information Service) (2012), *Bioplastics from Agricultural Waste* [online]. Available at: www.techno-preneur.net/technology/new-technologies/imp2/agricultural-waste.html (accessed July 2, 2013).

Turley, D. B., Copeland, J. E., Horne, M., Blackburn, R. S., Stott, E., Laybourn, S. R., Harwood, J. and Hughes, J. K. (2009), *The Role and Business Case for Existing and Emerging Fibers in Sustainable Clothing: Final Report to the Department for Environment, Food and Rural Affairs (Defra)*, London: Defra.

Valero, I. (2010), "Aesthetic(s) of the Common(s)" and the "Economies of Desire," Ignacio Valero, "EcoDomics: Beyond Palm Trees, Orangeries and the Ecology of Illusions," in Natasha Wheat (curator) and Susan Magrish Cline (designer), *Here/Not There* (Chicago: Museum of Contemporary Art Chicago): 22–33.

Worldwatch Institute (2011), *Vital Signs 2011: The Trends that Are Shaping Our Future*, Washington, DC: Worldwatch Institute.

23

FASHION DESIGN

Dilys Williams

I trained and am practised as a fashion designer, taught to evolve and apply skills and imagination in the creating of collections of desirable, press-worthy and sellable pieces. I have travelled across Europe, Asia and the US, leading teams in the making of runway, retail and wholesale collections, enjoying fantastic experiences and creating pieces for the enjoyment of wearing along the way. This journey has involved intersecting networks of makers, finance and press, to assimilate collection after collection as marks of success. But most of those pieces now lie redundant, probably in landfill, a slur on the landscape, owing to my ability to capture, but not to hold, the intention of design: to delight, connect and have meaning in the world. So I came to question what I have done to honour those whom I involved and to ask, what if, in the race for sales, I and others like me have lost the essence of what I set out to do and to be? In questioning fashion through the lens of sustainability, I have drawn together a collective of curious minds, connected through a deep engagement in nature and humanity as a means for exploring fashion's expressions of our lives and times. In creating a place for exploration to take place, by establishing the Centre for Sustainable Fashion, now a University of the Arts Research Centre, I am now able to guide the world's first academic research centre with sustainability as its starting point and fashion as its means of application.

Fashion, whether bespoke or mass production, is a human experience, an exchange with others, activated through the designer as relationship and shape maker. Fashion designers are well placed to explore what this engagement between people and materials might mean. Its practitioners however, notwithstanding pioneering people and organizations, seldom actively express the breadth of contribution or the authentic marks of time and place that fashion, seen from this broader way, might identify. Sustainability exploration offers such an opportunity, seeking radical re-imagining and redesigning of ways in which we can connect, and co-operate, through fashion.

Fashion design is commonly distracted from its role of helping us to distinguish and connect ourselves in the world by questionable imperatives of contemporary commercial practice. Therefore, it frequently deprives style of its meaning through its churn over its charm. It is full of 'stuff', but can be empty of significance. Fashion design is too often reactionary rather than radical, a restricted position for a discipline that sets out to shape, as well as respond to, cultural change. Fashion weeks the world over exemplify incredible aesthetic and technical prowess, but do they reduce design's agency just to the selling of clothes? Such a suggestion sits uncomfortably alongside the kernel of fashion design's practice: its roots in making, often with others. Indeed, over 30 million people around the world make clothes and textiles (UNITE, 1999), but, as a 'phenomen[on] that lies near the centre of the modern world' (Svendsen, 2006), it has become a test case for global business practice based on short-term profitability through exploitation of 'likes', rather than drawing together elements of what it is to be human.

Many large-scale industry and governmental narratives around fashion and sustainability focus on improving existing industrial practices, as an attempt to mitigate risk associated with existing products and production processes, predominantly via application of technologies. These seldom sit in partnership or discourse with design. A risk-reduction approach often puts in place restrictions to solve problems, while accepting the underlying conditions that created them. This does little to engage design experimentation or its potential to 'resolve' or even 'dissolve' such problems, perhaps by changing context (Ackoff in Ehrenfeld, 2008: 72). Such a disjuncture between approaches and actors can 'burden' designers with concern, leading to action more through personal moral judgement than through design thinking and doing as a powerful tool for change (Fletcher and Williams, 2012: 6). When starting with a design ethic, before engaging with appropriate technologies, other responses emerge, speaking to spiritual value as well as a technical transaction (Gore, 2013). In the fashion sector, it appears that we have an abundance of technical transactions, but little osmosis with human and spiritual value: an uncomfortable conversation for some, perhaps (also see Chapter 11)? Zakee Sharriff, designer and artist, finds that, 'there always has to be a spiritual connection . . . to make the print very connected to my soul is how I make my work more meaningful' (personal communication, 24 June 2013). She is not alone; designers across the spectrum, from Dries Van Noten to Mara Hoffman, display the pervasiveness of their values through their work (Figure 23.1).

By stepping back from the focus on runway showstoppers, is it possible to view the undertaking of fashion design quite differently? I would argue so. By embarking on a weaving of relationships mediated by garment creation and interaction, experience can be seen as embodied in the essence of a piece (Dorst, 2013). Looking from the perspective of human relationships within fashion design processes, it is clear that fashion is only made possible through its interactions, and the integrity and dignity of those involved depend upon the nature of those relationships. Contrary to the hylomorphic[1] model of creation, assuming making as the imposition of form upon resources, human and material, by the dictation of a design, Tim Ingold (2011) argues that the shape of things arises within flows (of material). If, in the case of fashion, we talk of flows between materials and people, and the role of designer as guide, then, as Ingold suggests, rather than reading creativity 'backwards' from a finished object to an initial intention in a designer's mind, we can read it forwards, in an ongoing, generative movement that is at once itinerant, improvisatory and rhythmic.

Examples of rhythm in fashion can be seen inside and outside its formalized structures, where those involved are active participants in the relationships of fashion. In creating the London Style Project, a space for designers to share ideas and listen to concepts relating fashion design to sustainability, I have been able to gather stories of such rhythms and flows. Eleanor of Partimi describes her practice and business as each design having a thread that runs through it from first ideas to product, a path, kept clear through simplicity and a sense of gentleness. Where designers can directly interact with the making process, they can attune their way of working with the materials and people involved. Ruth Ferguson of Olga Olsson, a Rio-based designer working co-operatively with marginalized women, forefronts the skills of the women, as much as her own design input, to ensure the quality and desirability of the product. Elsewhere, notable examples include David Hieatt, who depicts making jeans in Cardigan, Wales, as an interaction within a community, whereas William Kroll of Tender Denim speaks of the process of design

Figure 23.1 Finding connection that is true to the spirit of designer and design, Zakee Sharriff, AW2003

flowing through the weaving, dyeing and finishing process, each garment the result of the maker's skill and disposition, so each slightly different. In these situations, there exists the potential for dynamic interactions and trusted and empathic relationships. However, the perception in many (mainly larger) fashion businesses is that time spent in the developing of these relationships is a 'cost' and impracticability, whereas time spent on stripping back interaction is a gain.

This way of constructing *through* processes is at odds with the mechanistic convention of fashion creation based on replicability, where, aside from bespoke and other one-off or small-scale orders, each piece is deemed acceptable in a 'batch' only if it conforms to exactly the same specifications as its thousands of neighbours. Extreme examples of this can be witnessed in jeans factories, where, if pieces alter even slightly from the template of artificial wear marks for 'accelerated living', they are rejected as inferior goods. There exists little interaction here between designer, maker and wearer in exploring the parameters of what is deemed a desired quality within a piece. Improvisation, however, can and does take place, even at scale, as expertise and ingenuity sit across the making line. While working in China, through a machinist's suggestion, I was able to refine a style on an order for global distribution, increasing its quality for all those involved, but this example is rare and only possible with the receptivity of the idea via the designer, through negotiation and communication skills, in proposing and accepting reconfiguration over repetition to UK production and sales teams.

The recognized skills of fashion design, while valuing practical and technical qualities, tend not to value less explicit qualities of collaboration, co-operation and synthetic thinking that are the glue that sticks fashion design together. Skills and qualities in design that cover attentiveness, an ability to balance risk with opportunity and negotiation, as well as sketching and pattern-making, may together have the propensity to problem-solve through making, in ways different to benchmarks of efficiency that efforts towards sustainability currently suggest to design. In seeking the qualities and characteristics of such thinking and doing, considerations of *designer as host*, the multiplicity of voices involved and the simultaneous linking back and forth, an attentiveness to presence can be discussed.

Hosting

In considering the practices of the designer, it is possible to visualize them as 'hosting' relationships across a series of spaces, distinctive qualities and characteristics at play. Re-imagining these interactions amplifies the actions of designer as guide. Richard Sennett (2012) speaks of the skills that people need to sustain everyday life, with observations on our lack of understanding of how best to engage with materials and objects. His focus on our interactions might offer a spotlight for viewing fashion design as reciprocal actions. Networks of people brought in touch with each other create fashion's endeavours. However, dialogic skills in co-operation are not those usually mentioned when describing attributes for fashion design. These skills include listening well and behaving tactfully, skills Barry Schwartz (2009) illuminates in describing our 'loss of wisdom', discerning the value of empathic actions over prescribed ones.

Designers work in challenging new contexts where they are given mandates around sustainability as targets that they sometimes find difficult to achieve. In reframing questions around sustainability in the fashion creation process, we might better understand fashion designers' work within the social worlds in which it takes place. This is described by Lucy Kimbell (2011) as understanding design as a situated, contingent set of practices carried out by professional designers and those who engage with designers' activities. These potential human interactions are not always cross-referenced with sustainability targets, which tend to segment materials and components, industrialized practices and ethical considerations in the garment-making process.

This reductive approach may be appropriate to some parts of business, but designers can show distinctive qualities in visualizing a landscape around questions, over looking for direct answers, enabling a more interwoven, systemic, design-suited contribution to sustainability. A designer might start out as an individual evolving concepts, but can become engaged in a narrative of community with diverse skills and ambitions, mediated through product creation. This participatory ecosystem of design creates artefacts that emerge through a more dynamic bringing together of parts.

Relational viewpoints of design practices can also be superimposed on to wider societal systems, to cross-reference our roles as individuals, within communities and related infrastructures of society, and how each co-operate. This gives the designer a 'political' voice relating to the individual through fashion's distinction of self, to community through an ethic of design, and to economy through fashion as commodity. This gives agency to the designer as host, or moderator, creating an environment for interconnection.

Multi-voicedness

Fashion design and creation involve a diversity of participants with different types of usually tacit knowledge, personality, position, location, need and agenda. Engeström (2001: 4) describes such 'multi-voicedness' as, 'a source of trouble and innovation'. The rich diversity and opportunity that this affords are often stifled by command and control business structures as a means to negotiate its complexity. In seeking a way to create an environment for collaborative creativity, Leadbeater (2009) explores how digital spaces can facilitate mutually beneficial contributions by conceptual thinkers, practised makers, savvy business minds, mathematicians, visualizers, planners and voices of experience.

For designers in firmly established industry settings, explorations of 'multi-voicedness' may take quite different forms. The visible, tangible elements in fashion design are manifest in conceptualizing, drawing, draping, pattern creation, prototyping, materializing, sampling, fitting, tweaking, refining, producing and bringing garments to life on a body. The distinction of each piece lies in the hands and minds in these processes. The project Shared Talent, its foundations laid in 2007, has sought to activate and guide a series of interactions, charting points of collaboration, co-operation and competition, mediated through fashion creation. In it, actors are brought together to embody the experience of making, from ideation to wearing, to better understand their own and others' roles, possibilities and tension points across the process. This method for sustainability skills development intersects diverse ideas, practical knowledge of materials and processes, and consideration of needs and purpose to locate something of what Obama expresses as 'our lost sense of shared prosperity' (2008).

It would be naive to think that this alone evaporates the problems of price-led decision-making de-valuing expertise and power imbalances broadly prevalent in industry and society. However, with more than 99 per cent of all European businesses being small-to-medium-sized enterprises (SMEs) (European Commission, 2013), the true backbone of the European economy is held at small, human scale. This suggests that problem-facing and -solving take place through dialogue and contact. Contact can develop empathy and understanding, which in turn can create change. Multi-voicedness is not confined within geographic and cultural boundaries, as the IOU project (www.iouproject.com) exemplifies, through linking a variety of weavers in India and makers in Portugal or Italy, in dialogue with those seeking to purchase. This suggests far more scope than technical online fitting sessions as an application for global communication capabilities.

Look back, around, up, down and forward

Fashion design draws on past, present and future, giving reverence to practised technique, in juxtaposition with untested discovery. However, it rarely critiques normalized systems upon which many fashion rituals are based. The ontology of fashion design and making is out of sync with some of the very technologies, usually applied to sales and ordering, that now dictate fashion's speed. Often, elements that are not so easily digitized, such as research, experimentation and risk-taking, no longer have space to breathe. These design processes make sense of what we have around us, our daily lives, and make them extraordinary in delightful and practical ways. Taking insights from watching parkour, Emma Ranger developed styles that look better upside down! (CSF Nike project, 2012). The value given to such elements is often overlooked, not just in fashion design, but also across society. Manzini (2002: 4) refers to our loss of contemplative time, a notion often cited by designers and non-designers alike as a missed chance for imaginative thought. The practical skills of fashion design can in themselves facilitate reflection through their own rituals, acting as a filter to reject 'damaging' prototypes, but this space is often squeezed out of ideation, aesthetic conceptualization, experimentation, prototyping and refining, owing to focus on signing, sealing and auditing, creating 'damage' down the line. Working at the pace of 'practised technique' is what Nottingham-based company Albam sets out to do. Although time-consuming at the outset, their matching of products to resources in materials and making has enabled them to create pieces that are distinctive and resilient, as they are skills and location appropriate. This authenticity has earned them a reputation and an understanding by customers of what is involved in their creation (Westminster Media Forum, 2012).

Tensions and contradictions

The monological tendencies evident today within fashion hierarchies, and wider societal ones, challenge a notion of balance between individual aspirations, community wants and needs and the enabling infrastructures of governance. The logic behind their tendencies is clear: industrialization, combined with developments in science, technology and communication, has brought humans possibilities not previously seen or imagined. The materialization of tasks in the form of new products, such as creating a good impression being materialized through a new purchase, suggests 'access to possibility' but ties us into a cycle of 'dependency on' over 'delight in' what we might wear or use. The perceived options offered by global brands are leading to dramatic changes in how we make, sell, buy and value or 'consume' these materialized tasks. This mode of production and consumption is 'sold to us' as an aspiration of 'ease', but translates into passivity, a sad and precarious prospect for an ingenious species. This situation is exacerbated by weakening local community interactions, through perceived lack of time or interest and ambivalence towards our infrastructures of governance, through a growing mistrust of their handling of economy and society. Innovations of market lions, therefore, powered by a nation of pleasure-seeking individuals, offer distraction and excitement, but are built on models of insatiability, with the role of designer as enticer rather than provider of life-affirming interactions.

A designer who breaks free from this wheel to work outwards towards the creation of interactions can have more autonomy and space to grow. Cut x1 (made in collaboration with Evenings Code) (www.cutx1.com) is a simple making-based interaction between designer, maker and network facilitator, aiming to encourage curiosity for learning and making. It offers workshops, giving the opportunity to engage, in a group, in the process of making something to value and later enjoy. Each participant can experience constructing and growing value towards the garment and other makers, through learning what it takes to make something.

This experience is scaled through an iOS app, which visually describes ways to make a series of designs exist as garments. The scale of connectivity is global, whereas the scale of making is local. This offers a means of fulfilment that is visible eye to eye and to the world through a screen. Although design in fashion is part of the problem, in creating collections at increasing speeds and for immediate consumption, examples such as these expand products and services that act as positive agents in regenerating the contexts of life (Manzini, 2002).

Reconfiguration: next steps

This last section summarizes the ideas presented through the chapter and identifies paths for practice and research in fashion design that engage sustainability interactions where alternatives to the current model, with all its attendant ecological, social and cultural effects, come into view. These highlight delightful, political, viable, sociable, connective and adaptive facets of fashion. Notions of hosting, multi-voicedness and temporal awareness offer narratives for fashion design that embody empathy, holism and connection with human and ecological realms, ultimately contributing towards prosperity for all. They place value on the process of design and the products. This dialogue gathers some of the vitality around designing with space to move and to take effect, responding to and shaping the surroundings.

Fashion is greater than the current capitalist model presented to us

Building individual and collective confidence offers a space that fashion design does not always make time to consider. It invites an ethic in design, making more vivid its connections. This can be implemented in radical, political, poetic and awe-inspiring works, or in seemingly tiny but impactful interventions in the big machine of fashion realization. It can be evolutionary or transformational in showing the significance of fashion beyond a global sales-centred system to the place of facilitation in better lives and ecological flourishing. Building on research in constructing new working structures and networks in design and society (Simon, 1969; Kimbell, 2011; Elkington, 2012; Nowakowski, 2012), the emergence of networked holarchies and frames with osmotic membranes demonstrates a shift from management through hierarchies of control, to active interconnections with a more diverse sense of prosperity (Figure 23.2). Acts of reciprocation become more than just financial contracts and involve exchange and empathic consideration. This takes us deep into questioning assumptions about human nature and involves cross-disciplinary working and experience-rich research into people and nature relationships, through fashion's material and non-material practices.

Design as an empathic process

Collaborating is the human face of systems thinking. This is more than good intentions, it requires improving your convening skills.

(Senge, 2008)

Herbert Simon (1969) talks of design thinking as concerned with what ought to be, in contrast to the sciences, which are concerned with what is. This distinguishes design as constructing a landscape of exploration, as opposed to seeking answers to questions, and rather than looking for the 'truth' takes us beyond a refinement of the status quo to a place of curiosity. By considering cause and effect, we engage empathic practices, capturing enchantment to get a sense of what others feel, think and value. This necessarily entails skills to navigate a path of co-operation,

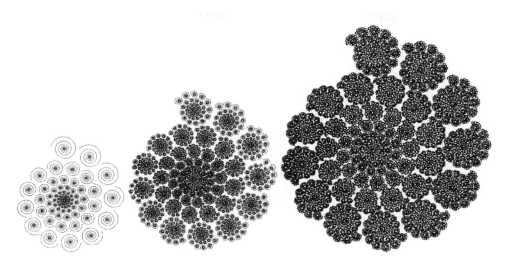

Figure 23.2 Notions of hosting, multi-voicedness and temporal awareness offer narratives for fashion
design that embody empathy, holism and connection with human and ecological realms
Source: Adapted from the Holon Ecosystem, Folke Günther

collaboration and competition, just as our natural ecosystems do. However, with a deeper
connection to, and understanding of, each other and the world, we get a greater sense of self
and our lives as individuals, within connected communities, and as contributors to governance and society.

Design in a changing context

Bauman (2000), described by Till (2013), defines the condition of our time as liquid modernity:
reflexive, possible, dynamic, contingent, a state that necessitates design thinking, with its
inherent ability to negotiate complexity. Its characteristics are ingenuity, imagination, empathy
and an ability to improvise and connect. Al Gore refers to an ability to engage in camaraderie
as a means to create 'energy fields' when people commit together to purposeful change (2013).

It now behoves us to frame an empathic, tangible, applicable design method that recognizes
and honours the many relationships that make up the life-enriching elements of our world, and
then we can joyfully celebrate and develop our skills with purposeful intention. Through such
an invigoration of the context of their work, designers can shape environments for relationships
to flourish and for artefacts of beauty and relevance to be formed.

Note

1   Hylomorphism (from Greek *hylē*, 'matter'; *morphē*, 'form'), in philosophy, is the metaphysical view
    according to which every natural body consists of two intrinsic principles, one potential, namely, primary
    matter, and one actual, namely, substantial form.

References

Ackoff, R.L. in Ehrenfeld, J. (2008), *Sustainability by Design: A Subversive Strategy for Transforming Our Consumer
Culture*. New Haven, CT, and London: Yale University Press.

Bauman, Z. (2000), *Liquid Modernity*. Cambridge, UK: Polity Press.

CSF Nike Project (2012), *Mobilize Makers*, student project. Nike, Centre For Sustainable Fashion, London College of Fashion.

Dorst, K. (2013), Up the down escalator: design thinking for the 21st century. *Design for Social Innovation and Sustainability (DESIS) Public and Collaborative Lecture Series (Lecture 5)*. London: Central Saint Martins College of Arts and Design.

Elkington, J. (2012), *The Zeronauts: Breaking the Sustainability Barrier*. London: Earthscan.

Engeström, Y. (2001), Expansive learning at work: toward an activity theoretical reconceptualization. *Journal of Education and Work*, 14(1): 133–56.

European Commission (2013), *Small and Medium-Sized Enterprises (SMEs): Facts and Figures About the EU's Small and Medium Enterprise (SME)* [online]. Available at: http://ec.europa.eu/enterprise/policies/sme/facts-figures-analysis/index_en.htm (accessed 3 June 2013).

Fletcher, K. and Williams, D. (2012), Fashion education in sustainability in practice. *Research Journal of Textile and Apparel*. ISSN 1560–6074.

Gore, A. (2013), *Marks & Spencer Plan A Conference*. Wembley Stadium, London, 13 June.

Ingold, T. (2011), *Being Alive: Essays on Movement, Knowledge and Description*. Abingdon, UK: Routledge.

Kimbell, L. (2011), Rethinking design thinking: Part I. *Design and Culture*, 3(3), 285–306.

Leadbeater, C. (2009), *We-Think: Mass Innovation, Not Mass Production*. London: Profile Books.

Manzini, E. (2002), Context-based wellbeing and the concept of regenerative solution: a conceptual framework for scenario building and sustainable solutions development. *The Journal of Sustainable Product Design*, 2(304), 141–8.

Nowakowski, L. (2012), Evolutionary education, in Rees, B. (ed.) *Pathways for Sustainable Education: From Hierarchy to Holarchy*. Cambridge, UK: Anglia Ruskin University: 47–57.

Obama, B. (2008), Economic speech at Cooper Union, New York [online]. Available at: www.nytimes.com/2008/03/27/us/politics/27text-obama.html?pagewanted=all&_r=0 (accessed 14 June 2013).

Schwartz, B. (2009), *Our loss of wisdom* [online]. Available at: www.ted.com/talks/barry_schwartz_on_our_loss_of_wisdom.html. Manuscript available at: https://dotsub.com/view/d71f6d0a-535f-4806-b8ec-28342c00c25d/viewTranscript/eng (accessed 23 May 2013).

Senge, P. (2008), *The Necessary Revolution: How Individuals and Organizations Are Working Together to Create a Sustainable World*. Boston, MA: Nicholas Brealey Publishing Limited.

Sennett, R. (2012), *Together: The Rituals, Pleasures and Politics of Cooperation*. New Haven, CT, and London: Yale University Press.

Simon, H. (1969), *The Science of Design: Creating the Artificial*. Cambridge, MA: MIT Press.

Svendsen, L. (2006), *Fashion, A Philosophy* (English trans.). London: Reaktion Books.

Till, J. (2013), *What is the point of art school?* Central Saint Martins College of Arts and Design, London, 14 May.

UNITE (1999), *A Union Activists' Guide to 'Stop Sweatshops' Campaigning* [online]. Available at: www.unpac.ca/economy/g_clothes.html (accessed 20 June 2013).

Westminster Media Forum (2012), *The UK fashion industry – challenges, opportunities and policy options*. Westminster Media Forum Keynote Seminar. London, 13 November.

24

FASHION AND COMMUNITY

Lizzie Harrison

Introduction

Notions of *community* are pluralistic and wide ranging and, in this chapter, I trespass into disciplines as diverse as sociology, politics, communications and ecology to explore its interconnectedness with fashion and its potential to further sustainability goals. My work at the boundaries of community development and fashion design over the past decade has challenged me as a designer and researcher. This intersection draws upon theoretical frameworks from sustainability-related and community development literature, yet has most life in a growing number of varied examples that emerge through grassroots ventures. Over these years, I have sought to experiment with live projects in this field, collaborating with fashion designers, public-service providers, academics, community development agencies and active local communities. This challenging approach has established 'Antiform' – a fashion label that seeks to find new methodologies for producing clothing locally in the UK – and 'Remade in Leeds' – a social enterprise that incubates fashion services to look for new ways to bring communities together, which will be discussed as a case study.

Exploring community

In the UK, the term *community* has become a political buzzword, implied in initiatives such as the 'Big Society' (thebigsociety.co.uk, 2013) and used extensively in everyday language, often with very different meanings. Broadly viewed, a community is 'a collection of people (or animals) who interact together in the same environment' (Bacon, 2009: 4). Many researchers, across disciplines, have described community as a contested concept that defies easy categorization (Field, 2010; Bertotti *et al.*, 2011; Crow and Mah, 2011). Drawing on these multiple ideas, community can be seen to comprise three types:

- *Geographical community* describes a community of people connected by their local physical place, sharing space and resources.
- *Community of culture or interests* is a community of people who have come together through a shared interest or hobby.
- *Community organizations* are more formalized groups, such as community childcare schemes and social-service providers.

As such, most of us can be seen as simultaneously part of many different communities, which may be nested within each other or overlapping and may co-exist at a local and global level. In this chapter, I refer to community as a collective of people who are interacting on varying levels, brought together by shared space, resources, values or experiences. Critically, it is not just the grouping of people that generates community but the interactions between them (Bacon, 2009). The network of interactions between individuals that makes a community is referred to as *social capital* and is described by Wilson as, 'the glue that holds a community together' (Wilson, 2012: 5). Social capital is based on relationships and trust; people connect through networks with members who share values, and these networks become a resource. In general, the more people you know, the more you share a common outlook, the richer you are in social capital (Field, 2010). When social capital is *bridged*, it links different communities and their networks (Cantle, 2005), bringing together different members through mutual interests or values. This has been shown as an opportunity to increase community cohesion, which aims to overcome divisions within a community by making multi-faith, multi-ethnic and multicultural communities work together (Cantle, 2005). This theory is built on the understanding that it is with positive values that communities create positive outcomes. This is distinct from these same principles being applied with negative values, which are the core tenets of gang culture (Leadbeater, 2009; Field, 2010; Sennett, 2013). The act of increasing social capital attempts to directly influence the social richness and quality of a community. Such 'social' features are intrinsically linked to the health of a community's local and global environment. It is within this theoretical context that practitioners working in the fashion and community space look to use fashion and its touchpoints as a tool to build and bridge social capital, and to use the skills and practice of making clothes and repairing them to work across generations, cultures and languages.

Transitioning communities

Under the broad rubric of sustainability, there has been considerable work to foster community feeling, action and social capital for positive ecological and cultural change. Perhaps one of the best known is the Transition Town Movement, which is based on the premise that well-networked communities can better deal with the environmental challenges brought on by *peak oil* and climate change (Hopkins, 2008). Initiated in 2005 by founder Rob Hopkins, the ideas emerged from a permaculture course he was running with students to explore roadmaps for strategic, sustainable community planning in Kinsale, Ireland (Hopkins, 2008; Hopkins and Lipman, 2009). These ideas acted as a catalyst and were adopted in Totnes, UK, in 2006 and have continued to grow. The movement focuses on transitioning communities towards a more sustainable future, through relatively radical grassroots thinking, and it hangs on the power of communities to self-organize and set the agenda for their own future by harnessing local opportunities and overcoming local threats.

The Transition Town Movement champions the idea of *act local* and now has 1,107 initiatives in more than forty-three countries worldwide, connected through the Transition Network platform (transitionnetwork.org, 2013). Each initiative or *transition town* is bound by a geographical area and promotes social, economic and environmental development through diverse emerging actions, such as repair cafes, energy descent plans and local currencies. Acting locally is perhaps not something readily associated with clothing, and yet there are already local hubs appearing across the UK to facilitate the making, altering and repair of clothing. These spaces, such as Fabrications (fabrications1.co.uk, 2013) and ECHO Community Centre (hamara.org.uk/echo-centre, 2013) are offering the facilities and expertise for individuals and communities to make clothing locally.

The key principle of the Transition Town Movement is to increase *resilience*, that is to foster the capacity of a system to hold together and maintain its ability to function, in the face of change and shocks from the outside (Hopkins, 2008; Wilson, 2012). Hopkins believes that community resilience is imperative; a resilient community is one that is able to adapt to changes, seen as critical in the face of climate change and the global energy crisis (Hopkins, 2008). Wilson frames the Transition Town Movement as part of a wider theoretical framework of transition theory, addressing the loss of community resilience caused by the global capitalist system and globalization (Wilson, 2012). Fashion practices within the community contribute to resilience through the skilled actions of making and using clothing and the creation of identity, and they further contribute to a shared language to engage people in social activities that link to wider community agendas.

Central to the idea of resilience is the concept of diversity; economist David Fleming, cited in *The Transition Handbook*, states that one of the main benefits of a resilient community is that, 'there is a diversity of character and solutions developed creatively in response to local circumstances' (Hopkins, 2008: 55). Such an approach lends itself well to fashion projects based within communities, each applying different thinking to create niche responses based on various local opportunities. This approach to fashion could see communities assessing local needs and local resources to create unique products, services and events in response to their geographical locations, local skills and local capabilities. A project doing just this is Glasgow-based Karibu Fashion, founded by Henriette Koubakouenda to support African refugees and asylum seekers in Scotland. The project has developed a range of tartan cloth produced from local Scottish yarns, using African weaving techniques (Adewunmi, 2012). The cloth produced is not only supporting the group to access services and meet people, but it also connects their cultural traditions with Scottish heritage. Koubakouendu has creatively brought together the skills of these women and local textiles knowledge to create a project that is about acting locally to support the integration of asylum seekers. This approach challenges current commercial mainstream fashion, with individuals and community-based initiatives actively engaging with fashion.

What makes the Transition Town Movement so transferable is that it is an example of a call to action that goes beyond asking people to simply participate in activities, instead supporting them to self-organize and create the activities themselves, mobilized by shared belief in building a more sustainable future (Cornwall, 2011). The idea of *mobilizing communities* is supporting them to be empowered to actively participate towards a shared goal. Much of the discourse around mobilizing communities in the Transition Town Movement and wider community development literature is around localizing food and energy (Hopkins, 2008) and improving health and reducing crime (Barnes *et al.*, 2007), perhaps because these are seen as pressing issues and fundamental human needs. Yet clothing is also regarded as a basic need, but fashion and craft practices fit less neatly into these conversations and the actions of this space. The Transition Town Movement only shows a few signs of initiatives including fashion, such as the sewing repairs at the Repair Cafes, and yet alongside this are emerging grassroots fashion initiatives that also focus on acting locally, responding to local opportunities and creating diverse responses to local circumstances.

The activation of transition town initiatives and community fashion initiatives depends on educating communities, the time of individual people and widening access to participation. Passion for Fashion, set up by a group of social housing providers in the north of England, is a project that widened participation in financial support services and fashion by using sewing as a tool to engage with their hard-to-reach, unemployed young tenants. The project runs workshops that bring participants together to learn basic sewing and garment remaking skills and presents the chance to meet people and various social support agencies. Here, fashion activities are used as a tool to support vulnerable young people by offering an interface with public service providers, such as debt and job advisers, allowing them to connect with service users in new ways (passion4fashionleeds.wordpress.com, 2013).

Another factor that is often raised in this field is whether such ideas are scalable and able to contribute significant change in the norms of how people engage with clothing. As mentioned, the Transition Town Movement has illustrated that there is a global appetite for communities to participate in connected practices, whether it is growing food, repairing household objects or preserving local woodland. The community arts scene in the UK, which refers to art-based practices that are undertaken within a community (McCabe *et al.*, 2010), provides an indication that there is also an appetite for community activity that is more focused around culture. In a recent scoping study, amateur arts activities were found to be thriving, with participation on the increase, involving an estimated 9.4 million participants and volunteers in England (McCabe *et al.*, 2010). The level of participation in both these sectors suggests that, given the right educational platforms, access and support, fashion initiatives created by local people could flourish.

Community arts projects can be examples of *cultural communities*. Communities can crystallize around shared interests rather than shared physical space, which, in the field of fashion, might include knitting, upcycling old clothing or wearing vintage fashion, showing the fluid definition of community from being geographically bound to culturally linked. Communication made possible by the Internet has led to more possibility for people to associate with communities of culture (Bertotti *et al.*, 2011). Cultural communities, whether they overlap with a geographical community or exist only online, allow like-minded people to connect, network and support the formation of real and virtual initiatives. Knitting circles such as Stitch 'n Bitch (stitchnbitch.org, 2013) are an example of how individuals with a shared interest can gather locally, through word of mouth and through online networks, to make collectively in a social setting, illustrating how the Internet has also allowed local networks to thrive with online social support (Thomas et al., 2012).

Communities maintained by social networking and supported by technology are often referred to as *virtual communities*. Large-scale virtual communities offer the prospect of linking like-minded individuals, regardless of location, coming together around a shared task or interest. Their significance for local action is that they provide open-source platforms for local knowledge and ideas to be exchanged between different communities around the world. The Transition Town Movement has harnessed this through the Transition Network, which connects members worldwide (transitionnetwork.org, 2013). Pioneering fashion and craft platforms in this space include the Craft Mafia, an international network for local socially focused craft groups (craftmafia.com, 2013), and The Amazings, a platform supporting community elders to share wisdom with others, including fashion, textiles and craft knowledge (theamazings.org, 2013). These sites take the role of allowing communities to self-educate, gather supporters locally and globally and share knowledge in an open-source space. Local, cultural and virtual communities form a layered and interconnected network, each operating and communicating in different ways, but all ultimately able to contribute to participation and local action.

In 2008, I embarked on trying to join the dots between community development and fashion by exploring how initiatives might offer some tangible ideas for how this field could be developed. Underpinning my work as a fashion designer and driving my practice are principles around inclusivity and diversity. I believe we need to expand the touchpoints of fashion beyond the creation of new products (see, for example, the chapters by von Busch (Chapter 27) and Fletcher (Chapter 1)) to include new services and new experiences; this broader view of fashion allows more possibilities for interactions on a community level. I also take the viewpoint that creativity is not exclusive to 'outstanding', formally trained individuals, but that everyone, including non-experts, has creative potential (Gauntlett, 2011). The projects that have interrogated this philosophy are Antiform and Remade in Leeds, which I present here as a case study.

Antiform: a fashion and community case study

The projects were developed in Leeds, UK, in a very socially and culturally diverse neighbourhood. The area is impacted by a large, transient, student population (Headingley Development Trust, 2009) and, as part of the city rim, is characterized by low-quality housing stock, deprivation and low levels of official economy (Julier, 2008). The project took an entrepreneurial approach to expand the knowledge around the practical application of act-local theory in a fashion context.

The main objective was to use local skills and undervalued material resources to create local fashion. This was mainly to be delivered through Antiform – a concept fashion brand – with a 20-mile supply chain using local waste textiles, both pre-consumer and post-consumer, remanufactured in our own factory and sold in our shop based within the community. The project started as a textile reuse initiative, but quickly shifted to a focus on the social value of the work. The activities also aimed to combine service design with the fashion brand, to create new experiences for fashion within the community and, further, to ensure these services were well designed, with high production values associated with a boutique fashion experience.

The project worked with a multi-stakeholder group, including local makers, local community centres and social enterprise support agencies. The activities included trialling Antiform by manufacturing in a hyper-local setting, working with skilled members of the local community. The project uncovered cross-cultural skills, including machine-sewing, crochet, embroidery and machine- and hand-knitting. The project went on to form Remade in Leeds, a social enterprise experimenting with new services creating touchpoints between the local community and fashion, including monthly clothes swaps, a repairs and alterations service, sewing cafes, youth and community workshops and a local boutique selling clothing made in Leeds. In 2010, after a 15-month research project, Antiform and Remade in Leeds started to operate on a commercial basis. Three years later, Antiform is an international wholesale brand, based in an old sewing mill in Leeds and still manufacturing with local people (antiformonline.co.uk, 2013). The Remade in Leeds services have developed into independent community initiatives, run and owned by the community, most notably the Leeds Community Clothes Exchange, which now has over 800 members, actively connected through a Facebook page, who swap over 2,500 items of clothing each month (Figure 24.1) (www.facebook.com/LeedsCommunityClothesExchange, 2013).

Since the project's inception in 2008, it has worked with thousands of people in various capacities and connected well with the larger community. By working so closely with the local community, what started as an entrepreneurial initiative has taken root in the local area in such a way that it has created its own cultural community around its activities. The project successfully increased access to its activities by working closely with existing social groups in the neighbourhood and introduced new ideas of how fashion can connect with the people in this field. The project also allowed the team to experiment with different business models, to understand how such initiatives might become financially sustainable. The projects have grown organically over the 5-year timeframe, and scalability has come through sharing knowledge and opportunities with others and allowing services to find new owners and develop autonomously. Locally, nationally and globally, new initiatives have appeared in this space, and both Antiform and Remade in Leeds have shared learning and experience widely with peers, through structured research and informal dissemination.

Figure 24.1 Leeds Community Clothes Exchange, 2013
Source: Photography Lana Armaghan

Figure 24.2 Antiform, 2013
Source: Photography Giles Smith

Developing and managing Remade in Leeds has been time intensive, but finding community partners to support development work mitigated much of this. Limitations with Antiform have been the same as for any new fashion brand in this economic climate, and, although it has remained true to its principles, financial restraints have, at times, hindered development. More significantly, Antiform has challenged the surrounding fashion industry, and it has been difficult to fit alongside the current fashion system; this has been overcome by working to educate buyers and customers to change the perception of handmade clothing (Figure 24.2).

Conclusion and future research directions

The project I have described and the others mentioned in this chapter do not often appear within the fashion narrative, nor do they feature in the Transition Town Movement theory or community development approaches. Yet they are intrinsically linked to the communities in which they are born. They personify the idea of acting locally and offer inclusive and accessible platforms for local communities to participate in fashion events, run fashion services and create new kinds of fashion product. The activities in themselves address sustainability through their very nature, often focusing on repairing, remaking and reducing waste, but they also contribute to larger ideas set out in this chapter around building resilience and creating diversity.

In order to populate this intersection of fashion and community, new projects need to be more ambitious and have the space to experiment. Facilitation of this might need to include supporting those initiating projects, having space to operate, being part of greater networks and accessing funding and new technologies. Many of the projects mentioned in this piece are formed and facilitated by an individual or core group who commits to creating new ways of doing with an entrepreneurial spirit. It is currently a female-dominated field, and, from my experience, projects take a very open approach to knowledge sharing. Individuals, specifically women, need to be encouraged and supported to become *community champions* to ignite new projects around the world. The best people to mentor this transition are those who have already done it and are actively involved in the field. In order to connect, communities need to be better networked, so that people might meet and be inspired. Sennett feels we have more forms of communication now, but less of an understanding of how to communicate well (Sennett, 2013: x), so it is essential that the networks create support communication between projects, communities and their community champions.

Supporting communities to more actively participate in the production of clothing, fashion workshops and related services and events demands space to come together for ideas to grow. This requires communities to rethink the space available. Owing to changing consumption patterns, it is estimated that nearly one in six shops in the UK is vacant (Portas, 2011); often placed in the heart of communities, this is valuable, underused space that could be reimagined, not only for retail, but also for meeting, making and participating. The Meanwhile Use as Performance Research Project looked at how to secure social value from vacant space and how local communities can be supported to do so. The research highlighted that the space offered valuable opportunity for community enterprises to experiment with their activities in a low-cost and, therefore, low-risk environment (Dearden *et al.*, 2013). These set-ups could be flexible and light, allowing them to move and adapt as space becomes available, experimenting with their activities in different locations. Such a model relies on communities being able to access advice on the legal implications of taking on a building and on local councils to broker relationships between initiatives and property landlords.

Another barrier for new projects is initial set-up and development funding. Many community enterprises in the past have been reliant on government funding, but being financially sustainable allows greater independence (Social Enterprise UK, 2012). Supporting the potential for fashion initiatives is the revolution in raising finance created by crowdsourcing websites, such as Kickstarter (kickstarter.com, 2013) and People Fund It (peoplefund.it, 2013). These platforms allow anyone to make a pitch to a global investment community to fund an idea. This simple concept has provided new ways for community initiatives to raise funds. If finance were raised in this way on a local level, for local enterprises, perhaps the act of investing in itself could become a tool to galvanize communities and ensure they support local enterprise. This has been the case for Leeds Bread Co-op, which raised money to buy a community-owned oven to make bread locally (leedsbread.coop, 2013). In the future, a co-operative of local fashion makers could use the same approach to fund production, equipment and activities.

Community fashion initiatives could also use crowdfunding to invest in new technologies, such as laser cutting and 3D printing, allowing them to experiment with innovative processes. These technologies exist within specialist colleges and universities, but widening access to them in a community and domestic setting could have the power to create a new industrial revolution according to supporters (Anderson, 2012). Importantly, these new technologies could support non-specialists to take new roles as designers, producers and distributors, making in a hyper-localized setting. As the technology is based on shareable code, wider virtual communities will be able to support local communities, who can adapt ideas to their own needs. It does not need to replace traditional crafts, but rather could integrate with them to create new forms of making. It is not the technology itself that will empower and mobilize communities, but rather how it is used (Thomas *et al.*, 2012), but it does offer space in which communities can experiment.

Through this chapter, I have started to position fashion initiatives based within geographical and cultural communities, and supported by virtual communities, as tools for community development and ultimately to contribute towards a more resilient future society. These fashion activities may include, but are not limited to, local production models, sewing cafes, clothes swaps, repair and alteration services, local fashion brands and community workshops. As a whole, these initiatives have the potential to connect people, developing networks, building social capital, bridging communities, increasing community cohesion and bringing diversity to fashion and clothing.

The research agenda I wish to set out in this realm is to widen understanding of the impacts of such work and gather deeper knowledge of its role in the wider sustainability discussions, and it includes:

- investigating the process of using fashion as a tool for community development and how this supports thinking around sustainable communities;
- understanding how to consolidate knowledge around the different services, events and products being produced in this space, and how organizations are presenting them in a fashion context;
- research into how strengthening networks and increasing access to space, funding and new technologies can facilitate work in this field that could support the development of new initiatives;
- exploration of how to understand the ways in which local knowledge, created through projects, discussions and research, can be accessed by virtual communities to connect communities worldwide to such knowledge and practice.

References

Adewunmi, B. (2012), How African women are making tartan and supporting each other in Scotland, *The Guardian* [online]. Available at: www.theguardian.com/lifeandstyle/2012/oct/01/african-women-making-tartan-scotland (accessed 3 April 2013).

Anderson, C. (2012), *Makers: The New Industrial Revolution*. London: Random House Business.

Bacon, J. (2009), *The Art of Community*. Sebastopol, CA: O'Reilly.

Barnes, M., Newman, J. and Sullivan, H. (2007), *Power, Participation and Political Renewal: Case Studies in Public Participation*. Bristol, UK: Policy Press.

Bertotti, M., Jamal, F. and Harden, A. (2011), A review of conceptualisations and meanings of 'community' within and across research traditions: a meta-narrative approach. *Connected Communities Report* [online]. Available at: www.ahrc.ac.uk (accessed 16 July 2013).

Cantle, T. (2005), *Community Cohesion: A New Framework for Race and Diversity*. Basingstoke, UK: Palgrave Macmillan.

Cornwall, A. (2011), *The Participation Reader*. London: Zed.

Crow, G. and Mah, A. (2011), Conceptualisations and meanings of community: the theory and operationalization of a contested concept. *Connected Communities Report* [online]. Available at: www.ahrc.ac.uk (accessed 16 July 2013).

Dearden, D., Hill, K. and Light, A. (2013), Meanwhile Use as Performance: securing social value from vacant spaces. *Connected Communities Report* [online]. Available at: www.ahrc.ac.uk (accessed 27 June 2013).

Field, J. (2010), *Social Capital*, 2nd edn. London: Routledge.

Gauntlett, D. (2011), *Making Is Connecting: The Social Meaning of Creativity, from DIY and Knitting to YouTube and Web 2.0*. Cambridge, UK: Polity.

Headingley Development Trust (2009), *Headways*, 27, January.

Hopkins, R. (2008), *The Transition Handbook: From Oil Dependency to Local Resilience*, 1st edn. Totnes, UK: Green Books.

Hopkins, R. and Lipman, P. (2009), *Who we are and what we do* [online]. Available at: www.transition network.org (accessed 18 November 2013).

Julier, G. (2008), Design Activism as a Tool for Creating New Urban Narratives, *Changing the Change.* Leeds, UK: Leeds Metropolitan University.

Leadbeater, C. (2009), *We-Think: Mass Innovation, Not Mass Production*, 2nd edn. London: Profile Books.

McCabe, A., Phillimore, J. and Ramsden, H.(2010), The role of grassroots arts activities in communities. A scoping study. *Connected Communities Report* [online] Available at: www.ahrc.ac.uk (accessed 16 July 2013).

Portas, M. (2011), *The Portas Review: an independent review of the future of our highstreets* [online]. Available at: www.maryportas.com (accessed 8 July 2013).

Sennett, R. (2013), *Together: The Rituals, Pleasures and Politics of Cooperation*, 2nd edn. London: Penguin.

Social Enterprise UK (2012), Social Enterprise and Youth Policy Paper. Catalyst Consortium.

Thomas, N., Hackney, F. and Bunnell, K. (2012), Connecting Craft and Communities. *Connected Communities Report* [online]. Available at: www.ahrc.ac.uk (accessed 16 July 2013).

Wilson, G. (2012), *Community Resilience and Environmental Transitions*. New York: Routledge.

25

OPENNESS

Amy Twigger Holroyd

Introduction

To commence this discussion of openness, I will first share a little about myself. I have been active in fashion and sustainability for the past decade, working as a designer–maker through my UK-based knitwear label, Keep & Share. Like Lizzie Harrison in the previous chapter, I have sought to put my sustainable design ideas into practice in order to demonstrate alternative possibilities and identify hidden issues and opportunities. In recent years, I have distanced myself from industrial initiatives, making a conscious decision to support grassroots amateur activity that could contribute towards a sustainable fashion system.

In my doctoral research, I have been investigating openness: opening garments, opening my practice as a designer–maker and opening the wider fashion system. I see a natural affinity between a holistic, systems view of fashion and activity at the micro scale; I feel that individuals are more able to reorient their practices and explore radical alternatives than larger organisations with various vested interests.

In this chapter, I will explore theoretical ideas of openness and share my attempts to explore openness through making, drawing on data from my own research. I worked with seven female amateur knitters, aged between 43 and 66, conducting individual, garment-based interviews before embarking on a series of experimental knitting workshops.

Openness

Openness is both an abstract concept and an identifiable trend that can be observed in many fields of life; for example: open-source software, open science, open gaming and open data (van Abel *et al.*, 2011). In each case, if we compare the conventional culture with its open equivalent, we see the breaking down of centralised authority and the erosion of the division between professional experts and amateur users. In many cases, the role of the user is fundamentally shifted from passive observer to active contributor.

The growth of open culture is often related to the rise of the Internet and, in particular, Web 2.0 technologies. Rather than experts creating static content for audiences to read, Web 2.0 involves 'everyday' people coming together to work collaboratively (Gauntlett, 2011). This is a significant shift in media culture, which Gauntlett describes as a shift from a 'sit back and be told' culture (typified by broadcast television) towards a 'making and doing' culture (typified by YouTube and Wikipedia). Jenkins (2006) argues that the desire for participation will spread, transforming institutions across society.

The qualities of openness have much in common with an ecological paradigm that is associated with a 'third-order' approach to sustainability (Sterling, 2001). This paradigm is informed by understandings of ecosystems and an appreciation of the characteristics – such as diversity – that allow such systems to be resilient in the long term. For example, openness is characterised by participation, which in turn is regarded as a key characteristic of an ecological paradigm (Sterling, 2001). Openness can also be seen as an organisational alternative to the rational, closed systems that arguably created the massive environmental and social problems that we face. As Thackara (2011: 44) argues, 'open research, open governance and open design are preconditions for the continuous, collaborative, social mode of enquiry and action that are needed'.

Fashion as a commons

Having established the qualities of openness, we can now ask: how open is fashion? Mainstream fashion certainly portrays an image of freedom and participation through its media and advertising. However, von Busch (2011: 33) argues that the current fast-fashion regime actually 'encourages a surrogate or receiving attitude for the . . . consumer'.

In order to interrogate this question more deeply, I have constructed a metaphor of fashion as land. According to Kaiser (2008: 140), 'metaphors suggest analogies that enable us to visualize and understand concepts that might otherwise be difficult to grasp'. Most metaphors for fashion are associated with industrial capitalism. For example, fashion can be described as a pipeline; this sets up production and consumption as fundamentally separate activities and encourages the idea that materials can continually flow through the system, without limits. Kaiser argues that a sustainable fashion system requires circular and weblike metaphors, because existing models 'contribute to binary thinking [and] ultimately limit our ability to envision new possibilities' (Kaiser, 2008: 143). The metaphor of fashion as land focuses on the experiences of wearers, rather than the professionals usually seen as 'producing' fashion. Furthermore, I find that comparing a transitory culture such as fashion with the tangible reality of land brings hidden issues into focus and enables an activist attitude.

As I look out from my workshop in rural Herefordshire on this summer's day, I am treated to the glorious view of Lugg Meadow: over 300 acres of wildlife-rich grassland. This vantage point provides the ideal opportunity to illustrate my metaphor: I can imagine the whole world of fashion superimposed on the meadow. Distributed around this space, I see all of the garments – new, old, fashionable, unfashionable – existing in the world. I see, too, every desirable way of appearing through dress, throughout history: the huge diversity of archetypal garment styles, shapes and details from different geographical areas and historical periods, and the enormous variety of ways of wearing clothes that make up the world's fashion and clothing cultures.

If I look a little closer, I see wearers – all of us – moving around the meadow. Because fashion reflects preferences at a particular time, areas of the meadow are accessed at different times and by different people. The way individuals move around the commons depends upon the degree to which they wish to stand out or conform. Dant (1999: 93) describes how fashion 'acts as a living museum' and 'plays promiscuously with the past'; thus, particularly fertile areas may return to favour time after time, renewed and layered with new meanings.

Lugg Meadow is one of the few surviving areas of common land in the country, having been managed in this way since medieval times (Brian and Thomson, 2002). Whereas most land in Britain is privately owned, the use of the meadow is shared by commoners. I would like to see 'fashion land' as a commons, too, because I believe the resource needs to be open – that is, with all areas accessible – in order to meet the needs of wearers. To explain the need for openness, we must take a brief detour into fashion theory (see also Chapter 2).

Identity and participation

Drawing on the work of Max-Neef (1992) and his idea of fundamental human needs, Fletcher and Grose (2008) argue that we use fashion to meet our human need for identity. As Rogers and Smith-Lovin (2011: 121) explain, 'sociologists use the term "identity" to refer to the many meanings attached to a person, both by the self and others'. We gain these meanings from our roles in society, the groups we belong to and our personal characteristics. Because leisure and lifestyle are now more important for identity than work, religion and class, 'the consumption of cultural goods, such as fashionable clothing, performs an increasingly important role' (Crane, 2000: 11). Our clothes are a particularly significant type of possession, because of the intimate relationship they have with our bodies (Dant, 1999). Woodward (2007) describes the act of choosing what to wear as a practice of identity construction, and dressing as an act of 'surfacing' particular aspects of the self. Identity construction relies on the meanings associated with our clothes, although such meanings are not universal or fixed (McCracken, 1990).

Fletcher and Grose point to participation as another human need that can be met through fashion. As Dant (1999: 107) explains, 'wearing clothes is social in that what people wear is treated by those around them as being some sort of indicator of who they are'. Thus, clothes – and, therefore, fashion – connect the individual with others in society. An important dynamic that shapes this connection can be found in the processes of identification and differentiation. First identified by Simmel (1904), identification, or conformity, describes a need to belong and carries a sense of solidarity; differentiation, or individualism, describes a need to feel unique. Uniqueness is a self-correcting process, and so, when individuals start to feel too similar to others, they will find ways to reassert their individuality (Snyder and Fromkin, 1980). Because of their ubiquity and visibility, clothes play an important part in this dynamic.

I argue that, in order to effectively express and resolve our identities and connect with others, a diversity of options is required. To meet our needs for identity and participation, we need space to move around the commons, to identify with and differentiate ourselves from others, and to make gaps and juxtapositions between styles.

Enclosure

Although I believe it is important to have an open fashion commons, I find that our access to this resource is restricted by various factors. By extending the metaphor of fashion as land, we can frame this restriction as 'enclosure'. The Enclosure Acts of the eighteenth and nineteenth centuries enclosed the vast majority of common land in England, shifting the land into private ownership and taking away the rights of commoners (Neeson, 1993). In an open fashion commons, we would have access to the full diversity of styles and ways of wearing them; enclosure would mean a restriction on these choices.

It could be said that fashion has always been enclosed. For several centuries, fashion was only available to the elite. During the nineteenth century, an industrial system was developed that helped to spread fashion to a much broader section of society; however, 'class fashion' prevailed, with strict rules governing the use of certain items and stylistic norms dictated by designers in Paris. Although this traditional form of fashion authority has dramatically diminished in recent decades, less obvious modes of restriction have taken over.

There are various perspectives that could be taken on this restriction, such as the influence of body image and the way in which the fashion media judge 'right' and 'wrong' fashion statements. The social norms that shape our dress choices could be seen as another, arguably unavoidable, type of restriction. As a maker, I am particularly interested in the role of manufacture as a mechanism of enclosure. Clothing production has become increasingly industrialised and professionalised in recent decades and concentrated in the hands of a small number of powerful companies. Fine and Leopold (1993) discuss 'systems of provision': the unique economic and social processes that affect the production and consumption of different types of good. I agree that the means by which clothing is produced affects, not only the characteristics of the garments themselves, but also the workings of the entire fashion system (see also Chapter 1).

Many would argue that, in today's culture, we enjoy a truly diverse fashion offer. According to conventional economic thinking, capitalism allows the consumer to choose from a wide range of products. However, Kean (1997: 172) suggests that, although customers perceive choice, what the fashion industry actually offers is a 'homogenous assortment of like items at varying price points'. In the interviews I conducted, one participant described her frustration at the choice of clothing available: 'I suppose I do feel constrained sometimes. You search from shop to shop to shop to shop, thinking I've got this image in my head, and you never can find quite what you want.'

Other interviews revealed disappointment with the quality of the fabrics used in high-street clothing, further restricting choice. Options are also limited for individuals whose bodies do not conform to the standardised size ranges of high-street shops. Another participant talked in detail about how size and fit restrict the choice of clothing available to her:

> There's a lot of disappointment. Mainly to do with fit. What is fashionable isn't cut to suit my figure. And it's . . . do they want to sell clothes to my age group? I think, is it my fault for trying to wear something which is unsuitable for me, or is it their fault for only cutting for one shape?

A further consequence of the industrialisation of clothing manufacture is the separation of the roles of producer and consumer. Today, the vast majority of clothing worn in Britain is produced overseas, and most wearers have little knowledge of how their clothes are made. Fletcher and Grose (2008: 5) argue that homogenous products mystify the practice of making clothes; they describe 'closed, ready-made products with little opportunity for self-expression'. These comments lead us to another type of enclosure: the sense that we cannot make or adapt our own garments. The ubiquity of mass-produced, 'closed' garments engenders a feeling that our homemade items are not good enough, and that, once items are made, they should not be repaired or altered. As I will explain later, although amateur fashion making is currently enjoying a surge in popularity, my research indicates that people are often unhappy with the items they have made.

I am proposing that the standardisation associated with industrial production is a mechanism of enclosure. I argue that those who produce our clothes restrict our use of the fashion commons, because they make many choices about what is available, and, as dependent wearers without an independent means of production, we can only choose from the limited options provided.

Reclaiming the commons

Happily, the story does not end here. We can use the metaphor of fashion as land to consider methods of challenging enclosure and opening up the fashion commons. One particularly inspiring example can be found in the Diggers of the seventeenth century. Instead of obediently abiding by the laws governing access to land, this group occupied and cultivated an area as a way of symbolically demonstrating its view that everyone should have a free allowance to dig and grow food (Hazeldine, 2011). A contemporary version of this attitude can be found in the guerrilla gardening movement, described as 'the illicit cultivation of someone else's land' (Reynolds, 2008:

16). Like the Diggers, guerrilla gardeners are motivated to claim the shared use of land. Through their actions, they force this resource back into a conceptual commons and demand the right to be actors, not just consumers, within public space.

In fashion terms, a similar reclamation would involve gaining access to a more diverse range of styles and ways of wearing clothes, and actively contributing to fashion culture. Of course, any attempt to challenge enclosure will be shaped by the type of enclosure that is perceived to exist. For example, the enclosure associated with glossy fashion magazines – which promote fashion as a globalised culture of conspicuous consumption – could be challenged through an alternative fashion publication. The experimental Syntax/144 project created by Otto von Busch is an inspiring example: a locally produced, editor-less fashion zine, distributed through insertion into copies of established magazines at local shops (von Busch, 2009). I am particularly motivated to challenge the enclosure associated with industrialised clothing production, supporting wearers to take a more active role in the material aspects of their clothes through engagement with making and remaking.

Amateur fashion making

Fashion and textiles have a long and continuous history of amateur making. There has been a resurgence of interest in recent years, with knitting, in particular, experiencing a noticeable revival (Lewis, 2011). Amateur making can open up access to the fashion commons, as higher-quality, better-fitting garments of any style can (in theory) be made. The ability to make clothes brings power to the hands of the wearer, making them less dependent and passive. Interestingly, the culture of craft has much in common with openness, with activities such as knitting, quilting and embroidery drawing on a rich resource of traditional designs and an ethos of communal evolution (Freeman, 1987) that can be linked to the participatory culture of Web 2.0.

I want to use my design practice to encourage grassroots activity that gives agency to wearers, opening up the production of garments – specifically, knitwear. This is not as straightforward as it might seem; knitters tend to use patterns to guide their projects, and my research shows that many have problems finding patterns they want to knit and wear. Although, like sewing patterns, knitting patterns can be adapted and used in 'unorthodox' ways (Szeless, 2002), many knitters do not have the confidence to do so. For those who manage it, there is sometimes a sense that their adaptations are remedial, helping them achieve the intended design with a different yarn, for example, rather than delivering creative satisfaction. Hence, we can see that amateur making is not a free pass to an open fashion commons and does not necessarily create a strong sense of empowerment among makers.

Amateur design

In my research, I explored the potential for knitters to design their own patterns, while reworking (re-knitting) existing items of knitwear. Although I am passionate about supporting amateur making, I am conscious that, because the vast majority of knitters produce new items, their efforts mirror – rather than challenge – the linear production–consumption model of the mainstream fashion industry. I see re-knitting as a more radical type of amateur making that disrupts the prevalent fashion system and engages with the mountains of existing garments found in the fashion commons. Hence, the opening of individual garments is linked with a more conceptual opening of fashion. Re-knitting is an ideal area in which to explore amateur design skills; it would be impossible to write a conventional re-knitting pattern, given that each project must respond to the unique materiality of the garment in question.

Figure 25.1 Completed re-knitting project (replacement sleeves using reclaimed yarn)

Figure 25.2 Completed re-knitting project ('cardiganised' jumper and afterthought pocket)

In the early stages of the project, I developed methods of altering knitted garments using knit-based techniques, exploiting the fact that the knitted structure is inherently open: the rows of intermeshed loops can be unravelled, laddered and reformed. I shared the re-knitting techniques with the group of knitters at a series of workshop sessions and guided them through a series of design tasks, intended to build their skills. At the first workshop, we discussed the professional mystique that surrounds design, and the fact that most knitters do not experiment with stitches and yarn – for me, a key element of the design process. As one of the participants explained: 'There's no culture of playing with wool, unless you're trying to do fancy odd things. There's no culture for ordinary knitters of playing around.'

Despite their lack of experience, the knitters enthusiastically embraced the opportunity to design. The project culminated in each participant designing and executing a knit-based alteration to an item from her own wardrobe. The tacit knowledge the knitters had gained from working with patterns allowed them to consider the technical, as well as aesthetic, aspects of knitwear design. By working together, they were able to generate ideas and develop them to suit their preferences, both as knitters and as wearers. Although the participants were wary of opening their garments at first, by practising on sample fabrics, they gained confidence in their skills and were able to overcome the closed nature of the manufactured garment. This project demonstrates the possibility of overcoming the enclosure of mass production through amateur making; the participants accessed, and contributed to, the fashion commons on their own terms.

Confidence

The conversations I have had with knitters over the years reveal another issue affecting amateur making: whether projects 'turn out' as desired and actually pass into use. I have met many people who are successful in making garments for themselves to wear and do so with pride. However, I know that many items do not turn out as intended. Walker (2006: 57) discusses the value of homemade items and somewhat idealistically argues that, 'such an object will be valued despite any lack of value evident in its creation, and whether or not it actually functions well or as intended'. The accounts I have gathered from knitters tell a different story. Although they may have enjoyed the process of making, they are unlikely to value – or wear – a finished item if it does not meet their standards.

I feel that many negative feelings stem from a cultural ambivalence around homemade clothes. Although homemade items are often seen in a romantic, positive light, there is also an association between homemade and poverty that endures, despite the cheapness of today's ready-made clothes. Homemade items are often the butt of jokes; negative comments about itchy, uncomfortable, ill-fitting jumpers are overwhelmingly familiar. Hence, makers are sometimes unsure of the way in which their homemade garments will be received by those around them.

When amateurs design their own projects, their doubts about the success of their creations may deepen; they no longer have the sanctioning effect of a pattern, designed by a professional 'expert'. This can be seen as one potential danger of de-professionalising fashion design. However, the participants in the re-knitting project did have confidence in the garments they produced. The structure of the workshops gave them space to experiment and try out ideas for their projects and the opportunity to reflect and select their preferred option. Crucially, they did so with the aid of feedback from their peers, as one participant noted: 'I think it's really exciting to design. But it's something I couldn't do on my own. I need to feed off other people, I think, to get ideas, and then to gain confidence in my ideas, I suppose.'

When dressing, we anticipate the gaze of others; our self-image is largely informed by external appraisals (Kaiser, 1997). In the project, the knitters tested out their ideas under that gaze, in a safe environment, and thus developed confidence in their work.

Conclusion

I will conclude by reconnecting with the overarching theme of sustainability. A lack of making skills among wearers weds identity construction to consumption, and all of its associated impacts; as Finkelstein (1991: 145) says, 'if we are relying upon the properties of procured goods for our sense of identity, then we are compelled to procure again and again'. A greater engagement with making – and, crucially, remaking – among wearers starts to break this link and build an alternative fashion culture. Like fashion, making enables us to connect with others and provides a means of constructing and expressing identity. By integrating making into fashion, we create an alternative, more materially grounded – but less materially intensive – means of meeting our human needs for identity and participation. Through opening individual garments and demystifying design, we can challenge the enclosure of the fashion commons that relates to industrialised clothing production. Although I have explored the idea of openness in my own specialism of knitting, these principles could be transferred to many other areas by consideration of the mechanisms of enclosure and creative methods of overcoming them.

I see an important role for designers in supporting openness: my project indicates that amateur design requires support in order to flourish. The participants described the project as a catalyst for their activity: a structure within which they could work creatively. Von Busch describes this new role for the designer as an 'orchestrator and facilitator . . . designing material artefacts as well as social protocols' (von Busch, 2009: 63). From a similar perspective, Jones (1991: 205) describes the designer who opens their practice to support amateurs as a 'professional encourager'.

Finally, I would like to note that, when wearers engage with making in a new way – whether a non-knitter learning the skill for the first time, or an experienced knitter starting to design – the activity often prompts reflection on the wider fashion system. Thus, my own research agenda for the next decade is to explore ways of encouraging amateur making, while constructively disrupting established ways of operating in order to prompt reflection and behaviour change.

References

van Abel, B., Evers, L., Klaassen, R. and Troxler, P. (eds) (2011), *Open Design Now: Why Design Cannot Remain Exclusive*. Amsterdam: BIS Publishers.

Brian, A. and Thomson, P. (2002), *The History and Natural History of Lugg Meadow*. Almeley, UK: Logaston Press.

von Busch, O. (2009), *Fashion-able*. Gothenburg, Sweden: Camino.

von Busch, O. (2011), The virus of fashion, in A. Trumpfheller and O. von Busch (eds) *The Virus of Fashion*. Istanbul: Rage Against the Sage Press: 27–34.

Crane, D. (2000), *Fashion and Its Social Agendas: Class, Gender and Identity in Clothing*. Chicago, IL: University of Chicago Press.

Dant, T. (1999), *Material Culture in the Social World: Values, Activities, Lifestyles*. Buckingham, UK: Open University Press.

Fine, B. and Leopold, E. (1993), *The World of Consumption*. London: Routledge.

Finkelstein, J. (1991), *The Fashioned Self*. Oxford, UK: Polity Press.

Fletcher, K. and Grose, L. (2008), Fashion that helps us flourish, in C. Cipolla and P. P. Peruccio (eds) *Changing the Change: Design, Visions, Proposals and Tools*. Turin, Italy 10–12 July. Turin: Allemandi Conference Press.

Freeman, J. (1987), Sewing as a woman's art, in G. Elinor, S. Richardson, S. Scott, A. Thomas and K. Walker (eds) *Women and Craft*. London: Virago: 55–63.

Gauntlett, D. (2011), *Making is Connecting*. Cambridge, UK: Polity.

Hazeldine, T. (2011), Foreword, in A. Hopton (ed.) *Gerrard Winstanley: A Common Treasury*. London: Verso: vii–xix.

Jenkins, H. (2006), *Convergence Culture: Where Old and New Media Collide*. New York: New York University Press.

Jones, J. C. (1991), Continuous design and redesign, in J. C. Jones (ed.) *Designing Designing*. London: Architecture Design & Technology Press: 190–216.

Kaiser, S. B. (1997), *The Social Psychology of Clothing: Symbolic Appearances in Context* (rev. 2nd edn). New York: Fairchild Publications.

Kaiser, S. B. (2008), Mixing metaphors in the fiber, textile and apparel complex: moving toward a more sustainable fashion, in J. Hethorn and C. Ulasewicz (eds) *Sustainable Fashion: Why Now?* New York: Fairchild Books: 139–64.

Kean, R. C. (1997), The role of the fashion system in fashion change: a response to the Kaiser, Nagasawa and Hutton model. *Clothing & Textiles Research Journal*, 15(3): 172–7.

Lewis, P. (2011), Pride in the wool: the rise of knitting. *The Guardian* [online] 6 July. Available at: www.guardian.co.uk/lifeandstyle/2011/jul/06/wool-rise-knitting (accessed 29 June 2013).

McCracken, G. D. (1990), *Culture and Consumption: New Approaches to the Symbolic Character of Consumer Goods and Activities*. Bloomington, IN: Indiana University Press.

Max-Neef, M. (1992), Development and human needs, in P. Ekins and M. Max-Neef (eds) *Real-life Economics: Understanding Wealth Creation*. London: Routledge: 197–213.

Neeson, J. M. (1993), *Commoners: Common Right, Enclosure and Social Change in England, 1700–1820*. Cambridge, UK: Cambridge University Press.

Reynolds, R. (2008), *On Guerrilla Gardening: A Handbook for Gardening Without Boundaries*. London: Bloomsbury.

Rogers, K. B. and Smith-Lovin, L. (2011), Action, interaction, and groups, in G. Ritzer (ed.) *The Wiley–Blackwell Companion to Sociology*. Oxford, UK: Blackwell: 121–38.

Simmel, G. (1904), Fashion. *International Quarterly*, 10: 130–55. Available at: www.modetheorie.de/fileadmin/Texte/s/Simmel-Fashion_1904.pdf (accessed 29 June 2013).

Snyder, C. R. and Fromkin, H. L. (1980), *Uniqueness: The Human Pursuit of Difference*. New York: Plenum.

Sterling, S. R. (2001), *Sustainable Education: Re-visioning Learning and Change*. Totnes, UK: Green Books.

Szeless, M. (2002), Burda fashions – a wish that doesn't have to be wishful thinking: home-dressmaking in Austria 1950–1970. *Cultural Studies*, 16(6): 848–62.

Thackara, J. (2011), Into the open, in B. van Abel, L. Evers, R. Klaassen and P. Troxler (eds) *Open Design Now: Why Design Cannot Remain Exclusive*. Amsterdam: BIS Publishers: 42–5.

Walker, S. (2006), *Sustainable By Design: Explorations in Theory and Practice*. London: Earthscan.

Woodward, S. (2007), *Why Women Wear What They Wear*. Oxford, UK: Berg.

26

MENDING

Jonnet Middleton

If you've found the joy of mending, pass it on. It's a gift for life.[1]

Perched between thumb and forefinger is the threaded needle. I am finally ready to mend. I anchor in a couple of inches of turquoise ribbon under the fraying lining and with satin stitch I reinforce the tear, turquoise thread on duck egg satin. I wallow in the luxury of the finish, and in the joy of this small act of repair. I am entranced. In herringbone stitch I go on to fix the hem, and with buttonhole stitch I reinforce the belt loop. Before the sun is too high Turquoise Backless Dress is in a fit state once again.

I call myself a mending activist and yet I have never mended like this before. I'll come clean and admit that I have hardly ever mended anything at all. There is no need, and try as I might even I can't find the incentive or the time. I inspire others to mend but can't defeat my own apathy as a victim of material abundance. I made a zero consumption pledge in 2008 to wear nothing but the clothes that I already owned for the rest of my life, but it failed to make a mender of me. By then, my hoard far exceeded what I can physically wear out in my own lifetime. The mending pile keeps growing, but I still have plenty of wearable clothes left in the wardrobe. Mending is always postponed. To become a mender, more drastic measures were required. I had to make mending irresistible and unavoidable. And so it was that I set out for Cuba in the spirit of a pioneer mending tourist, with a suitcase of unwearable clothing in need of repair and a pledge to mend every last thing by my return a month later.

I sit in a former art deco cocktail bar looking out over Havana rooftops to the turquoise blue Straits of Florida, mending out of necessity so that I have something to wear, but mending also out of pure delight as a privileged visitor to a mending paradise. Here in Cuba, everything is mended, and every person is a mender. I admire the fearlessness, the determination and the unexpected creativity of the ad hoc results. There are no rules, just a basic instinct to extend the useful life of material goods way beyond what a visitor from the West could ever imagine. I am inspired to put my whole mending pile in order. Suddenly, mending is contagious, uplifting, spontaneous and easy.

The belt loop broke as I was hurrying to a party, aged 17. I fastened a nappy pin inside the waist, and there it has stayed in a favourite dress for 25 years, all for the want of a 5-minute repair. Belatedly, I have mended, and finally it is fixed.

Figure 26.1 Mended Turquoise Backless Dress

Reinforcement required

Who will join me in mending paradise? This tale is a true story and also a dream. I am a UK-based artist living a lifelong experiment to overcome a disarming addiction to consumer excess. Mending is currently at the outer extreme of the fashion system. My mission is to help bring it into the centre. This chapter shares some thoughts on mending as commodity activism from a UK perspective.[2] I start with a brief contextual review of mending in fashion, followed by a confrontation with some of the obstacles to mending. I then tackle some of the deeper, political transmutations that are necessary for mending to get inside fashion, to increase its visibility and to get wearers and their clothing ready to mend.

Mending has been a fundamental human activity throughout history and continues to be so in the vast majority of the world, but, as consumerism has tightened its grip, mending has become very hard to do. It is not about cost. Many basic mends require but a needle and thread. It is not about time. Iron-on patches, strips and bonding powders make some mending jobs almost instant. It is not about skill. Mending has, perhaps, the lowest entry level of all crafts and is based on improvisation. Lack of skill, time and cost are the reasons most commonly cited for the demise of mending (Fisher *et al.*, 2008; Gibson and Stanes, 2011), and, granted, these obstacles loom large at the very contemplation of repair. It is contentious of me to shun their very tangible nature, but we find the time and money to feed our consumption habits, which is hard work in itself (Tranberg-Hansen, 2000), and likewise to launder clothes, regularly, sometimes with great care. I contend that the real obstacles are psychological and systemic in nature. Elsewhere in this volume, Otto von Busch's articulation of the psychological resistance to breaking fashion conventions serves to explain why mending is unthinkable for today's fashion consumer

(Chapter 27). The psychological and embodied character of fashion, coupled with the deeply stigmatised and gendered nature of repair, and the conflicting forces of consumerism and nature, throws the humble act of mending into a complex and multilayered arena of identity politics and commodity activism. In this chapter, I focus on the systemic barriers to mending created by consumerism on the social and material level.

Definitions

In the narrowest sense, mending is the gesture that sustains and prolongs the functional life of a garment by remedying malfunction and material wear. Mending lies between laundering, a regular practice of maintenance, and alteration, transformation and reuse, which are irregular practices to increase wearability and extend clothing life cycles on both the material and immaterial level. It is futile to seek a clear distinction between mending and these other practices, because the mender has recourse to the widest spectrum of techniques to craft a unique solution in a given context. As we shall see later, the mend follows the matter.

The term 'mending' carries subtle inferences of non-professional work done by hand, often by females, and particularly in textiles. 'Repair' is the more common, more generic and more gender-neutral term for mending practices across all fields. In this chapter, I use both terms, although I focus on the mending of clothing[3] as a DIY activity rather than as an entrepreneurial opportunity. I explore the political significance of consumers becoming menders, as opposed

Figure 26.2 Tom of Holland's meta-darning of Sanquhar socks
Source: Tom of Holland

to the provision or consumption of mending services within the fashion system (WRAP, 2012) or the design of repairable fashion consumables (Rissanen, 2011). As such, I refer to the most intimate moments of mending as 'small tactical interventions at a personal micro-level' (von Busch, 2012).

Mending is a post-growth fashion activity that everyone can do. Expectations and standards of repair vary from the stapled hem of the office trouser leg to the bespoke Sanquhar sock darning of Tom of Holland.[4] There are how-to guides for novices and manuals for quality repair, the most exigent from earlier eras[5] that testify to the consummate skill of menders past and the huge shift that has since taken place in matters of quality and care. Today, quality and success are contingent on context. The stapled hem or the nappy pin belt loop may be plenty good enough. The crudest mends can ooze kudos from their sheer daring or joviality, whereas, at the opposite extreme, the most exquisite mends go well beyond function in their expression of mastery, creativity and love.

Context

What sort of a mender are you? Hedonist? Activist? Artist? Specialist? Bodger? Thriftster? Traditionalist? Professional? New entrepreneur? Survivalist? Fashionista? Station stitch?[6] At an urban repair cafe, mending is a hip pursuit; in a dimly lit kitchen, it's a drudge; in a war zone, it's a matter of life and death.[7] The occurrence of mending in the clothing sector can be broken in two, the remains of traditional practices, and the emergence of what I shall term 'new mending'. The former includes domestic mending, high-street repair and alteration services often linked to dry cleaners or sewing-supplies shops, and traditional retailers who provide mending services for their high-end or specialist products.[8]

Of the latter, new mending manifestations have mushroomed over the last 5 years. Entrepreneurial pioneers such as Rapha and Nudie Jeans have made online mending services the ultimate in cool. Upcycling fashion label Antiform (see also Chapter 24), which restyles pre- and post-consumer waste, offers a 'mending boutique' service as a natural extension of its activities, an idea it takes on the road to festivals. Mending is coming into sight in edgy fashion capitals such as Berlin,[9] and fashionista hysteria broke out when Prince Charles nonchalantly donned a jacket mended to the extreme on UK television.[10] Signs of a mending resurgence are most evident at the grassroots level. Mending events, social initiatives and workshops are germinating in large cities and small towns alike, typically linked to craft-supplies shops, transition towns[11] and artisan and activist individuals within fashion and craft communities, a great example being mending champion Scrapiana's Big Mend, based in Bath, UK. Mending bloggers, experts and artists such as Tom of Holland and Celia Pym in the UK and Michael Swaine in the US have earned niche celebrity status through social media among a new generation of aspiring menders.

This new mending subculture is rooted in the recent revival of sewing, knitting and crafting, the resurgence of the 'make do and mend' mentality, the Second World War UK government campaign to promote fashion austerity, and, beyond fashion, in the fervent fixer community that has developed out of hacker and maker culture, ad hocism and craftivism, where digital repair, electrical and electronics repair and cycle repair predominate. To name but three examples, iFixit is a grassroots, open-source online repair community whose aim is to teach everyone in the world to fix everything; the Restart Project advocates a future economy of maintenance and repair by organising repair events in communities and workplaces in London and inspiring similar initiatives around the world; the Repair Cafe, started in the Netherlands and now across Europe, visits a new town in a tour bus, stages a launch event and identifies local individuals to make the repair cafe a regular fixture once the bus leaves town. iFixit, Sugru and the legendary and now defunct Platform 21 of Amsterdam have penned impassioned and influential repair manifestos that serve as inspiration to menders in the field of fashion.[12]

Academic research into repair in the fashion industry is negligible and patchy (Gorowek *et al.*, 2013). Significant exceptions are projects that encompass the social practices of mending, such as Local Wisdom and Craft of Use[13] and Community Repair (von Busch, 2011). Other research proposes specific, sector-wide changes: tax breaks to make repair affordable (Fletcher and Grose, 2012), a 'lifetime policy' for garments that includes repair services (Cataldi *et al.*, 2013) and a 'green clothing care' labelling system that informs about and encourages repair (Dombek-Keith, 2009, in Dombek-Keith and Loker, 2011). Most significant and comprehensive as advocacy tools are the Defra (Fisher *et al.*, 2008) and WRAP (2012) reports, which survey UK consumers' attitudes to repair and present the ecological imperative and economic opportunities, while recording a sizeable consumer demand for an increase in garment repair. At the same time, the policy relevance of repair is being recognised across the UK economy as a whole (Lee *et al.*, 2012; Ellen MacArthur Foundation, 2013).

The mending deterrent

Although vibrant mending cultures advance fresh-faced from the fringes, mending is still invisible to the majority of consumers. When, as an art activist, I entice people to mend in a pop-up high-street mending shop, mending suddenly appears to them to 'make so much sense'.[14] The idea of mending offers respite from a growing disquiet with the consumerist lifestyle, but to convert this idea into action requires facing up to the obstacles ahead. I list some of the more troublesome.

1 *Consumerism has made mending obsolete.* Mending has become increasingly obsolete in fashion systems that are based on the high availability and turnover of low-cost, low-quality clothing. Skills are forgotten, and mending becomes unnecessary, anachronistic and even absurd. Fashion is not physically and cryptically black-boxed in the way that digital products increasingly are; in fact, it is one of the few sectors where mending is still an easy option in practical terms (Brook, 2012), but psychological black-boxing has an equally paralysing effect. Neo-liberal economic ideologies have caused the 'complete rebuttal of the subtle cultures of repair' (Graham and Thrift, 2007: 14), while at the same time affording the consumer every convenience to discard clothes and buy more. Our habits follow the logics of consumption.

2 *There is nothing to mend.* Mending is an activity that, by necessity, follows on from wearing or, more precisely, from wearing out. Our clothes aren't ready to be mended yet because today's clothes are so rarely worn out (Farrant *et al.*, 2010; Fletcher and Grose, 2012; WRAP, 2012). It could take years, if not decades, of wearing the booty from the last two decades of 'normalised overconsumption' (Gibson and Stanes, 2011) before holes appear, but it's a radical thought to allow things to get old (Ryan, 2012). It's daring enough to wear a party dress twice (Jensen and Jørgensen, 2013). Recommendations to wear clothes for just 9 months longer, at significant environmental benefit (WRAP, 2012), are extreme by many people's standards, and yet, if we were to wear and care for our garments with the utmost degree of wartime discipline, the need for mending could be postponed for many years yet (Guilfoyle Williams, 1945, in Rissanen, 2011).

3   *Fast fashion is not worth mending.* Turquoise Backless Dress is a 1960s creation from a reputable brand. It boasts a material quality worthy of repair, unlike the majority of recently produced clothing stock that, were we ever to wear it out, would make an impoverished material arsenal for a future mending culture. How can we be moved to care, emotionally and practically, for a vast and nasty legacy of unmendable tat? Why prolong the misery of short-lived fashions and poorly constructed garments that mock us of our 'failings as uncareful consumers' (Gregson *et al.*, 2009)? Who has the perverse obstinacy to mend these things back into fashion, not only to sustain, but to restore (Hawken, 2012)? Who can imagine a new aesthetics of poor fashion, such as the gritty 'suboptimal' underwear of Dym Products.[15] The easy task, laudable though it is, is to design a brand new set of repairable attire. But who will design the repair of the existing waste-clothing stock to confront the problem of overconsumption immediately, head on?

4   *There's no need to mend.* Almost all the menders of the world do so out of necessity. Without that necessity, how do we mend our way out of a problem, when we can buy our way out instead? How can we find the intrinsic motivation to mend when, with such overabundance, no one is short of things to wear? Can we make our necessity a political or ecological one, in the absence of economic or material need? Can we mend, not out of need, but out of desire?

Resistance

Everyday, people are falling in love with mending, especially people who have made pledges to reduce or eliminate their fashion consumption.[16] To stop shopping for a period of time proves extremely effective in transforming consumption habits (Cline, 2012; Smithers, 2013).[17] The desire to shop soon fades, and mending, as well as making, gains currency as 'the new shopping'. These new menders may not be engaged in conscious political action, but their behaviour clearly sits within practices of commodity activism (Mukherjee and Banet-Weise, 2012). In fact, I suggest that mending within fashion is a particularly complex and compelling form of commodity activism that is layered with tension and irony. New practices of mending go beyond ethical consumerism and boycotts, by offering an alternative to consumption itself. Mending postpones or eliminates the need to consume. The perceived need for a new product is actively dismantled, as life-affirming actions are performed upon an existing commodity. Within the very intimacy and humility of mending lies a deep political power. Formerly situated outside the official fashion economy, mending is now increasingly performed on the fashion fringes, both as anti-consumerist activism and as a marketised mode of resistance to unsustainable fashion, but, whatever form critical consumerism and new mending economies take, they can't escape the dynamics of neo-liberal power. There is no 'outside' of contemporary capitalism (ibid.). Mending can easily be co-opted by market forces and reduced to fad or representation, to next season's 'pre-darned in Bangladesh', must-have jumper. But equally, the new vanguard of menders offers a persuasive vision of mending as a new form of desire, of self-expression and of self-realisation (see Soper, 2009). They offer alternative leadership; they mend to show the way.

Mending hedonists mend as a lifestyle choice, as a luxury in which, to quote Suzy Menkes, 'the essence of the luxurious [is] a private joy in something that [is] crafted to last' (cited in Church Gibson, 2012: 23). They wait for new holes to appear because they love to mend.[18] They are beyond the stigma of shame, because, frankly, in this age of overconsumption, no one needs to mend anything anymore. Pleasure overshadows necessity. The ability to repair redefines prosperity and can increase social status. The pauper is he or she who lacks the intelligence and imagination to repair.

(In)visibility

Shrouded in shame, mending has traditionally been hidden away in the dark recesses of under-arms, back rooms and side streets, and a large shift is required to lift the persistent stigma of wearing visibly mended clothes (Fisher *et al.*, 2008). Invisibility retains a high premium in traditional garment repair, where the finest-quality work is that which is never perceived. Invisible menders reconstruct the warp and weft of a fabric, replicating complex patterns in the weave, and leave nothing but a few loose threads on the reverse. More mundane repair continues to take place in the traditional domestic setting, and, if the resulting patches aren't quite invisible, the practice itself is. And silent. Few traditional menders spare a comment on the sock they darned the night before. And gendered. The most invisible mending has been women's work. Tedious, and thankless. Traditional mending is an emotional labour whose burdens and shames have been kept extraordinarily silent.

The invisible menders have all but disappeared as clothing becomes less and less worthy of luxury repair. The last Parisian workshop of invisible mending recently closed,[19] and, in London, the sole remaining British company is a family business with no heir.[20] Since the 1970s, domestic mending has also all but vanished, since consumerism swept in to liberate the domestic female workforce, and the load shifted from the mending basket to the shopping basket. Daughters were not taught to darn, sometimes by virtue of feminist politics, more often out of indifference. Today, following on from the subjugated mender and the non-mender is the new mender, who reclaims mending as a 'liberating feminist action' within the politics of the 'new domesticity' (see Fletcher and Grose, 2012).

The invisibility of repair has left traces in academic literature. Jackson (2013) talks of the secret history of repair that has always invisibly sustained globalisation. However, sociologists concur that repair practices become visible at the moment of breakdown (Henke, 2000; Graham and Thrift, 2007). The world is briefly disrupted until 'hi-vis' repairmen fix cars, hospitals, offices and power grids and, triumphant, they depart. I argue that feminine mending practices have rarely shared the brief moments of visibility and glory of their masculine counterparts. What is more, with the advance of consumerism, what was once an invisible practice is now a practically non-existent one, as replacement is the new repair.

As invisible mending practices quietly vanish, new menders herald a new era of visible mending,[21] be it out of pride and delight in the durational aesthetics of repair, or be it rooted in an urgent political, social or ecological agenda. Visibility is one of the most pressing tasks of the mending activist. To reveal is to make political. Visibility does not mean insisting that every mend be 'hi-vis'. Traces of repair can linger in our conversations, our status updates and the mending basket in the lounge. Retailers, ads, apps, fashion press, bloggers, garment-care labels, policymakers and education curricula can all signpost repair.

Readiness to mend

I have treasured Turquoise Backless Dress for a quarter of a century, but, consumed by nostalgia and broken promise, I have never raised a needle to it. We appreciate how emotional rela-tionships with our clothes help us to value and wear them more and to keep them for longer (Chapman, 2005; Fletcher and Grose, 2012), but an emotional relationship alone can be passive and sentimentalising. However much love is bestowed on a garment, there is no guarantee that feelings of care translate into action. Care itself has become a practice of consumption: buying organic cotton to care for the environment, fair trade to care for workers, and a new pair of shoes to care for ourselves (see Puig de la Bellacasa, 2012).[22] I assert that, to be ready to mend,

Figure 26.3 Mending in Cuba in Turquoise Backless Dress

we need to go beyond the emotional tie and establish a deeper form of relationship, one that exists on the material and the bodily level, at the intersection between cloth and fingertip. The feminist sociologist Puig de la Bellacasa maintains, 'caring is more than an affective–ethical state: it involves material engagement in labours to sustain interdependent worlds, labours that are often associated with exploitation and domination' (ibid.: 198). Henke (2000: 64) adds that, 'the body is the link between social and material forms of order'; it brings order to our psychological addiction to fast fashion and to the obscene accumulation of matter that it keeps generating.

To illustrate the transmutation of values required for consumers to become menders, I draw on a distinction made by Ingold (2012) between 'object' and 'sample of material'. Following Ingold, we currently relate to clothes as objects, in the Heideggerian sense of 'ready-made'.[23] We know our clothes only in their finished form, as a fixed, or 'undisturbed' (Rissanen, 2011), fashion object. We can touch, but we cannot disturb or 'correspond' with them. Our garments are aliens. Cloth and fingertip cannot converse. The fashion industry churns out static fashion statements that outlaw any thought of mending or transformation (see Fletcher and Grose, 2012: 143–4, 167).

In contrast to the 'object', Ingold positions the term 'sample of material', which is rooted in Heidegger's notion of the 'thing,' the 'gathering of materials in movement'. I argue that to approach a garment as a 'sample of material' indicates a readiness to mend. Mending starts from matter. When repair beckons, fingertips 'follow the materials' (Deleuze and Guattari, 2004, in Ingold, 2012: 437) to outsmart the physical wear and the psychological obsolescence of the garment. The mender thinks 'from materials, not about them' (ibid.). Materials invite us to unlock the worlds of possibility that are latent within their fibre. Materials are always 'becoming something else . . . overtaking the formal destinations that, at one time or another, have been assigned to them' (Ingold, 2012: 435). So, in Rissanen's (2011) turn of phrase, the wardrobe of a consumer is impotent with 'undisturbed' fashion objects, while the wardrobe of a mender is alive with material resources that are 'never finished'. Having licence to override the fashion object's premature ending is liberating and generative, in the sense not only of material transformation, but also of transformation of the self. 'Repair and maintenance activities have not just more grip but more emancipatory potential than may be thought by those who want to write them off as simply mundane or slavishly repetitive' (Graham and Thrift, 2007: 2). Mending has the potential to meet basic human needs, where fashion consumption can only ever be a poor surrogate (see Fletcher and Grose, 2012; Cataldi et al., 2013).

The mending imperative

No one will force us to mend, and yet mending is ever our obligation. Care is 'not something forced upon living beings by a moral order; yet it obliges in that for life to be liveable it needs [to be] fostered', because, 'a world's degree of liveability might well depend on the caring accomplished within it' (Puig de la Bellacasa, 2012: 198). Repair helps fashion to fit within the limits of the material world and restores relations of care in the social world. It disengages fashion from consumption, and, as such, its potential as a change agent is as yet unrecognised. This chapter has placed an emphasis on mending one's own clothes, because, at fingertip level, the shift from passive fashion consumer to active wearer and carer is, I believe, more visceral and acute. Mending one's own clothes creates a direct relation or 'correspondence' between 'the wear the wearer does' and 'the wear the cloth endures'. Mending helps us create relation to the vast, insensible material world. Second, mending for oneself is more radical and politically transformative than consuming a mending service, as it fully renounces consumer passivity. Otto von Busch (in the following chapter) talks of the 'microaggressions' that breed the violence of fast fashion. Mending is a kindness that launches an antidote to this violence, and the accumulation of millions of acts of 'microkindness' have untold promise. All forms of mending are valid and invaluable, but to experience mending first-hand pushes the mending ethic deep inside our consciousness and rewires our consumer brains.

At the outset, this chapter defined mending as a gesture to extend the functional life of clothing. I end with a more personal, activist definition that embraces the social and political promise of mending today: Mending is the liberation of the self through the nexus of cloth and fingertip, in defence of matter, in defiance of consumerism and in the generation of new codes of fashion. The power to mend is held on the tips of fingers.[24]

Research agenda[25]

For fashion educators, students and fashion-sector workers alike, the underlying task is to engineer the complex transition towards making less and mending more, as part of the shift towards post-growth fashion.

Education

- Embed mending across fashion curricula; encourage students of all fashion disciplines to respond to the challenge of the mending imperative.
- Prepare students to forge career pathways in a new mending sector.

Research

- Mending economies: generate new business models and mending enterprises.
- Mending data: compile data on the wear and repair of clothing, from fibre level to social, economic and environmental levels, to assess the limits and possibilities of the current clothing stock as a basis for future research, practice and advocacy.
- Mending skills: recover advanced mending skills and practices relevant to contemporary clothing culture and lifestyles, drawing both from traditional techniques and new innovations and fashions in repair.
- Mending technology: increase durability and mendability through garment construction and textile technology, e.g. the quick-repair jeans zip, recoverable fibre properties such as stretch.
- Mending standards: introduce industry standards for repairability, provision of care and repair information and services.
- Mending studies: these could include history, sociology, feminist studies, ethnography, psychology of mending, gender, power, politics, conservation, care, global studies of repair.

Advocacy

- To peers: mend in public, talk about mending, wear visibly mended clothes, teach children to mend, create new mending fashions to bring novelty to repair.
- To legislators: show how economic incentives and legislation could promote a new mending sector in a circular economy.
- Disseminate mending know-how: mending directories, skills guides, maps and recommendations for mending services, classes and groups, bespoke menders, celebrity menders and more manifestos.

Questions

- How can the deeply felt creative urge of the designer–maker to create new, original fashion be satisfied by the creative act of repair and rechannelled towards the challenge of generating fashion by caring for existing clothing?
- How can fashion marketing and media invent new fashionable subjects around repair, in which the practice rather than the commodity is desirable, where the act of repair is replicated rather than the aesthetic alone? How do consumers become creative custodians of clothes?
- What happens when we mend? How can mending meet human needs for novelty and social identity?
- What are the wider consequences and opportunities of reengineering the fashion industry away from mass production and into care and maintenance?

Notes

1 Adapted from the Fixer's Manifesto, available at: sugru.com/blog/the-fixer-s-manifesto (accessed 11 March 2013).
2 This text is the product of three forms of enquiry: my art activist work to facilitate mending shops and other pop-up mending initiatives (see futuremenders.com), the establishment of a research community around mending (see mendrs.net) and my PhD research into mending activism at Lancaster University (highwire.lancs.ac.uk). I am indebted to my ever-enthusiastic colleagues in these overlapping communities and gratefully acknowledge the financial support of EPSRC, UK. Special thanks to Liz Parker and my Cuban hosts, Analcy, Javier and Ronny.
3 Shoe and accessory repair, both as enterprise and as DIY practice, would paint a different picture.
4 tomofholland.com/2012/05/09/meta-darning-my-sanquhar-socks/
5 The most valuable contributions are historical texts in the form of early-twentieth-century mending manuals, chapters in sewing and home-management handbooks and government wartime publications (see Rissanen, 2011), although there is a recent resurgence in sewing-repair publications.
6 Station stitch is the role assigned to that member of a UK military base or field camp responsible for the repair of uniforms and kit.
7 www.silverdoctors.com/one-year-in-hellsurviving-a-full-shtf-collapse-in-bosnia (accessed 12 May 2013).
8 e.g. www.barbour.com/repairs_reproofing
9 Personal communication with fashion students, Nottingham Trent University.
10 'How Prince Charles' raggedy jacket became a hit with fashionistas', *The Guardian*, 11 March 2013, www.guardian.co.uk/fashion/shortcuts/2013/mar/11/prince-charles-jacket-hit-fashionistas (accessed 11 March 2013).
11 http://en.wikipedia.org/wiki/Transition_Towns_(network) (accessed 11 March 2013).
12 www.ifixit.com/Manifesto, sugru.com/blog/the-fixer-s-manifesto, www.platform21.nl/page/4375/en
13 www.localwisdom.info, craftofuse.org
14 An oft-repeated comment at the Mending Shop, Peterborough, UK, 2012, was that 'every High Street should have one', see: themendingshop.wordpress.com. WRAP (2012) reports that over half of women and nearly a quarter of men are keen to learn repair skills.
15 www.dymproducts.com/suboptimal-underwear.html
16 There are many such pledges comprising personal and public initiatives of varying duration, e.g. for 1 month, (Six Item Challenge); a year (Free Fashion Challenge, The Uniform Project, The Great American Apparel Diet, artist Alex Martin (in Gwilt and Rissanen, 2011; Fletcher and Grose 2012); and for a lifetime (Sarah Kate Beaumont, who makes all her clothes herself, in Cline, 2012, and myself. Since 2008, and for the rest of my life, I will wear only the clothes I already own).
17 See also *Dear Fashion*, a post-consumption magazine edited by a group of fashionistas after completing the Free Fashion Challenge.
18 Lone Koefoed Hansen, presentation at Reclaiming Repair workshop, CHI 2013.
19 http://parisiangentleman.co.uk/2012/01/11/invisible-mending-an-amazing-craft-under-threat/ (accessed 2 November 2012).
20 Personal communication with the British Invisible Mending Service; www.invisible-mending.co.uk

21 tomofholland.com/tag/visible-mending/

22 Anecdotally, my mother finds it hard to come to terms with my pledge and frequently buys me clothes as an act of care.

23 See also Graham and Thrift's (2007) application of Heidegger's ready-to-hand concept to the field of repair.

24 Inspiration credit to Seb Rochford for this thought from the 2005 Polar Bear album, *Held on the Tips of Fingers*.

25 I welcome any correspondence regarding mending in general, or the research agenda in particular. Please contact futuremenders@gmail.com

References

Brook, I. (2012), Mend, Make and Do, in Brady, E. and Phemister, P. (eds) *Human–Environment Relations*. Dordrecht, the Netherlands: Springer: 109–120.

von Busch, O. (2011), Community repair [online]. Available at: www.kulturservern.se/wronsov/selfpassage/CoRep/CommunityRepair_cat-w.pdf (accessed 2 March 2013).

von Busch, O. (2012), The game of fashion and LOOKBOOK.nu, in Black, S. (ed.) *The Sustainable Fashion Handbook*. London: Thames and Hudson: 16–19.

Cataldi, C., Dickson, M. and Grover, C. (2013), Slow fashion: tailoring a strategic approach for sustainability, in Gardetti, M. and Torres, A. (eds) *Sustainability in Fashion and Textiles: Values, Design, Production and Consumption*. Sheffield, UK: Greenleaf: 22–46.

Chapman, J. (2005), *Emotionally Durable Design: Objects, Experiences and Empathy*. London: Earthscan.

Church Gibson, P. (2012), Sustainable fashion in the age of celebrity culture, in Black, S. (ed.) *The Sustainable Fashion Handbook*. London: Thames and Hudson: 20–3.

Cline, E. (2012), *Overdressed*. New York: Portfolio Penguin.

Deleuze, G. and Guattari, F. (2004), *A Thousand Plateaus* (transl. Massumi, B.). London: Continuum.

Dombek-Keith, K. and Loker, S. (2011), Sustainable clothing care by design, in Gwilt, A. and Rissanen, T. (eds) *Shaping Sustainable Fashion: Changing the Way We Make and Use Clothes*. London: Earthscan: 101–16.

Ellen MacArthur Foundation (2013), *Towards the Circular Economy, Vol. 2: Opportunities for the Consumer Goods Sector*. Ellen MacArthur Foundation.

Farrant, L., Olsen, S. and Wangel, A. (2010), Environmental benefits from reusing clothes, *International Journal of Life Cycle*, 15: 726–36.

Fisher, T., Cooper, T., Woodward, S., Hiller, A. and Gorowek, H. (2008), *Public Understanding of Sustainable Clothing: A Report to the Department for Environment, Food and Rural Affairs*. London: Department for Environment, Food and Rural Affairs (Defra).

Fletcher, K. and Grose, L. (2012), *Fashion and Sustainability: Design for Change*. London: Laurence King.

Gibson, C. and Stanes, E. (2011), Is green the new black? Exploring ethical fashion consumption, in Lewis, T. and Potter, E. (eds) *Ethical Consumption: A Critical Introduction*. London: Routledge: 169–85.

Gorowek, H., Hiller, A., Fisher, T., Cooper, T. and Woodward, S. (2013), Consumer's attitudes towards sustainable fashion: clothing usage and disposal, in Gardetti, M. and Torres, A. (eds) *Sustainability in Fashion and Textiles: Values, Design, Production and Consumption*. Sheffield, UK: Greenleaf: 376–92.

Graham, S. and Thrift, N. (2007), Understanding repair and maintenance, *Theory, Culture & Society*, 24(3): 1–25.

Gregson, N., Metcalfe, A. and Crewe, L. (2009), Practices of object maintenance and repair: how consumers attend to consumer objects within the home, *Journal of Consumer Culture*, 9(2): 248–72.

Guilfoyle Williams, J. (1945), *The Wear and Care of Clothing: A Practical Guide to the Correct Choice and Care of Clothing*. London: The National Trade Press.

Gwilt, A. and Rissanen, T. (eds) (2011), *Shaping Sustainable Fashion: Changing the Way We Make and Use Clothes*. London: Earthscan.

Hawken, P. (2012), Foreword: To be clad, in Fletcher, K. and Grose, L. (eds) *Fashion and Sustainability: Design for Change*. London: Laurence King: 4–5.

Henke, C. (2000), The mechanics of workplace order: toward a sociology of repair, *Berkeley Journal of Sociology*, 44: 55–81.

Ingold, T. (2012), Toward an ecology of materials, *Annual Review of Anthropology*, 41: 427–42.

Jackson, S. (2013), Rethinking repair, in Gillespie, T., Boczkowski, P. and Foot, K. (eds) *Media Technologies: Essays on Communication, Materiality and Society*. Cambridge, MA: MIT Press.

Jensen, C. and Jørgensen, M. (2013), Young academic women's clothing practice: interactions between fast fashion and social expectations in Denmark, in Gardetti, M. and Torres, A. (eds) *Sustainability in Fashion and Textiles: Values, Design, Production and Consumption*. Sheffield, UK: Greenleaf: 344–57.

Lee, B., Preston, F., Kooroshy, J., Bailey, R. and Lahn, G. (2012), *Resource Futures: A Chatham House Report*. London: The Royal Institute of International Affairs.

Mukherjee, R. and Banet-Weise, S. (2012), Introduction: commodity activism in neoliberal times, in Mukherjee, R. and Banet-Weise, S. (eds) *Commodity Activism: Cultural Resistance in Neoliberal Times*. New York: New York University Press: 1–18.

Puig de la Bellacasa, M. (2012), 'Nothing comes without its world': thinking with care. *The Sociological Review*, 60: 197–216.

Rissanen, T. (2011), Designing endurance, in Gwilt, A. and Rissanen, T. (eds) *Shaping Sustainable Fashion: Changing the Way We Make and Use Clothes*. London: Earthscan: 127–38.

Ryan, T. (2012), Can fashion ever be sustainable? in Black, S. (ed.) *The Sustainable Fashion Handbook*. London: Thames and Hudson: 63.

Smithers, R. (2013), How I gave up retail therapy and learnt to love mending, in *The Guardian* [online]. Available at: www.guardian.co.uk/money/2013/jan/04/how-gave-up-retail-therapy (accessed 4 January 2013).

Soper, K. (2009), Introduction: the mainstreaming of counter-consumerist concern, in Soper, K., Rule, M. and Thomas, L. (eds) *The Politics and Pleasures of Consuming Differently*. Houndmills, UK: Palgrave Macmillan: 1–21.

Tranberg-Hansen, K. (2000), *Salaula: The World of Second Hand Clothing and Zambia*. Chicago, IL: University of Chicago Press.

WRAP (2012), Valuing our clothes: the true cost of how we design, use and dispose of clothing in the UK. Waste and Resources Action Programme [online]. Available at: www.wrap.org.uk/clothing (accessed 2 March 2013).

27

'A SUIT, *OF HIS OWN EARNING*'

Fashion supremacy and sustainable fashion activism

Otto von Busch

Thoreau and independence

It is no coincidence that Henry David Thoreau starts off his *Walden* (1992 [1854]) experiments on independence, self-determination and autonomy with a critique of what he sees as people's everyday relation to fashion, a relation that affects us all, whether we want it or not. Thoreau draws parallels between our obedience to fashion, our submission before fate, and our surrender to power, as we uncritically adhere to the authority of trends:

> When I ask for a garment of a particular form, my tailoress tells me gravely, 'They do not make them so now', not emphasizing the 'They' at all, as if she quoted an authority as impersonal as the Fates [. . .] We worship not the Graces, nor the Parcæ, but Fashion. She spins and weaves and cuts with full authority. The head monkey at Paris puts on a traveller's cap, and all the monkeys in America do the same.
>
> *(Thoreau, 1992 [1849/1854]: 16f.)*

For Thoreau, clothes are not unimportant, they are instead remarkable instruments from which to build independence, and they can reveal our relationship to power, fate, fashion or government, if we just take them seriously. Not only are clothes 'assimilated to ourselves' (Thoreau, 1992 [1849/1854]: 14), but simple clothing is part of an independent life, 'where is he so poor that, clad in such a suit, *of his own earning*, there will not be found wise men to do him reverence?' (Thoreau, 1992 [1849/1854]: 16; original italics). Following Thoreau, independence starts from the production of our social skin, with a position that questions the fate, or power, of fashion.

For Thoreau, we must govern ourselves by our conscience, and not seek to be ruled, not even democratically. As he notes in his essay *Resistance to Civil Government* (1992 [1849/1954]), 'Even voting *for the right* is *doing* nothing for it. It is only expressing to men feebly your desire that it should prevail' (Thoreau, 1992 [1849/1854]: 231; original italics). To Thoreau, democracy is only a convenient delegation of power and responsibility to a parliament; thus we acquit ourselves from necessary action for justice.

Thus, following Thoreau, at the core of independence lies our relation to fashion, as it mirrors our relation to government and power. Obeying fashion consists of the same behaviour as obeying laws not set by ourselves. With a suit of *one's own earning*, there is, however, a possibility of building independence, justice and responsibility.

Fashion supremacy

Being considered unattractive can be a subjective or individual experience between peers, and this is a part of any human life. However, being unattractive can also be part of subjugation under a structural regime of domination, where ideals of beauty and hierarchies of values are weapons of repression and where ideals reinforce submission. Such a system also promotes various forms of indifference and willing blindness to injustice. This type of regime I would like to call *fashion supremacy*, an aesthetic, political and ontological category, which has become an intrinsic part of today's social life. It is also ingrained in the collective psyche of consumer society's dressed and embodied normativity. As in white supremacy, it is a mechanism of what sociologist and civil rights activist W. E. B. du Bois called 'double-consciousness', which implies that 'of looking at oneself through the eyes of others', producing a derogatory sense of self (Cowan, 2003: 22f.). Here, I learn to see myself through the eyes of a system that looks down on me, a system I can neither influence nor escape, and yet it still defines me. Similar to the mechanisms of racism experienced, for example, in the US, where one may live *in* America, while not feel part *of* America, a consumer may temporarily feel he or she is *in* fashion, while also definitely not part *of* it.

Power may be inherent in almost every social relation, but fashion supremacy is so mendacious today, where cheap consumer goods allow the consumer to feel as if one can change one's world, or at least oneself, by what one buys and owns. With access to goods, a consumer can, at least temporarily, change social position and access new arenas. Yet, as cultural critic Henry Giroux writes, the role of the agent is still limited to that of consumer, object or billboard (Giroux, 2009: 14). It is never a position of authority, even if it may appear so from the perspective of a self-proclaimed fashion blogger, who still achieves their position by excessive consumption. This tendency amplifies an individualist subjectivity based on commodity competitiveness, where 'it becomes difficult for young people to imagine a future in which the self becomes more than a self-promoting commodity and a symbol of commodification' (Giroux, 2009: 17). Similarly, cultural critic Zygmunt Bauman frames the marketplace as the main arena today for a formation of the self, where citizens are 'simultaneously, *promoters of commodities* and the *commodities they promote*' (Bauman, 2007: 6; original italics).

> In the society of consumers, no one can become a subject without first turning into a commodity, and no one can keep his or her subjectness secure without perpetually resuscitating, resurrecting and replenishing the capacities expected and required of a sellable commodity.
>
> *(Bauman, 2007: 12)*

What makes fashion supremacy so deceitful today is the imagination that cheap and accessible fashion is a form of democracy, a system governed by and for the people. This type of con-sumer democracy is a severe deception of the democratic promise. The democratic promise of change is a social one, based on equal access to influencing power through the vote, whereas the consumerist promise is an individual, private and egocentric one, based on economic assets. The democratic promise of social change tells us we can hold people of power accountable, change the regime, and we as citizens are part of the ruling order of society. The inherent choices of consumer democracy hold nothing but the promise of individual change of style, and only within the commodity economy. As philosopher Jean Baudrillard notices, 'Fashion embodies a compromise between need to innovate and the other need to change nothing in the fundamental order' (Baudrillard, 1981: 51). Nothing in individual consumer choices, as offered to the larger part of the population through fast fashion, can change the order of consumerism itself: 'to the illusion of change is added the illusion of democracy' (Baudrillard, 1981: 78).

No consumer choice will change the order of power in fashion supremacy. In direct opposition to political democracy, the 'democratization' of fashion perpetuates ideals that reinforce submission and indifference to suffering, such as social exclusion, even producing a blunt denial of consumer society's inequities and injustices. I can consume, as the advertisement says, 'Because I am worth it', and those who cannot are simply not worth it.

Fashion consumption is a powerful tool to avoid, sublimate or ignore discomfort, and it resonates well with cultural critic Cornel West's perspective of Western societies as a *hotel civilization*, 'obsessed with comfort, convenience, contentment' (Cowan, 2003). When you leave the room it is dirty, but, as you come back, it is clean, and you never saw how it happened, as those doing the labour at the hotel are meant to be unseen, quite like the sweatshop workers overseas. As a guest at the hotel, you are shielded from the unjustified suffering of the world, and, in this perfect comfort, there is no need to talk about injustices or inequities, as they are simply not allowed into the lobby. The hotel is a perfect fusion of home and market that makes you feel at home, as long as you have the cash to pay (West in Cowan, 2003: 25).

As fashion consumers, and hotel guests, we become complicit in the mechanisms of injustice, or deeply planted within the hostile terrain of exploitation. This is not only an exploitation happening overseas in hidden sweatshops, but we are enacting the power of fashion every day. The power of fashion is not residing in some buildings in Paris or New York, but is repeated between us every day. The fashion system happily supplies us with the micro-weapons of oppression we use against each other. As British media theorist Nick Couldry says, 'every system of cruelty requires its own theatre', drawing on the rituals of everyday life to legitimize its norms, values and social practices (Couldry, 2008: 1). A 'democratized' fashion system is such a theatre of cruelty.

Fashion as everyday fear

Every fashion is enacted between peers, within the horizontal comradeship of a real or imagined community, and it has its own mechanisms of inclusion and exclusion, its icons and leaders, its unwritten 'rules of the street'. And, just like any other style, it is both a force of empowerment as well as a culture driven and reproduced by systemic reproduction of fear, a social fear of losing popular ground, being ridiculed or isolated. Through fear, the social mechanisms of control are internalized in all of us. As political scientist David Cortwright notices,

> We fear the loss of job security or position; we worry how family, friends, and employers will view us. We are so entangled in the comforts of society that we find it difficult to take risks, even for causes we hold dear.
>
> *(Cortright, 2009: 33)*

As sketched out by anthropologist James Scott (1990), we overcome fear and domination by our hope of one day having the opportunity to dominate. One can endure domination today, if one will eventually be able to exercise it later, and this gives a strong incentive to emulate patterns of domination, even if the revenge 'must be exercised on someone other than the original target of resentment' (Scott, 1990: 82). Similarly, by wilfully engaging in these activities, we do not question our compliance. Gossip may be an example of this type of exercise of distributed compliance, reinforcing 'normative standards by invoking them and by teaching anyone who gossips precisely what kinds of conduct are likely to be mocked or despised' (Scott, 1990: 142f.).

An example from fashion can be paparazzi photos. They show how ordinary looking the Hollywood stars are when they wake up in the morning, but the photos, at the same time, verify the stars' power over us. Similarly, as the photos show, the stars may not look good all the time, but they sometimes look amazing, and, thus, we come to ask ourselves: why can't I look as good sometimes? (– 'It must be their commodities, I got to get more of that fancy stuff they have!').

Street fashion photography can be seen as a merger of emancipatory fashion imaging, paparazzi surveillance and politics of individuation. Just like any other technology, street fashion photography can be seen as 'neutral', and yet it is also employing specific 'technologies of self' that distribute power in a certain way. Parallels could be drawn to ultrasonic imaging, which produces a special moral position (Verbeek, 2011), which in turn makes us judge the world accordingly. Street fashion produces the subject as an isolated individual (rather than part of a social community), as an object (rather than agent), as a consumer (rather than producer), and it amplifies visual primacy, setting visual 'style' and the submission to fashion ideals higher than personal skills or capabilities. It makes the visually documented consumption patterns idealized by the fashion industry the everyday mode of subjectification, or what Foucault would call a 'technology of the self', reinforced by a scopic 'regime of truth' (Foucault, 1973, 1988). Even if fashion blogging may demonstrate some agency as that of the 'prosumer', or producer–consumer (Toffler, 1980), it is still a position totally within the regime of fashion supremacy, with no means to affect the ruling order, and it even strengthens the domination of fashion supremacy.

Enactment of supremacy: fashion violence and microaggressions

Fashion supremacy makes our peers the 'judges' of our fashionability, referencing our dressed expressions to the latest shared trends. The social comments, of approval or condemnation, are the verdicts of the jury. And no law is upheld without systems of judgment, execution and punishment. In the social world of fashion, punishment takes the form of *violence* and *microaggressions*. Our peers are the 'fashion police'.

The violence of fashion is not a physical force or assault, but rather a transgression, humiliation, harassment or a violation of integrity. As political theorist Vittorio Bufacchi proposes, also seemingly non-violent acts, such as imprisoning and starving someone to death, are acts of violence (Bufacchi, 2007: 14f.). Fashion may not be violent, but it still enforces violence on the social and psychological environment, on social relations and subjects. It reproduces a social sorting and pecking order based on dress. A micro-act of violence conducted through fashion may be wilfully ignoring someone, a degrading comment, or sustained harassment on the basis of clothing. Such micro-acts, or microaggressions, are parts of a larger scheme of culturally, structurally and directly sanctioned violence.

Following the typology of violence from peace researcher Johan Galtung, three levels of violence could be amplified through fashion: 'direct', 'structural' and 'cultural' violence (1990). Cultural violence is the soft power that legitimizes an order that supports the fact of structural violence and the acts of direct violence. Cultural violence makes structural discrimination seem 'natural' and endorses individual acts of direct violence, with the help of mechanisms of inclusion/ exclusion, social hierarchies and norms: 'The culture preaches, teaches, admonishes, eggs on, and dulls us into seeing exploitation and/or repression as normal and natural, or into not seeing them (particularly not exploitation) at all' (Galtung, 1990: 295).

In the realm of fashion, cultural violence may make the slim Caucasian model body an explicit standard of beauty, discriminating against other bodies both implicitly and explicitly, and it may even play with this ideal in an 'ironic' way in media, while still perpetuating it (see also Chapter 10). Structural violence may manifest these fashion ideals in sizes and patterns and also produce social or racial sorting mechanisms in the layout of stores or names of sizes. The direct violence may happen in forms of blunt harassment or microaggressions, by a shop attendant, a bouncer at a restaurant or fellow pupils at school.

Microaggressions is a term sprung from psychologist Derald Wing Sue's studies of racism, and they are 'everyday verbal, nonverbal, and environmental slights, snubs, or insults, whether intentional or unintentional, that communicate hostile, derogatory, or negative messages' towards the marginalized (Sue, 2010: 3). Microaggressions are most detrimental when delivered by well-intentioned individuals who are unaware of their harmful conduct.

> Because most people experience themselves as good, moral, and decent human beings, conscious awareness of their hidden biases, prejudices, and discriminatory behaviors threatens their self-image. Thus, they may engage in defensive maneuvers to deny their biases, to personally avoid talking about topics such as racism, sexism, heterosexism, and ableism, and to discourage others from bringing up such topics. On the one hand, these maneuvers serve to preserve the self-image of oppressors, but on the other, they silence the voices of the oppressed.
>
> *(Sue, 2010: 5)*

By executing a 'conspiracy of silence', the perpetrators keep their oppression from being acknowledged (– 'don't be so oversensitive'), maintain their innocence and leave inequities from being challenged. Sue divides microaggressions into *microassaults*, *microinsults* and *microinvalidations*, where the last form is perhaps the most insidious and harmful form, 'because microinvalidations directly attack or deny the experiential realities of socially devalued groups' (Sue, 2010: 10). The reality of the powerful is imposed on the less powerful groups, making them judge their experiences through the values and hierarchies of the powerful. Even a flattering compliment can still reflect oppression, as it both confirms the position of the powerful, who is allowed to judge, and it allows the perpetrator to cling to his or her belief in the subject's inferiority (Sue, 2010: 13). The seemingly well-intentioned comment creates an 'attributional ambiguity', a 'motivational uncertainty in that the motives and meanings of a person's actions are unclear and hazy', to which the victim has trouble responding, or ends up in a double bind (Sue, 2010: 17). The comment 'nice shoes' may be a seemingly harmless compliment, but the context may speak the opposite, making the statement clearly derogatory.

Classist microinvalidations 'broadly negate or demean the lived experience of poor or working-class people' (Smith and Redington, 2010: 279). The reality of the poor is not worth anything:

> Fashion and lifestyle programming spotlights the wardrobe, dinner parties, and daily activities of wealthy people; issues relevant to them and to middle-class individuals, such as the stock market, comprise the entire programming schedules of cable networks. Simultaneously, we are fed images and narratives evoking our sense that anything is possible and that in this winner-take-all society, we have as good chance of taking it all as anyone.
>
> *(Smith and Redington, 2010: 279)*

Like in Scott's example earlier of how the marginalized endure domination because of the hope of one day exercising revenge, here, the belief that they will one day 'make it' can lead the poor to endure large-scale poverty and nullification, for a glimpse of status through cheap consumer goods, such as the ephemeral glamour of fashion. Simultaneously, the powerful are simply 'worth it'.

As Sue notes, microaggression happens in the small gestures, usually from our peers, not our outspoken enemies. Enemies are easy to ignore – the opposition is explicit – but the comments and looks among friends are what expose and hurt us the most, and this is what makes fashion supremacy so socially deceitful. In order to challenge fashion supremacy, other values that build courage and self-esteem beyond consumerism need to be embraced and practised (see also Chapter 1). The disarmament of fashion supremacy needs to be a constructive one; as is often noted in non-violent resistance, it needs to work with two hands: one that opposes and one that builds the alternative.

Resistance to fashion supremacy

The power wielded by fashion icons, such as editors of authoritative magazines, is manifested between us because *we* obey them, not because they have some inherent power. *We give them power*. Resistance means withdrawing that power, by us withdrawing obedience and fear, while simultaneously creating alternative values and forms of togetherness through fashion.

Yet, as Simmel (1957) and others have noted, we always dress both to assimilate and differentiate, so that even an alternative to fashion will reproduce fashion itself. The tension is part of fashion's inherent energy, making it a *'perpetuum mobile'* (Bauman, 2010), possibly enacting similar mechanisms of violence. However, a constructive fashion may have different emphasis, and it can be a dress-practice coming from different moods, skills and positions. Empowerment in fashion can mean self-esteem, courage and confidence based in *other* personal expressions than buying new clothes in a competitive setting. Building courage is the act of making and believing in one's skills and value in the act of making. Even if the material outcome may look similar to a commodity, making allows for training the capability of independence and courage, and reflecting on their social characteristics.

One powerful example of constructive resistance could be the Salt March, coordinated by Mohandas Gandhi in 1930, where *Satyagraha* (or Truth–Force) was manifested through the hands-on production of independent salt. Instead of buying British salt, which was taxed, Gandhi proposed that Indians marched to the Indian Ocean to make their own salt, which existed there in superabundance. This salt would basically be the same salt as the one they bought from the British, but without the tax. Salt without imperialism. It would be independent salt, where every grain of salt was a manifestation of Indian freedom. Although the act itself was very simple and easily reproduced by the participants, Gandhi had developed a very powerful strategic perspective of the simple action, not basing it on a reaction to oppression, but taking a proactive stance. The act was not *against* British taxed salt, but *for* independent salt. Thus, the act disarmed some of the violence of opposition. Several components in the action made it a strong statement of proactive resistance:

- The act mobilized participants through simple and palpable means.
- The act was a non–reproduction of domination.
- The act was an exposure of oppression by making something useful, but illegal (salt).
- The act showed how tangible result, however small, can emerge from protest.
- The act showed how resistance, even on a small scale, builds momentum towards self-rule.

All these components produced a situation where power was *displaced* from the salt. The salt produced by the Indians themselves was purified from imperialism. Violence was no longer in the salt, but the British had to reconquer it by using force, imprisoning the people who made their own salt. The British had to be reactive.

Similar to Thoreau's idea of starting autonomy from a suit of *one's own earning*, Gandhi also manifested Indian independence through his own, small-scale production of cloth, as it evoked a debate about independence, truthfulness and justice. What Gandhi did, by producing his own cloth (*khadi*), was to raise the debate about independence built from self-sufficiency. For Gandhi, a suit of one's own earning would mean to build autonomy from the ground up, detoxing the everyday, taking one type of cloth-bound supremacy out of our social relationships.

One simple act of proactive resistance can be repair (see also Chapter 26). It is not an act of reactive non-consumption, but it is a proactive act of amplifying emotional attachment to a garment. It displaces some of the garment's fashion commodity status to instead highlight its role as a companion, a co-traveller through the adventure we call life. The act of care builds self-esteem and independence, and active restoration reframes the object from a subjective position, with new values and skills attached. A social example of repair can be the workshop, Refuge in Restoration, I organized at the Green Gulch zen centre in Sausalito, California, in 2011. All participants brought a garment that needed repair, but, instead of simply restoring the garment back to its original status, everyone had to cut a small piece of his or her garment that would become a patch for someone else's garment. Each garment became a vessel for community, as every garment carried a patch from another. A more strategic method can be 'fashion hacktivism', which aims at decoding the larger fashion 'operating system' in order to produce more open and inviting alternatives, where the user can contribute and also easily learn skills to build a sustained co-authorship and a position of empowered participation (von Busch, 2008). However, if we only look at the outcomes, as most of these initiatives are still centred on garments, we miss the part that displaces fashion supremacy. Just like the Salt March, the outcome may still look (or taste) the same, but the process of acquirement and production makes all the difference in building independence and empowerment.

As designers and activists take on fashion supremacy, it is important to shift the focus from the objects, or commodities, and their meanings, to the strategic and social value of the capabilities produced through the engagements:

- The act makes clothes open and public, creating a counter-system of clothes.
- The act is based on fashion, not some form of anti-fashion (not violent rejection).
- The act is constructive, building values that challenge fashion supremacy.
- The act breaks the pacifying consumerist order of the dominant system.
- The act highlights the social and ethical resistance to fashion supremacy.
- The act mobilizes people to share the experience of empowerment.
- The act uses the garment to produce personal and social consequences, such as new forms of togetherness.

For designers and users, such a manifestation of *fashion-ability* means building self-esteem by social making. A suit of one's own earning does not mean to literally make our own clothes, but having the ability to co-produce self-esteem that challenges fashion supremacy. It means to be grounded in political autonomy, in a position of independence beyond the means offered to me through commodity democracy or consumer culture. Fashion-ability means the capability to engage in fashion on one's own terms, yet in relation to the zeitgeist, *displacing* fashion supremacy, and doing so from a position of independence and ethical responsibility.

With the help of engaged designers, we all need to keep on training and generate hope and shared visions that may one day extend to full civic engagement.

In a time of fashion surplus, to mobilize action on fashion self-reliance is not primarily an act of anti-consumerism. It is not a frugal boycott. As cultural critic Raj Patel notes, 'the opposite of consumption isn't thrift – it's generosity' (Patel, 2009: 29). Fashion-ability means the capability to act together in generosity, in order to *do the right thing*.

References

Baudrillard, J. (1981), *For a Critique of the Political Economy of the Sign*, St Louis, MO: Telos Press.

Bauman, Z. (2007), *Consuming Life*, London: Polity.

Bauman, Z. (2010), *Perpetuum mobile, Critical Studies in Fashion and Beauty*, 1, 1: 55–63.

von Busch, O. (2008), *Fashion-able: Hacktivism and Engaged Fashion Design*, Gothenburg, Sweden: ArtMonitor.

Bufacchi, V. (2007), *Violence and Social Justice*, Basingstoke, UK: Palgrave Macmillan.

Cortright, D. (2009), *Gandhi and Beyond: Nonviolence for a New Political Age*, Boulder, CO: Paradigm.

Couldry, N. (2008), Reality TV, or the secret theater of neoliberalism, *Review of Education, Pedagogy, and Cultural Studies*, 30, January–March: 1.

Cowan, R. (2003), *Cornel West: The Politics of Redemption*, Cambridge, UK: Polity.

Foucault, M. (1973), *The Birth of the Clinic: An Archaeology of Medical Perception*, New York: Pantheon Books.

Foucault, M. (1988), *Technologies of the Self: A Seminar with Michel Foucault*, Amherst, MA: University of Massachusetts Press.

Galtung, J. (1990), Cultural violence, *Journal of Peace Research*, 27, 3: 291–305.

Giroux, H. (2009), *Youth in a Suspect Society: Democracy or Disposability?* New York: Palgrave.

Patel, R. (2009), *The Value of Nothing*, New York: Picador.

Scott, J. (1990), *Domination and the Arts of Resistance*, London: Yale University Press.

Simmel, G. (1957), Fashion, *The American Journal of Sociology*, 62, 6: 541–58.

Smith, L. and Redington, R. (2010), Class dismissed: making the case for the study of classist micro-aggressions, in Sue, D. W. (ed.) *Microaggressions and Marginality*, Hoboken, NJ: Wiley.

Sue, D. W. (ed.) (2010), *Microaggressions and Marginality*, Hoboken, NJ: Wiley.

Thoreau, H. D. (1992 [1849/1854]), *Walden and Resistance to Civil Government*, New York: Norton.

Toffler, A. (1980), *The Third Wave*, London: Collins.

Verbeek, P.-P. (2011), *Moralizing Technology: Understanding and Designing the Morality of Things*, Chicago, IL: University of Chicago Press.

28

FUTURES OF FUTURES STUDIES IN FASHION

Mathilda Tham

Introduction

Often, I look at my young daughters, Paloma and Rosa Lulu, future wearers, makers, crafters, or perhaps best described as collaborators of fashion (and, of course, many, many other things) and think: 'who am I, that only know the past, to guide these magical beings into the future?'. And yet, I sometimes call myself a futurist.

Disturbingly–hopefully–naturally, I won't be alive for a big part of my daughters' future. Significantly and thankfully, I am not their only guide. Still, and despite the vertigo-like sensation that fills me as I consider the deep and far void of time and experience that lies ahead of my daughters, nothing can keep me from squinting, trying to discern it, listening to the murmurs of this future and, foremost, hoping, willing for the very, very best.

I believe this volume well reflects the rich body of knowledge that now exists, some of it already well rehearsed and some emerging, on issues of concern, as well as strategies to make fashion more compatible with a paradigm of sustainability. This chapter, instead and complementarily, explores auspicious *implementation* of such knowledge and auspicious *processes of change*. It argues that futures studies, as manifested in fashion forecasting, can constitute a powerful driver for change in the endeavour of creating fashion futures of sustainability.

It positions fashion forecasting as a strategic tool that can synergise levels of products, systems and even paradigms. It further suggests that forecasting can offer a free zone for risky and playful exploration, the bringing together of personal and professional values systems and experiences, an agile dance between micro and macro perspectives, and operational and strategic design.

To explain the conceptual space that forecasting may offer fashion, and thus its potential as an auspicious driver of change, I will draw on some interwoven ideas, predominantly from systems-thinking, action-oriented research, peacework and futures studies. To me, they find a designerly shape and agency through an emerging field of metadesign, a design of design itself, seeds for change, a collaborative and inclusive design process (see, e.g. Giaccardi, 2005; Wood, 2007; Tham and Jones, 2008). The ideas I propose reflect the focus of my research and practice for the past decade or so. A fashion designer and forecaster, uneasy in a paradigm of unsustainability, a PhD project allowed me to design myself out of it. I found a positive, creative and activist place through what I term the *lucky people forecast* approach, which I use in research, education and organisational change.

Fashion forecasting

Below follows a description of forecasting as relevant for this chapter, drawing on existing literature and an empirical study. For further guidance, the reader may consult Brannon (2005), McKelvey and Muslow (2008), Tham (2008), Kim *et al.* (2011) and Rousso (2012).

Brief history

Fashion forecasting (trend forecasting, fashion prediction or prognosis) as an organised phenomenon appeared in the 1960s in Paris, where *agences de style* such as MAFIA, Promostyle and Precler (founded 1970) started developing and selling seasonal advice to fashion companies. Giertz-Mårtenson (following Giddens, 1991) views the development as part of the post-modern condition:

> when the institutional thinking with firmly established authorities gradually disappeared from fashion, the risk element of fashion design became much more significant. There was no longer a given institution (the haute couture of Paris) or a clear manifesto (for every season the declared and approved new fashion) to rely upon. The fashion press's accelerating reports on constantly new styles and the subcultures' expression emphasised this even further.
>
> *(Giertz-Mårtenson, 2006: 17; my translation)*

How it works

Forecasting constitutes an integral part of – at least – the mass-market segment's process of conceptualising, designing and bringing to market a fashion offer. *Formal trend work* is offered by specialised agencies, including WGSN (World Global Style Network), Promostyle and TrendUnion, through seminars, trend books, trend magazines and, increasingly, designated websites. The reports range from directions on style (as specific as the positioning of a pocket) to directions on lifestyle and social/cultural/technological/economic trends. In addition to the use of such services, design teams (and especially designers) also conduct their own *informal* trend work by, for example, conducting market research in shops, visiting trade fairs and second-hand shops, perusing websites for catwalk trends (see e.g. www.style.com) and documenting personal style in capitals and emerging fashion locations around the world. Depending on interest and time, designers may also be drawing on films, exhibitions and literature to inform the work on a new collection (Tham, 2008). The reports resulting from both formal and informal trend work often constitute tantalizing documents, rich in visual material and using emotive language.

My empirical study (with representatives from H&M, Gap, Levi's, Topshop) showed that, alongside the sales figures of current and previous seasons, fashion forecasting constitutes the most important driver of fashion in the mass-market domain. With many and very quick decisions to make, and a highly competitive market, such 'evidence' serves an important role in the dialogue between designer, buyer and the sales organisation. My study also showed that the forecasting work, 'looking at the big picture', was a highly appreciated aspect of designers' work. They lamented the shortage of time to dedicate to first-hand exploratory trend research.

Forecasting and sustainability

My empirical study showed little alignment between trend work and sustainability work in the mass-market industry context. Sustainability featured only as a theme (or trend), alongside others within a report (whether bought or produced in house), with suggestions mainly concerning product level choices, such as the specification of organic cotton (Tham, 2008). Literature on forecasting to date reflects this lack of integration. However, sustainability has increased presence in the reports generally, and examples exist of formal trend reports dedicated entirely to sustainability. Typically, these provide examples/case studies of initiatives in the market and from niche practitioners, including product-level approaches (such as design for longevity) and systems-level approaches (such as an innovative take-back scheme) (see e.g. Prahl, 2012). In 2010, Forum for the Future launched a scenario and workshop resource dedicated to fashion and sustainability, with the aim of inspiring educators and companies (Forum for the Future, 2010). These constitute positive developments, but I see a larger potential for forecasting to support fashion futures of sustainability.

Futures studies

Fashion forecasting can be understood as a branch of futures studies. Here, I highlight some aspects of this larger field that I believe can enrich the fashion application, particularly in the context of sustainability.

While existing as pockets in various academic fields before, futures studies emerged as a discipline in its own right after the Second World War, out of the need for cohesive strategic planning and an interest coming from scholars, writers and artists in conceptualising and creating a more positive future (Slaughter, 1996). By the late 1970s, several international futures organisations had developed, of which the Club of Rome and its publication *The Limits to Growth* are notable in this context (Meadows *et al.*, 1972). Non-fiction future-oriented bestsellers by, for example, Alvin Toffler and Faith Popcorn, popularised the field and established it in a marketing context. In recent years, a Critical Futures Studies movement has emerged that promotes a self-reflexive stance of the futurist, and predominant world-views (a Western hegemony) are challenged, and a wealth of social realities are engaged with. The word *futures* in plural signifies this important shift (see e.g. Slaughter, 1996; Inayatullah, 1998).

Futures studies makes a key distinction between probable futures, which answer the question 'what is likely to happen?' by extrapolating data (for example, meteorology and population-growth studies), and preferable futures, which answer the question 'what would we like to happen?'. In reality, the approaches are often combined, and the role of futurists is to create 'new, alternative images of the future – visionary explorations of the possible, systemic investigations of the probable, and moral evaluation of the preferable' (Toffler, 1978: x). Futures studies can, therefore, integrate rationality and value – or analysis and care.

Muslim futures scholar Ziuddin Sardar, a strong advocate for need for a diversity of voices engaged in futures work and critic of a Western bias in the field, powerfully articulates the circular nature and resulting potentially disastrous effects of the forecast: 'forecasting is one of the major tools by which the future is colonised. No matter how sophisticated the technique . . . forecasting simply ends up by projecting (the selected) past and the (often-privileged) present on to a linear future' (Sardar, 1999: 9).

The circular argument is exemplified in the fashion forecast, where, anecdotally, if influential players, let us say the trend forecaster Li Edelkoort, propose the poncho as the next big thing, it is likely that it will be, because of fearful ears of companies who 'cannot afford' to get their offer wrong (and she was right last time), because of the media's acquiescent promotion of the poncho, and because, when the user hits the shops, they find the poncho in prime place and not much else. I want to emphasise that this does not mean I view fashion users as mindless victims, nor that I ignore the diversity of fashion offers that exist, if fashion is regarded as a collaborative effort, and its many niche practices and creativity (at both designer/producer and user ends) are acknowledged. Yet, many readers will, with me, have noticed how the influence of some brands and the global media result in the dominance of certain styles and colours, not only on the high street in London and similar, but also in a shopping centre in Amman, Shanghai or Rio de Janeiro.

The role of powerful forecasts in shaping the future (and, therefore, in editing away less marketable versions of it) resonates with ecofeminist, philosopher and historian Carolyn Merchant's salient description of how 'controlling imagery' guides us at least as powerfully as does legislation. Descriptive metaphors and images (as when nature is perceived as a dead resource, detached from humans, instead of alive with us) operate at the deep level of our individual and societal mindsets, giving ethical restraints or sanctions (Merchant, 1982: 4).

Karl-Erik Edris, scholar of the rise and fall of civilizations through history, attributes their longevity to a strong religious root (Edris, 1987). The role of politics, he argues, has been to legalise, formalise and organise the vision; the role of economics to provide for the vision – to resource it. According to Edris, the dire predicament of contemporary Western society is a result of how, in affluent, Western, secularised society, a spiritual imperative is no longer the starting point for visions (see also Thomas, Chapter 11). In modern history, political conviction came to overtake religious belief as the root of new visions. In postmodernity, politics is no longer a viable platform for visions, as ideologies are giving way to issue politics, and there is an overall mistrust of politicians. Therefore (in extreme terms), we are left with economics as the foundation of visions (Edris, 1987), which is problematic, as its primary goal is never sustainability in holistic terms (see also Fletcher, Chapter 1). Edris's interpretations of the rise and fall of civilisations thus highlight how a flawed vision, or world-view, results in a flawed operation of the system.

Counterfactuals

Let us momentarily return to Paloma and Rosa Lulu, future collaborators of fashion (and more), who are already creating futures scenarios. 'Psychologists have found that counterfactual thinking is absolutely pervasive in our everyday life and deeply affects our judgments, our decisions, and our emotions' (Gopnik, 2009: 21).

Gopnik writes powerfully of the role of human childhood in human civilization and the survival of the human species. She discusses recent developments in cognitive science, which reveal that, not only can even very young children discern between fantasy and reality, they also purposefully explore alternative realities to make plans and create the world. She means that what in philosophy is known as counterfactuals – alternatives to reality in the past, present and future – is a central facet of the human condition and our evolutionary success; the ability to imagine such alternative realities means we don't need to rely on trial and error in all decision-making. Whereas factual knowledge and imagination are conventionally perceived as opposites, they become a sophisticated whole in counterfactuals. So futures imagination is vital for our survival. We *must* give space for it.

Discussion

The explicit forecast shapes the future of fashion. I argue that, in addition, fashion proposals (products, collections, imagery) act as implicit forecasts that shape the future. Fashion proposals that are influential (through their ubiquity, a strong designer name or brand, or powerful marketing and alliances) cast not only subsequent product types, but also actions, attitudes, values and meaning – accumulatively a future. To forecast, of course, in effect means *to shape before*: the cast constituting the boundaries of an object in the making and, consequently, the boundaries of our imagination. The future or legend that has been powerfully and persuasively articulated takes precedence over such futures that have not been articulated at all, or articulated in weaker voices.

That forecasts are published that integrate fashion and sustainability is positive, yet they have severe limitations. One problem is that scenarios appear as choices, just like commodities (this or that future); another is the many voices and perspectives they, by necessity (or not), exclude, by ultimately adhering to an overarching financial framework. To me, most significantly, the forecast as report will remain abstract to its perusers (or consumers). The true power of forecasting, I believe, comes from participating in imagining our shared futures. Participation affords the personal situatedness, commitment, empathy and the drawing on an extended epistemology (Heron and Reason, 2001). There is no sustainability by proxy. It must start in the individual. Yet, we cannot be holistic on our own. We must imagine together.

Futures of futures studies in fashion: proposal 1

I developed the *lucky people forecast* approach to explore the potential of forecasting to mobilise holistic and systemic engagement with sustainability, across a broad range of fashion stakeholders, by drawing on insights presented above, as well as the inspirational qualities of fashion and fashion forecasting. The approach has been evaluated in, and evolved through, various industry and educational contexts in Sweden, the UK, Turkey, China and Indonesia. The approach, its use and effect have been described elsewhere (see e.g. Tham and Jones, 2008; Tham, 2010). For the purposes of this chapter, two findings are especially relevant.

The first concerns the approach's *generative quality*. Creative scenario work that starts from personal, and communal, negotiated *values* allows fashion stakeholders to unleash creativity and extend tacit and explicit knowing beyond product-focused and operational realms towards proposals of nested ideas at levels of products, systems and even paradigms. These have potential for real application. The scenarios become cohesive, personable and portable holders of a wealth of insights and ideas, thus forging integrated knowing and a sense of ownership. The scenarios constitute new legends that are alternative to dominant narratives deriving from the commercial framework. Metaphors representing an epistemological leap into a realm of 'what ifs' serve as a particularly auspicious force in extending participants' imagination, and as potent provocations or seeds to take out into the world after a session.

Metadesign can be an integrator of systems (Wood, 2007). The agile dance afforded by creative scenario work can be formalised in the framework in Figure 28.1.

Systems thinking has informed my understanding of unsustainability in the fashion organism (yes, it is alive!) as caused by severed or missing feedback loops (see also Fletcher, 2008; Meadows, 2008). This is manifested in the alienation of fashion professionals and consumers *here* and workers *there*; humans *here now*, and other species, and humans in *other places* and in the *future*. It is staged in a lack of engagement with the complex resource flows the garments we wear depend upon, and the many messages embodied in our clothing. It is manifested in a lack of confidence and, perhaps, a lack of creativity many of us display, which prompts us to overconsume.

The framework joining up nested levels of design can help us to identify paths between the fashion object, the infrastructures it necessitates and the narratives it cements – or breaks against. A real or imagined system 'trend' (such as, 'what if I shared my wardrobe with four other people') gives parameters with space for many viable interpretations for the product design (such as size

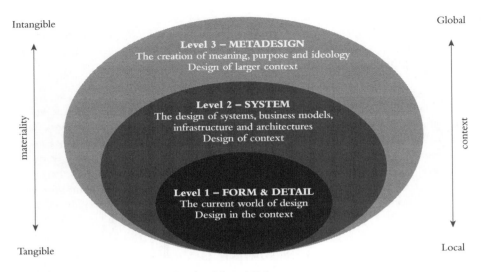

Intangible

Global

Level 3 – METADESIGN
The creation of meaning, purpose and ideology
Design of larger context

Level 2 – SYSTEM
The design of systems, business models,
infrastructure and architectures
Design of context

Level 1 – FORM & DETAIL
The current world of design
Design in the context

materiality

context

Tangible

Local

Figure 28.1 Nested levels of design (after Lundebye, 2004)

'openness', material durability or transparent making, facilitating repair). The product design can cause ripples across the layers, challenging, for example, paradigmatic assumptions of gender, a narrative of inexhaustible resources or technological determinism. By restoring or creating an understanding of the complex paths between the levels, we can start imagining the healing, or mending, of vital feedback loops.

As practically applied in the fashion–industry context, formal forecasting can have a role in providing broad outlooks on socio-economic–ecological trends, and best available lifecycle science can contribute to the robustness of the agile dance. However, the situated deep exploration needs to take place within the fashion organisation (involving as many stakeholders as possible), where knowledge and understandings are held (or should be held) about specific contexts of design, production, use, care and disposal.

A second key insight yielded from the *lucky people forecast* approach concerns the pivotal role of the experience of agency in fostering comprehensive engagement with sustainability. An *increased sense of agency* (in personal/professional realms) inspires curiosity to *learn more*, enables understanding of *relationships* (between micro and macro phenomena, environmental, social and financial concerns, and the situating of the self in these) and the enhanced *appreciation of the significance of sustainability*. In addition, the extraordinary space that the creative scenario session offers enables perspectives to cut across disciplines and specialisms, fostering a healthy empathy between stakeholders. Experiencing the lucky people forecast approach has constituted for many fashion stakeholder participants a threshold moment between their identification as outsiders and that as insiders of sustainability (or between culprits and helpers). This points to a further potential for application in organisational change towards sustainability.

A place called reconciliation: an inspiring framework from peacebuilding

Professor Paul Lederach, a key scholar and actor in peacebuilding, powerfully critiques conventional approaches to peace negotiation and offers frameworks towards holistic and systemic peacebuilding (Lederach, 1997). The predicament we are in, as regards human-driven detrimental changes to the environment and interlinked socio-economic concerns, is not war (but may cause wars), and yet, like extreme conflicts characterised by hatred, violence and severely divided societies, it is a crisis of international proportions. Below, I describe some core and interwoven tenets of Lederach's text that I find offer valuable insights into the processes of change that the sustainability imperative provokes, at both individual and societal levels, and an expanded scope for forecasting.

Simplistic definitions of problems

Lederach points out the limitations of how problems or reasons for conflicts have predominantly been defined, focusing on issues instead of relationships. I argue that un/sustainability as constructed in the realm of fashion (for example, codes of conduct), and beyond (for example, the Millennium Development Goals), has been shaped (or cast) as *a series of issues* – whether concerning human rights or environmental management – over underlying fluid relationships (between the social, cultural, economic, technological, ecological and more) (see also relational aspects of fashion and sustainability in Fletcher, Chapter 1).

Simplistic categorisation of stakeholders

Similarly, Lederach highlights flaws in the focus on conflicting parties as nation–states over aspects of identity and belonging. The fashion sustainability discourse polarises stakeholders (producers/ brands versus consumers, legal/fiscal top–down initiatives versus grassroots movements). Yet, brands and institutions are built and operationalised by *people*, who are also consumers (or, my preferred term, users), and have fluid and complex loyalties – and a range of affiliations aside from, and sometimes at odds with, the organisations they work for.

Unproductive separation between rationality and emotion

Lederach powerfully places emotions in understandings and resolution of international crises, remarking that, while 'contemporary conflicts are indeed hard-core situations . . . and require political savvy, traditional mechanisms relying solely on statist diplomacy and realpolitik have not demonstrated a capacity to control these conflicts, much less transform them toward constructive, peaceful outcomes' (Lederach, 1997: 25). His description of how, in the peace work community, 'a big brother of International Relations admonishes a little sister of Conflict Resolutions for emotionalism and sentimentality' reminds me of how, within fashion and sustainability work, legal and fiscal frameworks and metrics are placed apart from (and above) experiential dimensions.

Simplistic understanding of solution and identification of solution holders

Lederach argues that ceasefire is not a viable definition of peace, but must be accompanied by, for example, health, well-being, education and financial stability (which he means necessitates female voices to be included in negotiations and onwards) (see also Southwell, Chapter 10). The peace process he proposes, therefore, is a long-term investment and commitment – albeit with initial urgent action – that should, ideally, be preventative. It necessitates a broad involvement from communities – ultimately everyone. In the fashion and sustainability context, ceasefire can be compared with the incremental measure invented and actioned in isolation.

Truth, mercy, justice and peace

'Truth and mercy have met together, peace and justice have kissed' (Lederach, 1997: 28).

Inspired by a hymn that recurred in the negotiations he advised on between the Sandinista government and the Yatama, an indigenous resistance movement of Nicaragua, Lederach identifies four key ingredients requisite for sustainable peace building: truth, mercy, justice and peace. Reconciliation, he describes, is the place or locus where these meet, as well as an ongoing focus. All four are necessary; for example, truth alone leaves us raw, and mercy alone is superficial (like the frequently said sorry) (Figure 28.2) (Lederach, 1997: 31).

> Reconciliation-as-encounter suggests that space for the acknowledging of the past and envisioning of the future is the necessary ingredient for reframing the present. For this to happen, people must find ways to encounter themselves and their enemies, their hopes and their fears.
>
> *(Lederach, 1997: 27)*

Discussion

The simplistic and binary definitions that Lederach identifies as typical in the construction of war and peace, and I argue also are prominent in the construction of un/sustainability, are unsurprising. Distinct points (and dichotomies) seem fathomable, tangible and actionable and resonate with a Newtonian Lego logic that still pervades our societies here (see also Thackara, Chapter 4). They reduce the mess in our heads. But the mess is still there!

Systems thinking teaches us the danger of steering away from the mess of the complexity of intertwined socio-economical–ecological systems. Because of the non-linear and asymmetric causal structures of systems, fix-its risk precipitating larger problems ahead and transferring a problem to other parts of the system or linked systems. My experience of facilitating

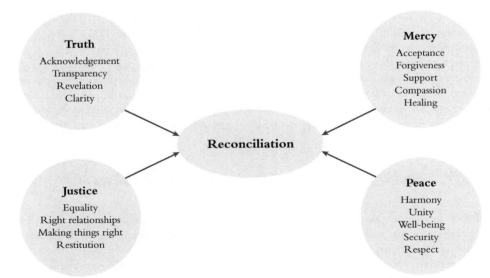

Figure 28.2 The place called reconciliation
Source: Lederach, 1997: 30

organisational change towards sustainability, as well as my readings (see e.g. Macy and Johnstone, 2012), has alerted me to the danger of steering away from the mess of human emotions. True peace cannot be without giving attention to deeply harboured feelings of sorrow, animosity and fear. Sustainability will not be without giving attention to, for example, the strong urge to communicate through fashion, or the fear of change.

When an individual or an organization is asked to adapt to sustainability (whether the change concerns design choices, business models, waste streams or personal habits), this entails leaving the status quo to enter new territories, provoking us as whole human beings. We can feel fear (for ourselves, children, whether we can live up to the task ahead), anger (at previous generations or an authority that tells us to act differently from what we are used to), sorrow (for a lost world, a lost lifestyle), critique (that what we were, did and knew was wrong), apathy, confusion, frustration, shame, guilt and more. Rarely do we feel undivided enthusiasm when asked to leave behind much of what we knew to be true and who we were – which we thought was good/enough.

Most awkwardly, profound change requires encountering ourselves in our less attractive guises. In all honesty, we (yes I) enjoy getting our knickers in a twist or having a chip on our shoulders (how I love these English expressions, and, sometimes, in the company of small children both can be true); we have uncomfortable biases, resentments, egos and ambitions. But, directing ourselves to the fruitful space of reconciliation and turning our capabilities towards the future (Fry, 2011) require that we confront and leave churlish enjoyments behind, for the reward of better and stronger relationships. The space of encounter affords this, as well as closure, by providing a pivotal point in time, the drawing of a line in the sand, and (just as Rob Hopkins, founder of the transition movement, said, while symbolically holding a can of oil) 'loving and leaving' this no longer viable past behind (Hopkins, 2009).

Futures of futures studies in fashion: proposal 2

I forecast that futures of futures studies in fashion can offer a place to lay bare and process the multifarious hard and soft, small and large, close and far dimensions of fashion and sustainability: a place of reconciliation for all us collaborators of fashion. The process of four stages of encounter – truth, mercy, justice and peace – can become a new integral practice of fashion work, assigned dignity on a par with annual reports and global brand meetings. I recommend that research onwards should explore platforms, formats and facilitation for the inclusion of a wide range of stakeholders in such bold and celebratory meetings.

Lederach describes how the moment of reconciliation readdresses the wrongs of the past and envisions a common, shared future (Lederach, 1997). That this future is shared is crucial, and, as transferred to the context of fashion and sustainability, we could understand this as casting fashion and sustainability as one, and their various stakeholders as one heterogeneous team working towards one rich, multifaceted and deeply held vision.

Conclusion

The systems and even paradigms we live with are created by humans, and so we can create other systems and paradigms that are better suited for our present and future well-being, and that of fellow humans and fellow species. This seems simple and obvious, but often gets forgotten in the stream of tasks, technologies and more, so that we often resort to 'diddling with the deck-chairs on the Titanic' (Meadows, 1997), instead of beginning with the most fundamental questions, 'who do we want to be, and how do we want to live our lives?'.

Every time I think and write about, or try to do, fashion and sustainability, I need to remind myself of my love for fashion. In the fashion moment at its best, vibrant with creativity, play and experimentation, I encounter extended possibilities of myself and of being together with others. I forecast fashion moments where we, collaborators of fashion, can encounter ourselves and each other, and our messy-disturbing-beautiful world, raw. Then we can imagine our shared futures.

References

Brannon, E. L. (2005), *Fashion Forecasting*, New York: Fairchild Publications.

Edris, K. E. (1987), *Vision eller Vanmakt*, Uppsala, Sweden: Hallgren & Fallgren.

Fletcher, K. (2008), *Sustainable Fashion and Textiles: Design Journeys*, London: Earthscan.

Forum for the Future and Levi Strauss (2010) *Fashion Futures 2025: Global Scenarios for a Sustainable Fashion Industry*. Available at: www.forumforthefuture.org/project/fashion-futures-2025/overview (accessed 12 November 2012).

Fry, T. (2011), *Design as Politics*, New York: Berg.

Giaccardi, E. (2005), Metadesign as an emergent design culture, *Leonardo*, 38 (4): 342–9.

Giddens, A. (1991), *Modernity and Self-Identity*, Cambridge, UK: Polity Press.

Giertz-Mårtenson, I. (2006), *Att Se in i Framtiden: En undersökning av trendanalys inom Modebranschen*, Masters thesis, Ethnology, Stockholm University, Stockholm.

Gopnik, A. (2009), *The Philosophical Baby*, London: Bodley Head.

Heron, J. and Reason, P. (2001), The practice of co-operative inquiry: research with rather than on people, in Reason, P. and Bradbury, H. (eds) *Handbook of Action Research: Participative Inquiry and Practice*, London: Sage Publications: 179–88.

Hopkins, R. (2009), Rob Hopkins: Transition to a world without oil [video file]. Available at: www.ted.com/talks/rob_hopkins_transition_to_a_world_without_oil.html?quote=599 (accessed 12 February, 2012).

Inayatullah, S. (1998), Causal layered analysis: poststructuralism as method, *Futures*, 30 (8): 815–29.

Kim, E., Fiore, A. M. and Kim, H. (2011), *Fashion Trends: Analysis and Forecasting*, London: Berg.

Lederach, J. P. (1997), *Building Peace: Sustainable Reconciliation in Divided Societies*, Washington, DC: United States Institute of Peace.

Lundebye, A. (2004), *Senseness*, Masters thesis, Goldsmiths, University of London.

McKelvey, K. and Muslow, J. (2008), *Fashion Forecasting*, Oxford, UK: John Wiley and Sons.

Macy, J. and Johnstone, C. (2012), *Active Hope: How to Face the Mess We're In Without Going Crazy*, Novato, CA: New World Library.

Meadows, D. H. (1997), Places to intervene in a system, *Whole Earth Review*, (91): 78–84.

Meadows, D. H. (2008), *Thinking in Systems: A Primer*, White River Junction, VT: Chelsea Green Publishing Company.

Meadows, D. H., Meadows, D. L., Randers, J. and W. Berhens. (1972), *The Limits to Growth*, London: Earth Island.

Merchant, C. (1982), *The Death of Nature: Women, Ecology and the Scientific Revolution*, London: Wildwood House.

Prahl, A. (2012), Design for sustainable consumption: trend analysis. Report. 18 April. WGSN.

Rousso, C. (2012), *Fashion Forward: A Guide to Fashion Forecasting*, New York: Fairchild Books.

Sardar, Z. (ed.) (1999), *Rescuing All Our Futures: The Future of Futures Studies*, Twickenham, UK: Adamantine Press.

Slaughter, R. A. (ed.) (1996), *The Knowledge Base of Futures Studies*, Melbourne: DDM Media Group.

Tham, M. (2008), *Lucky People Forecast: A Systemic Futures Perspective on Fashion and Sustainability*, PhD thesis, Goldsmiths, University of London.

Tham, M. (2010), Languaging fashion and sustainability – towards synergistic modes of thinking, wording, visualising and doing fashion and sustainability, *The Nordic Textile Journal*, Special Issue Fashion Communication, 1: 14–23.

Tham, M. and Jones, H. (2008), Metadesign tools: designing the seeds for shared processes of change, in Cipolla, C. and Peruccio, P. P. (eds) *Changing the Change: Design, Visions, Proposals and Tools. Proceedings*: 1491–505. Turin: Allemandi Conference Press. Ebook available at: www.allemandi.com/university/ctc.pdf (accessed 9 April 2011).

Toffler, A. (1978), Foreword, in Maruyama, M. and Harkins, A. M. (eds) *Cultures of the Future*, The Hague: Mouton: ix–xi.

Wood, J. (2007), *Design for Micro-utopias: Making the Unthinkable Possible, Design for Social Responsibility*, London: Ashgate.

CONCLUSIONS

The *Handbook of Fashion and Sustainability* is a gathering of contributions that variously cleave to, interrogate and reimagine fashion and sustainability ideas and practices, within and towards a futures-oriented agenda. For us, this book is an indication of the emergent potential of non-linear exploration of a field; a vindication of the power and unruliness of collaborative work; an expression of hope that fashion can – and indeed will – be different when experienced as thriving; and, moreover, that this can shape and inspire activity in the field and beyond. On a personal note, we would like to acknowledge that three children were born to our author–collaborators in the making of this book; testament, we think, to the vitality of work in this area and to its futurity – welcome!

In the course of editing this book, we were reminded, among many other things, of the multiplicity of possible approaches to change. Those reflected by the voices of our contributing authors, including those of the people and projects they draw upon, show that change takes many forms: paradigmatic, systemic, attitudinal, behavioural and incremental. Not only are the manifestations and possibilities for change diverse, but also they inscribe clearly a sense that fashion for sustainability is a process that is both deep and long term. Yet, the chapters also reflect the stark reality that the time available to effect change is diminishing, in the light of multiple transgressions of planetary boundaries (Rockström *et al.*, 2009). Importantly, in this light, although the mainstream fashion sector has been slow to change, this book provides evidence that this is not the only response.

In this book, we can see indications of ideas and practice beyond accommodatory approaches or first-order change to engaging with sustainability, that is, beyond acting within accepted boundaries, where underlying values are left unexamined and unaffected (for more on levels of change, see Sterling, 2001: 78). Rather, many contributions reflect second-order change, which examines the assumptions that influence accepted practices, and occasionally third-order change, expressing a deep awareness of other world-views and ways of doing things. Their cumulative contribution should not be read as a static instrumental blueprint for change in the sector, but a flavour of a multifactorial, continuous process of change. This is a message of hope!

That an ongoing process of change is sketched out within these pages is, for us, a reflection of an inchoate shift in culture of the field (see Chapters 20–8 for particular examples of this). We see this shift enacted in pluralistic ways, both within the academy and beyond it, in societies and fashion communities around the world. Further, it portrays the potential of a closer integration of ecological and economic thinking, where economic value is seen to follow from environmental and social value, and understanding is built about what that means in theory and practice (Chapters 4–8). It is also manifested in a renewal in emphasis on local democracy and activity, and personal practice and meaning as a key route to further fashion futures for sustainability (Chapters 14, 24–7). We sense that there is a strong requirement for a culture shift, an integration of environment and economy and personal and democratic action to develop in step with each other, so that the broadly held, changed values and norms of sustainability are facilitated by a system of material provision and expression with other goals and rules, and for this to be enacted at a networked, connected, human scale.

Transformation of the fashion sector depends on a vision for fashion provision and experience in futures aligned to a notion of sustainability, of thriving or (in John Ehrenfeld's term, Chapter 5), of flourishing. In many ways, the work of this book can be seen as an attempt to augment and bring to life this vision and to help create the conditions for change to happen. That is, to design, in an open and non-deterministic way, fashion systems that promote healthy emergence, nurturing the living qualities that arise and change from dynamic interaction. Central to this is a fashion education system based on learning as change. We see the articulation of a continuing learning process about sustainability as an essential component of all chapters, a process that is identified explicitly by some authors (for example, Louise St. Pierre, Chapter 3; Carolyn Strauss, Chapter 8; Timo Rissanen, Chapter 20; and Lynda Grose, Chapter 22). This learning as changing must also include space to examine and encounter ourselves, our assumptions, values, fears and dreams (see Mathilda Tham, Chapter 28). Work is underway in this regard in a range of formal education contexts, as well as in less formal places, to reverse the loss of 'the habit of learning and the freedom to learn' (Sterling, 2001: 79). That they succeed is critical for a view of fashion that is extended, connective and integrative.

Research agenda

To that end, we invited all contributors to set out a research agenda within their chapters, to make recommendations about what they would wish to see as future priorities for new knowledge generation, processes of change, alternative structures and other directions in the field. We offer an accumulative research agenda in Figure C.1 that is the intellectual property of all contributors, whom we thank again for their generosity and spirited insights.

System purpose and paradigm

- Explore how fashion can be greater than the view the current capitalist model presents to us (and reconfigure over-consumption towards use or participation).
- Work to understand the potential of a relational fashion system shaped by an understanding of our world and the interdependencies that we face.
- Explore the ways to help all of us develop 'visceral, tangible and unshakeable relationships with the Earth: an embodied ecological literacy' (see Louise St. Pierre, Chapter 3).
- Explore what becomes possible if we envision fashion in service of a whole new range of clients – people outside the conventional fashion remit, fashion's others (see Else Skjold, Chapter 17), people of the future, other species of the present and the future.
- Explore the role of language in general to further understandings and practices of fashion and sustainability, and which language in particular can be most helpful in shaping and mobilising healthy actions.

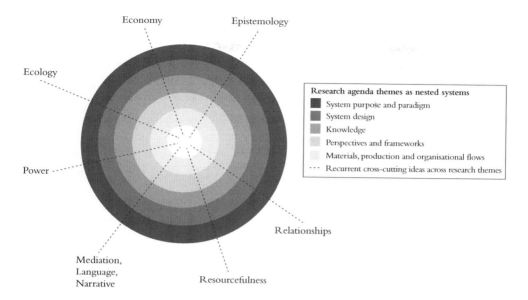

Figure C.1 Research agenda themes and recurrent cross-cutting ideas

- Explore epistemological underpinnings of research into fashion and sustainability, and the range of knowledge sources that can support futures of fashion and sustainability.
- Reveal and explore ways to reconcile divisive assumptions and structures, within and between disciplines, organisations and communities, that slow down or hinder creative constructive work forwards.
- Explore alternative indexes and understandings for success to that of growth, embracing both quantitative and qualitative possibilities.
- Explore which new possibilities can emerge from challenging assumptions and perspectives of what constitutes valid centres of fashion (geographically, culturally, chronologically, humans and other species).

System design

- Further explore the fashion commons, consider the mechanisms of enclosure and creative methods of overcoming them.
- Explore clothing as shaped by the capacities of the land and the regional community, where material flows are resituated in co-existence with local economy, place and people.
- Investigate ways of encouraging the taking of action, while constructively disrupting established ways of operating, in order to prompt reflection and behaviour change.
- Explore ways to slow the pace of consumerism and rekindle long-term commitment.
- Reinvigorate the civic realm as an important resource for relieving pressures from the realm of private consumption.
- Consider the wider consequences and opportunities of reengineering the fashion industry away from mass production and into care and maintenance.

- Explore how 'the energetic enthusiasm of women across the boundaries of class and ethnicity for fashion could be used to transform it into a better place of work rather than allowing it to remain a space of exploited production and guilt consumption' (McRobbie, 1997: 87; see also Mirjam Southwell, Chapter 10 and Liz Parker, Chapter 21).
- Explore what becomes possible if we articulate a whole new set of problems for fashion design to solve.
- Explore how consumers become creative custodians of clothes.
- Explore new roles for designers beyond the realm of the product and the operational.

Knowledge

- Establish multiple and effectively linked fundamental platforms of knowledge and knowing in fashion and sustainability, towards a rich and diverse knowledge ecology.
- Establish new modes and platforms of disseminating knowledge effectively and engagingly towards accessibility for, and participation from, a wide range of audiences and knowledge holders.
- Build knowledge about actual clothing use – that is, what real people *do* – such as comparisons between countries, gender and clothing, or users with different social and physical abilities.
- In order to embrace fashion in multiple registers of speeds, draw a more comprehensive map of fashion's assets and stakeholders, based on an engagement with the people, places and information around us.
- Establish interdisciplinary research investigating if and how emerging sustainability-driven businesses are contributing to change.
- Investigate the ways in which local knowledge created through projects, discussions and research can be accessed by virtual communities and connect them to such knowledge and practice.
- Consider the effect and influence of gender on ideas and practice of fashion and sustainability.

Perspectives and frameworks

- Explore the potential of actor network theory to offer innovative ways of thinking through fashion and sustainability in more sustained and integrated ways, so as to better understand our relationship to fashionable clothing and a cultural–ecological continuum.
- Investigate the mechanisms for new practices in fashion journalism that embrace a critical stance to issues such as over-consumption and lack of diversity.
- Explore how fashion marketing and media can entice interest and agency around repair or mending, in which the practice rather than the commodity is desirable, and where the act of repair is replicated rather than the aesthetic alone.
- Explore how fashion forecasting can support fashion futures of sustainability.
- Explore what happens when we mend. How can mending meet human needs and desires for novelty and social identity?
- Explore the well-being of workers 'with' rather than 'about' workers, including fostering holistic understandings of workers that see them as people with lives outside the workplace.
- Establish a series of comparative ethnographic projects to allow an understanding of what people do in different locations, both in terms of cross-cultural comparisons and also in terms of different points within the flows of fashion.

- Build understanding of the ways in which theopraxy in sustainability practice may be a model paradigm.

Materials, production and organisational flows

- Increase the visibility and acknowledgement of social and environmental costs of the current fashion (and sustainability) system.
- Evaluate existing and emerging technological innovations.
- Investigate a shift beyond discrete focus on the material object in and of itself, to include the vast territory of real and imagined experiences that it can deliver.
- Explore the process of using fashion as a tool for community development and how this supports thinking around sustainable communities.
- Research how strengthening networks and increasing access to space, funding and new technologies can facilitate work in this field and could support the development of new initiatives.
- Map second-hand clothing commodity chains.
- Work to fill the gap between the macro level of sustainability marketing theory and the micro level of sustainability-driven fashion business and branding.
- Investigate possibilities for the sustainable development of clothing industries, in places such as Africa, by imaginative knowledge and skills sharing.

Bisociations

We would like to draw this book to a close by offering a small number of *bisociations* between chapters. Bisociation (Koestler, 1964; see also Jones, 2007, for a process) is the blending of ideas and practices from two contexts or categories that are normally considered to represent contrasting frames of reference and starting points. It offers one way to think with originality about the territory opened up by fashion and sustainability, and to be guided by subconscious processes to access ideas and understandings not open or restrained in a formal logical process. We invite you to explore those we identified below, and others that excite you towards new, disturbing, revealing, tantalising scenarios for futures of fashion and sustainability.

- Big picture politics and activism (John Thackara, Chapter 4) – Specific technological innovation (Carole Collet, Chapter 19).
- Personal narratives of technological and historical change (Joe Smith, Chapter 14) – Scientific improvement (Greg Peters, Chapter 18).
- Detailed exploration of change for well-being (of workers) (Liz Parker, Chapter 21) – Exploring theopraxy in sustainability (Sue Thomas, Chapter 11).
- The view from consumption (Ingun Grimstad Klepp and Kirsi Laitala, Chapter 12) – The view from design and production (Timo Rissanen, Chapter 20).
- A critique of fashion branding (Simonetta Carbonaro and David Goldsmith, Chapter 16) – A critique of fashion supremacy (Otto von Busch, Chapter 27).
- Exploring fashion as nature–culture hybrid (Joanne Entwistle, Chapter 2) – Exploring adaptive resilience in fashion (Jonathan Chapman, Chapter 7).
- Exploring mending as metaphor and practice (Jonnet Middleton, Chapter 26) – Exploring mediation of fashion and sustainability (Else Skjold, Chapter 17).
- A critique of consumer-led economic growth (Ann Thorpe, Chapter 6) – Mobilising communities through fashion (Lizzie Harrison, Chapter 24).

- Exploring new roles for fashion designers (Dilys Williams, Chapter 23) – Exploring flows of materials as nested systems (Lynda Grose, Chapter 22).
- Exploring ecological literacy for fashion (Louise St. Pierre, Chapter 3) – Exploring fashion as situated evolving micro-practices (Sophie Woodward, Chapter 13).
- Reflections on time and speed (Carolyn Strauss, Chapter 8) – Reflections on past behaviour and patterns (Sasha Rabin Wallinger, Chapter 15).
- Reforming material flows of fashion (Amanda Ericsson and Andrew Brooks, Chapter 9) – Reimaging fashion as commons (Amy Twigger Holroyd, Chapter 25).
- Exploring other fashion systems (Kate Fletcher, Chapter 1) – Exploring fashion and sustainability from the perspective of gender (Mirjam Southwell, Chapter 10).
- A futures view of sustainability (John R. Ehrenfeld, Chapter 5) – Futures framework for fashion and sustainability (Mathilda Tham, Chapter 28).

The exploration of sustainability and fashion is emergent, ethical and impassioned. Change is urgent. Many possibilities remain unwritten and unpractised. We hope you will join with us and activate rich regenerative potential: fashion and sustainability, living qualities of inter-connected natural and human systems.

References

Jones, H. (2007), Bisociation within keyword-mapping; an aid to writing purposefully in design, *Journal of Writing in Creative Practice*, 1 (1): 19–31.

Koestler, A. (1964), *The Act of Creation*, London: Hutchinson.

McRobbie, A. (1997), Bridging the gap: feminism, fashion and consumption, *Feminist Review*, 55 (Spring): 73–89.

Rockström, J., Steffen W., Noone, K., Persson, Å., Chapin III, F. S., Lambin, E., Lenton, T. M., Scheffer, M., Folke, C., Schellnhuber, H., Nykvist, B., De Wit, C. A., Hughes, T., van der Leeuw, S. Rodhe, H., Sörlin, S., Snyder, P. K., Costanza, R., Svedin, U. Falkenmark. M., Karlberg, L., Corell, R. W., Fabry, V. J., Hansen, J., Walker, B., Liverman, D., Richardson, K., Crutzen, P. and Foley, J. (2009), Planetary boundaries: exploring the safe operating space for humanity, *Ecology and Society*, 14 (2) [online]. Available at: www.ecologyandsociety.org/vol14/iss2/art32/ (accessed 29 January 2014).

Sterling, S. (2001), *Sustainable Education: Re-Visioning Learning and Change*, Totnes, UK: Green Books.

INDEX